watching Wildlife

East Africa

Kenya, Tanzania, Uganda, Rwanda

WATCHING WILDLIFE EAST AFRICA
2ND EDITION
Published September 2009
First published January 2002

Published by
Lonely Planet Publications Pty Ltd ABN 36 005 607 983
90 Maribyrnong St, Footscray, Victoria 3011, Australia

LONELY PLANET OFFICES
Australia
Head Office
Locked Bag 1, Footscray, Victoria 3011 ☎ 03 8379 8000,
fax 03 8379 8111 talk2us@lonelyplanet.com.au
USA
150 Linden St, Oakland, CA 94607 ☎ 510 250 6400,
toll free 800 275 8555 fax 510 893 8572 info@lonelyplanet.com
UK
2nd fl, 186 City Rd, London EC1V 2NT ☎ 020 7106 2100,
fax 020 7106 2101 go@lonelyplanet.co.uk

ISBN 9781741042085

text & maps © Lonely Planet Publications Pty Ltd 2009
photos © as indicated 2009

Photographs
Front cover photograph: Giraffe, Gabor Geissler/Getty Images
Cover flap photographs: Lion (Ariadne Van Zandbergen/Lonely Planet
Images), zebras (Dennis Jones/Lonely Planet Images), gorillas (Ariadne
Van Zandbergen/Lonely Planet Images), leopard (Christer Fredriksson/
Lonely Planet Images), elephant (Ariadne Van Zandbergen/
Lonely Planet Images)
Back cover photographs (from left to right): leopard (Mitch Reardon/
Lonely Planet Images); monkey (Ariadne Van Zandbergen/Lonely Planet
Images); flamingo (Anders Blomqvist/Lonely Planet Images)
Many of the images in this guide are available for licensing from Lonely
Planet Images: www.lonelyplanetimages.com.

Printed by Markono Print Media Pte Ltd, Singapore.

CONTENTS

AUTHORS

MATTHEW D. FIRESTONE
Coordinating Author

Matt is a trained biological anthropologist and epidemiologist who is particularly interested in the health and nutrition of indigenous populations. His first visit to East Africa in 2001 brought him deep into the Tanzanian bush, where he performed a field study on the traditional diet of the Hadzabe hunter-gatherers. Unfortunately, Matt's promising academic career was postponed due to a severe case of wanderlust, though he has relentlessly traveled to over fifty different countries in search of a cure.

MARY FITZPATRICK
Tanzania

Mary is from the USA, where she spent her early years in Washington, DC – dreaming, more often than not, of how to get across an ocean or two to more exotic locales. After finishing graduate studies, she set off for several years in Europe. Her fascination with languages and cultures soon led her further south to Africa, where she has spent the past 15 years living and working all around the continent, including in Tanzania and South Africa. She has authored and co-authored many guidebooks and articles on the continent, and heads off on safari at every opportunity.

ADAM KARLIN
Kenya

Clichéd as it may sound, Adam Karlin's first trip to Africa, as a student and volunteer, changed his life. It set him on the path of travelling and writing for a living, and seven years later he closed a circle by coming back to the continent to work on this seventh edition of Lonely Planet *Kenya*. In the course of his research, he drove a RAV4 full of elephant poop around Meru National Park, explored the ruins of the Kenyan coast by dhow, and became one of the first Westerners allowed into the kaya (sacred forest) of the Kausa Mijikenda.

KATE THOMAS
Uganda

Growing up in an English seaside town, Kate would sit on the pebbly beach contemplating life on the other side of the sea. After finishing her studies in Paris and London, she flew to Melbourne, returning by cargo ship, road and rail. When she took a job on the foreign desk of a British newspaper, she pinned a map of Africa above her desk. It soon became torn and tattered and she knew she had to see the real thing. For the past few years she's been writing from Africa, where she's watched mountain gorillas in DR Congo and tried to find pygmy hippos in Liberia.

Watching Wildlife East Africa was first published in 2001. It was researched and written by:

DAVID ANDREW

David created *Wingspan* and *Australian Birding* magazines; edited *Wildlife Australia* magazine; and among other jobs has been a research assistant in Kakadu NP, a birding guide for English comedian Bill Oddie and an editor of Lonely Planet guides.

SUSAN RHIND

A wildlife biologist, Susan ventured to Africa for a break following the completion of her PhD, and spent nearly two years working and travelling around seven of Africa's countries. Susan has scientifically studied dolphins, monkeys and Australian marsupials.

OLIVE BABOON, LAKE NAKURU NATIONAL PARK

INTRODUCTION

FROM the coral reefs off Kenya and Tanzania to the summits of Africa's highest mountains, nowhere else on earth within a similar geographical area is so great an assemblage of large animals supported by such a range of environmental and climatic variation – elements which continue to shape animal distribution and behaviour today.

But too often watching wildlife in East Africa involves being shuttled from one herd or pride to the next, a two-dimensional experience not unlike watching a TV documentary. A more expansive experience can be had by understanding the elements of an ecosystem and their inextricable linkage. For example, the abundance of tiny insects at the bottom of a food chain can affect the behaviour of predators at the top; and entire habitats can appear or disappear according to the behaviour of animals – and people.

The stimulation of the sheer variety and endless activity of forest and savanna should be justification in itself to find out why, how and when it all started, and what makes the cogs turn. And if the emotions stirred by the experience prompt you to take further action for the conservation of what you have seen, then a greater understanding will make that action more effective.

Few visitors come away unmoved from tracking mountain gorillas or our closest living relatives, chimpanzees; for many the experience challenges preconceptions about human nature and evolution. Yet habitat favoured by early humans – mosaics of riverine forest, savanna and lake shore – remain today much as they did a million years ago. Extensive fossil beds in Kenya and Tanzania show that large numbers of existing animal species shared the savannas of East Africa when our ancestors first began to walk upright. If not for the evolutionary pressures that caused their extinction, those early hominids could still be living and reproducing alongside modern lions, antelopes, giraffes…and human beings.

So in a sense the East African wildlife-watching experience is also a direct and profound link with the origins of every human being on the planet. As Karen Blixen wrote in her famous book, Out of Africa: 'In Africa…you woke up in the morning and thought: Here I am, where I ought to be.'

HIGHLIGHTS & ITINERARIES

WHAT TO SEE & WHERE TO SEE IT

THE GREAT MIGRATION
SERENGETI NP, TANZANIA & MASAI MARA NR, KENYA

SEE WILDEBEEST **PAGE 221** SERENGETI NATIONAL PARK **PAGE 108** MASAI MARA NATIONAL RESERVE **PAGE 62**

From July to October each year, millions of wildebeests and zebras travel across the Serengeti Plains, ford the Mara River and – for the lucky survivors – reach fresh grasslands in Masai Mara. This dramatic wildlife drama plays out in reverse from November to April when the herds return to Tanzania and complete the great migration.

EASTERN MOUNTAIN GORILLAS
PN DES VOLCANS, RWANDA & BWINDI IMPENETRABLE NP, UGANDA

SEE GORILLA **PAGE 190** PARC NATIONAL DES VOLCANS **PAGE 179** BWINDI IMPENETRABLE NATIONAL PARK **PAGE 146**

On a continent rife with unparalleled wildlife experiences, tracking gorillas through the equatorial rainforests of Rwanda and Uganda is truly in a class of its own. The first encounter with a silverback, which is more than 90kg of muscled primate, is impossible to describe in words alone.

HIGHLIGHTS

CHIMPANZEE TRACKING
PN DE NYUNGWE, RWANDA & KIBALE FOREST NP, UGANDA

SEE CHIMPANZEE **PAGE 191** PARC NATIONAL DE NYUNGWE **PAGE 178** KIBALE FOREST NATIONAL PARK **PAGE 150**

Lying just beneath humans on the evolutionary ladder, chimpanzees are highly intelligent and sociable primates. Tracking them through the dense underbrush takes time, energy and a little bit of luck, but you'll know you've found them when you're greeted by their distinctive pant-hoot vocalisations.

WHITE RHINOCEROSES
LAKE NAKURU NP, KENYA

SEE WHITE RHINOCEROS **PAGE 208** LAKE NAKURU NATIONAL PARK **PAGE 91**

The more commonly spotted of Africa's two rhinoceros species, the near-threatened white rhino has made a spectacular comeback from the brink of extinction. Tracking these surprisingly gentle giants through hotspots like Lake Nakuru is a chance to test your safari skills.

HIGHLIGHTS

BLACK RHINOCEROS
NGORONGORO CONSERVATION AREA, TANZANIA

SEE BLACK RHINOCEROS **PAGE 209** NGORONGORO CONSERVATION AREA **PAGE 104**

With a quick temper (and a heaving bulk to match), black rhinos were dubbed one of the Big Five dangerous game by early hunters on foot. In the crater at Ngorongoro – and in the safety of your car – you can bathe in adrenaline while you stare down this formidable but charismatic beast.

LIONS ON THE HUNT
SERENGETI NP, TANZANIA & MASAI MARA NR, KENYA

SEE LION PAGE 196 SERENGETI NATIONAL PARK PAGE 108 MASAI MARA NATIONAL RESERVE PAGE 62

Lions are more commonly spotted than you might imagine, though that doesn't mean they're common by any means. They are one of nature's most perfect predators and to catch them on the hunt is to have a front-row seat to the drama of life and death.

HIGHLIGHTS

HYENAS ON THE PROWL
SERENGETI NP, TANZANIA & MASAI MARA NR, KENYA

SEE SPOTTED HYENA **PAGE 200** STRIPED HYENA **PAGE 201** SERENGETI NP **PAGE 108** MASAI MARA NR **PAGE 62**

A highly evolved predator with a killer instinct and massive jaws, the hyena can hold its own alongside larger cats and bring down prey as it pleases. As the sun drops over the Mara and the Serengeti, you will feel chills run down your spine as their haunting but distinctive calls echo through the African bush.

RECLUSIVE LEOPARDS
SERENGETI NP, TANZANIA & QUEEN ELIZABETH NP, UGANDA

SEE LEOPARD **PAGE 197** SERENGETI NATIONAL PARK **PAGE 108** QUEEN ELIZABETH NATIONAL PARK **PAGE 158**

HIGHLIGHTS

Topping the wish list of most safari-goers and Big Five seekers is the leopard, the most reclusive of Africa's big cats. Most often spotted on a branch in the treetops – sometimes directly in front of your vehicle – leopards are nocturnal predators that are masters of stealth and ambush.

CHEETAHS IN FLIGHT
SERENGETI NP, TANZANIA & MASAI MARA NR, KENYA

SEE CHEETAH **PAGE 195** SERENGETI NATIONAL PARK **PAGE 108** MASAI MARA NATIONAL RESERVE **PAGE 62**

You have to look quick if you want to catch a cheetah in flight – these graceful but deadly felines have been clocked at speeds of more than 110 km/h and can leap more than 7m in a single bound. Prey is knocked off balance and dispatched with a lethal bite to the throat.

HIGHLIGHTS

ELEPHANT HERDS
AMBOSELI NATIONAL PARK, KENYA

SEE AFRICAN ELEPHANT **PAGE 205** AMBOSELI NATIONAL PARK **PAGE 74**

HIGHLIGHTS

Weighing in at more than 6000kg and reaching heights of more than 3m, African elephants are the largest terrestrial animals on the planet. Huge herds can quickly surround a vehicle and make you feel positively diminutive, though it's the old and solitary bulls that command the most respect.

FLAMINGOS & PELICANS
LAKE BOGORIA NATIONAL RESERVE, KENYA

SEE GREATER AND LESSER FLAMINGOS **PAGE 240** GREAT WHITE PELICAN **PAGE 235** LAKE BOGORIA NR **89**

Colourful flocks of flamingos use their angular bills to scour the shallows for algae, while aerial formations of pelicans duck, dive and dart for whatever hapless creatures happen to get caught in their pouches. Along the soda lakes of the Rift Valley, you can quite literally spot thousands upon thousands of these birds in a single breathtaking scene.

HIGHLIGHTS

HORNBILLS
TSAVO NP, KENYA & MURCHISON FALLS NP, UGANDA

SEE HORNBILLS **PAGE 266** TSAVO NATIONAL PARK **PAGE 66** MURCHISON FALLS NATIONAL PARK **PAGE 154**

Few birds are as distinctive of the African savanna as the hornbill, a toucan-like omnivore that numbers more than 20 separate species. Easily identified by their enormous but highly specialised bills, and impossible to forget once you've heard their noisy yet engaging call, hornbills are true safari staples.

HUNTING DOGS
SELOUS GAME RESERVE, TANZANIA

SEE HUNTING DOGS **PAGE 193** SELOUS GAME RESERVE **PAGE 118**

Although they were the progenitors of man's best friend, wild hunting dogs have been decimated by common canine diseases and are presently endangered throughout Africa. However, Selous Game Reserve in Tanzania protects a healthy number of these playful pack animals, which are fortunately protected by strong conservation measures.

NILE CROCODILES
LAKE TURKANA, KENYA

SEE NILE CROCODILE **PAGE 290** LAKE TURKANA **PAGE 92**

HIGHLIGHTS

Spotting a crocodile in the wild is a mixed blessing and your reaction usually depends on the distance between you and the lizard. Indeed, crocs are best given a healthy berth, though it's difficult not to stare in awe at this prehistoric predator. At Lake Turkana, don't unpack the swimsuit – crocs congregate in their thousands.

CLASSIC EAST AFRICA
THREE WEEKS TO ONE MONTH / NAIROBI TO ARUSHA

East Africa is one of the world's top destinations for wildlife, and this classic route highlights the best that the region can offer. Starting off in the Kenyan capital of Nairobi, your first port of call is the **Masai Mara National Reserve (p62)**, arguably the finest safari park on the continent, especially from July to October when the wildebeest migration takes place. Heading southeast towards the Tanzanian border, make a brief stop at **Amboseli National Park (p74)**, where enormous elephant herds congregate in the shadow of Mt Kilimanjaro, Africa's tallest peak. In Tanzania, **Lake Manyara National Park (p128)** is one of the many soda lakes lining the floor of the Rift Valley and is home to massive colonies of pink flamingos. Don't miss the nearby **Ngorongoro Conservation Area (p104)**, a veritable lost world of big-game animals, including the critically endangered black rhino. Your final stop is none other than **Serengeti National Park (p108)**, which is contiguous with Masai Mara and positively teems with wildlife, particularly from November to April when the great migration swings south. This itinerary ends in Arusha, a tourist-friendly city where you can swap travel stories over a few rounds of cold beers.

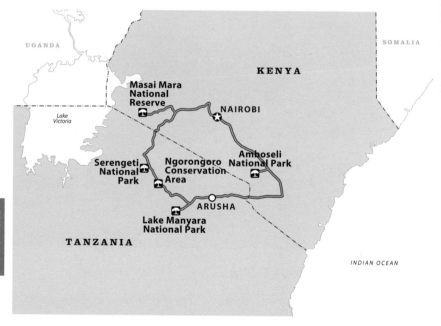

In order to immerse yourself in the classic East Africa experience, it's good to take an entire month to fully explore the extents of this incredible collection of safari parks. However, if you're a bit short on time, or if you want to cut down on the long cross-country drive, you can always take an internal flight or two.

UP-AND-COMING EAST AFRICA
TWO TO THREE WEEKS / KAMPALA TO KIGALI

While Kenya and Tanzania may steal the spotlight in East Africa, both Uganda and Rwanda are up-and-coming players on the safari circuit, allowing you to seek out wildlife while leaving behind the crowds. Starting off in the Ugandan capital of Kampala, head north to **Murchison Falls National Park (p154)**, which is bisected by the mighty Nile River and supports increasingly large herds of herbivores among the papyrus swamps. After backtracking through Kampala, turn west to **Semliki Valley Wildlife Reserve (p170)**, where you can penetrate the eastern extents of the Ituri Forest and get a taste for what lies beyond in the Congo. Turning south, you'll soon reach Uganda's crown jewel, **Queen Elizabeth National Park (p158)**, which protects the country's biggest offering of large animals, including a healthy complement of predators. For a decidedly different take on the safari experience, cross the border and visit **Parc National de l'Akagera (p176)** in eastern Rwanda, which is back on the map with a new conservation mandate. Wind things down in the Rwandan capital of Kigali, where you can pick up a gorilla-tracking permit and set out on the next wildlife adventure.

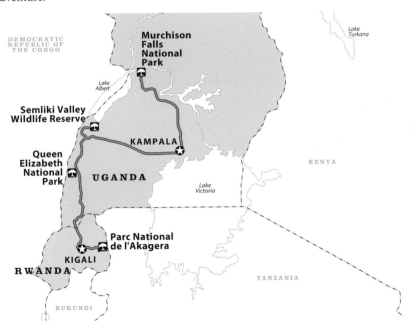

The going can be a bit slow at times, though Rwanda and Uganda are two countries where the journey is often more invigorating than the destination. Depending on how much time you spend in Kampala and Kigali, a few weeks is all you need to escape the tourist trail and check out these emerging parks.

PRIMATE SAFARI
TWO TO THREE WEEKS / KIGALI TO KAMPALA

East Africa is the cradle of humanity, which is why it should come as no surprise that our closest living ancestors are alive and well in the equatorial forests. After registering with the tourist office and picking up your permit in Kigali, try to contain your bursting excitement as you track eastern mountain gorillas in **Parc National des Volcans (p179)** along the Rwandese–Congolese border. Although gorillas are by far the largest primates on the planet, and garner most of the attention in Volcans, the national park is also home to a sizeable population of rare golden monkeys. The next stop on the primate safari is **Parc National de Nyungwe (p178)**, an ecologically vital strip of primary forest that fosters 400-strong habituated troops of colobus monkeys, which bound playfully through the trees and are, at times, an overwhelming sight. Crossing the border into Uganda, you can track our closest genetic cousin, the chimpanzee, underneath the verdant canopies that comprise **Kibale Forest National Park (p150)**. At this point, you can either hightail it to Kampala or have another go at gorilla tracking in **Bwindi Impenetrable National Park (p146)**, a stunning swath of ancient trees that protects these gentle giants.

If you have the time to spare, primate tracking in Uganda and Rwanda pairs wonderfully with more traditional game drives in East Africa's safari parks. While it takes two to three weeks to follow the itinerary above, you can alternatively choose just one or two primate locales and tack them onto your trip to make a custom tailored itinerary.

ROUGH & RUGGED
ABOUT ONE MONTH / NAIROBI TO DAR ES SALAAM

While some safaris parks are, at times, saturated with trains of tourist vehicles, this itinerary is perfect for anyone who wants to leave civilisation – and the paved road – behind. Starting in Nairobi, ease into your wilderness adventure with a brief visit to the **Samburu, Buffalo Springs & Shaba National Reserves (p84)**, a scorched scrubland where you can spot arid specialists in patches of thorny trees. Things really start to get extreme when you reach nearby **Lake Turkana (p92)**, a shimmering jewel of jade surf in the middle of a baking-hot red desert. Heading briefly back into the modern human world, pass through Nairobi en route to **Tsavo National Park (p66)**, a massive and largely undeveloped reserve that is roughly the same size as Wales. After crossing the border into Tanzania, skip the well-trodden northern circuit and instead focus your time on **Selous Game Reserve (p118)** and **Ruaha National Park (p134)**. Despite getting the short stick from tourists, both reserves protect some of the largest populations of hunting dogs in Africa. If you find yourself in need of some sand and sea, this itinerary ends in the steamy port city of Dar es Salaam.

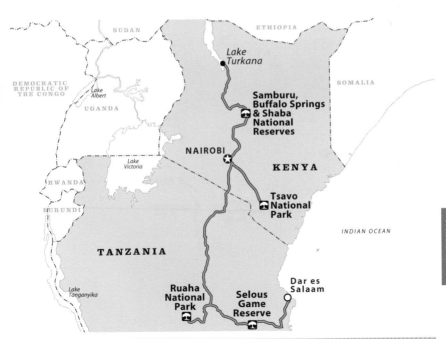

This itinerary takes in large stretches of poorly developed roads and remote wilderness, which means you're going to need time and patience to tackle whatever gets thrown your way. However, your reward will be a brief but impossible-to-forget glimpse at some of East Africa's wildest and least-known game parks.

ITINERARIES

SAND & SEA
AT LEAST TWO WEEKS / DAR ES SALAAM TO MOMBASA

While most people's image of East Africa entails dusty savannas and dried-out landscapes, all you need to do is head for the coast to indulge in a healthy measure of white sand and tropical sea. From Dar es Salaam, either take a ferry or hop a small plane to Africa's Spice Islands, **Zanzibar** and **Pemba (p114)**. Centred on Stone Town, a Swahili port steeped in rich architectural history, Zanzibar is dotted with pristine, palm-fringed beaches and surrounded by dazzling coral reefs that are home to dolphins, sea turtles and tropical fish galore. The nearby island of Pemba sees far fewer tourists, though its Ngezi Forest Reserve is inhabited by rare endemics from the Pemba flying-fox to the Pemba scops owl. Back on the Tanzanian mainland, **Saadani National Park (p138)** is a unique wildlife destination that combines traditional safari drives with more holiday-like beachcombing. Continue north across the border into Kenya until you reach **Malindi & Watamu Marine National Parks (p93)**, prominent snorkelling and scuba-diving hotspots where you stand a high chance of spotting whale sharks and manta rays. This itinerary ends in the Kenyan port city of Mombasa, where you can work on getting your land legs back.

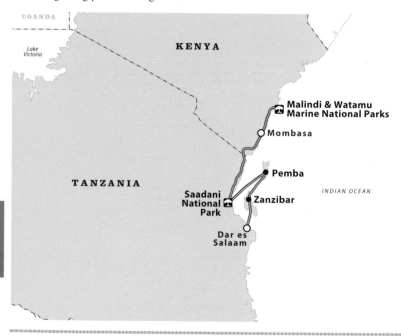

It takes about two weeks to travel the Swahili Coast and visit the sights mentioned in this itinerary, though you really can't set a time limit on rest and relaxation. On the contrary, this is one trip where it's worth taking things slow, ignoring the time and date and helping yourself to yet another coconut.

EAST AFRICAN BIRDING
ABOUT ONE MONTH / NAIROBI TO DAR ES SALAAM

East Africa is regarded as one of the world's top birding destinations, which means that you don't have to look too hard to spot African standards, localised species and rare endemics. Startiwng in Nairobi, your first stop on the birding tour is **Lake Nakuru National Park (p91)**, a Rift Valley soda lake that is famed for its enormous populations of flamingos and pelicans. For rainforest avians, head west into **Kakamega Forest (p76)**, which is the easternmost stronghold for West African species, especially during the June-to-August breeding season. For a different set of birds altogether, head to the **Arabuko Sokoke Forest Reserve (p70)** on Kenya's coast in search of weavers, sunbirds, turacos and many, many more. Tanzania is also home to a couple of high-profile sanctuaries, especially **Tarangire National Park (p122)**, where sparse vegetation leads to simply stunning birdwatching. A comparatively new player on the birding circuit is **Udzungwa Mountains National Park (p136)**, a protected patch of the Eastern Arc Mountains that is comprised of lowland, submontane and montane forests. Just in case you need some time to update your checklists with your travel companions, this trip conveniently ends in Dar es Salaam.

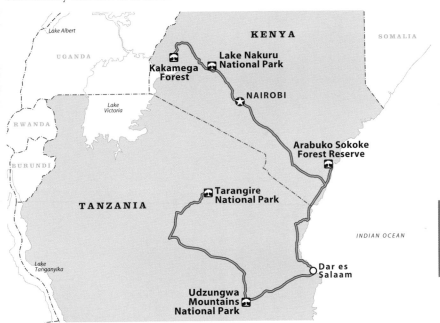

ITINERARIES

Patience is a virtue, especially when it comes to birdwatching, which is why you should give yourself plenty of time to explore some of East Africa's most famous birding spots. Truth be told, virtually every national park in the region is home to rare endemics worth seeking out, though the parks mentioned in this itinerary are some of our favourites.

ENVIRONMENT & CONSERVATION
UNDERSTANDING THE LAND & ITS HISTORY

STRADDLING THE EQUATOR, and edged by the Rift Valley and the Indian Ocean, East Africa is a region of primeval natural splendour and untamed rawness that is both geographically and environmentally diverse. Boasting one of the world's most impressive collections of national parks, East Africa is defined by its rich concentration of wildlife, which has been fostered through generations of increasingly comprehensive conservation measures.

THE EAST AFRICAN ENVIRONMENT

NATURAL HISTORY

Africa was once joined to South America and Australia as part of the supercontinent Gondwana, which broke up between 270 and 200 million years ago. For another 30 million years, Africa and Eurasia were periodically linked by land bridges, which enabled the spread of mammals between the two continents. Extensive volcanic activity in East Africa 12 million years ago uplifted the land by around 1300m and formed the great mountain peaks. The last million years have been marked by violent tectonic activity and further development of the rift valleys.

Climatic changes caused by ice ages in the northern hemisphere caused the expansion and contraction of habitats in Africa. The icy peaks of Mt Kenya, Mt Kilimanjaro and the Rwenzoris are remnants of once-extensive glaciations, which during the ice ages would have linked these great mountains. During glacial periods, the climate at lower altitudes was drier than at present, enabling savanna to expand and restricting forests to isolated pockets. Between ice ages, wetter conditions prevailed and forests spread while drier habitats retreated.

Even today, the East African environment is far from stable and is constantly reshaped by complex elements. For example, fire has long swept through coarse grassland during the dry season, promoting new growth. In the absence of fire and grazing animals, woody growth dominates until elephants open it up and it reverts to grassland. Now, however, it is humans who are the main shaper of the landscape, forming high population densities while destroying habitats at unsustainable rates.

WILDLIFE

The mammals of East Africa have reached an extraordinary diversity, particularly in the savanna and at the eastern edge of the rainforests of the Zaïre River basin. The total number of species depends on which classification system is accepted, and varies because some species become locally extinct, others are discovered or rediscovered and still others are reclassified in light of new research. To a tally of about 30 primates (monkeys, apes etc) can be added 41 carnivores (cats and dogs as well as mongooses, otters and weasels) and 59 more peaceable large mammals such as antelopes, elephants and rhinos. Other groups include hyraxes, elephant shrews, pangolins and hares and hundreds of species of rodent, shrew and bat.

ENVIRONMENT

East Africa's hugely varied and abundant birdlife has inspired many a passive observer to take up birdwatching. Approximately 15% of the world's bird species have been recorded in the region, with well over 1000 different species recorded in Kenya, Uganda and Tanzania. Several bird families are also unique to Africa, including turacos, mousebirds and four monospecific families (ie containing only one species): the ostrich, secretary bird, hamerkop and shoebill.

Of course, mammals and birds are just peak groups in a complex web of codependent plants and animals numbering thousands of species. Other groups that reach particular abundance or diversity are reptiles, amphibians, butterflies and the incredibly varied life forms of coral reefs. Lake Tanganyika, the second-deepest in the world, supports 300 fish species, 90% of which are endemic, and molluscs similar to those known from marine fossils dating back to the Jurassic era.

HUMANS & WILDLIFE

Evidence from extensive fossil beds in Tanzania, Kenya, Uganda and other parts of Africa now leave little doubt that Africa, if not East Africa, is where ancestral apes evolved into hominids and, hence, modern human beings. From its early beginnings as just one of many predators in the savanna,

THE GREAT RIFT VALLEY

The Great Rift Valley is part of the East African rift system – a massive geological fault slicing its way almost 6500km across Africa, from the Dead Sea in the north to Beira (Mozambique) in the south. The rift system was formed more than 30 million years ago when the tectonic plates that comprise the African and Eurasian land masses collided and then diverged again. As the plates moved apart, massive tablets of the earth's crust collapsed between them, resulting over the millennia in the escarpments, ravines, flatlands and lakes that mark much of East Africa today.

The rift system is especially famous for its calderas and volcanoes (including Mt Kilimanjaro, Mt Meru and the calderas of the Crater Highlands) and for its lakes. Some of these lakes, including Lakes Tanganyika and Nyasa, are very deep, with floors plunging well below sea level, although their surfaces may be several hundred metres above sea level.

The East African section of the Rift Valley consists of two branches formed where the main rift system divides north of Kenya's Lake Turkana. The western branch, or Western Rift Valley, makes its way past Lake Albert in Uganda through Rwanda and Burundi down to Lake Tanganyika, after which it meanders southeast to Lake Nyasa. Seismic and volcanic disturbances still occur throughout the western branch. The eastern branch, known as the Eastern or Gregory Rift, runs south from Lake Turkana past Lakes Natron and Manyara in Tanzania before joining again with the Western Rift in northern Malawi. The lakes of the Eastern Rift are smaller and shallower than those in the western branch; some of them are only waterless salt beds.

Places where the escarpments of the Rift Valley are particularly impressive include Kenya's Rift Valley Province, the Nkuruman Escarpment east of Kenya's Masai Mara National Reserve, and the terrain around Ngorongoro Conservation Area and Lake Manyara National Park in Tanzania.

ENVIRONMENT

THE GREAT MIGRATION

There are probably more wildebeests in Kenya and Tanzania now than ever before. European explorers found the Maasai tribes of southern Kenya and northern Tanzania tending their cattle in apparent harmony with grazing plains mammals, which they did not as a rule hunt for food. But in 1891, an outbreak of rinderpest decimated the Maasai's herds and wiped out nearly 90% of the region's buffaloes and wildebeests. Famine struck and the tribes abandoned the area for several decades. The resulting proliferation of woodland in the absence of wild and domestic grazing animals made ideal habitat for tsetse flies, which carry *trypanosomiasis* (sleeping sickness), and the area was shunned by people and their livestock.

The wildebeest population recovered for several decades, but until 1920 numbered only 120,000 to 130,000. However, WWII fires set by hunters and honey gatherers destroyed much of the woodland, once again opening the region up to grazing animals. Subsequently, the wildebeest population exploded from about 250,000 to 1.3 million.

The famous great migration between the Serengeti and Masai Mara – on its current scale – is only a recent phenomenon. Before 1960, most of the Mara wildebeests came from a separate population in the Loita Plains, and reached the Mara from the Serengeti only in very dry years. Following the massive population increase, however, the Mara emerged as a dry-season refuge for 500,000 to one million wildebeests, which give birth during the wettest part of the year in the Serengeti, moving north as their food supply diminishes.

obliged to fortify itself against a hostile environment, the adaptable, increasingly populous and aggressively inventive human species now dominates the planet.

The early traces are scanty, but from assemblages of bones at famous digs such as Olduvai Gorge and Sibiloi, a picture is gradually building up to show that humans evolved in Africa an estimated three million years ago among rich plant and animal communities. Carl Linnaeus, the father of modern taxonomy, correctly classified human beings as apes, although it can only have been the genteel behaviour he observed in the bourgeois drawing rooms of 17th-century Europe that led him to name his fellow species Homo sapiens – 'wise man'. Yet the environmental pressures affecting the evolution of every other species also applied to the rise of Homo sapiens, and its continued survival depended on the same factors – the availability of water

and food, the ability to avoid predation and the survival of disease.

The nearest living apes to humans are the two species of chimpanzees, and recent research has provided biological, behavioural and ecological evidence of early humans' metaphorical walk out of the forest. But things didn't get off to a good start, and for many highly specialised large mammal species, contact with early human hunters proved to be fatal at a time when climate change was causing their habitats to contract. Three species of African elephant alone are known to have died out during the rise of Homo sapiens, and other species known to have become extinct include giant species of pig and buffalo and several giraffes, hippos, horses and hyenas.

Apart from hunting, the first great change wrought on the landscape was fire, which, until about 350,000 years ago, was lit either accidentally or deliberately, to smoke out beehives and aid progress through grassland. Within the last 5000 to 6000 years, however, pastoralists dependent on livestock, and cultivators dependent on crops, have further modified vegetation over large areas.

EXPLOITATION & POPULATION EXPLOSION

East Africa's pastoral peoples have always lived alongside wildlife, and their cultures and traditions reflect the plants and animals with which they came into daily contact. Some tribes, such as the Maasai, are famously indifferent to wildlife, respect turning to malice only when crops, livestock or human life are at stake. The Maasai consider the hunting of wild animals for food beneath them and would rather starve than eat birds or reptiles – thus large numbers of large mammals remain in former or current pastoral areas. The Waliangulu, on the other hand, were master bushmen of the arid plains and active hunters of elephants, pursuing them with poisoned arrows fired from great bows.

The arrival of Europeans and the advent of firearms ushered in the most enduring mass slaughter of wildlife – or 'game'. Their legacy is the modern tourists' pursuit of the Big Five – lion, leopard, rhino, elephant and buffalo, so called because they were reputedly the most dangerous to hunt. These safaris spawned numerous legends about both the game and its adversaries, among them famous miscreants such as Theodore Roosevelt and Ernest Hemingway. But 100 years ago, large animals were abundant and people few – nobody saw where it was all leading and the hunting safaris took an immense toll.

The last 50 years have seen a complete reversal in the roles of people and nature in East Africa. Environmental change has accelerated, owing to livestock and overgrazing, the clearance of natural systems for agriculture and an exploding human population. While most hazards to human life have been conquered, one natural adversary still holds the trump card – disease. Africa is an evolutionary hothouse – malaria and sleeping sickness have affected the spread of people in East Africa, and another killer, AIDS, is now rampant.

CONSERVATION

PARKS & RESERVES

The cornerstone of wildlife conservation in East Africa has historically been national parks and other reserves declared under colonial governments. Management problems notwithstanding, these continue to provide the highest level of official protection to wildlife and ecosystems across the region and remain the focus for most wildlife

ENVIRONMENT

EAST AFRICAN ENDANGERED SPECIES

ANIMAL	STATUS	BEST PLACE TO SEE	PAGE
BLACK RHINOCEROS	CRITICALLY ENDANGERED	SERENGETI NATIONAL PARK	108
CHIMPANZEE	ENDANGERED	KIBALE FOREST NATIONAL PARK	150
DUGONG	LOCALLY ENDANGERED	MALINDI MARINE NATIONAL PARK	93
GREVY'S ZEBRA	ENDANGERED	SAMBURU NATIONAL RESERVE	84
HIROLA ANTELOPE	CRITICALLY ENDANGERED	TSAVO NATIONAL PARK	66
HUNTING DOG	ENDANGERED	SELOUS GAME RESERVE	118
MOUNTAIN GORILLA	CRITICALLY ENDANGERED	PARC NATIONAL DES VOLCANS	179

tourism despite the fact that many were created with no regard for preserving biodiversity. On paper at least, national parks protect all wildlife from exploitation, such as hunting, and prohibit cultivation, settlement and all other disturbances.

The establishment and maintenance of protected areas in each country is handled by a national body, but in practice, law enforcement and reserve management are hampered by lack of funding and other chronic problems. Conservation is a low priority when resources are thinly spread, though fortunately nongovernment organisations (NGOs) such as the International Union for Conversation of Nature (IUCN) and the World Wide Fund for Nature (WWF) maintain a permanent presence in the region under the United Nations Environment Program (UNEP). Other big players include the United Nations Educational, Scientific and Cultural Organisation

(Unesco), the Flora and Fauna Preservation Society (FFPS), the African Wildlife Foundation (AWF), the Wildlife Conservation Society (WCS) and the International Gorilla Conservation Programme (IGCP).

High-profile mammals such as gorillas, elephants and rhinos presently benefit from intensive study, donor aid and funding from tourism, though the threats to their survival are very real. Black rhinos were nearly wiped out in the space of 30 years – from an estimated 70,000 in 1960 to about 2500 in 1990 – which vaulted the issue of conservation to the international stage. Today, East Africa has an abundance of protected areas, but it continues to suffer from grave environmental scourges.

POACHING & CULLING

The most notorious environmental issue in East Africa is arguably poaching, which occurs throughout the region.

VICTORIA'S LAST GASPS?

Lake Victoria once supported one of the world's most diverse community of freshwater fish, with around 500 species – and most were endemic. Today, Nile perch and tilapia introduced as food fish have wiped out half the native species, and even the commercial fisheries are threatened. Fertiliser run-off from agriculture and effluent from the 30 million people who live around the lake, both increasing, have raised the level of nutrients entering Lake Victoria. This results in decreased oxygen levels and encourages algal blooms that choke the surface.

However, the most pressing problem is the dense, floating mats of water hyacinth, introduced to East Africa as an ornamental plant. The weed is now so thick, and spreading so rapidly, that it surrounds entire islands and blocks the passage of cargo boats. Without the collective presence of native fish, which once thrived on decaying plant and animal matter, mosquitoes and snails proliferate among hyacinths rotting in shallow water – spreading malaria and bilharzia.

Scientists warned against upsetting Victoria's ecological balance three decades ago; now even its partial restoration will be prohibitively expensive and will require the long-term commitment of all regional players. To date, attempts at controlling the water hyacinth have included hauling it out by hand, spraying it with herbicides and introducing weevils that feed exclusively on the weed.

In one sense, it's not difficult to see why: 1kg of elephant ivory is worth as much as US$1000 wholesale, and rhino horn is valued at thousands of dollars per kilogram. This amounts to tens of thousands of dollars for a single horn, or more than 100 times what the average East African earns in a year. Poaching is also difficult to control due to resource and personnel shortages and the vastness and inaccessibility of many areas. Entrenched interests are also a major contributing factor, with everyone from the poachers themselves (often local villagers struggling to earn some money) to ivory dealers, embassies and government officials at the highest levels trying to get a piece of the pie.

In 1989, in response to the illegal trade and diminishing numbers of elephants, a world body called the Convention on International Trade in Endangered Species (CITES) internationally banned the import and export of ivory. It also increased funding for antipoaching measures. When the ban was established, world raw-ivory prices plummeted by 90% and the market for poaching and smuggling was radically reduced.

Although elephant populations recovered in some ravaged areas, human populations continued to grow and another problem surfaced. Elephants eat huge quantities of foliage, but in the past, herds would eat their fill then migrate to another area, allowing time for the vegetation to regenerate. However, an increasing human population pressed the elephants into smaller and smaller areas – mostly around national parks – and the herds were forced to eat everything available. In many places, the bush began to look as if an atom bomb had hit.

POPULATION CONTROL

Increasingly across the region, park authorities are facing elephant overpopulation. Proposed solutions include relocation (where herds are permanently transplanted to other areas) and contraception. The only other alternative is to cull herds, sometimes in large numbers; this seems a bizarre paradox, but illustrates the seriousness of the problem. In the West, people generally hold a preservationist viewpoint, that elephant herds should be conserved for their own sake or for aesthetic reasons. However, the local sentiment maintains that the elephant must justify its existence on long-term economic grounds for the benefit of local people, or for the country as a whole.

This is an issue sure to generate much debate, with proponents citing the health of the parks, including other wildlife and the elephants themselves, and organisations such as the International Fund for Animal Welfare (IFAW) appalled at such a solution, which they claim is cruel, unethical and scientifically unsound. IFAW believes aerial surveys of elephant numbers are inaccurate, population growth has not been accurately surveyed and that other solutions have not been looked at carefully enough, including more transfrontier parks crossing national borders.

Furthermore, there is much dispute about whether controlled ivory sales should be reintroduced, with countries with excessive elephant populations and large ivory stockpiles pushing hard for a relaxation on the ban. Some argue that countries with large tracts of protected land are paying for the inability of other African countries to properly manage and protect their wildlife. Indeed, it remains to be seen whether a lift on the ban will occur but, meanwhile, debate about the ivory trade, and the culling solution to overpopulation, rages on.

ENVIRONMENT

ECOLOGICAL DEGRADATION

Parks and reserves are now effectively islands in a sea of cultivation, ranches and humanity, and many priority areas for conservation still lie outside the system. At present, East Africa includes some of the poorest and most resource-stressed nations in the world. The population of the region has doubled in the last 20 years and is predicted to multiply another three times in the next 20 years. In times of crisis, such as famine and political instability, conservation can fall off the agenda altogether.

To illustrate this point, consider that Rwanda, one of the most densely populated countries on the continent, downsized Parc National de l'Akagera in the 1990s by 70% to accommodate refugees. A decade later, the Rwandan government is struggling to once again attract foreign revenues earned from wildlife tourism. Gorilla-tracking permits in Parc National des Volcans bring in over US$1 million per year alone, as well as all of the secondary income generated by the tourist presence in and around the national park. However, if beleaguered reserves disappear, then wildlife tourism will quickly lose its focus and a much-needed source of hard currency will dry up.

Just as worrisome as overpopulation is deforestation, with East Africa's forest areas today representing only a fraction of the region's original forest cover. On the Zanzibar Archipelago, for example, only about 5% of the dense tropical forest that once blanketed the islands still remains. In sections of the long Eastern Arc mountain chain, which sweeps in an arc from southern Kenya down towards central Tanzania, forest depletion has caused such serious erosion that entire villages have had to be shifted to lower areas. In Kenya, agriculture, land grabbing, charcoal burning and illegal logging have all taken their toll over the years.

Deforestation brings with it soil erosion, shrinking water catchments and cultivable areas, and decreased availability of traditional building materials, foodstuffs and medicines. It also means that many birds and animals lose their habitats and that local human populations risk losing their lifeblood. While the creation of forest reserves, especially in Kenya and Tanzania, has been a start in addressing the problem, tree-felling prohibitions are often not enforced.

Introduced plant species also present a real threat to East African ecosystems. There are hundreds and hundreds of invasive alien plant species in the region – that is, they thrive to the detriment of endemic species. For example, Australian wattle trees and Mexico mesquite flourish by sinking their roots deeper into the soil than indigenous trees, wich then suffer from lack of nourishment. Additionally, the Australian hakea shrub was introduced to serve as a hedge and is now rampant, displacing native trees and killing off smaller plants.

THE SOLUTIONS?

For years, the conservation establishment regarded human populations as a negative factor in environmental protection, and local inhabitants were often excluded from national parks or other protected areas because it was assumed that they damaged natural resources. A classic example is that of the Maasai, who were forced from parts of their traditional grazing lands around Serengeti National Park for the sake of conservation and tourism. Fortunately, the tide has begun to turn and it's now recognised that steps taken in the name of conservation will ultimately backfire if not done with the cooperation and involvement of local communities.

In the new millennium the traditional role of conservation bodies, such as reserve management, protection of wildlife and fulfilling the obligations of international conservation treaties, must be achieved in a climate of unprecedented population growth and the manifold demands it creates. Wildlife management must involve politically and socially acceptable solutions that are ecologically sustainable and economically viable, against a backdrop of regional poverty, endemic corruption, powerful market forces and, in some countries, political instability.

Fortunately, governments and NGOs are now aware that policies shaped without local participation inevitably lead to local opposition. Community conservation projects encourage local involvement, leading to a strong sense of ownership and benefits such as crop protection and health and education funding. For example, Bwindi Impenetrable National Park in Uganda has a multi-use forest program; income from tourism is shared among local

WANGARI MAATHAI, NOBEL LAUREATE

On Earth Day in 1977 Professor Wangari Maathai planted seven trees in her backyard, setting in motion the grassroots environmental campaign that later came to be known as the Green Belt Movement. Since then, more than 40 million trees have been planted throughout Kenya and the movement has expanded to more than 30 other African countries. The core aim of this campaign is to educate women – who make up around 70% of farmers in Africa – about the links between soil erosion, undernourishment and poor health, and to encourage individuals to protect their immediate environment and guard against soil erosion by planting 'green belts' of trees and establishing tree nurseries.

Maathai, who served as assistant minister for the environment between 2003 and 2005, has worked extensively with various international organisations to exert leverage on the Kenyan government, and was awarded the Nobel Peace Prize in 2004 (the first African woman to receive it) for her tireless campaigning on environmental issues. However, the Moi regime on several occasions vilified her as a 'threat to the order and security of the country' due to her demands for free and fair multiparty elections.

In addition to environmental issues she is also heavily involved in women's rights (her first husband divorced her because she was 'too strong-minded for a woman' – the judge in the divorce case agreed and then locked her in the slammer for speaking out against him!) and in 2006 was one of the founders of the Nobel Women's Initiative, which aims to bring justice, peace and equality to women. Maathai's personal views have also attracted controversy in some circles, particularly on the subject of AIDS – it's claimed that she said AIDS was created by scientists for use in 'biological warfare' against blacks. However, she has denied making this statement.

Whatever her beliefs, Maathai is certainly a fascinating figure and the Green Belt Movement is still one of the most significant environmental organisations in Kenya. Maathai's book *Unbowed: One Woman's Story* was published in 2006.

ENVIRONMENT

communities; and several international groups cooperate on aspects of gorilla tourism training and management. Such projects have shown sometimes sceptical locals that wildlife can benefit all, not just overseas tourists and government.

Indeed, community-based conservation has become a critical concept as tour operators, funding organisations and others recognise that East Africa's protected areas are unlikely to succeed in the long term unless local people can obtain real benefits. If there are tangible benefits for local inhabitants – benefits such as increased local income from visitors to wilderness areas – then natural environments have a much better chance of evading destruction.

Much of this new awareness is taking place at the grassroots level, with a sprouting of activities such as Kenya's Green Belt Movement (see the boxed text, p41) and community-level erosion-control projects.

TRAVELLING SUSTAINABLY

As one of the world's iconic destinations, East Africa spoils visitors with a never-ending assortment of wildlife-watching activities. At the same time, the greatest challenge to travellers in the region is preserving the purity of the environment for future generations. Quite simply, each of us bears the responsibility to minimise the impact of our stay and to travel in the most sustainable way possible.

The continuous growth of the travel industry has brought incredible economic success to parts of East Africa. However, this growth has also placed enormous stress on both biological and cultural habitats and threatens to destroy the very destinations that tourists are seeking out. In recent years, the term 'sustainable tourism' has emerged as an industry buzzword and refers to striking the ideal balance between travellers and their surrounding environment.

One of the most important tenets of sustainable tourism is the notion of respecting local communities. Cultural ruin of a destination is irreversible, but community preservation is one area where travellers can make the biggest individual difference. While in East Africa, talk to locals and ask them about their customs and traditions. An eagerness to learn on the part of the traveller may reassure a local that others value their customs, even if everything is changing around them.

An immediate benefit of tourism is a strong financial boost to the local economy. Regardless of whether you're shoestringing or living it up in five-star hotels, please respect the fact that international travel in any capacity is a luxury that the majority of the world's people will never be able to enjoy. With that said, if the opportunity arises to spend money at a locally run business or vendor, don't hesitate to give a little back.

Finally, one of the simplest things you can do before embarking on a trip to East Africa is to learn about pressing conservation and environmental issues, which are highlighted throughout this chapter. Keeping these issues in mind, do your best to do business with and support hotels, lodges, tour operators and environmental groups that promote conservation initiatives and have public long-term management plans.

VOLUNTEER TOURISM

There are quite a large number of volunteers in East Africa, which is certainly cause for celebration as voluntourism is a great way to travel sustainably while simultaneously reducing the ecological footprint of your trip. It's also an amazing forum for self-exploration, especially if you touch a few lives and meet a few new friends along the way.

Some general places to start your search include **Volunteer Abroad** (www.volunteerabroad.com), **Frontier** (www.frontier.ac.uk), **Working Abroad** (www.workingabroad.com), **Global Volunteers** (www.globalvolunteers.org) and **Volunteer Africa** (www.volunteerafrica.org), which are all well-organised online directories of volunteer placements. There are also various volunteer holiday opportunities included in the online listings of **ResponsibleTravel.com** (www.responsibletravel.com) and **Camps International** (www.campkenya.com).

For more long-term placements, consider **Voluntary Service Overseas** (VSO; www.vsointernational.org), the largest independent (nongovernment) volunteer organisation in the world, the **US-based Peace Corps** (www.peacecorps.gov) and the **Unesco-sponsored Coordinating Committee for International Voluntary Service** (www.unesco.org/ccivs).

If you have professional skills and are looking for more specific wildlife-related volunteer or work placements, consider the following organisations:

- **African Wildlife Foundation** (AWF; www.awf.org)
- **Fauna & Flora International** (www.fauna-flora.org)
- **International Fund for Animal Welfare** (IFAW; www.ifaw.org)
- **International Gorilla Conservation Programme** (IGCP; www.igcp.org)
- **International Union for Conversation of Nature** (IUCN; www.iucn.org)
- **United Nations Educational, Scientific and Cultural Organisation** (UNESCO; www.unesco.org)
- **United Nations Environment Programme** (UNEP; www.unep.org)
- **Wildlife Conservation Society** (WCS; www.wcs.org)
- **World Wide Fund for Nature** (WWF; www.panda.org)

HABITATS

SAVANNA

The popular image (thanks to numerous documentaries, films and books) of East Africa as a land of rolling plains of grass dotted with acacias, perhaps with a dramatic montane backdrop, pretty closely matches the reality. This habitat, generally called savanna, covers vast areas and straddles all the countries of the region, reaching its greatest extent in Kenya and Uganda, but merely poking into Rwanda via river valleys across the Albertine Rift Valley.

Under a multitude of definitions and conditions, East African savanna is a dynamic ecosystem that supports more herds of large mammals and their predators than any other habitat on earth. Broadly speaking, savanna develops where annual rainfall falls in one long wet season followed by a long dry. Usually it is characterised by an understorey of grassland and taller vegetation such as various species of acacia, many of which have distinctive

ENVIRONMENT

SAVANNA, TARANGIRE NATIONAL PARK, TANZANIA

shapes and can withstand the grass fires that sweep through during dry seasons. Think of it as a vast mosaic: over long periods of time, savanna advances into adjoining woodland destroyed by fire and elephants; but if fire and elephant damage become too concentrated, savanna may be reclaimed by grassland.

The relationship between some savanna plants and animals is subtle and complex and reflects cyclical patterns that may take decades to complete. For example, the seed pods of the flat-topped umbrella acacia are shed in the dry season and are covered in nutritious pulp, that attracts browsers such as antelopes and giraffes when other food is scarce. Animals that eat the pods transport and distribute the seeds in their dung, and germination and resistance to insect predation appears to be higher in seeds that have passed through an animal's digestive tract than those in that haven't.

OPEN-TOP SAFARI

Much of your time in the savanna will be spent peering out the roof of an open-top safari vehicle, but you'll still get a feel for this important habitat and start to appreciate its fragrant smell. The great and famous parks of the region all have huge areas of savanna in which you are going to see large animals. There's no real knack to it, other than putting in the hours and getting in the field early.

Look down from a ridge with the vehicle as a vantage point to spot large mammals; elephants, giraffes and buffaloes stand out because of their sheer size, although even they can get lost at a distance. Watercourses are marked by lines of tall trees and denser bush – these are productive areas to seek the heat of the day; leopards in particular like this habitat. Birds are abundant; expect several species of raptor at any time and a constant parade of weavers, hornbills, barbets, woodpeckers and others throughout the day. Finding some animals takes patience, but watch for the signs – vultures volplaning down to a kill, birds mobbing a mongoose or antelopes fleeing a predator.

Rocky outcrops that rise, sometimes dramatically, from the plains as jumbled piles of massive boulders, provide islands of shelter in the savanna. Known as koppies, the natural crevices and overhangs are dens for predators such as leopards and spotted hyenas; pythons hunt between the boulders and small carnivores such as mongooses and genets chivvy out prey – a favourite of which are hyraxes, the quintessential koppie dwellers. Take care when walking around koppies: they are a favourite shady spot for lions.

SEE IT AT...

» Serengeti NP (p108) » Masai Mara NR (p62) » Amboseli NP (p74) » Queen Elizabeth NP (p158)

GRASSLAND & WOODLAND

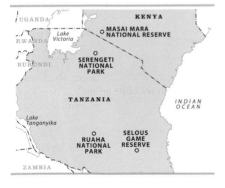

In a long succession from east to west, woodland probably represents a transition from savanna to the rainforest of the Zaïre River basin, and thrives where 800mm to 1200mm of rainfall is concentrated between November and May. Normally woodland has a more or less continuous canopy, but during dry months the combined effects of fires and elephant activity break it into a mosaic of vegetation at different stages of growth. Grazing animals often concentrate around areas of regrowth after these periodic disturbances, but where too much interference occurs, woodland can eventually revert to grassland.

Cycles of wet and dry, flood and fire dictate which grasses dominate and, consequently, which animals graze. Each species has a different preference for type and age of grass, and the actions of each shape the grassland to the benefit or detriment of others. Thus, zebras crop the coarsest species, seed heads and all, followed by the more selective wildebeests; topis, hartebeests and gazelles are even more specialised. The huge herds recycle nutrients in a vast cycle of mowing, trampling and fertilising, paving the way for the next wave and carried on over vast areas. Least selective are the elephants, whose actions help shape grassland by destroying woody growth and even tree cover.

Fires become more frequent as the habitat reverts to grassland, further encouraging grass and grazers. Once the grazing herds moved over empty plains in a great cycle that took centuries or even millennia to complete, and allowed grassland to recover in their wake. But modern pastoralists, who graze their livestock in competition with native herbivores, also encourage fires. Ironically, because they overstock the land, their herds of cattle and goats kill off the grassland and encourage woody growth again.

ENVIRONMENT

ENVIRONMENT

SCANNING THE CROWDS

Large tracts of grassland are at times virtually empty – just endless ripples in the wind – but at others, crowded with herbivores. Although they look simple, grasslands are complex communities that vary dramatically according to rainfall, aspect, drainage and soil chemistry, and the further effects of fire, elephants and other grazers. Look at a head of grass; the shape of the seeds and flowers is distinct for each species, forming a canopy over which you and other large animals tower – a bonus for the observer, of course, because the wide vistas make for easy watching.

Low down lives a host of insects and ground-nesting birds, such as larks, pipits and bustards, and a few reptiles. But out there in the fields, most larger animals are vulnerable and camouflage or mobility are the secrets to success. Small mammals, such as mongooses and bat-eared foxes, shelter in thickets or termite mounds, or dig their own burrows. Apart from the prospect of death from above, there is the very real danger of being trampled by millions of hooves. Of course, this is what most people come to see in the grassland – the great herds of herbivores and the well-organised gangs of predators that hunt them.

Fingers of woodland frequently extend into adjoining savanna, where a tall, spreading acacia, the yellow fever tree, grows along permanent and semipermanent waterways. This is not a habitat with specialised inhabitants, but leopards, in particular, like to lounge on the sometimes huge boughs of fever trees. The dense understorey can also shelter antelopes and ground birds such as francolins, primates such as vervet monkeys and black-and-white colobus, and birds such as woodpeckers, barbets and wood-hoopoes.

SEE IT AT...
» **Serengeti NP (p108)** » **Masai Mara NR (p62)** » **Selous GR (p118)** » **Ruaha NP (p134)**

RAINFOREST

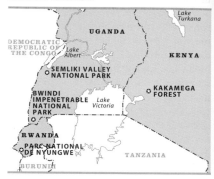

Incredibly rich in biodiversity, and much studied yet little understood, rainforests support more animal species than any other terrestrial ecosystem. In past ages, vast rainforests formed an evolutionary hothouse in the Zaïre River basin and stretched east across the Rift Valleys, before retracting with climatic change to leave far-flung relics. However, some of these forests are still extensive enough to support large mammals, such as gorillas and chimpanzees, and most are heaving with hundreds of bird species and uncountable insects and other small animals.

To enter the rainforest is to walk into a luxuriant world of growth and decay, with the humid air full of the rich smell of dampness. Deep leaf litter makes a spongy carpet through which grow 3m-wide buttressed trees with trunks that barrel straight up to the canopy 30m or more above your head. Massive interlocked branches sprout bracket fungi, deep cushions of moss and miniature gardens of epiphytic orchids and ferns. Shafts of light piercing the gloom form pools on the ground that explode in a cloud of butterflies as you approach. At times bustling with activity, at others silent, the rule in rainforests is much variety but small numbers. Thus, mammals (apart from primates) are usually few and far between.

Birds tend to move in feeding parties sometimes comprising two dozen or more species, but only one or two individuals of each kind. But when you hit a wave, all hell breaks loose in the scramble to see the hornbills, barbets, flycatchers, woodpeckers, warblers and cuckoos moving through; squirrels also may join the fray and monkeys ahead of the pack disturb insects that are snapped up by the bird party.

From the wildlife-watcher's point of view, the most productive part of the forest is where it adjoins another habitat, such as savanna or cultivated land. Here sunlight reaches all levels, allowing a great diversity of plants to grow, often in a tangle of competing creepers, herbage and saplings. Monkeys sun themselves, and birds and butterflies are at their most active, feeding on insects, fruits and blossom. It's also worthwhile staking out a fruiting fig tree and watching for the birds and primates that visit.

THREE-DIMENSIONAL HABITAT

Rainforests present a three-dimensional habitat for animals and observers alike. The forest floor, with its cover of fallen vegetation, is a thoroughfare for large mammals. Insects, snails and spiders thrive in the rich layer of rotting vegetation and, in turn, become prey for amphibians, reptiles, birds and mammals. Trunks, branches and hollows are utilised as shelter, nesting and resting places and as highways to the bounty of fruits and blossom in the canopy. Birds, bats and primates in turn disperse seeds around the forest in their droppings. Trees fruiting at different times ensure a year-round supply, and vegetation dislodged from the canopy helps sustain ground-dwelling animals such as antelopes, pigs and rodents. Birds, flying squirrels and bats take advantage of the comparatively open forest interior to move about.

Lowland rainforest is richer in mammal and bird species than any other. It is thought to be ancient and acted as a refuge for early rainforest species as surrounding habitats became increasingly arid. Evidence for this is provided by the presence of birds and mammals in the Zaïre River basin whose only close relatives live in the rainforests of Southeast Asia (Africa and Southeast Asia were connected millions of years ago).

Highland rainforest grows on mountain ranges as high as 2700m where rainfall is sufficient, but lowland rainforest usually supports different species – birds in particular show remarkable variation between the two habitats. In only a few surviving patches, however, have lowland and highland forest survived contiguously (ie growing adjacently and running together).

Watching wildlife in rainforest can be frustratingly difficult. Undergrowth hides skulking birds; monkeys crash through the trees then give only tantalising glimpses as they silently scamper away; and looking up into the canopy can be neck-breaking work to see something that may be only a silhouette high in the leafy ceiling. Vegetation can rustle only a couple of metres from your nose, yet an animal can remain completely hidden or, worse, cross the path behind you and start to rustle about on the other side. A day in productive rainforest is by turns tiring – be prepared to sweat – challenging and exhilarating. But be warned: rainforests can be addictive – few environments on earth house such bizarre, colourful and spectacular creatures.

ENVIRONMENT

ENVIRONMENT

SEE IT AT...
» Kakamega Forest (p76) » Bwindi
Impenetrable NP (p146) » Semuliki NP
(p169) » Parc National de Nyungwe (p178)

HIGH MOUNTAINS

The isolated peaks of massive extinct volcanoes and high ranges represent islands of distinctive vegetation rising from the surrounding savanna. Forest covers the lower slopes (if it hasn't been cleared for agriculture) and, above it, vegetation grows in distinctive bands dominated by one or more species according to altitude and aspect. Broadly speaking, dense forests grow as high as 2700m; thickets of bamboo straddle the slopes between 2500m and 3000m; an ericaceous zone – so-called because it is dominated by giant heathers of the genus *Erica* – grows above the bamboo, usually between 3000m and 3500m; and swathes of soft, blonde and waist-high tussock grassland, also known as alpine moorland, reach down from the snowline to the giant heather zone, punctuated by the so-called big game plants – giant examples of common herbs like groundsels and lobelias. This unique Afro-alpine vegetation grows at its densest above 4000m; various species of giant lobelia and groundsel grow on all the great peaks, some towering 4m high with tall flowering spikes that attract sunbirds.

The high peaks are a barren world of rocky crags, white snow and permanent ice; a place where few animals venture and none survive permanently. Swifts and large raptors (particularly lammergeiers) patrol the greatest heights, the former ranging far for insects, the latter for carcasses of animals that have perished.

FROM FOREST TO MOORLAND
Forest grows thickly below the bamboo; the bark of tall olives and junipers is encrusted with lichen and their branches are festooned with beard moss. Biologically, this is the most diverse part of the montane habitat, although there are few specialists and many of the inhabitants are also found in lowland forests. For example, elephants and buffaloes, numerous antelopes and even black rhinos ascend the forests of the great mountains. Birdlife is profuse and, again, many species are found only in these high forests. And while bamboo usually marks the upper limit of primates, the forests lower down can support several species, of which black-and-white colobus and blue monkeys are conspicuous.

The bamboo zone can be a pure stand of these woody grasses, or mixed with other ground-covering plants. Bamboo shoots are a favourite food of primates, such as gorillas and golden monkeys. Numerous birds live in this zone, particularly warblers and various skulking members of the thrush family. The change from forest to bamboo occurs quite dramatically in some places, such as along the Naro Moru Route on Mt Kenya.

The ericaceous zone is dominated by *Erica* heaths that in wet conditions, such as those in the Rwenzoris, can grow as high as 15m. Other distinctive trees scattered among the giant heathers can include scattered hagenias, a giant form of St John's wort and lobelias, with an

MOUNT KENYA'S MAIN SUMMIT FROM THE HEAD OF THE TELEKI VALLEY

often-sodden understorey of deep moss, tall spikes of orchids and sticky bogs. Where they occur in sufficient numbers, duikers and tree hyraxes attract leopards and African golden cats, in addition to birds such as sunbirds, seedeaters and wood-hoopoes.

The only permanent residents in alpine moorland are birds and hyraxes, and rodents that burrow to escape the cold, although many large mammals ascend the great peaks during dry seasons. Thus elephants, plains zebras, common elands, duikers and hartebeests might all be encountered along walking trails, and predators such as lions, spotted hyenas and leopards are seen occasionally. Verreaux's eagles feed on the abundant rock hyraxes, and mountain buzzards hunt rodents. Several bird species, such as scarlet-tufted malachite sunbirds, alpine chats and Jackson's francolins, are found only at these altitudes.

SEE IT AT...
» **Mt Kenya NP (p80)** » **Mt Elgon NP (p96)**
» **Arusha NP (p126)** » **Kilimanjaro NP (p132)**

ENVIRONMENT

SEMIARID ZONE

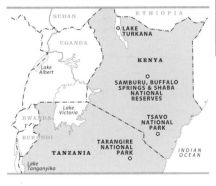

At the northern extremity of East Africa, rainfall declines considerably and occurs irregularly. The driest and harshest areas support little plant life

ENVIRONMENT

and a low diversity of animals, although the popular conception of drifting sand dunes doesn't apply until still further north in the Sahara. Kenya's deserts are mainly stony – the remains of ancient lava flows through which grows sparse vegetation able to withstand high daytime temperatures and scouring winds. Adjoining true desert is a much larger area of semidesert, where rainfall is slightly higher (and more regular) and the vegetation thicker. Between 250mm and 500mm of rain falls annually in semidesert, usually from April to May and in November, but up to six months may pass without any at all. Shrubs, rather than trees, dominate, with an understorey of hardy grasses.

Among the few permanent animal inhabitants in the true desert, those that burrow or have low moisture requirements are the most successful – rodents, lizards and scorpions are often abundant. Dry, sandy river beds cut across the landscape, their course marked by denser stands of thorny vegetation that support browsers such as gerenuks, kudus and dik-diks. When rain does fall, these dry watercourses fill quickly and plant life puts on a spurt of growth before the precious water drains away or evaporates. Oryxes, Grant's gazelles and Grevy's zebras move in from adjoining habitat to graze on the sudden bounty, and birds such as larks, sandgrouse and bustards eke out a living, the strongest flying species following showers to arrive in the wake of seeding plants.

As in true desert, those animals least dependent on water most successfully exploit the semiarid zone. Insects – grasshoppers, termites and beetles – are the staple of small mammals such as hedgehogs, mongooses and elephant shrews. Larger mammals include herbivores that can live independently of permanent drinking water, such as gerenuks and oryxes, and elephants, zebras and black rhinos move through when conditions are suitable. A nocturnal lifestyle is one strategy commonly employed to escape daytime heat; to this end many animals, such as the highly specialised bat-eared fox, spend the day below ground, emerging to feed after dark.

WATERHOLE PROCESSIONS
Few animals go completely without water if it is available, and waterholes become the focus of much activity as the dry season wears on in the semiarid zone. Some animals make a visit to the waterhole a regular part of their daily routine and there's even a drinking hierarchy (if you have the time it's worth staking out a waterhole for a few hours to watch the procession). Mixed herds aggregate, zebras rubbing shoulders with antelopes and giving way to elephants and rhinos – predators take advantage of the situation to lay ambushes. Birds flock to waterholes, especially in the early morning, when a constant turnover includes sandgrouse lining up to drink, pigeons, doves and weavers and other finches.

As the waterholes in an area dry up completely, most of the animals must move on. Some can linger a little longer: Grevy's zebras dig in dry stream beds for water and defend the resulting puddle; elephants, which suck up water with their trunks before squirting it into their mouths, have the ability to extract water from deep holes that are beyond the reach of other animals; and baboons also dig for water. But eventually the struggle of moving between feeding grounds and the increasingly scattered remaining water becomes too difficult, and mammals, especially those that must drink every day, such as elephants and buffaloes, move out of the semiarid areas until the next rains bring them back. Birds too may be fewer and further between, but their mobility enables many to remain in these areas and exploit the desiccated country in all but the driest of years – strong-flying nomads such as sandgrouse and bustards are among the most successful.

SEE IT AT...

» **Tsavo NP (p66)** » **Samburu, Buffalo Springs & Shaba NRs (p84)** » **Lake Turkana (p92)** » **Tarangire NP (p122)**

LAKES, RIVERS & SWAMPS

Water appears in many forms and quantities across the region, from the great lakes to dew trapped in alpine plants, savanna waterholes, and solid masses frozen in glaciers. Rain in the high watersheds of the Albertine Rift Valley feeds the mighty Nile River that flows 2000km to the Mediterranean Sea. And the greatest lake of all, Lake Victoria, creates its own weather patterns and is a major source for evaporation – which together waters the rainforests of Uganda. Water sustains all life: hundreds of species of fish and invertebrate equipped with gills draw oxygen from water and live all or part of their lives in it; it's a reservoir of prey for many air-breathing animals that wade, swim, fly or perch; a refuge for creatures that also spend much

time on land; and essential for the daily drinking or bathing routine for many large animals.

Shallow water margins are packed with life, and water is a great medium for witnessing first hand the often complex biological web. Sunlight filtering through the shallows promotes the growth of algae, which is fed upon by huge numbers of tiny crustaceans and single-celled animals. These support fish (which exploded in diversity in Lakes Victoria and Tanganyika), tadpoles and the larvae of many insects, all of which in turn become prey for larger aquatic animals and land-based predators such as otters and birds. Larger fish living in deeper water feed crocodiles, pelicans and African fish eagles; and the water itself supports and cools the largest aquatic animal of all, the hippo, between its nocturnal forays into adjoining grassland.

The great lakes of the Eastern Rift Valley are high in minerals, which favour the proliferation of algae and tiny crustaceans, but are not conducive to fish and most other aquatic life. These conditions favour a few specialised species and what the saline (also called alkaline or soda) lakes lack in diversity of large animals, they tend to make up for in numbers – sometimes millions of one species (lesser flamingo), thousands of another (greater flamingo) and at most a few hundred other waterbirds. Apart from flamingos, other birds present may include assorted ducks and grebes, shorebirds and predators such as African fish eagles, which, in the absence of fish, have taken to preying on the flamingos themselves.

THE WATER'S EDGE

A succession of vegetation between the floating mats and the shore can, over time, alter the course of rivers by choking and silting up bends that eventually are claimed by land plants and animals. Where water levels remain more or less constant, dense ranks of tall bulrushes, reeds and grasslike sedges mark the transition to dry land. Snakes hunt amphibians and marsh mongooses hunt both; and bitterns, crakes and rails live almost exclusively in these grass forests. The tall stems are too slender for most predators to ascend and many small birds build their nests, and sometimes thousands roost, in the security of reed beds. Where running water is slowed and trapped by vegetation, otters hunt for fish, crabs and shellfish; waterbucks graze, often belly-deep in water; and the semiaquatic sitatunga feeds, walking over submerged vegetation on splayed hooves.

Great papyrus stands choke swamps, but support a number of birds specialised to this habitat, such as papyrus gonoleks, papyrus canaries and shoebills. Drowned trees and large, overhanging branches along rivers and lakeshores make secure nest platforms for colonies of herons, pelicans and cormorants, which sometimes form mixed colonies; sandbanks are basking sites for hippos and crocs, and roosts for gulls, terns and ducks; kingfishers and bee-eaters dig nest tunnels in steep banks; and de Brazza's monkeys live in the protection of flooded forests. Where banks are not too steep, a procession of animals large and small visits the water's margin to drink, wallow or bathe. At this point, all but the largest are at their most vulnerable, and even lions and leopards occasionally fall prey to large crocs.

SEE IT AT...
» Murchison Falls NP (p154) » Parc National de l'Akagera (p176) » Lake Nakuru NP (p91) » Lake Bogoria NR (p89)

SHORE & SEA

Where rivers empty into the sea, suspended silt deposited over millennia has formed expansive mudflats rich in nutrients and small animals such as molluscs and crustaceans. In places the fine, fertile mud supports underwater meadows of seagrass, grazed by animals as large as the dugong (or sea cow) and sheltering fish and crustaceans different to those of coral reefs. Some have adapted to spend short spells out of water at low tide, like mudskippers, which lie partly submerged in puddles or burrows and flip between pools across the mud; and fiddler crabs, which emerge to pick food particles from the surface. Mudflats attract birds, such as herons, kingfishers and the thousands of shorebirds that pass through the region on migration twice each year. Mudflats are excellent places to watch wildlife at low tide, but don't expect any large mammals (although jackals and baboons are known to exploit the rich pickings).

Few other habitats are as challenging to survival as the zone where land meets the sea. Shore inhabitants must be adapted to a daily pattern of inundation with sea water (with its high salt concentration) and, often, a pounding by the waves, followed by exposure to freshwater if it rains or baking sun for hours at a stretch.

But this is a classic edge habitat, a zone rich in resources exploited by human and animal predators alike. Shorebirds pick over the incoming tide and hermit crabs scavenge from dead animals washed up on the sands. The largest users of the beaches visit only briefly, and then at night: female marine turtles haul themselves up the sand to dig nest chambers and lay their eggs.

Forming a buffer between shore and sea, mangroves are trees unique for their ability to withstand daily inundation in sea water. Mangrove seeds are carried away by the tides and take root wherever conditions are suitable, but usually on sheltered points and in calm back waters. Silt accumulates around the roots and eventually forms a deep ooze in which crustaceans and fish burrow. Zones of different mangrove species develop – those less able to withstand salt grow closer to land, trapping more debris and eventually allowing land plants to grow. Their extensive root systems calm wave action, slow coastal erosion and shelter hatchling fish and crustaceans.

THE DEEP BLUE SEA

From the soup of plankton, which originates in the warm surface waters and underlies most of the ocean's food chains, to rocky shelves supporting hardy molluscs and crustaceans, the shallow waters above the continental shelf support one of the most diverse faunas on earth. Where conditions are suitable, coral reefs put on a show rivalled only by the wildlife of tropical rainforests, and best appreciated underwater. A dazzling display awaits anyone who dons snorkel and mask: fish in every shape and colour, from neon blue to fluorescent orange; crustaceans, many also in bright colours, but often camouflaged with weed, pebbles or even living sponges; and the many coloured corals themselves, supported by solid lime skeletons constructed over millennia by tiny organisms.

Open ocean beyond the continental shelf is the realm of great hunting fish, such as sharks, tuna and marlin; marine mammals such as whales and dolphins; sea turtles that return to land only to lay their eggs; and birds, such as cormorants, boobies, terns and frigatebirds, that wander far in search of fish. Cruising the channels between the islands and the mainland could yield sea mammals or pelagic birds.

SEE IT AT...
» **Arabuko Sokoke Forest Reserve (p70)**
» **Zanzibar Archipelago (p114)** » **Saadani NP (p138)** » **Malindi & Watamu Marine NPs (p93)**

OTHER HABITATS

While we tend to think of East African habitats as forests, savanna and grassland, there are many other, less obvious habitats that animals use – some of which overlap the boundaries of our own 'habitats'. And there are good reasons for animals to partake of human hospitality: our endeavours provide extra sources of food, shelter and breeding sites for creatures equipped to make the transition from natural to human-designed environments. But not all of these habitats are human-engineered.

VILLAGES, TOWNS & CITIES

Although generally bereft of large animals, urban environments are utilised by some species opportunistically and, in a few cases, are the habitat of choice. Into the latter category fall various rodents, but birds fare better than mammals as a rule, because the latter are often sought for food and discouraged as competition or carriers of disease. What this means for the visitor is that large city parks can support at least some

ENVIRONMENT

MINIATURE MUSHROOM FARMERS

Termite mounds are a wonder of natural engineering. Alone, these insects are helpless, but somehow colonies (sometimes numbering millions) cooperate to build protective fortresses by cementing together grains of earth with saliva. Inside, the temperature and humidity remain more or less constant, regulated by ventilation shafts and chimneys; other passages serve as brood chambers. The hub of the colony is the queen, whose main task in life is to squeeze out millions of eggs. Most eggs hatch into workers, who tend the queen, forage for food and build and repair the mound; others become soldiers that defend the nest. A mound's inhabitants can consume tonnes of vegetation annually; once chewed, the vegetation is deposited in storage chambers in the mound where it sprouts a fungus that is consumed by the termites. Pretty impressive so far, but consider this: during the rains, termites of several species spread the fungus on the ground outside, where it sprouts edible mushrooms that set spores, which the termites gather to renew their underground supply. Not bad for tiny, blind insects.

living things, including squirrels, roosts of bats and even troops of monkeys.

Opportunistic birds such as pied crows and black kites swoop for scraps near markets; starlings and sparrows nest in buildings with vertical faces that are effectively cliffs; and marabou storks perch like sentinels overlooking savanna and city squares alike. Several species of weaver build colonies of nests right in the middle of settlements, and fruit-bats also roost in towns, both probably because the risk of predation is less – although raptors hunt above city streets through the canyons created by buildings.

AGRICULTURE & CULTIVATION

Where land is cleared for cultivation, the result is comparatively poor in regard to both plants and animals. Most large animals quickly desert these changes or, if unable to move far, die out – others are hunted to local extinction. And when elephants, absent for months in other parts of their range, return along traditional migration routes to find crops and dwellings in their way, conflict with people inevitably develops. Similarly, the fencing of fields across wildebeest

migration routes causes the animals to change course.

Nonetheless, some animals, particularly birds and small mammals such as mongooses and genets, readily adopt agricultural land as an extension of their natural habitat. While driving along highways, you can expect to see various weavers and sparrows, doves and blossom-feeding sunbirds, the ubiquitous common bulbul and orchard-raiding hornbills, crows and starlings. Watch for secretary birds, bustards and storks picking over burnt fields, cattle egrets among livestock, and shrikes perched on overhead wires. Ironically, when agriculture does benefit a species, it can be to such a degree that animals such as rats, normally held in check by natural predators, become a major pest. Thus baboons are expanding their numbers and range at the interface between cultivation and savanna, and red-billed queleas can descend on crops in millions, causing widespread damage.

THE AIR UP THERE

Habitat is usually described in terms of objects, but for many animals the main event is actually the space above or between objects. Although generally transparent, air is not just empty space. It behaves like other matter except that it's much lighter than most and there's a lot more of it. It stands still and moves – sometimes very quickly or in circles. Air heats up and cools down, sometimes rapidly and in quick succession. It bumps into things and fills voids such as great caves. It also acts as an agent of dispersal, carrying the seeds of plants and the young of spiders and insects over many kilometres.

All these factors are exploited by a few mammals, a myriad of insects and by most birds. To them it is a dining room, highway, playground, courtship arena or observation post. Air can communicate the presence of food: thunderheads on the horizon stimulate termites to hatch – millions drift upward like plumes of smoke, attracting birds and mammals alike – and swifts move ahead of the storm front to feast on the bounty. Vultures take advantage of thermals as they look for a kill; their volplaning is a clear signal to predators to move onto a kill themselves. And smoke, often visible from kilometres away, signals a grass fire to which bustards, raptors and jackals are drawn in their search for a meal.

TERMITE MOUNDS

Termite biology and behaviour is itself fascinating, but the earthen mounds of these silent armies play an important role in the life cycles of many other creatures. At various stages, termitaria form important refuges for other animals. For example, monitor lizards lay their eggs and various birds dig nest tunnels in mounds, aardvarks and pangolins dig out shelters in abandoned mounds and animals ranging from small bats and snakes to warthogs, ratels, porcupines and jackals use hollow mounds as shelters and nurseries. Topis and cheetahs use mounds as vantage points and elephants and rhinos rub against them for a scratch.

Termite mounds also help to shape the environment by encouraging the growth of certain plants. For example, mounds on floodplains become islands during wet seasons that plants colonise, in turn sheltering more plants and animals and encouraging the growth of thickets. It's pretty hard to miss termite mounds on the savanna, but look also for arboreal termitaria – in which kingfishers excavate nest tunnels – and the mushroom-shaped structures made by some termite species.

ENVIRONMENT

DESTINATIONS
AFRICA'S TOP WILDLIFE SPOTS

KENYA

KENYA

CAPITAL NAIROBI **AREA** 569,250 SQ KM **NATIONAL PARKS** 33 **MAMMAL SPECIES** APPROX 400

Sometimes the stereotype has its basis in fact. Sometimes the cliché is justified. Sometimes the hyperbole is actually understatement. Welcome to Kenya. This is textbook outdoors Africa: dry, vast savanna, deep jungle, empty desert, sugar-powder beaches, all a dream.

THE LAND From coral reefs to the icy peaks of Africa's second-highest mountain (Mt Kenya), and vast savanna stretching to northern deserts, Kenya is famous as one of the world's great wildlife-watching destinations. A staggering biological diversity is generally easy to see: there are hundreds of mammal species, including all of Africa's Big Five; birds are abundant, common and diverse, with over 1000 species – several of which are endemic; and other highlights include succulent plants and 871 species of butterfly.

Although Kenya is wholly tropical, its climate (and therefore its habitats and wildlife) varies greatly with rainfall and elevation. At one extreme, high rainfall affects Aberdare, Mt Kenya and Mt Elgon National Parks (where montane forests and giant herbs are best appreciated in the dry seasons) and biologically rich rainforests in the west – now restricted to patches such as Kakamega Forest – abound with birdlife, animals and plants of West African origin. Vast areas of semiarid scrub in the north and east support a high diversity of wildlife protected in Samburu National Reserve and Tsavo and Meru National Parks. Little rain falls in the arid far north, where ancient fossil beds, specialised animals and lava flows border Lake Turkana.

KENYA

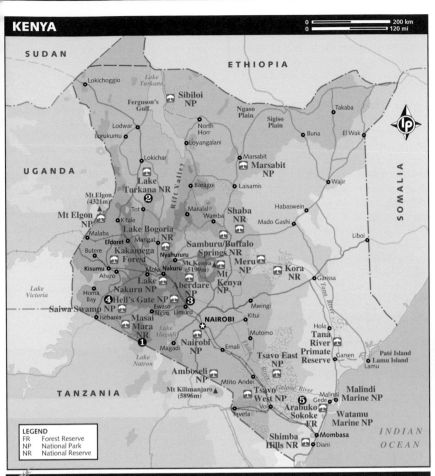

LEGEND
FR   Forest Reserve
NP   National Park
NR   National Reserve

KENYA

⭐ TOP SPOTS

1. MASAI MARA NATIONAL RESERVE (p62) Herds of zebras, prides of lions, hooting elephants and graceful gazelle leap across an African landscape so clichéd it'd be a story – but it's real and waiting in the Mara.

2. LAKE TURKANA (p92) Nile crocodiles, nomads, shifting sands and a stark, harsh landscape carved out of wind

and rock surround a green, watery, desert wonder.

3. ABERDARE NATIONAL PARK (p86) Shifting from the windswept moorlands and alpine meadows of the high country into the thick jungle of the Salient is one of Kenya's most diverse hidden gems.

4. HELL'S GATE NATIONAL PARK (p87) Don't just spot zebras, giraffes and klipspringers from

a jeep – walk among them in this park's thorn-bush desert, where enormous vistas are complemented by its intimately accessible size.

5. ARABUKO SOKOKE FOREST RESERVE (p70) Feel the stars rain down on an estuarine mangrove forest and spot rare birds and small mammals in this reserve where dramatic overstatement is eclipsed by serene, user-friendly beauty.

Rainfall and elevation rise in the south and west, where rolling savanna attracts tourists who flock to the famous Amboseli National Park and Masai Mara National Reserve (scene of the annual migration of 500,000 wildebeests from the Serengeti plains – the greatest concentration of large animals on earth). East of the Rift, most rain falls in two distinct periods: the so-called 'long' (March to May) and 'short' rains (November to December). Dry seasons make access and wildlife viewing easier but rains bring fewer tourists and a flush of green to the savanna, and trigger the breeding of many species.

The eastern arm of the Great Rift Valley forms sheer 1km-high cliffs and a chain of shallow freshwater and alkaline ('soda') lakes, which attract concentrations of flamingos and other waterbirds. Lake Bogoria National Reserve and Lake Nakuru National Park support masses of flamingos, while Lake Baringo offers a suite of other waterbirds in a semiarid setting.

Arabuko Sokoke Forest Reserve is East Africa's most important coastal forest as well as the last refuge for many endemic species. Malindi and Watamu Marine National Parks protect the great biodiversity of Kenya's inshore coral reefs, with migrating whale sharks an added attraction. And Kenya's numerous wildlife conservancies and private ranches boast successes in breeding rare species such as rhinos.

WHEN TO GO Many visitors cram into Kenya in late July and early August to witness the annual great wildebeest migration; others try to time their visit to coincide with the choicest climate conditions, which generally adhere to a similar June-to-August time frame. Of course, coming at this time means crowds – you may be doing more van spotting than lion spotting if you safari during these months. Don't be put off visiting in the off season (spring and

autumn); the marked reduction in crowds makes up for any reduced chance you may have – and these are small – of spotting animals in wildlife-rich Kenya.

WILDLIFE HIGHLIGHTS
» Getting a prime front row for the wildebeest migration (p108), the greatest wildlife-watching show on earth
» Watching a cheetah in a 100km/h sprint after its prey in Samburu National Reserve (p84) » Searching for endangered black rhinos amongst the scrub along the shores of Lake Nakuru (p91) » Weaving past Nile crocodiles as you boat along the jade waters of Lake Turkana (p92) » Watching herds of buffalo amble, drink, bathe and dust-bathe in the shadow of Mt Kilimanjaro at Amboseli National Park (p74)
» Scanning Kakamega Forest (p76) for hundreds of rainforest specialities to bolster your birding count » Being a passive observer as herds of elephants surround your safari vehicle in the wilderness of Tsavo National Park (p66)

MT KENYA NATIONAL PARK

KENYA ITINERARIES

1. SODA LAKES, SAVANNA LOOKS & SNORKELING LIGHT From Nairobi, head to **Hell's Gate National Park** (p87) and take a walk on the wild side amid herds of zebras

in this dry, thornbush–studded stretch of semidesert. Pop north to **Lake Naivasha** (p90) and **Lake Nakuru** (p91) to see the bubbling geographic detritus that is the soda lakes of the Rift Valley. Now pop down to **Masai Mara National Reserve** (p62) to see Kenya at its most textbook 'African'. Spend a few nights here, then head for the coast via **Tsavo National Park** (p66) for more semiarid wildlife, or snorkel at **Malindi** or **Watamu Marine National Park** (p93) and finish in **Arabuko Sokoke Forest Reserve** (p70).

2. MOUNTAINS, OCEANS & MAYBE MONKEYS Head north to the Central Highlands and follow the ring road around Mt Kenya, stopping to see buffalos in the Salient of

Aberdare National Park (p86) and a *Lion King*–worthy sunrise over **Meru National Park** (p95). Then get your alpine gear out and take a hike into **Mt Kenya National Park** (p80) itself. Afterwards, head east to the coast and ride the Tana River up to the **Tana River National Primate Reserve**.

KENYA

3. FLY ME TO THE MOON Kenya abounds with dramatic vistas of both semidesert and full-on moonscapes of sun-blasted brown plains and rocky escarpments, all hiding a wide variety

of hardy wildlife. Start this trip in the appropriately named **Hell's Gate National Park** (p87), then amid the steaming soda lakes of **Lake Nakuru National Park** (p91) and **Lake Baringo** (p88). Now head north into the fat horizons and unending deserts of **Marsabit National Park** (p94) before turning west towards the jade shores and crocodiles of **Lake Turkana** (p92). On your way back to Nairobi, grace yourself with a little green in the wilds of **Samburu National Reserve** (p84).

LOCATION 270km southwest of Nairobi. Good roads as far as Narok and Ngorengore can become atrocious further south – 4WD is recommended in wet seasons.

FACILITIES Rangers can be hired at park headquarters (Sekenani Gate). Most lodges have resident naturalists. Game walks are possible in the Sekenani Valley and Siria Escarpment. Night drives outside the reserve are run by various operators.

ACCOMMODATION Large range of lodges and tented camps in the reserve; camping grounds and lodges outside.

WILDLIFE RHYTHMS Wildebeests and zebras present during dry season (mid-June to mid-October). Buffaloes calve March to May and many carnivores are born early in the Wet (April to June). Great flocks of Abdim's and white storks feed on termites and frogs in October-to-November rains; long rains trigger breeding displays of widowbirds.

CONTACT Masai Mara National Reserve (☎ 0305-2178/2337).

MASAI MARA NATIONAL RESERVE

All wildlife viewing in this popular reserve must be done from a vehicle, and the Mara has developed a reputation as a minivan circus during busy times (such as the wildebeest migration and school holidays); but at other times, especially during the long rains, it can be virtually deserted. To get the most out of your visit use a reputable company with accredited guides and preferably a 4WD vehicle. Since the Mara isn't fenced, don't ignore the surrounding areas – the Loita Plains north of the Sekenani Gate, the Sekenani Valley and the dispersal area north of the Musiara Gate are all productive.

The Sekenani Gate in the east leads into the rolling Ngama Hills, dominated by stands of dense *Croton* bushes, soft silvery leleshwa (used by the Maasai as a deodorant), candelabra euphorbias and thorny acacias. Plenty of animals can be seen along tracks leading off the main access road: **warthogs**, **lions**, **elephants** and **buffaloes** are generally about, and this habitat is favoured by antelopes such as **Grant's gazelles**, **impalas** and the **common eland**, as well as the park's 40-odd **black rhinos**, which disperse across the central Olmisigiyoi region and southeastern corner of the reserve. **Kirk's dik-diks** (which live only in the thickets) and **steenboks** are also common in this habitat. Birdwatching is excellent and features several species not seen in other parts of the Mara, such as **Denham's bustard**, **magpie shrikes**

WILDLIFE HIGHLIGHTS

» **Vast grasslands stretch south to Tanzania's Serengeti National Park, from where hundreds of thousands of wildebeests migrate annually into the Mara, accompanied by herds of plains zebras and many lions** » **Mammals include Masai giraffes, buffaloes, elephants, topis, kongonis (Coke's hartebeests), elands, defassa waterbucks, impalas, Thomson's and Grant's gazelles** » **Hippos live in the Mara and Talek Rivers, and a few black rhinos remain in the east and centre of the park** » **Leopards and spotted hyenas are commonly encountered, cheetahs less so and striped hyenas and hunting dogs rarely** » **Smaller attractions include black-backed jackals, servals, caracals and four species of mongoose** » **The 540 bird species include 57 raptors; sought-after birds include Denham's bustards, rock cisticolas and Jackson's widowbirds; birds of prey range from the grey kestrel to large eagles and six species of vulture.**

KENYA

(especially near Siana Springs) and **African penduline tits**. **Kestrels** – grey, common and lesser – hunt rodents over the grasslands; **white-bellied go-away birds** mock from the top of trees; and **yellow-mantled widowbirds**, **purple grenadiers** and **cinnamon-breasted rock buntings** all feed along the tracks. A night drive in the Sekenani Valley will almost certainly clock up **spotted hyenas**, **black-backed jackals**, **Kirk's dik-diks** and **springhares**; **pearl-spotted owlets** and **African scops owls** are also common.

BROWSERS IN SHELTERING THICKETS

The Talek Gate opens onto the undulating grassland of the Posee, Meta, Central and Burrungat Plains that stretch between the Ngama Hills and the Mara River. Lone euphorbias, *Balanites* and flat-topped acacias – browsed by the distinctively marked **Masai giraffes** – dot a landscape once covered in woody shrubs. Herds of **elephants** slowly destroyed the thickets, allowing grasses to proliferate, and now the central and western Mara is one of the best areas to see grazing animals and their predators. **Kongonis** (Coke's hartebeests), **topis** and **Thomson's** and **Grant's gazelles** are present year-round, although they may be absent from great swaths of grassland and concentrated in others; several species can sometimes be seen milling together, especially at the top of ridges as night approaches. Troops of **vervet monkeys** and **olive baboons** fan out to forage and the dry season brings the great herds of **wildebeests** and **plains zebras**. **Lions**, **cheetahs**, **servals** and **caracals** could all be encountered. Large grassland birds include **common ostriches**, **secretary birds**, **southern ground hornbills** and three species of **bustard**, while **dark chanting goshawks**, **vultures** and **eagles** nest in the surviving trees. This grassland is incredibly beautiful during the rains,

GRASS WIDOWS

During the long rains (beginning in March) the normally drab male Jackson's widowbird moults into glossy-black breeding plumage and grows a long, flowing tail. But his courtship display is even more dramatic: he tramples an arena of grass in which he sways sideways and jumps forward while vibrating his wings and calling, then jumps up to 1m in the air, as if trying to see over the grass heads, with wings outstretched, head arched back and feet thrashing the air. Several males perform in loose colonies and the display is repeated until a watching female either loses interest or decides to mate with him. It is thought the famous jumping of Maasai warriors is partly based on this display; and when a lion in long grass flicks up its tail, from a distance the tuft looks uncannily like a little black bird jumping in the grass.

KENYA

when the sound and smell of **buffaloes** and **elephants** ripping the grass is punctuated by the plaintive whistling of **rufous-naped larks**, and cloud shadows move across the softly riffling swards littered with wastepaper flowers.

Millions of termites ceaselessly chew through the grassland digesting cellulose, and in turn become a valuable source of protein for other animals – nocturnal **aardvarks** and **aardwolves** feed almost exclusively on them.

👀 WATCHING TIPS

Arrange with Kenya Wildlife Service to accompany the Rhino Patrol, which leaves from the Sekenani Gate. Patas monkeys are most often seen in grassland near the Tanzanian border, and red-tailed monkeys live in the small patch of forest at Kichwa Tembo. Rock cisticolas inhabit the Siria Escarpment and hills behind Mara Safari Club.

Large earthen termite mounds dot the plains and during the rains active colonies build funnels, out of which fly vast numbers of adults relished by **jackals** and **mongooses** and birds such as **lilac-breasted rollers**, which gather to hawk them on the wing, and **capped wheatears**. Derelict termite mounds serve as shelter for mongooses, nest chambers for jackals and **hyenas** and lookouts for **cheetahs** and sleek tan-and-gunmetal **topis**. The grassland also supports a rich community of small birds, including 12 species of **cisticola** (whose identification poses a birdwatcher's headache); **quail**, **francolins** and **red-necked** and **yellow-necked spurfowl**; drably coloured **larks** and **pipits**, **yellow-throated** and almost neon-bright **rosy-breasted longclaws**; and many **finches**, **weavers** and **widowbirds**.

THE GREATEST GAME SHOW OF ALL

The vast, bleating herds of **wildebeests** usually enter the Mara from the adjoining Serengeti in June or July, although the timing and exact route changes from year to year. Waves of **plains zebras** arrive first, mowing through the tall, coarse grass stems that shot up during the rains, and exposing the green, leafy grasses preferred by the wildebeests following behind them. At several points the herds cross the Mara and Talek Rivers, trotting down in single file then charging across in an attempt to avoid waiting **Nile crocodiles**. Thousands are eaten, crushed or drowned in the crossings; **lions** (and minivans) wait in ambush at the other side; and **vultures** and other scavengers enjoy good pickings. Large numbers of lions follow the herds, although some stay to slug it out for dominance of an established territory. A smaller population of about 100,000 wildebeests heads west from the Loita Plains to mingle with the Serengeti herds in the Mara dispersal area north of the reserve. As the grassland dries out in late October or early November the wildebeests and zebras move back to the Serengeti and Loita Plains.

For much of the day, lions and **spotted hyenas** laze around, panting off the night's meal and twitching flies. But as the afternoon draws on, ears prick and noses dip into the breeze, and the prides and packs stalk zebras, wildebeests, **antelopes** and even dangerous prey such as **buffaloes**. Most of the action takes place at night (infrared spotting gear is used on night drives by Mara Intrepids Club), but in the morning there is usually plenty of activity around a kill: **vultures** circling overhead attract hyenas and **jackals** that wait for the lions to finish; if the hyenas outnumber the lions they may drive off a pride. Jackals wait in line – **black-backed jackals** are most common – and vultures and **marabou storks** pick over the bones when the mammals have departed. Kills are most frequently seen during the wildebeest migration. Of the Mara's three spotted cats, the most glamorous and eagerly sought is the **cheetah**, though they are more abundant

THE DIK-DIK & THE ELEPHANT

The Mara's smallest antelope, Kirk's dik-dik, stands only 40cm high and marks territories in patches of dense woody vegetation such as *Croton,* acacia or *Commiphora* with scent glands and by depositing middens of little dung pellets.

'One day a careless elephant crapped on a baby dik-dik and buried it; its parents looked everywhere but couldn't find their missing fawn,' Maasai guide David tells. 'When the parents realised what had happened, grief turned to anger and, to seek revenge, from that day on all dik-diks started to pile up their droppings high enough to bury a baby elephant.'

n the short grass plains to the north. **Leopards** are probably best seen along wooded rivers such as the Talek and Mara, and in dense vegetation at the foot of the Siria Escarpment. Seeing smaller cats such as **servals**, **African wild cats** and **caracals** is a matter of luck, and **hunting dogs** are the scarcest predator of all, although a pack is thought to live in the Aitong area north of the Mara. **Striped hyenas** are occasionally encountered on night drives.

WESTERN WETLANDS & RIVERS The steep Siria Escarpment, overlooking the reserve's western reaches, is inhabited by **Chanler's mountain reedbucks**, **klipspringers** (both also found in the Sekenani Valley), **steenboks** and **Kirk's dik-diks**. The Musiara Marsh, a permanent wetland drained by the Mara River, supports **defassa waterbucks**, **impalas** and large herds of **elephants** and **buffaloes**. **Lions** are common in this area, and several well-established – and fiercely defended – territories take advantage of the abundant **antelopes** and seasonal **zebras** and **wildebeests**. The rivers support around 2000 **hippos**, which wallow in pools during the day and emerge to graze the adjacent grassland at night; early risers often see them far from water, but they can always be seen at well-established hippo pools along the rivers. **Nile crocodiles** bask on sandbars and **Nile monitors** are common, and the riverine forest is home to **olive baboons**, **vervet monkeys**, **bushbucks**, **Harvey's duikers** and nocturnal **tree hyraxes** and **greater galagos** (which visit feeding stations at lodges). This area and a small patch of forest at Kichwa Tembo offer some of the Mara's best birdwatching: **African fish eagles** hunt along the rivers; Musiara itself attracts seasonal, resident and migrant **waterbirds**; and fruiting fig trees attract **Schalow's turacos**, **African green pigeons**, laughing parties of **green wood-hoopoe** and **black-and-white-casqued hornbills**.

KENYA

BALLOONS RISING OVER MASAI MARA AT SUNRISE

KENYA

TSAVO EAST
NATIONAL
PARK

TSAVO WEST
NATIONAL
PARK

LOCATION 300km southeast of Nairobi, 200km northwest of Mombasa – accessible year-round to 2WD vehicles.

FACILITIES Various observation and picnic points, nature trail and underwater viewing tank, rhino sanctuaries (open from 4pm to 6pm daily), waterholes at lodges and camping grounds.

ACCOMMODATION Several lodges, permanent tented camps, self-service bandas and camping grounds.

WILDLIFE RHYTHMS Large-animal concentration is highest during the dry seasons (September to October and January to March).

CONTACT Kenyan Wildlife Service (KWS), Tsavo West headquarters (☎ 0456-22483); KWS, Tsavo East headquarters (☎ 043-30049).

TSAVO EAST & WEST NATIONAL PARKS

At around the size of Wales, Tsavo National Park is the largest reserve in Kenya and one of the largest in the world. Split into East and West sections by the main Nairobi–Mombasa highway, it contains the biggest **elephant** population in Kenya (in excess of 6000) and is famous for its **lions**. Tsavo is also home to many mammals able to tolerate drought conditions, such as **gerenuks**, **fringe-eared oryxes** and **black rhinos**. But for all its diversity, Tsavo is not a park where you will see animals constantly: it is a huge, semiarid wilderness straddling the Taru Desert and much of its appeal lies in its dramatic scenery and sense of space. If possible, go to Tsavo with some time to spare – it is not a place to dash about and tick off animals; it's a place to soak up atmosphere – and if you get off the beaten track (the roads are good) you could have it to yourself.

VIEWS FROM BELOW & ON HIGH Tsavo West is smaller, better watered and more often visited than Tsavo East. Mzima Springs is the highlight and 220 million litres of water gushes out of the ground every day to form a river 70m wide – home to **Nile crocodiles** and **hippos**. **Elephants**, **plains zebras**, **gazelles** and other animals drink at the river; **blue** and **vervet monkeys** frequent the surrounding fever trees and *Acacia tortillis*; and fringing reeds, vines, figs and palms are prime spots for birds.

The river is crystal clear at its source and an underwater observation chamber has been built. The **hippos** stay out of range of the chamber, but you will see various freshwater

WILDLIFE HIGHLIGHTS
» **Kenya's largest reserve supports the Big Five and features the country's largest elephant population (which includes released orphans) and lions in good numbers**
» **Two rhino sanctuaries make Tsavo Kenya's most important rhino conservation location, and other large mammals include buffaloes, hartebeests, lesser kudus, elands, waterbucks, Grant's gazelles, impalas and giraffes; steenboks, Kirk's dik-diks and klipspringers are common**
» **The park has over 600 bird species, including birds of the semiarid zone such as Somali ostriches (Tsavo East) and common ostriches (Tsavo West), golden pipits and golden-breasted starlings; bird banding at Ngulia Lodge is a major annual event**

KENYA

POACHING & PESTILENCE

Tsavo has had a chequered history and the effects linger. Poaching for rhino horns in the 1970s nearly took the black rhino to extinction, and poaching for ivory in the 1980s reduced the park's elephant population from around 17,000 to about 8000. The Kenyan Wildlife Service's war on poachers started in 1989 and was won and mostly fought in northeast Tsavo, which remains largely closed to the public. But drought (1993–94) followed by an outbreak of rinderpest in eastern Kenya in 1994–95 decimated Tsavo's hoofed animals: buffalo numbers in the region crashed from an estimated 34,600 in 1991 to 5500 by 1997; kongonis (Coke's hartebeests) from 16,000 to 4100, and elands from 10,000 to 760. Most hoofed species declined over the 1990s, including greater kudus, waterbucks, Grant's gazelles, gerenuks, impalas, Masai giraffes and fringe-eared oryxes. But herds of up to 200 buffaloes are now being seen so a recovery could be on the horizon.

fishes, such as **barbels** and **suckers**, close up. The best place to watch hippos is from the lower pool lookout; the stream here is also a favourite with small **crocodiles** and the huge fig around which the viewing platform is built attracts fruit-eating animals.

Not far north from Mzima is Kilaguni Lodge, where you can indulge in some wildlife-watching at a waterhole. Roaring Rocks observation point is well worth a visit: **eagles** cruise at eye level and the westerly vista takes in the Chaimu Hills, Chyulu Hills and – on a clear day – Mt Kilimanjaro. The easterly view looks down on the winding watercourse of Ngulia Spring in Rhino Valley: you're likely to see **elephants**, **hippos** and **gazelles** from up here. Drive down into the valley and follow the watercourse to get closer, and search among the trees for animals seeking shade. Looking up, the face of the rocky scarp is the place to locate raptors such as **bateleurs**. A road here leads to Chaimu Crater (lava flow) and winds through rocky terrain that is ideal habitat for **klipspringers**. Although they are shy and frequent dense thickets, **lesser kudus** are readily seen here.

Tsavo West is dotted with features of recent volcanic activity: the Chyulu Hills are composed of cinders resulting from volcanic activity less than 500 years ago and are one of the world's newest mountain ranges. Water

percolates straight down through the porous soil before hitting solid rock and flowing underground to emerge at Mzima and other springs. Eastwards, at the base of the Ngulia Hills, Ngulia Rhino Sanctuary protects between 30 and 40 **black rhinos** plus a suite of other animals, including **giraffes**, **zebras**, **lesser kudus** and **leopards** (the surrounding fence is quite low so many animals are not confined). The sanctuary's five waterholes are the obvious places to look for rhinos; otherwise rhino spotting is mighty difficult because of the thick vegetation. **Kirk's dik-diks** thrive in this habitat and you are sure to see many pairs. Keep an eye out for the **golden pipit**, which in flight and coloration resembles a giant golden butterfly – it and the gorgeous **golden-breasted starling** are quite abundant.

WATER IN THE DESERT Tsavo East is less visited than the park's western

👀 WATCHING TIPS

A succession of animals come to drink in the mornings at Voi Lodge waterhole. Aruba Dam is a busy spot for animals and if lions are your thing, camp here – their roaring will probably keep you awake at night. A leopard is seen at bait at Ngulia Lodge just about every night. Hirolas (Hunter's hartebeests) translocated from Arawale National Reserve in northern Kenya can sometimes be seen between Aruba Dam and Buchuma Gate in Tsavo East.

section and only the southern part, below the Galana River, is open to the public. This permanent river is a feature of the park, and its greenery contrasts with the endless grasses and occasional saltbush thicket or thorn tree that characterise much of Tsavo East. Except during the rains (May to June, and November), when large animals disperse, sightings of **elephants** are virtually guaranteed by following the river route from Sala Gate to Manyani Gate – especially around Sala Gate itself and the Sobo Camp area. Herds of **waterbucks**, **plains zebras** and **impalas** are common, and **hippos** and **crocodiles** are found at Crocodile Point below Lugard's Falls. A pride of **lions** is frequently seen near Sala Gate, and another small family of lions lives near the Sobo area. **Giraffes** are regulars along the river route, as are numerous **dik-diks**, a few **gerenuks**, **Somali ostriches**, **kori bustards**, **bateleurs**, **carmine bee-eaters**, **waterbirds** and an East African speciality: the **vulturine guineafowl**. A highlight in this area is a family of melanistic (black) **servals**.

Near Lugard's Falls is the Black Rhino Sanctuary, which now has over 50 **black rhinos**. This can be visited and explored on foot (escorted by an armed ranger) with prior permission of the Kenyan Wildlife Service (KWS) or if you are staying at Galdessa Camp. Numerous **black-backed jackals** and **bat-eared foxes** inhabit this area but, being nocturnal, they are seen most often in the early morning or late afternoon.

Yatta Escarpment forms a backdrop to the Galana River for most of its length through Tsavo. This ancient lava flow is the largest in the world and runs along the north bank of the river almost all the way to Nairobi, 200km away. By driving along the Galana you should see a good selection of Tsavo's wildlife. Away from the river, towards Manyani Gate, the vegetation becomes thicker and visibility decreases, but this area is worth searching for **lesser kudus** and **black rhinos**. Between Manyani Gate and Voi is Mudanda Rock, a favourite spot for taking panoramic photos and a great vantage point for looking down on a dam that attracts many **elephants**. This area is a known **leopard** haunt, but daytime sightings are rare. As you approach Voi the bush thins out to grassland, which can be covered in herds of **impalas**, **buffaloes**, **plains zebras** and **elephants**.

Voi is well known for elephants: several orphans raised by the Daphne Sheldrick Trust roam the area, the older released

TSAVO'S BIRD BEACON

Each November and December Eurasian birds migrating south at night along the eastern flyway become disorientated in the rainy-season mists. Both birds and birders descend on Ngulia Lodge, in Tsavo West, where bright game-viewing lights become Tsavo's bird beacon. Graeme Backhurst and David Pearson run the Ngulia Bird Ringing Project – Africa's foremost Eurasian migratory bird-banding project. Since 1969 around 274,000 birds have been banded and individuals have been relocated in 38 different countries as far-flung as Kazakhstan, Finland, Russia and Zimbabwe. In all 57 Palaearctic species and 197 Afrotropical species have been banded. Graeme describes the whole experience as magic. 'As we are at the mist nets at night...migrating birds are constantly flitting past us and often alight on our heads, shoulders or even hands. All this takes place in misty conditions which tend to deaden sound, although we do hear the occasional hyena and lion roaring. In the early days of Ngulia, elephants and rhinos were frequent visitors to the lodge's salt licks and proved to be major hazards!'

elephants acting as guides for the younger orphans (the KWS rangers at Voi Gate generally know their whereabouts). The savanna around Voi is punctuated by isolated rocky hills that are worth exploring for **lions**, and the waterhole at Voi Safari Lodge is normally visited in the mornings by herds of **buffaloes**, **zebras** and **elephants**. There are also plenty of bold **yellow baboons** in this area so keep your vehicle windows closed if you don't want your lunch to disappear up a tree.

Near Voi Gate is Kanderi Swamp, which in the drier months provides one of only two drinking areas this side of the park: **buffaloes**, **impalas** and other **antelopes**, **yellow baboons** and **lions** are quite often found here. Further on is Aruba Dam, which usually holds water throughout the year and is frequented by huge numbers of **ibises** and many **grey herons** and other **waterbirds**. The tall trees in the camping ground and deserted lodge are home to **woodpeckers**, **sunbirds**, **starlings** and **pigeons**. Aruba Dam is part of the territory of a large pride of **lions**, which can usually be seen in the vicinity of the dam.

KENYA

MT KILIMANJARO FROM TSAVO NATIONAL PARK

KENYA

ARABUKO SOKOKE FOREST RESERVE

ARABUKO SOKOKE FOREST RESERVE

Arabuko Sokoke ('Sokoke') Forest is the largest and most important patch of coastal forest remaining in East Africa. Its uniqueness is apparent from the number of species that bear the forest's name, such as the **Sokoke scops owl**, **Sokoke pipit** and **Sokoke bushy-tailed mongoose**. An abundance of interesting small creatures makes up for a dearth of big animals, and birders will find several coastal endemics in Sokoke – species otherwise found only in the nearby Shimba Hills and in Tanzania's Usambara Mountains. This is the last stronghold of the **golden-rumped elephant shrew** and one of only two places where **Aders' duiker** survives; Sokoke also features an amazing variety of **butterflies** and has one of the richest diversities of **frogs** in Kenya. You are free to drive and walk about unescorted as long as you stick to designated tracks (**elephants** and **buffaloes** occur in low numbers, but you're unlikely to bump into them).

For the energetic there is a long-distance walking track (the 14km Elephant Track) and those with transport can explore 50km of tracks. Although you won't see much wildlife from a car, the main driving track gives a perspective of the three different vegetation zones: it begins in mixed forest before passing through a large area of *Brachystegia*; on higher ground, you'll encounter dense thickets of *Cynometra*. The denser vegetation is a favoured habitat of duikers. While you are unlikely to encounter the rare **Aders' duiker** (see the boxed text, p71), keep a lookout for other duikers – **blue**, **red** and **common duikers** all inhabit the forests. The main drive is topped off by Nyari Viewpoint, which is best visited in the afternoon or at sunset. On the way there, take an amble around the Whistling Duck Pools: apart

LOCATION 1.4km from the Gedi junction on the Malindi–Mombasa road. Accessible year-round (high-clearance vehicles advised).

FACILITIES Well-equipped visitor centre with comprehensive information. Marked nature trails and a treetop platform.

ACCOMMODATION A wide range in nearby Malindi and Watamu; camping in the reserve (fee applies).

WILDLIFE RHYTHMS Good any time; waders present October to April, frogs best April and May, Clarke's weavers return in March.

CONTACT KWS tourism ranger (☎ 042-3246; kwsarabuko@africaonline .co.ke).

👁 WATCHING TIPS

To see Kenyan crested guineafowl, drive about just after rain – the guineafowl then come out of the forested areas and should appear on the open tracks. Bird the *Brachystegia* woodland in the early morning then concentrate on the cooler mixed and *Cynometra* forest after 9am, when bird activity starts to slow down. Carry the butterfly identification chart (available from the visitor centre) while wandering about. The best birding at Mida Creek is one to two hours before high tide.

WILDLIFE HIGHLIGHTS
» A bird list in excess of 230 includes six globally threatened species and coastal specialities such as Fischer's turaco and the Kenyan race of the crested guineafowl » Rare mammals include the golden-rumped elephant shrew and Aders' duikers » Sokoke is renowned for butterflies (263 species have been recorded), and frogs make it a rainy season delight » Nearby Mida Creek offers superb birdwatching: it is a significant area for migratory waders and crab plovers are a highlight

from any **waterbirds** that might be here, there is a fine specimen of *Encephalartos hildebrandtii* – one of Sokoke's cycads – on the trail (this plant is ancient both in evolutionary terms and because some live for centuries).

BIRDING WITH & WITHOUT A GUIDE

Arabuko Sokoke is recognised by BirdLife International as an internationally Important Bird Area (IBA) because of the number of near-endemic species present. Three distinctive habitats dominate Sokoke and it's worth spending time in each as they all support different animals. The wetter parts of the reserve support a rich mixed closed-canopy forest formerly dominated by *Afzelia* trees (most have long since been felled for timber). Interspersed with the mixed forest is more open *Brachystegia* woodland. This woodland offers ideal birding, especially when, as often happens, a feeding flock composed of several species moves through. Two specialities are found only in this habitat: **Clarke's weaver**, which often moves through the canopy in large flocks (try the Lower Mida Track), and the **Amani sunbird**, which is relatively common and can be seen rapidly gleaning insects among the upper leaves. The woodland is also important for the **Sokoke pipit** – it can be seen in virtually any patch, but the Kararacha Track is a good bet. A summer visitor that you won't see in Kenya outside the Sokoke area's forests is the **spotted ground thrush**, but even here finding it will be hard work.

Forest dominated by *Cynometra* trees, punctuated by candelabra euphorbias, covers almost half the reserve and is home to Sokoke's real birding prize – the **Sokoke scops owl**. Although this diminutive owl is quite common, it is virtually impossible to see without assistance: to see it, you'd best

A SPECIES IN CRISIS

Aders' duiker is a small forest antelope that survives only in two places: Arabuko Sokoke Forest Reserve (where it lives in pairs among *Cynometra* thickets) and Zanzibar. The International Union for Conservation of Nature (IUCN) states that the Sokoke population is in 'danger of immediate extinction' unless it can be effectively protected. Numbers are not known for Sokoke, but the Zanzibar population is under serious threat: in 1995 there were estimated to be only 1400 remaining. On Zanzibar they are still hunted for meat and the population continues to dwindle because of habitat destruction. The Friends of Arabuko Sokoke Forest (www.watamu .net/foasf.html), established in 1996, helps protect Sokoke and its rare and restricted species. Support by local and international visitors aids the cause; information on providing support is available at the reserve's visitor centre.

hire a specialised guide and be prepared to squeeze though the bushes bent double and for long waits in the darkness.

Birders without transport should try the track between the visitor centre and the Nature Trail car park. In addition to the resident birds commonly seen – **white-browed coucal**, **green barbet**, **scaly babbler** and **collared sunbird** – watch for migratory **Eurasian** and **white-throated bee-eaters** between October and April. The northern race of the large and spectacular **carmine bee-eater** is generally abundant from September to January. This scrubby area backing onto forest is also excellent for spying **Fischer's turaco**, a coastal speciality (its loud call makes it easy to detect early in the morning).

KENYA

Among the mixed forest along the Nature Trail, you'll have to rely more on hearing to find birds and it's probably best to hire a guide. The **Sokoke pipit** can also be found here, but it takes an expert ear to locate it by call. **Blue monkeys** and **yellow baboons** are the most commonly seen animals on this circuit – a troop of about 70 inquisitive baboons frequents the area. There is also a good chance you'll find the **golden-rumped elephant shrew**. About the size of a rabbit, this diurnal insectivore has a gold-coloured rump and is largely restricted to Sokoke (90% of its population survives here). It can often be heard scuffling about pursuing insects in leaf litter, and when alarmed taps a foot or thumps its tail. Elephant shrew territories often span both sides of the trail, so you may see one scamper across the path as it does its rounds of boundary reinforcement.

SEASONAL FROG POOLS Seasonal pools occur on both the Nature Trail and the track leading to the sand quarry. These are the places to look for **frogs** in the rainy season (April to May). Of the 25 frog species in the area, there's the wonderfully named **Bunty's dwarf toad** (which mates belly-to-belly), the **marbled shovel-snout**, the **common squeaker** (the young skip the tadpole stage and develop straight into froglets), various **leaf-folding frogs** and the **red-legged pan frog**. White masses dangling from branches overhanging water are the nests of the communally breeding **foam-nest tree frog**. A platform 10m up in a tree overlooking the quarry gives great views over a revegetated area: in the wet season there is a good chance of seeing **waterbirds** in the pools, and **raptors** are often overhead during mornings and evenings.

Butterflies are abundant and many common species have names that double as

BLUE MONKEY

descriptions, such as **large striped** and **narrow green-banded swallowtails, banded gold tips** and **dark blue pansies.** Whenever you're near water in Sokoke, check the damp edges for butterflies mud puddling (congregating on wet soil). The **gold-banded forester** is often encountered gliding close over forest tracks in front of you as you walk, and is recognisable by purple and gold bands on its wing tips. The **white flip-flop butterfly** is another common species – it flies in a jerky motion around knee height.

THE MIDA TOUCH It is essential that birders visit Mida Creek adjacent to the reserve: the extensive, mangrove-fringed mudflats are Kenya's most important site for overwintering waders. From November to April large numbers can be seen feeding on the mudflats; the wader line-up includes a host of long-distance migrants, such as **sandpipers, godwits, whimbrels, curlews** and **plovers**; and larger birds such as **greater flamingos, yellow-billed storks, egrets** and **black herons.** Birds to look out for in the mangroves include **Retz's** and **chestnut-fronted helmet-shrikes, mangrove kingfishers** and, overhead, **northern carmine bee-eaters.** But the prize sighting

here is the rare **crab plover** – this large wader is endemic to the Red Sea area and hundreds are occasionally recorded at Mida Creek. Some crab plovers are present all year, but your chances are greater between August and April, when numbers swell with the arrival of migrants from their breeding grounds. Getting to Mida Creek is a little tricky – ask one of the guides at Arabuko Sokoke to show you the best access tracks.

Visiting here also helps the local Giriama community, which works with A Rocha, a Christian-oriented conservation organisation, and Arabuko Sokoke Schools & Eco-Tourism Scheme (ASSETS, which also works in Arabuko Sokoke National Forest). Excellent Giriama guides will take you through the landscape of the creek and the nearby mangrove forest. A bird blind looks out over the surrounding wetlands, while a rope bridge leads back into the mangroves, where giant crabs cling to tree trunks and oysters can be taken from the ground. You can also organise canoe trips to the former slaving island of Kirepwe or the ruins of Gedi; there's no more magical way to approach that lost city than at a soft paddle, under the shadow of spider roots via a surrounding network of riverine tree-roofed channels.

KENYA

NATURAL TREASURES BENEFIT LOCAL COMMUNITIES

The Kipepeo Butterfly Farm (☎ 042-32380; www.kipepeo.org; ⊙ 8am-5pm), adjacent to Gedi Ruins, was established in 1993 to provide a small income for local farmers and partly compensate those whose shambas had been damaged by elephants and baboons living in Arabuko Sokoke Forest. Live pupae collected from the forest by the farmers are taken to Kipepeo, from where many are shipped to live butterfly displays around the world. But many pupae are also hatched under controlled conditions into adult butterflies and displayed in a large flight cage at Kipepeo (which means 'butterfly' in Swahili). Guides can show you the various stages of butterfly development, and in the flight cage you'll get close enough to photograph a few of the hundreds of species in the region (depending on what's hatching at the time of your visit). Arabuko Sokoke Forest is constantly under threat from the demands of local people for land and firewood. More than 500 farmers are now involved with the Kipepeo butterfly project, which has shown how local people can benefit economically from the preservation of this important woodland remnant.

LOCATION 265km southeast of Nairobi. Road access limited in wet seasons; all-season airstrip.

FACILITIES Lodges run game drives, some have nature walks. Guides can be hired from park headquarters.

ACCOMMODATION Two camping grounds and four lodges.

WILDLIFE RHYTHMS
Mammals easier to see near water during dry seasons; migratory birds peak November to March.

CONTACT Senior Warden (☎ 0456-22251).

AMBOSELI NATIONAL PARK

Lake Amboseli takes up a large part of this relatively small park (which is also an International Biosphere Reserve) and Mt Kilimanjaro provides it with an extremely picturesque backdrop. The lake is typically dry and the park's few patches of trees are mostly in the east, but run-off from surrounding mountains feeds Amboseli's permanent swamps and creates a marshy green belt across the middle of the park. The swamps are a centre of activity for **elephants**, **hippos**, **buffaloes** and abundant **waterbirds**, and the surrounding flat grassland is home to grazing **antelopes**. **Spotted hyenas** are plentiful and **jackals**, **warthogs**, **olive baboons** and **vervet monkeys** all occur. **Lions** can still be found in Amboseli, although the famous black-maned lions are no longer here. Black rhinos are also now extinct in the park.

MARSHY CENTRES OF ACTIVITY

Normatior, also known as Observation Hill, provides an ideal lookout from which to orientate yourself to the plains, swamps and roads below. From the top you can spot hundreds of dots on the plains (typically **plains zebras**, **Grant's** and **Thomson's gazelles** and **wildebeests**), with larger masses near the swamp edges and in the swamps themselves (**hippos**, **buffaloes** and **elephants**). Amboseli is well known for its 700-plus resident elephants, and herds can be seen raising dust as they cross the plains to drink and feed at the swamps.

From Observation Hill the northern route runs across the Sinet Causeway, which makes an excellent place from which to start birdwatching over the swamp. In and near the marshes, **African jacanas** are abundant and you'll typically find several species of **heron**, such as **squacco**, **grey**, **goliath** and **black-**

WILDLIFE HIGHLIGHTS
» Famous for large herds of elephants – and big tuskers at that » Open plains allow fabulous wildlife viewing and photography, and mammals are very relaxed after years of tourism » Wildebeests, buffaloes, plains zebras, gazelles, spotted hyenas and elephants are abundant; lions occur in small numbers and cheetahs are sometimes seen » Permanent marshes are frequented by hippos, elephants and buffaloes » Prolific birdlife – 425 species have been recorded – includes waterbirds and plains and woodland species; Amboseli is particularly good for grey crowned cranes

👁👁 WATCHING TIPS

Amboseli is one of only two places where you can see the Taveta golden weaver, which is common around lodges and camps.

headed, plus **great white egrets, glossy ibises, Egyptian geese** and **blacksmith** and **spur-winged plovers**. There's also great birding along the causeway between the airstrip and Ol Tukai if you travel slowly: the list is long, but includes **saddle-billed storks, white-faced whistling-ducks, African fish eagles, little egrets, red-billed teal** and the migratory **purple heron** (which winters at Amboseli). Large numbers of **flamingos** may be present in the wet season (March to May and October to early December).

Amboseli is also home to less commonly seen species, including **common redshanks, purple swamphens** and **Eurasian thick-knees**. Among the various weavers that you should encounter in the wooded areas are **white-headed buffalo-weavers** and **grey-capped social weavers. Superb starlings** will help themselves to leftovers, and **drongos, red-billed hornbills** and **grey-headed sparrows** are also common. Anywhere they can find a vantage point, **lilac-breasted rollers** – a favourite with photographers – are likely to be seen perching and scanning for ground insects and lizards. Look for **grey crowned cranes** out on the plains.

Birds migrating from the north begin to arrive in October (departing again in March), so a visit after the short rains begin in November could give you a good shot at Amboseli's full complement of birds. Depending on the rains, Lake Amboseli may hold water and other small lakes may appear; by meandering around these temporary wetlands (as the roads allow) you can get away from the congested main wildlife-viewing circuit.

If you leave Amboseli by the Kimana Gate on the way to Tsavo West National Park, you'll probably find **Masai giraffes** in the acacia woodland. Better still, this is the place to spot **gerenuks**, particularly just outside the park on the road leading away from Kimana. These unusual gazelles browse by standing on their hind legs and stretching their necks – this behaviour is fairly easy to observe.

TRUNK CALLS

Amboseli's elephants are probably the best known of all: Cynthia Moss and her team have studied them since 1972. And Moss knows *all* of the park's elephants by sight – 53 families and 900 individuals. How? Like a lion's whisker spots, a cheetah's tail bands or a zebra's stripes, each elephant has unique identifiers: the profile of the ear and its filigree of veins are the equivalent of fingerprints. Yet elephants probably don't rely on sight to recognise each other. Research shows that they can identify at least 100 individuals by their calls. They even remember the voice of dead companions: when researchers played the calls of an elephant that had died two years earlier, her family responded with the 'I know you' call.

KENYA

KENYA

KAKAMEGA FOREST

LOCATION 45km north of Kisumu; 418km northwest of Nairobi. 4WD recommended on forest roads after rain.

FACILITIES Marked walking trails. Guides can be hired at Buyangu KWS office and at Isecheno Forest Station. Night walks by permission.

ACCOMMODATION Camping ground and guesthouse at Isecheno, camping ground and bandas at Udo's; guesthouse at Rondo Retreat; hotels in Kakamega.

WILDLIFE RHYTHMS The end of heavy rains triggers breeding of forest birds (June to August) and the emergence of many butterflies (best in August and September). Up to 30 species of migrant bird arrive in October.

CONTACT Kakamega Forest KWS office (☎ 056-20425).

KAKAMEGA FOREST

Monkey activity is at its best once the day warms up and again a few hours before sunset. **Black-and-white colobus** are abundant and sometimes keep company with **blue monkeys**; both, plus **red-tailed monkeys**, can usually be seen near Isecheno Forest Centre. Red-tailed monkeys also associate with blues and both visit fruiting trees at Rondo Retreat to feast on brightly coloured fruit – **African crowned eagles** overhead send them into a screaming panic. **Olive baboons** loiter near camping grounds at Isecheno and Buyangu, and raid shambas around Kisere Forest. Kisere Forest is also a good place to look for **de Brazza's monkeys**.

Red-legged sun squirrels, easily identified by their rich-red thighs, and **giant forest squirrels** are both regular canopy visitors at Rondo Retreat. **Bushbucks** are becoming rare, but **blue** or **Harvey's duikers** might be startled on forest trails – they normally freeze to avoid detection. **Servals** have been seen occasionally in glades south of Buyangu Hill. **Rhinoceros** and **Gaboon vipers**, two superbly camouflaged snakes, are rarely seen, but **Nile monitors** may be seen wandering throughout the forest, especially around Isiukhu Falls. Forest edges and grassland are favoured habitat for **skinks**, and **dwarf chameleons** – a mere 10cm in length – are a Kakamega speciality. Butterflies are most active by late morning; large **charaxes** and **swallowtails** congregate around animal dung along trails.

PEERLESS FOREST BIRDWATCHING

Kakamega is the largest remaining stronghold in Kenya for 84 bird species whose main distribution lies further west. Rondo Retreat is an excellent place to start looking: **Mackinnon's fiscals** are common in the grounds; **starlings**, **barbets** and

WILDLIFE HIGHLIGHTS
» **Largest surviving stand of rainforest in Kenya, now marking the easternmost distribution of many West African species** » **Blue monkeys and red-tailed monkeys, plus black-and-white colobus, easily seen among seven primate species, and red-legged sun and giant forest squirrels frequent the canopy** » **First-rate rainforest birding includes turacos, bee-eaters and hornbills among a list of 330 species; others include a selection of greenbuls, finches, barbets and starlings** » **Butterflies are profuse – 400 species recorded – and reptiles with a West African spin include the Gaboon viper**

BLACK-AND-WHITE COLOBUS

weavers sun on top of great trees; **snowy-headed robin-chats** inhabit the gully behind the gardens; and **grey parrots** sometimes roost nearby. **Cinnamon-chested bee-eaters** pursue passing insects from prominent perches; **blue-headed bee-eaters** are another speciality best sought on the Ikuywa Trail; and **little bee-eaters** nest in banks near Buyangu Hill. **Great blue** and **Ross' turacos** are commonly seen at Rondo and Isecheno, and another noisy canopy dweller, the **black-and-white-casqued hornbill**, lives throughout Kakamega Forest.

Trails near the Ikuywa River also support abundant rainforest birds (plus **monkeys** and **butterflies**) such as **barbets**, **greenbuls**, **starlings**, **cuckoo-shrikes**, **wattle-eyes** and **cuckoos**; unsociable forest weavers such as **brown-capped** and **black-billed weavers**; and the **yellowbill**, a forest cuckoo. The dazzling **red-headed bluebill** is common along roads and trails. Forest glades – especially along the Hiking Trail – harbour **harlequin quails** and **button-quails**, **white storks** (a seasonal visitor) and **grey crowned cranes**. **African black ducks** and **giant kingfishers** frequent the river along the Isiukhu Trail and **crested guineafowl** are most common in the northern Buyangu area.

CREATURES OF THE NIGHT

After sundown the noise of insects and frogs is drowned out only by the frequent thunderstorms. **African giant snails**, **goliath beetles** and **fireflies** become active, and spotlighting along roads and trails could reveal some of Kakamega's nocturnal gems: **bushpigs** are quite common; **aardvarks** are recorded occasionally; and you might pick out the huge eyes of a **potto**. **Lord Derby's anomalure** glides across clearings, and mammals that fly include the **hammer-headed fruit-bat** (Africa's largest) and smaller **insect-eating bats**, which emerge en masse at dusk from old mine shafts in Lirhanda Hill. **Marsh mongooses** live near waterways throughout the forest, which are also patrolled by **African clawless otters**; **brush-tailed porcupines** favour valley bottoms; and **tree pangolins** are most common in habitat mosaics. Forest owls that might be encountered are the **African wood owl** and **red-chested owlet**.

● ● WATCHING TIPS

- The Pumphouse Trail near Isecheno Forest Centre is good for monkeys and birds – African broadbills and white-spotted flufftails are seen along here.
- Spotlighting is probably the best chance to see a hippo on the Yala River (rare), as well as a Kakamega speciality, the giant otter shrew.
- A night walk in Kisere Forest might turn up a genet or African civet.
- African grass owls and African white-tailed nightjars have been recorded on the Falls Trail.

A NATURAL MEDICINE CHEST

Local people have long used Kakamega Forest as a source of natural products: wood for building, cooking fires and charcoal; grass for thatches, lianas for rope and bark for making blankets; and the *Raffia* palms growing along forest rivers for weaving baskets. But with the rapidly increasing human population, the supply will soon be exhausted and perhaps more serious is the potential loss of an estimated 50 medicinal plant species that grow here. For example, the bark of *Croton megalocarpus* and *Olea* trees is soaked, pounded and used as a remedy for intestinal worms; *Fagaropsis* roots are boiled and used to treat chest pains; and *Diospyros* roots are burnt and licked as a cure for tonsillitis. Animal products also have remedial uses – antelope droppings are soaked and used as a remedy for stomach ache – but species that are eaten, such as antelopes and porcupines, are becoming scarce.

GREY CROWNED CRANE

LOCATION 193km northeast of Nairobi. 4WD essential to reach trailheads when wet.

FACILITIES Various walking trails to summits.

ACCOMMODATION Basic huts on main climbing routes; huts at Meteorological Station; bandas and lodges outside the park; hotels in Nanyuki.

WILDLIFE RHYTHMS Large mammals move to higher altitudes during dry seasons (January to March and July to October). High-altitude birds may move to lower elevations during rains (March to June and October to December).

CONTACT Mt Kenya National Park (☎ 061-55645).

👁👁 WATCHING TIPS

Earth mounds produced by Rüppell's root-rat (*Tachyoryctes splendens*), endemic to Mt Kenya, can be seen in the Hinde Valley. Mackinder's eagle-owl (a race of Cape eagle-owl) is common in the Teleki Valley – a park ranger may know of a roost. Leopards are the most common predator and have been seen even near the summit of Point Lenana. Spotted hyenas travel far up the Teleki Valley, cheetahs are occasionally seen on the Timau and Sirimon Trails, and lions hunt high on the Naro Moru Route.

MT KENYA NATIONAL PARK

Distinct vegetation zones form horizontal bands across the slopes and valleys that radiate from Mt Kenya's peaks. Tall forests of camphors, cedars and African olive cloak the lower slopes, their trunks fluted like Greek columns or twisted like giant sticks of barley sugar. Beard moss swaying in the breeze looks like the dangling tail tufts of **black-and-white colobus**, which leap into the overgrown ravines when spotted; **Sykes' monkeys** also feed along the roadsides. **Elephants** and **buffaloes** generally keep out of sight, but **bushbucks** and **defassa waterbucks** are common, and **black-fronted duikers**, **sunis** and **giant forest hogs** all live in the understorey.

Pairs of **Hunter's cisticolas** duet on top of bushes; **Hartlaub's turacos** glide across the road with crimson wing-flashes; **silvery-cheeked hornbills** and **red-fronted parrots** sun themselves on the topmost branches (especially near the Naro Moru park entrance); parties of **white-headed wood-hoopoes** probe cracks; and **cinnamon-chested bee-eaters** snap up prey from exposed branches. **Tree hyraxes** start screeching after sunset and **white-tailed mongooses** might be spotlighted along roads. This was once a stronghold of **black rhinos**, and about half a dozen are thought to remain in Mt Kenya's forests; other rarities include **golden cats**, melanistic (black) **servals** and **leopards**.

SUCH GREAT HEIGHTS At about 2400m, dense thickets of 12m-high bamboo appear, broken by the trails of **elephants** and **buffaloes**, their droppings littering the roads. **Bushbucks** are still common on grassy verges at this height, while **black-fronted duikers** and **bongos** are far more secretive. Above 2600m, spreading East

WILDLIFE HIGHLIGHTS
» Colourful wildflowers, giant groundsels and lobelias are among at least 10 endemic plants of alpine meadows
» Dense forests and bamboo shelter elephants, buffaloes and black rhinos; larger herbivores such as plains zebras and common elands graze as high as alpine meadows; bushbucks and defassa waterbucks are common in forests; and leopards reach the lofty passes » Sykes' monkeys (a local race of blue monkey), black-and-white colobus and tree hyraxes live in forests, where common birds include Hartlaub's turacos, white-headed wood-hoopoes and red-fronted parrots; high altitude birds are an attraction

African rosewood (*Hagenia*) trees grow in open glades, becoming stunted at the treeline; the mossy ground is pierced by wildflowers, bracken and tall forest lobelias. Beyond 2900m, head-high giant heather shelters herds of **buffaloes**, **common elands** and **plains zebras** (although large animals are sighted only occasionally by walkers); **lions** are also sometimes encountered. **Sunbirds** probe aromatic proteas, and other wildflowers include everlastings, gladioli and the brilliant blue *Delphinium*. **Alpine chats** perch fearlessly at arm's length if you stop long enough and **scarlet-tufted malachite sunbirds** sip from red-hot pokers (this popular garden flower is native to East Africa's highlands).

Above 3300m, vast swathes of tussock grass stretch to the snowline. Gladioli add a scarlet slash to the scene and, at about 3500m, fleshy lobelias and groundsels – the so-called 'big game plants' – reach gargantuan proportions: two species of giant groundsel grow as high as 6m. **Rock hyraxes** live among the outcrops, watchful of **Verreaux's eagles** and **mountain buzzards** patrolling overhead. **Elephants** and **buffaloes** have been seen as high as 4000m in the Teleki Valley; and the northern slopes support resident grazers such as **kongonis**, **steenboks** and herds of **plains zebras** (there's a chance of seeing all of these along the Timau Route). Herds of **elands** are also resident – the Sirimon roadhead is a good place to see them. Rodents abound up here: **groove-toothed rats** scuttle across the trails and chattering **African common dormice** keep hikers awake at night in the huts. Birds include **African snipe** in the grassland, **African black ducks** on tarns and **white-naped ravens** scavenging around huts. The mighty **lammergeier** cruises the greatest heights – try Sendeo or Terere Peaks on the Sirimon Route – **mottled** and **scarce swifts** are common, and **alpine swifts** can be seen near Two Tarn Hut.

SUMMER EVERY DAY & WINTER EVERY NIGHT

Giant groundsels and lobelias have various adaptations to Mt Kenya's extreme daily temperature fluctuations. Rosettes of densely packed leaves close at night around a central bud, like an artichoke, protecting them from bitter winds and subzero temperatures. Dead leaves hanging off groundsels insulate sap in the stem and hold heat absorbed during the day, and a fluffy white tuft (called a tomentum) on the underside of the cabbage groundsel (*Senecio brassica*) helps trap warm air.

Lobelia keniensis secretes a fluid into its rosettes – it looks like rainwater – that freezes to insulate the plant at night. Only a thin layer of ice has time to form overnight; the rising sun causes rosettes to reopen within minutes and the ice to melt. Each rosette grows about 2.5cm per year for several decades, produces one flowering spike then dies; ostrich plume *(L. telekii)* flowers once every 40 to 70 years.

LOCATION 9km south of Nairobi.

FACILITIES Animal Orphanage just inside the main entrance.

ACCOMMODATION None in the park. Hotels, hostels and backpacker accommodation in Nairobi.

WILDLIFE RHYTHMS Wildebeests disperse November to May, returning July to October and also in March. Fields of wildflowers appear after rains. Male Jackson's widowbirds display March to May.

CONTACT Nairobi National Park (☎ 02-500622).

NAIROBI NATIONAL PARK

First wildlife impressions of Nairobi city will probably consist of a few birds: opportunistic **pied crows** and **black kites** wheeling over the market; **red-winged starlings** clinging to walls as if they were cliff faces; platoons of **marabou storks** and **cattle egrets** on playing fields; and chittering flocks of **little swifts** near Nairobi University. It's not the most prepossessing city on earth, but this is Kenya, so something living can usually be seen in even the smallest patch of greenery: **variable sunbirds** (one of the most common city birds), a **common bulbul** or two, iridescent **greater blue-eared starlings** and a few **rufous sparrows** or **speckled mousebirds**. **Butterflies**, such as swallowtails, flit about in parks and hotel gardens; **silvery-cheeked hornbills** and showy **Hartlaub's turacos** are common in leafy suburbs; and even in the middle of town the comical honking of **hadada ibises** will be heard most days. The musical 'tink' of tree frogs at night is actually **epauletted bats**, a type of fruit-bat (some roost under eaves at Nairobi Museum); other nocturnal garden visitors include **African wood owls** and **montane nightjars**.

Fortunately, only half an hour's drive south from the city centre there is excellent – and safe – wildlife viewing available at Nairobi National Park. Most of the popular characters play out the drama of the plains right next to Jomo Kenyatta international airport: there are no elephants around, but **plains zebras, Masai giraffes, buffaloes, antelopes** and **gazelles** complement a cat list headed by **lions** and **cheetahs**. Nairobi National Park has Kenya's highest density of **black rhinos** (about 50) and there's a good chance of seeing **white rhinos** (which were introduced to the park). **Spotted hyenas** and **leopards** also occur – the latter a possibility in tall trees along rivers. Small antelopes – **oribis, steenboks, Kirk's dik-diks** and **bushbucks** – live among the whistling thorn and *Cordia* bushes on high ground in the park's west.

WILDLIFE HIGHLIGHTS

» Plains mammals such as black and white rhinos, Masai giraffes, plains zebras, buffaloes, kongonis (Coke's hartebeests) and wildebeests (in season) » A good chance of lions and cheetahs, and leopards and spotted hyenas are also resident; also olive baboons, vervet and blue monkeys, hippos and Nile crocodiles » Grassland birds prominent among 550 recorded bird species

KENYA

Impala Point is a good place from which to scan the grasslands for **rhinos**, **Masai giraffes**, **buffaloes**, and antelopes such as **common elands** and **kongonis** (Coke's hartebeests). **Grant's** and **Thomson's gazelles**, **impalas** and **warthogs** can be encountered virtually anywhere on the plains. **Wildebeests** cross the park's southern boundary to disperse across the Kitengala Plains during the rains, but a few are normally present year-round – try the Embakasi Plain. **Plains zebras** join the dispersal, but can usually be seen year-round in the park. **Marabou storks**, **vultures** and **hawk-eagles** sit in tall acacias, and grassland birds such as **secretary birds**, **ostriches**, **bustards** and **Jackson's widowbirds** are park specialities.

BABOON CLIFFS & HIPPO POOLS

Hippos wallow in the Athi River, emerging to graze on the banks at night, and **terrapins** and **Nile crocodiles** bask on exposed mud. A ranger guide should be available for the nature trail at the Hippo Pools, where **vervet monkeys**, **pigeons**, **barbets** and **starlings** feed in African fig trees along the banks. **Defassa waterbucks** are common along the Athi and **rock hyraxes**, **klipspringers** and **Chanler's mountain reedbucks** frequent the steep slopes of Mbagathi Gorge. **Olive baboons** and **vervet** and **blue monkeys** loiter at the top of the Baboon Escarpment, where **rock hyraxes** also wait for handouts and **red-headed agama lizards** nod to prospective mates.

KENYA

ZEBRAS IN NAIROBI NATIONAL PARK

LOCATION Buffalo Springs' main gate is 20km north of Isiolo, 355km north of Nairobi. 4WD recommended in wet seasons.

FACILITIES Guides can be hired from park headquarters.

ACCOMMODATION Camping grounds, tented camps and lodges in all parks.

WILDLIFE RHYTHMS Vegetation dies back in dry seasons (June to October and December to April) and large animals concentrate near springs and the Ewaso Nyiro River, dispersing across the parks soon after rain.

CONTACT Samburu National Reserve (☎ 020-244068).

SAMBURU, BUFFALO SPRINGS & SHABA NATIONAL RESERVES

Large, domed termite mounds among the dry, thorny shrubland make dens for **aardvarks**, **warthogs** and **bat-eared foxes**, as well as lookouts for **cheetahs**, which are commonly sighted in the open woodland of Buffalo Springs. In Shaba and Samburu, succulent aloes, euphorbias and desert roses grow on rocky ridges that shelter **hyraxes**, **klipspringers** and **leopards**. Shaba is famous for large prides of **lions**, which during the day laze under dense thickets of the leathery mswaki bush – used by lcals as a toothbrush. Nocturnal predators such as **golden** and **black-backed jackals**, and both **striped** and **spotted hyenas** live in all three reserves. **Aardwolves** are also occasionally seen. **Common genets** scrounge around camp sites, and **banded** and **dwarf mongooses** charge around in packs looking for small prey. **Unstriped ground squirrels** and **Cape hares** make tasty snacks for small cats and large raptors.

Browsers of the thorny shrubs include **common elands**, **impalas**, **Bright's gazelles** (the pale northern race of Grant's gazelle) and **gerenuks** (also called giraffe-gazelles). **Reticulated giraffes** also live here and browse even higher up the trees. Both **Grevy's** and **plains zebras** graze the plains, sometimes in mixed herds: Grevy's lives in all three parks, but plains are rarely seen north of the Ewaso Nyiro. **Warthogs** root for bulbs and **beisa oryxes** graze on short grass throughout the reserves, and both **lesser** and **greater kudus** are seen in small numbers on the densely vegetated slopes of Lowa Mara and Koitogor in Samburu. The scarlet rumps of **white-headed buffalo-weavers** in flight are a common sight. Other conspicuous birds include **Somali ostriches, secretary**

👀 **WATCHING TIPS**

Nile crocodiles are fed at various lodges along the Ewaso Nyiro River. Leopards lie up in tall acacias or dense vegetation near the river. Klipspringers may be seen on outcrops near Dakadima Hill in Shaba. Caracals are most frequently encountered in Shaba and northern Samburu.

WILDLIFE HIGHLIGHTS

» **Healthy numbers of predators, with lions, leopards and cheetahs frequently seen; also spotted and striped hyenas, bat-eared foxes and hunting dogs (rare)**
» **Elephants, buffaloes, hippos, plains zebras, reticulated giraffes, lesser and greater kudus complemented by herbivores typical of semiarid plains: Grevy's zebras, beisa oryxes, gerenuks, Kirk's and Günther's dik-diks, and the northern race of Grant's gazelle** » **Good pickings among 395 bird species includes 47 species of birds of prey, Somali ostriches, vulturine guineafowl, Verreaux's eagles, sandgrouse and hornbills**

KENYA

THE DANGERS OF DINING ON THORNY CROWNS

Acacias – the distinctive thorn trees of Kenya – grow in profusion in Samburu, Buffalo Springs and Shaba National Reserves, shading animals and supporting hanging colonies of weavers. During dry seasons many acacia species shed their leaves, quickly bursting into green again when their shallow, densely matted roots absorb the first rains. Most acacias are armed with sharp thorns, and stinging ants that take up residence in their branches are a further hazard to would-be browsers. Nonetheless, olive baboons feast on young pods; the protein-rich leaves are sought by antelopes such as gerenuks, impalas and dik-diks; and giraffes and rhinos hardly seem to notice the thorns as they munch away. Perhaps the most easily recognisable species is *Acacia tortillis*, the flat-topped umbrella acacia, which grows in large stands that provide shade for oryxes, giraffes, zebras, gazelles and cheetahs. *Acacia elatior* grows to 20m or more in height and is the most common tree along the Ewaso Nyiro River.

birds and **vulturine guineafowl**, which explode in a puff of red where they've been dust bathing. **Red-billed** and **Von der Decken's hornbills** are common and **sandgrouse** drink at the Ewaso Nyiro River in the evening.

RIVER TRAFFIC
The Ewaso Nyiro is the lifeblood of **hippos**, usually seen in the lower reaches near tributaries, and **Nile crocodiles** – some large specimens bask on exposed sand bars. **Buffaloes** shelter in dense riverside thickets, and **impalas** and **common waterbucks** also stay close to the permanent greenery. **Storks** feed along the banks, and **Verreaux's eagles** and **martial eagles** hunt from large trees. **Kirk's** and **Günther's dik-diks** – both favourite prey of leopards – hold territories in the dense bush but are also found far from water. Large animals that can negotiate the Ewaso Nyiro (and its crocs) pass freely between Samburu and Buffalo Springs. In the late afternoon, **elephants** – red from dust bathing – often file down to the river to drink or spray themselves with sand. Giant figs, acacias, Tana poplars and 20m-high doum palms line the banks and mark the course of the river to the horizon. The fruits of the palm are eaten by **elephants**, **vervet monkeys** and **olive baboons**; troops of

vervets and baboons raid unattended camping grounds and rest under riverside trees during the heat of the day. **African orange-bellied parrots** also feed on the doum fruits and nest in old palms. The **palm-nut vulture** also feeds on palm nuts; more conventional, carrion-eating **vultures** wait on large boughs for thermals to carry them over the plains. Quick-flying **African palm swifts** are active along the river at dawn and dusk.

KENYA

ELEPHANT BATHING IN DUST

ABERDARE NATIONAL PARK

LOCATION 160km north of Nairobi; 20km west of Nyeri.

FACILITIES Walking trails.

ACCOMMODATION
Camping grounds, cottages and lodges in park; hotels in Nyeri.

WILDLIFE RHYTHMS
Elephants and some antelopes disperse to higher altitudes during dry seasons, retreating to forested slopes in wet seasons.

CONTACT Aberdare National Park (☎ 061-55645).

Elephants and **buffaloes** are common in the densely forested Salient (the park's eastern extension), but the quickest way to see them is at the park's two game lodges. **Bushbucks, defassa waterbucks, warthogs, giant forest hogs** and **olive baboons** are also regular visitors and the night shift can include **lions, leopards, spotted hyenas, bushpigs, genets** and **white-tailed mongooses**. A few **ducks, herons, storks** and **coots** usually linger at the lodges' waterholes and **vervet monkeys** forage in open areas during the day. **Black-and-white colobus**, the park's most common monkey, and **blue monkeys** can usually be seen feeding along the roads to the high plains.

Elephant and buffalo dung litters the tracks, attracting fly-snapping **yellow wagtails**. A few **buffaloes** can generally be seen around the Salient's waterholes – **cattle egrets** often indicate their whereabouts. About 50 **black rhinos** live in the park – sightings are rare, but one occasionally visits a lodge's salt lick. **Defassa waterbucks** and **bushbucks** graze along ravines; other antelopes – **common elands, sunis** and **Harvey's duikers** – are less likely to be seen in the open. **Caracals,** and melanistic (black) forms of **leopards** and **servals** inhabit the Salient; **African golden cats** have been seen near camping grounds at the eastern end. Large forest birds include **silvery-cheeked hornbills, Hartlaub's turacos** and the monkey-eating **crowned eagle**.

Vegetation grows in distinct horizontal bands as altitude increases: **bongos** (now rare) inhabit dense bamboo thickets and moss-encrusted *Hagenia* glades above the tall forest. Giant heather grows at still higher elevations and, on the highest plateaus, giant fleshy lobelias and groundsels punctuate broad swathes of tussock grass. **Common elands, lions** (hairier and more spotted up here) and **leopards** venture above the treeline, and **servals** are regularly seen hunting rodents or **Jackson's francolins. Mountain buzzards** soar over moorlands, and **alpine chats** perch at arm's length around picnic sites.

👁 WATCHING TIPS

Black rhinos sometimes wander onto lawns at Tusk Camp. A black serval is a permanent resident around Kiandongoro Fishing Lodge.

WILDLIFE HIGHLIGHTS
» Expect to see elephants, buffaloes, defassa waterbucks and bushbucks; other possibilities are elands and black rhinos (rare), primates such as black-and-white colobus, vervet monkeys and olive baboons, plus wart-hogs
» Predators include lions, leopards and servals » A bird list of 200 species includes forest species such as silvery-cheeked hornbills, crowned eagles and Hartlaub's turacos

HELL'S GATE NATIONAL PARK

Ol Njorowa Gorge (Hell's Gate) makes a highway for both animals and people: it's lion-free so it's possible to walk or cycle among herds of **plains zebras** and **kongonis** (Coke's hartebeests), **impalas** and **Grant's** and **Thomson's gazelles**. **Warthogs**, **secretary birds** and **common ostriches** are also residents and **cheetahs** are sometimes encountered. **Masai giraffes** are breeding residents and **defassa waterbucks** might be seen where the gorge narrows towards steaming volcanic vents at the park's centre and west end. **Jackals** and **spotted hyenas** sometimes scavenge around camping grounds at night.

Rock hyraxes bask on Fischer's Tower, a 25m-high volcanic plug at the eastern entrance to the gorge, bolting into crevices should a **Verreaux's eagle** cruise past. **Augur buzzards** perch on the pillar and both raptors nest on the cliffs nearby. Five other bird-of-prey species use the 120m-high cliffs and there are plans to reintroduce the mighty **lammergeier**. **Olive baboons** lounge about on rocks at the base of the pillar, attracted to the fig trees growing near its base, and **Chanler's mountain reedbucks** may sometimes be seen grazing on the slopes nearby in the late afternoon.

WHITEWASHED CLIFFS Grass on the slopes and cliff tops is favoured by **steenboks** – look for their black nose stripe – and **klipspringers**, although the latter are never far from protective rock faces. **Common elands, buffaloes** and **Kirk's dik-diks** shelter among stands of dense *Croton* bushes. The cliffs themselves provide nesting sites for thousands of **Nyanza** and **mottled swifts**; their chief predators, **lanner** and **peregrine falcons**, perch on high ledges and cut swaths through the flocks. Colonies of nesting **Egyptian** and **Rüppell's griffon vultures** have whitewashed the walls near the western end of the gorge. You'll need sharp eyes to spot **Cape eagle-owls** on the cliffs, but they also nest in the gorge.

LOCATION 100km northwest of Nairobi; 18km west of Naivasha. Unsealed roads.

FACILITIES Visitor centre.

ACCOMMODATION Camping grounds in park; camping grounds, bandas and hotels at Lake Naivasha.

WILDLIFE RHYTHMS Grass shorter and animals more visible during dry seasons. Swifts breed on cliffs March to May.

CONTACT Hell's Gate National Park (☎ 050-50547).

KENYA

WILDLIFE HIGHLIGHTS

» The herbivore line-up includes plains zebras, common elands, impalas, waterbucks, kongonis, Masai giraffes, buffaloes, Grant's and Thomson's gazelles and warthogs
» Predators include spotted hyenas and (rarely) cheetahs
» The park's good for small antelopes such as steenboks and klipspringers » Nesting birds of prey, including Rüppell's griffon and Egyptian vultures, are a highlight

👀 WATCHING TIPS

Klipspringers may sometimes be seen on high cliffs near Elsa Gate. Stake out artificial waterholes in the gorge for mammals – the park is otherwise virtually waterless.

LOCATION 110km north of Nakuru; 266km northwest of Nairobi. Sealed roads.

FACILITIES Expert guides, boat hire and daily bird walks at Lake Baringo Country Club. Boat hire at Kampi ya Samaki.

ACCOMMODATION Lakeside camping, cottages and hotel; hotels in Kampi ya Samaki.

WILDLIFE RHYTHMS Migratory waders and ducks arrive October to November. Many local birds breed April to June.

CONTACT Lake Baringo ranger station (☎ 037-40746).

LAKE BARINGO

Abundant **waterbirds** and **African fish eagles** compete with **Nile crocodiles** for fish, and **hippos** that graze on the western shore at night loll in the shallows in the early morning. Colourful – and easily seen – bird species include **red-and-yellow barbets** and an assortment of **starlings**, **hornbills** and **sunbirds**. Nocturnal **Heuglin's coursers** lives in scrub north of Kampi ya Samaki – ask a local guide to help find them.

Drowned trees fringing the western shore make perches for waterbirds such as **long-tailed cormorants** and oodles of **pied kingfishers** – plus an occasional **giant kingfisher**. Apart from fish eaters, **Madagascar bee-eaters** hawk from the trees between May and October, and **blue-cheeked bee-eaters** use the same perches from November to April. South along the shore, **lesser moorhens** and **African jacanas** pick their way over lily pads and mats of Nile cabbage; **flamingos** are joined by **yellow-billed storks** and **African spoonbills**; **pelicans** feed in deeper water; **ducks** and **geese** loaf on muddy shores; and **glossy ibises** and **grey herons** are dwarfed by **goliath herons** – the latter breed year-round on rocky islands in the lake.

AT THE CLIFF FACE *Acacia-Commiphora* woodland 3km west of the shoreline, at the foot of 100m-high cliffs, has a rich bird diversity. For good birdwatching walk north along the cliffs from the lake turn-off in the early morning (bird activity dies off after about 9am). **Bristle-crowned starlings** perch high up and **rock hyraxes** bask on trees on top of the cliff. The fluting call of **white-shouldered cliff chats** echoes across rock walls; **white-faced scops owls** roost in rocky ravines; and fig trees attract **speckled pigeons** and **hornbills** – Jackson's and **Hemprich's** are two local specialities. Colourful **finches** in the undergrowth include **purple grenadiers**, **green-winged pytilias** and **red-cheeked cordon-bleus**. **Common kestrels** and **lanner falcons** nest on the ledges, and **pygmy falcons** are common in woodland.

WILDLIFE HIGHLIGHTS
» Hippos and Nile crocodiles » Brilliant birding (460 species recorded), with waterbirds, including flamingos, ducks, storks, herons and pelicans, a strong suit » African fish eagles are common and local specialities include lesser moorhens, giant kingfishers and, at the nearby escarpment, white-faced scops owls, Hemprich's hornbills and brown-tailed rock chats

LAKE BOGORIA NATIONAL RESERVE

An unbroken, pink collar of **lesser flamingos** (and many **greater flamingos**, standing almost twice the lesser's height) rings the lake's shores. Around 200 to 250 **greater kudus** live in dense woodland on the steep hillsides, but most large animals concentrate south of the hot springs and geysers that erupt from the lake's margins: **impalas, Thomson's** and **Grant's gazelles, plains zebras** and **warthogs** all graze near the shore. A small herd of **buffaloes** inhabits the park, **klipspringers** and **rock hyraxes** live on steep rock faces and **leopards** are present, though rarely seen. **Abyssinian ground hornbills** sometimes forage along wooded gullies near the lake's southern end.

WALKING BOULDERS & TERMITE CHIMNEYS The shores are strewn with boulders – but if one moves it's probably a **leopard tortoise**. Tall hollow towers built by termites on flat ground – like earthen chimneys – are used as lookouts by **grey-headed kingfishers, common fiscals** and **lilac-breasted rollers**. With no fish to eat, **African fish eagles** harass the flamingos by sweeping low and snatching stragglers. Late in the afternoon, **Kirk's dik-diks** step out from the thornbushes and a few **greater kudus** descend from the slopes to drink at springs near the lake – anywhere south of the (usually) dry riverbed is a good spot to wait.

Common **ostriches** and **grey crowned cranes** visit the plains north of the lake. The lake's high salinity offers limited nourishment for waterbirds, but a few **Cape teal, Egyptian geese** and **black-necked grebes** are usually present; and **hamerkops** and **storks** loiter at the water's edge. Otherwise it's **flamingos** all the way, sweeping their bills through water, roosting on one leg, floating like giant blossoms and upending in deeper water, their skinny legs kicking. Slow processions form lines along freshwater streams; in the late afternoon, some wander onto the road to drink or bathe in puddles.

WILDLIFE HIGHLIGHTS

» An estimated two million lesser flamingos – forming one of the great ornithological spectacles of East Africa – and the best place in Kenya to see greater kudus » Other wildlife includes plains zebras, buffaloes, impalas and warthogs, and 375 bird species have been clocked up, including lilac-breasted rollers, common ostriches and grey crowned cranes

LOCATION 38km north of Nakuru (southern end – 4WD essential); 150km to northern end (sealed road).

FACILITIES Guards can be hired for game walks.

ACCOMMODATION Camping grounds in the park; hotels just outside northern gate and in Marigat.

WILDLIFE RHYTHMS Migrant waterfowl, waders and swallows arrive October to November, leaving again between April and May.

CONTACTS Lake Bogoria National Reserve (☎ 037-40746).

KENYA

◉◉ WATCHING TIPS

Buffaloes are usually seen in woodland at the park's southern end. Swamps at the northern end support a higher diversity of waterbirds than the lake itself.

LAKE NAIVASHA

Lake Naivasha is a freshwater Rift Valley lake – the level of which fluctuates periodically – that supports resident **hippos** and, at times, the largest **waterfowl** population in Kenya. **Vervet monkeys** and **olive baboons** live in woodland adjoining the southwestern shore, and game corridors from nearby Hell's Gate National Park allow **buffaloes**, **kongonis** (Coke's hartebeests), **antelopes** and **Masai giraffes** access to grazing areas. Fish attract good numbers of **African fish eagles**, **cormorants**, **pelicans** and **herons** – birdwatching is a highlight, although populations of both predators and prey fluctuate. Mats of water lilies and Nile cabbage on the southern shore attract **jacanas** and **long-toed plovers**, and **weavers** and **warblers** breed in papyrus reed beds.

Crater Lake, an extinct volcanic crater at Naivasha's western end, is thickly wooded with yellow fever trees on which troops of **black-and-white colobus**, **vervet monkeys** and **olive baboons** drape themselves. A total of 38 mammal species has been recorded here: **buffaloes**, **warthogs**, **defassa waterbucks**, **bushbucks**, **Thomson's gazelles** and **impalas** can be seen by walking around the crater, and spotlighting on night drives may reveal **springhares**, **Senegal galagos**, **common genets**, **white tailed mongooses** or predators such as **servals** and **bat-eared foxes**. Antelopes sheltering in the dense vegetation include **Kirk's dik-diks**, **steenboks** and **common elands**. **Lesser flamingos** and various **ducks** and **grebes** feed in the flooded crater.

At Elsamere Conservation Centre, **hippos** graze on the lawns at night, **black-and-white colobus** frequent huge yellow fever trees in the gardens and **African fish eagles** and **Verreaux's eagles** feature among 200 bird species.

Crescent Island is the exposed lip of a submerged volcanic crater, and its area changes with the lake's water level. **Plains zebras**, **defassa waterbucks** and **Thomson's gazelles** were all introduced and wander free; **herons**, **storks** and **waterfowl** puddle around the edges and **pied kingfishers** are abundant.

LOCATION 89km northwest of Nairobi. All sites except Crater Lake accessible by matatu.

FACILITIES Boat hire at Elsamere, Fisherman's Camp and Lake Naivasha Country Club.

ACCOMMODATION Camping grounds, bandas, hotels and lodges along lakeshore; hotels in Naivasha.

WILDLIFE RHYTHMS Northern migrants – waterfowl and waders – swell bird numbers from October to March.

👀 WATCHING TIPS

Black-and-white colobus visit the lawns at Elsamere most Sunday afternoons. Hippos and good birdwatching can be enjoyed from the dock at Fisherman's Camp.

WILDLIFE HIGHLIGHTS
» **Hippos** in the lake, and **black-and-white colobus**, **olive baboons** and **vervet monkeys** are resident on the wooded southern shore, also frequented by **buffaloes**, **Masai giraffes** and **antelopes** such as **kongonis**, **impalas** and **gazelles** from nearby reserves » **Waterbirds** a highlight; they include **African fish eagles**, **pied kingfishers**, **yellow-billed storks**, **flamingos** and **waterfowl**

LAKE NAKURU NATIONAL PARK

Hippos wallow near the northern and southern ends of this shallow soda lake, which usually has a few hundred **flamingos** feeding on its edges. Rarities are a feature: **Rothschild's giraffes**, and **black** and **white rhinos** were all introduced and are now breeding – black rhinos favour acacia thorn scrub in the south. Rogue **leopards** translocated from other parts of Kenya have boosted the local population – this is one of the best parks to see this big cat. A small population of **lions** is also present, typically seen lounging about in thickets of fever trees.

THE GREAT PLAINS IN MINIATURE Grassland on the southern and western shores is grazed by **defassa waterbucks** – the most common antelope – and **white rhinos**. **Grey crowned cranes** and **warthogs** forage among **plains zebras, Thomson's** and **Grant's gazelles, bohor reedbucks** and **buffaloes** – **oxpeckers** picking parasites off their backs. **Olive baboons** fan out from cover while raptors such as **bateleurs** and **vultures** cruise overhead. Waterbirds are abundant at the southern end, including both **great white** and **pink-backed pelicans, greater** and the more abundant **lesser flamingos** and many **storks, egrets** and **herons. Rock hyraxes, rock pythons** and **agama lizards** frequent the Baboon Cliff, where **olive baboons** loiter for picnic scraps.

Yellow fever trees growing at the water's edge bubble with the calls of **tropical boubous** and **white-browed coucals**. **Leopards** are often seen draped over large boughs – the corner near the Lanet Gate is a good place to look; **impalas** also favour this area and **Rothschild's giraffes** browse on trees along the eastern shore. At the water's edge, **ducks** dabble among **herons** stalking in the shallows, while **cormorants** rest on branches overhead. **Black-and-white colobus** forage in the dense stand of candelabra euphorbias near the southeastern corner and **vervet monkeys** may be seen virtually anywhere among fallen timber and in trees.

LOCATION 155km northwest of Nairobi; 5km from Nakuru.

FACILITIES Good road networks, game-viewing and birdwatching tours.

ACCOMMODATION Camping grounds, bandas, hostel and lodges in park; lodges outside park; hotels in Nakuru.

WILDLIFE RHYTHMS Antelopes and hippos have young in March. Lion cubs born April to May. Migratory waterfowl and waders swell bird numbers from October to April. Lake waters contract during dry seasons, forcing waterbirds to feed at other Rift Valley lakes.

CONTACT Lake Nakuru National Park (☎ 051-44069).

KENYA

WILDLIFE HIGHLIGHTS
» **Large animals such as black and white rhinos, hippos, Rothschild's giraffes and buffaloes are easily seen** » **Lions and leopards head the predator list while plains zebras, defassa waterbucks and gazelles are common** » **Primates include vervet monkeys, olive baboons and black-and-white colobus** » **Flamingos, pelicans and other waterbirds feature on a bird list topping 400 species**

👀 WATCHING TIPS
White-shouldered cliff chats frequent Baboon Cliffs. A freshwater spring at the northeast corner of the lake attracts mammals and birds.

LOCATION Loyangalani 665km north of Nairobi, Koobi Fora 845km north of Nairobi.

FACILITIES Museum and KWS guides at Koobi Fora.

ACCOMMODATION Camping and bandas at Koobi Fora; camping at Allia Bay; camping and lodges at Loyangalani.

WILDLIFE RHYTHMS Crocodiles hatch April to May.

CONTACT KWS headquarters (☎ 02-50 10 81).

LAKE TURKANA

Hot winds scour ancient lava flows where **ground squirrels**, **crested larks** and **lizards** dart among sparse grass and hardy acacias. Rains bring on a flush of green and, despite treacherous roads, the wet season is the best time to visit: wildlife is abundant in Sibiloi National Park, a World Heritage site with fossil beds and a petrified forest on Mt Sibiloi. Central and South Islands are also national parks, and Central Island and Ferguson's Gulf are important staging posts for **migrating birds** (October to April). Birdwatching in Sibiloi National Park is excellent, and highlights include **Somali ostriches**, **kori** and **Heuglin's bustards**, **northern carmine** and **Somali bee-eaters**, **chestnut-bellied sandgrouse** and **fox kestrels**.

Thick avenues of *Acacia-Commiphora* scrub growing along Sibiloi's luggas shelter **greater** and **lesser kudus**, **gerenuks**, **warthogs** and **Günther's dik-diks**. **Reticulated giraffes** browse the tallest acacias, and grazing the adjoining plains of spear grass are **beisa oryxes**, **Jackson's hartebeests** and **tiangs**, a local race of topi. Large herds of **plains** and **Grevy's zebras** and **Grant's gazelles** are stalked by **lions**, **cheetahs** and **leopards**, while **caracals** and **servals** chase **hares** and **ground squirrels**. Other predators include **striped** and **spotted hyenas**, **jackals** and **bat-eared foxes**. **Scorpions** are abundant after rain.

ISLANDS OF BIRDS & CROCODILES Puffer fish, a group normally found in sea water, indicate Turkana's prehistoric connection to the Red Sea. But the lake's most famous inhabitants are **Nile crocodiles**, with up to 12,000 estimated to breed on Central Island. Some large crocs can usually be seen at Allia Bay, where **hippos** and at times hundreds of thousands of **flamingos** congregate. **African open-billed storks**, **ducks** and **gulls** feed along the shores and **African skimmers** are usually present, breeding on Central Island along with **goliath herons**. Central Island's volcanic lakes also attract **lesser flamingos**.

👀 WATCHING TIPS

Migrating warblers and wagtails shelter in scrubby *Salvadora* bushes on Central Island; the northward migration (March to April) is best.

WILDLIFE HIGHLIGHTS
» Africa's largest population of Nile crocodiles » Large animals of arid plains including plains and Grevy's zebras, Jackson's hartebeests, topis, beisa oryxes and lesser kudus; gerenuks and Günther's dik-diks in thorny scrub; and predators such as lions, cheetahs and spotted hyenas » Waterbirds, including large flocks of flamingos, feature among 350 recorded bird species

MALINDI & WATAMU MARINE NATIONAL PARKS

These two small parks protect fringing coral reefs, and are ideal for novice snorkellers. For best results, time boat trips to two hours either side of low tide; the tidal range can be as great as 4m so low tide will expose the greatest number of fish and other animals. Scuba dives entail a boat ride to reefs further out, but are typically shallow, nondecompression dives.

Malindi offers more snorkelling opportunities and the action inevitably begins at the coral gardens on North Reef. Glass-bottomed boats crowd the area, but the fish are used to being fed so you'll encounter lots of friendly **snappers**, **parrotfish**, **rubberfish**, **zebras**, **surgeons**, **sergeants** and **butterflyfish**. Other good snorkelling spots are Stork Passage and Tewa Reef, which is good for corals and smaller fish and is probably the best place for watching **octopuses**. On the way out you may see **barracudas** in the Barracuda Channel (they are present most of the year) – if not, sightings are guaranteed at Stork Passage (this is also a good place for **turtles** and **stingrays**). Generally the eastern side of North Reef has the best corals, and this is where you'll find higher numbers of the larger fish. Sometimes **reef sharks** can be spotted idling on the sandy bottom, facing into the current; rays and sharks are most common from September to May.

While Watamu's coral gardens are good for snorkelling and glass-bottomed boat rides, the big draws here are **whale sharks** and **manta rays** – sightings are almost guaranteed in January and February (the current carrying krill from Antarctica is deflected by the coast at Watamu and lies 2km offshore at Malindi – thus these big fish are not seen inshore at Malindi). Watamu is especially good for scuba diving and Turtle Reef is the most species-rich area in the park.

Further south, at the entrance to Mida Creek, are whopping big **groupers** (rock cods) – one rare species grows to over 3m and weighs 500kg. Groupers stick to the same spot for years and Mida Caves are a favourite site. This is a tricky spot to dive and you must get permission from the warden.

LOCATION Both parks adjacent to their namesake towns.

FACILITIES Glass-bottomed boats and several dive shops (most are closed May to July).

ACCOMMODATION Plenty in Watamu and Malindi.

WILDLIFE RHYTHMS Malindi best October to November and March to April (silt decreases visibility December to March). Watamu is best November to March – access to dive sites is restricted at other times.

CONTACT KWS (malindimnp@swiftmalindi.com).

KENYA

WILDLIFE HIGHLIGHTS
» Kenya's top spots for snorkellers – glass-bottomed boating is available » Hundreds of species of tropical fish and molluscs in coral gardens, plus pelagic animals such as turtles, rays, sharks and barracudas » Manta rays and whale sharks are commonly seen inshore at Watamu, and large groupers live at Mida Caves

👀 WATCHING TIPS

Make sure your boat operator will take you to Stork Passage at Malindi.

MARSABIT
NATIONAL
PARK

KENYA

LOCATION 310km north of Isiolo; 560km north of Nairobi. 4WD recommended.

FACILITIES Camel safaris, visits to local village watering wells.

ACCOMMODATION Camping on shores of Lake Paradise and at park headquarters; hotels in Marsabit.

WILDLIFE RHYTHMS Large animals more abundant in forest during dry seasons, dispersing to surrounding plains during wet seasons (March to May, October to early December).

CONTACT Marsabit National Park (☎ 069-2028).

KENYA

MARSABIT NATIONAL PARK

Marsabit's extinct volcanic craters are cloaked in moss-encrusted forests. They are home to herds of **elephants** and **buffaloes** and troops of **black-and-white colobus** and **blue monkeys** – these primates sometimes feed together. **Antelopes** such as **bushbucks** and **sunis** might be seen bolting into the undergrowth and you might even see a **leopard** by spotlighting along the road (but seek permission first). Clouds of **butterflies** swirl in pools of sunlight, **emerald-spotted wood doves** and **tambourine doves** clatter off the roads, and **olive pigeons** and **Hartlaub's turacos** – the latter's crimson wing-flashes are a giveaway – feed among trailing beard moss.

VOLCANIC OASIS Cliffs at the northern end of Lake Paradise (in Gof Sokorte Guda) are home to birds of prey, especially **Rüppell's griffon vultures** but also **peregrine falcons**, **mountain** and **common buzzards**, **black kites** and **African fish eagles**. The freshwater lake attracts ducks – **southern pochards**, **garganeys** and **teals** – which mingle with **little grebes** and rafts of **red-knobbed coots**. **Hamerkops**, **ibises**, **purple herons** and **saddle-billed** and **yellow-billed storks** feed in shallow water, and **darters** and **cormorants** rest on overhanging branches. Surrounding forest is inhabited by **black-and-white colobus**.

On Marsabit's lower slopes the forest peters out into scrubland and savanna – inhabited by **olive baboons** and **vervet monkeys** – where **Peters' gazelles**, **reticulated giraffes**, **beisa oryxes** and **plains zebras** are hunted by **lions** and **cheetahs**. Other predators include **striped hyenas**, **aardwolves** and **caracals**. Birds surrounding the massif include **Somali ostriches** and **vulturine guineafowl**, larks such as the **masked lark** and **Williams' lark** (endemic to northern Kenya), plus **Somali bee-eaters**, **Heuglin's bustards** and **cream-coloured coursers**.

WILDLIFE HIGHLIGHTS
» **Densely forested mountain with elephants, buffaloes and greater kudus, surrounded by semiarid plains with oryxes, zebras, giraffes, various antelopes and lions**
» **Black-and-white colobus and blue monkeys in the forest, vervet monkeys and olive baboons in savanna** » **Birdlife prolific – 350 species including 52 birds of prey, waterbirds in crater lakes and forest pigeons**

MERU NATIONAL PARK

Wildlife-viewing is best on Meru's northern plains, such as Murera, Bisanadi and Rojewero: **elephants** come and go, migrating as far as 60km away, but both species of **zebra**, **Grant's** and **Thomson's gazelles**, **impalas**, **beisa oryxes**, **kongoni** (Coke's hartebeests) and **reticulated giraffes** are easily seen. Further south, **gerenuks** browse dense woodlands that also shelter **common elands**, **Kirk's dik-diks** and **warthogs**. This is ideal habitat for **lesser kudus** but getting a good view of one takes luck and patience (you could come across one nearly anywhere). **Unstriped ground squirrels**, **vulturine guineafowl** and **yellow-necked spurfowl** scuttle off the roads where the industrious **naked mole-rats'** mounds puff up dirt like miniature volcanoes as the rodents dig inside.

BAOBABS, BUFFALOES & PALMS Lions are common on the plains and there's a fair chance of **cheetahs**. Baboons and their arch-enemy, **leopards**, lurk among the boulders of euphorbia-draped koppies. Honking groups of **hornbills** – sometimes several species together – feed among the woodland. Several species of palm line the waterways that dissect the park, providing feed for **palm-nut vultures** and lookouts for other birds of prey. The nuts of doum palms are a favourite of **elephants**, **vervet monkeys** and **baboons**.

Swampy grasslands are grazed by **defassa waterbucks** and (sometimes large) herds of **buffaloes**. **Hippos** are common in slower streams and in the broad Tana River, which is accessible at Adamson's Falls; **Nile crocodiles** also cruise the Tana and some large specimens travel far along its many tributaries. **Baboons** and **vervet monkeys** loiter in and around the fig trees that line the banks; tracks in the sand show where **impalas** and **lesser kudus** – or nocturnal **leopards** and **spotted hyenas** – have drunk, and where basking **crocs** haul themselves out. River birds include **ibises**, **herons** and **African fish eagles**.

LOCATION 60km east of Meru; 355km northeast of Nairobi. 4WD advisable.

FACILITIES Game drives to savanna and riverine forest areas.

ACCOMMODATION Bush camping grounds, public camping ground with bandas, and lodges in the park.

WILDLIFE RHYTHMS Grass is shorter and animals are easier to see in dry seasons; elephants use Meru as a dry-season refuge, wandering from the park in wet seasons (March to May, October to early December).

CONTACT Meru National Park (☎ 0164-20613).

KENYA

WILDLIFE HIGHLIGHTS
» Reticulated giraffes, buffaloes, abundant lions and seasonal elephant herds are the main draw; beisa oryxes, lesser kudus and gerenuks star in the antelope line-up; cheetahs are frequently encountered and other predators include spotted hyenas and leopards » Olive baboons and vervet monkeys are common » Hippos, Nile crocodiles and waterbirds along Tana River; 300 bird species in all

WATCHING TIPS

Lesser kudus, Kirk's dik-diks and gerenuks feed near roadsides at dusk. Pel's fishing owls hunt at night along the Tana River.

MT ELGON NATIONAL PARK

Elephants and, more commonly, **buffaloes**, **bushbucks** or **defassa waterbucks** are seen along roads through Elgon's densely forested lower slopes; **duikers** and **giant forest hogs** frequent the undergrowth. Troops of **black-and-white colobus** and **blue monkeys** share the canopy with **red-fronted parrots** and **Ross' turacos**; **olive baboons** loiter at forest edges near cultivation; and a small population of **de Brazza's monkeys** inhabits the park. Caves riddle the sheer cliffs: thousands of small insect-eating **bats** cling to the roof of Kitum Cave, and **roussette bats** – a type of fruit-bat – roost in the back reaches, their tongue-clicking sonar clearly audible.

ELEPHANTS AS EXCAVATORS Elgon's high rainfall encourages prolific plant growth, but leaches soluble mineral salts from the soil – salt-deficient food plants force most of Elgon's large mammals, including primates, to eat or lick salt-rich rocks from the caves. The most famous visitors are **elephants**, which make nightly forays deep into the caverns to tusk off and eat bits of the soft rock. This has been going on for generations and some researchers believe elephants actually excavated some of Elgon's caves. **Spotted hyenas** shelter in remote caves and **leopards** stake out the entrances for salt-hungry visitors; **servals** have been seen near Rongai camp.

Black-and-white colobus forage as high as bamboo thickets where the forest peters out. *Hagenia* trees and heather grow higher still, replaced on the peaks by moorland dotted with giant herbs – groundsels and lobelias – that can grow 6m high. Wildflowers grow on rocky slopes above the treeline, where **Verreaux's eagles** pick **rock hyraxes** off outcrops and **leopards** stalk rodents, **hyraxes** and **duikers**. Scarce and **alpine swifts** and huge **lammergeiers** cruise the thin air; **white-naped ravens** forage up to about 4000m and **moorland francolins** are common in the tussock grasslands even higher.

LOCATION 408km northwest of Nairobi.

FACILITIES Nature trails, self-hiking trails and cave exploring.

ACCOMMODATION Camping grounds and bandas in the park; camping and bandas 5.5km east of Chorlim Gate; hotels in Kitale.

WILDLIFE RHYTHMS Animals mine salt year-round. Antelopes graze on higher slopes in dry seasons.

CONTACTS Mt Elgon National Park (☎ 054-314056/7).

KENYA

WILDLIFE HIGHLIGHTS
» Salt-mining elephants are the most famous attraction, but dense forest hides buffaloes, bushbucks, defassa waterbucks and giant forest hogs, four species of primate (black-and-white colobus is most common) and predators such as spotted hyenas and leopards » Birds (240 species) are most abundant and diverse in forest, although alpine specialities include lammergeiers

SAIWA SWAMP NATIONAL PARK

Covering only 3 sq km, Kenya's smallest national park was established primarily to protect a population of **sitatungas** in a reed-choked stretch of the Saiwa River. Walking trails skirt the swamp through riverine and savanna woodland inhabited by monkeys. For the best chance at **sitatungas**, look down into the reeds from the eastern shore in the early morning, when these shy antelopes feed and bask. **Defassa waterbucks**, **bushbucks** and **bohor reedbucks** frequent swamp edges; **pottos**, **African civets** and **common genets** could be spotlit; and **leopards**, **ratels** and **aardvarks** are occasional visitors.

SWAMP WITH A VIEW Vervet monkeys are most likely to be seen in drier parts of the park. **De Brazza's monkeys**, also known as swamp monkeys, are mainly active near water – the canopy over the trail to observation tower four is a good place to look. **Blue monkeys** and **black-and-white colobus** can also be seen in this stretch. Fig trees attract **double-toothed barbets** (which sometimes nest in trees along the boardwalk), **crowned hornbills**, **Ross' turacos** (recognisable by crimson wing-flashes) and another turaco, the **eastern grey plantain-eater** (its call sounds like chimp hoots). **Grey crowned cranes** are regular visitors to the marsh.

Observation towers along the banks make ideal platforms from which to scan the reed beds for **sitatungas** and birds, and to see **red-legged sun squirrels** or **giant forest squirrels** scampering through the canopy at eye level. Channels worn through the aquatic vegetation are also patrolled by **African clawless** and **African spot-necked otters**, and throughout the swamp **ibises**, **ducks** and **herons** feed. **Cisticolas** and **warblers** skulk at the foot of the towers; birds of prey, including **African fish eagles** and **long-crested eagles**, perch on the trees poking through the reeds; and **blue-headed coucals** sun themselves on sturdy bulrushes in the morning.

WILDLIFE HIGHLIGHTS
» Kenya's best park for sitatungas and the localised de Brazza's monkey; other primates include black-and-white colobus, blue and vervet monkeys » Defassa waterbucks and bushbucks are commonly seen, and ratels and African civets are occasionally encountered » Birds are a draw – 372 species, including Kenyan rarities such as Ross' turacos and blue-headed coucals

LOCATION 26km north of Kitale, 5km east of the highway.

FACILITIES Viewing platforms, boardwalks, 7km nature trail.

ACCOMMODATION Camping ground at park; camping ground and lodge 5km north at Sirikwa Safaris.

WILDLIFE RHYTHMS Most sitatunga young are born in the dry season.

CONTACTS Saiwa Swamp National Park (kwssnp@ africaonlin.co.ke).

KENYA

WATCHING TIPS

The best (and safest) observation tower is number four, from where sitatungas, both otters and blue-headed coucals are regularly seen.

KENYA

SHIMBA HILLS
NATIONAL
RESERVE

LOCATION 37km from Mombasa with year-round access; can be reached by public transport.

FACILITIES Three observation points, a walking trail and a waterhole.

ACCOMMODATION Two camping grounds (one with self-catering bandas), a lodge and a tented camp.

WILDLIFE RHYTHMS Rains (November and late April to June) restrict walking and wildlife-viewing.

CONTACT Shimba Hills National Reserve (☎ 040-4159).

KENYA

SHIMBA HILLS NATIONAL RESERVE

One of the smallest parks in the country, Shimba Hills protects the bulk of Kenya's **black-and-white colobus** and its only population of a distinctive subspecies of sable antelope – **Roosevelt's sable**. Add to this 13 rare or restricted bird species, including the **spotted ground thrush**, **Sokoke pipit** and **east coast akalat**, about 35% (300 species) of the country's **butterflies** and one of Kenya's richest plant diversities, and Shimba Hills makes a very attractive wildlife destination.

A good place to start is at one of the hilltop observation lookouts. From these vantage points, **elephants, buffaloes** and **sables** should be seen in the glades below. Search for sables on the Marare Circuit; you can also find **Masai giraffes**. **Bushbucks, duikers** and **sunis** are there but not easily seen.

Easily located birds (mainly the large and noisy ones) include **Fischer's turaco** – it has a restricted distribution along the coast and Shimba Hills is one of the best places to see it. Forested areas, especially Longomwagandi Forest near the airstrip, are also good for **trumpeter, crowned** and **silvery-cheeked hornbills**. And scrutinize any guineafowl you see – Shimba Hills is one the few places where the distinctive Kenyan race of **crested guineafowl** can be seen. Both Longomwagandi and another small forest patch, Makadara, have strong plant, bird and butterfly presence and are great places to get out and walk (but keep an eye out for elephants).

SHIMBA HILLS RAINFOREST LODGE The Shimba Hills Rainforest Lodge (day visitors welcome) maintains a waterhole that attracts **African fish eagles, elephants** and **buffaloes**. And **red-bellied coast squirrels** skittering about the restaurant tables provide reliable daytime entertainment. When the squirrels retire in the evening, **greater galagos** take over. For the energetic, there is a 2.6km walk down to the 21m-high Sheldrick Falls. You'd be unlucky to encounter a **buffalo** or **elephant** on the trail, but an armed scout is still mandatory. On the walk down, look about in the trees for **blue monkeys**.

WATCHING TIPS

Meat hung from a tree at the lodge's waterhole (to lure a leopard that never shows) often attracts fish eagles and, at night, genets.

WILDLIFE HIGHLIGHTS

» **Elephants, buffaloes and Masai giraffes are easily seen, but large numbers of black-and-white colobus star and this is Kenya's only park with Roosevelt's sables** » **Wild but habituated red-bellied coast squirrels and greater galagos are a treat at the lodge**

OTHER SITES

BISANADI NATIONAL RESERVE
Savanna bounded by the Tana River serves as a wet-season dispersal area for elephants and buffaloes.
60km east of Meru

LAKE MAGADI Kenya's most southerly Rift Valley lake attracts great white pelicans, breeding lesser flamingos, African spoonbills and chestnut-banded plovers.
100km south of Nairobi

LEWA WILDLIFE CONSERVANCY
Working cattle ranch and self-financing rhino conservation project in Mt Kenya's northern foothills. Main attractions are breeding black and white rhinos and around 400 Grevy's zebras. Elephants, leopards, buffaloes, reticulated giraffes and translocated sitatungas also present.
35km south of Samburu National Reserve,
www.lewa.org

LONGONOT NATIONAL PARK
Dormant 2886m volcano with an almost circular crater. Scenic walks and steaming fumaroles are a feature, and artificial waterholes encourage animals, including buffaloes.
60km northwest of Nairobi

MWALUGANJE ELEPHANT SANCTUARY About 150 elephants use this trail as a corridor from Shimba Hills National Reserve to Mwaluganje Forest Reserve. Locals benefit financially as land use changes from agriculture to tourism, an electric fence resolves conflict and the sanctuary is gradually getting bigger. There's an information centre near the main gate.
35km southwest of Mombasa,
☎ *011-586121/6*

RUKINGA RANCH Semiarid grassland and scrub adjoining Tsavo East National Park lie on the elephant migration route between Tsavo and Kilimanjaro's foothills. Permanent water attracts herds of elephants (up to 1000 visit Rukinga), and other mammals include Grevy's and plains zebras, lesser kudus, gerenuks and abundant lions. Excellent dry-country birdwatching features abundant golden pipits, spotted eagle-owls and golden-breasted starlings.
50km south of Voi

RUMA NATIONAL PARK Tall grassland and acacia woodland protecting Kenya's only remaining roan antelopes. Large mammals include lions, cheetahs, leopards, buffaloes, Rothschild's giraffes and plains zebras – all little-disturbed because of tsetse flies and because locals believe the park's uranium deposits cause sterility.
34km west of Homa Bay

SOLIO RANCH Working cattle ranch famous for breeding rhinos: Solio has reared 91 black and 87 white rhinos in 27 years – setting an unprecedented annual birth rate of 12%. Many have been translocated to reserves such as Lewa Downs and Tsavo East and Aberdare National Parks.
180km north of Nairobi

TAITA HILLS FORESTS Isolated remnants (the largest only 220 hectares) of Tanzania's Eastern Arc Mountains supporting 13 endemic plants and endemic birds such as the Taita thrush and Taita white-eye. A globally important centre of plant biodiversity and source of species such as African violets.

TANZANIA

CAPITAL DODOMA **AREA** 943,000 SQ KM **NATIONAL PARKS** 14 **MAMMAL SPECIES** APPROX 370

Tanzania's vast plains teem with wildlife, its turquoise seas abound with colourful corals and fish, and its lush mountainside forests are filled with unique plants and birds. Its parks have no fences and the bush ambience is superb.

TANZANIA

THE LAND In Tanzania the sweeping plains of East Africa, with their fertile soils and flat-topped acacias, meet the nutrient-leached miombo woodland more typical of south-central Africa. This vast country is home to diverse wildlife, including around 430 mammal species and subspecies, 1060 bird species and 1370 butterfly species, and the famous Serengeti National Park boasts the greatest concentration of large animals on earth. Tanzania also features Africa's highest mountain (Kilimanjaro), its deepest and largest lakes (Tanganyika and Victoria, respectively), its largest protected area (Selous Game Reserve) and the world's

largest intact volcanic crater (20km-wide Ngorongoro). About one-quarter of the country is protected in 14 national parks, one conservation area and 14 wildlife reserves; and some of its coastal waters, including parts of the Mafia and Zanzibar archipelagos, are conserved as marine parks and reserves.

Most of Tanzania is high plateau, averaging 900m to 1800m in altitude and fringed by the two bowed arms of the Great Rift Fault. The course of the Western Rift Valley is marked by the deep, isolated, freshwater Lakes Tanganyika and Nyasa (Malawi), where hundreds of species of unique cichlid fish have evolved. The shallow

TANZANIA

0   200 km
0   120 miles

LEGEND
CA   Conservation Area
GR   Game Reserve
NP   National Park
NR   National Reserve

TANZANIA

⭐ TOP SPOTS

1. SERENGETI NATIONAL PARK (p108) Famed for its annual wildebeest migration, the Serengeti is also an excellent destination for lions, cheetahs, elephants and a host of others.

2. NGORONGORO CRATER (p104) With exceptionally high densities of predators, fine up-close Big Five viewing opportunities and stunning panoramas, Ngorongoro

is one of the jewels in Tanzania's safari crown.

3. SELOUS GAME RESERVE (p118) Lovely riverine landscapes, excellent birding, a pronounced wilderness ambience and the chance for both walking and boating safaris make Selous the choice of many wildlife connoisseurs.

4. RUAHA NATIONAL PARK (p134) Tanzania's largest park is

known for its elephants and wild dogs and for its unique mix of southern and East African species.

5. TARANGIRE NATIONAL PARK (p122) Tarangire, with its evocative, baobab-studded landscapes, is an outstanding destination in the dry season when wildebeests, elephants and other migratory mammals converge on the Tarangire River.

alkaline lakes of the Rift Valley's eastern branch, such as Lake Natron, are the birthplace of most of Africa's flamingos. Towards the plateau's eastern edge, the fragmented Eastern Arc Mountains feature many rare and unique bird and plant species. The country's narrow coastal belt consists of long, sandy stretches punctuated by dense stands of mangroves and fringed by waters rich with corals and other marine life.

Tanzania's so-called 'northern circuit' is comparatively crowded, but the wildlife and landscapes are unrivalled: Mt Kilimanjaro not only lures trekkers, but probably acts as a navigation beacon for many of the 600 million migratory birds that overwinter in tropical Africa. Other sights include Ngorongoro Crater, Olduvai Gorge (immortalised for its hominid fossils) and the Serengeti Plains, where 1.5 million animals (wildebeests, zebras and gazelles) make their spectacular annual trek following the seasonal availability of food.

The 'southern circuit' is ideal for more wilderness-orientated travellers: it takes in the vast Selous Game Reserve and Ruaha National Park; Udzungwa Mountains, where serious birders search out local and endemic species; and Mikumi National Park, part of the larger Selous ecosystem. In the far west are relatively untouched Katavi National Park and the chimpanzees of Mahale Mountains and Gombe Stream National Parks. Northwest of here is the shallow and enormous Lake Victoria basin, with Rubondo Island, a birder's paradise.

WHEN TO GO Tanzania's two rainy seasons are from November to January (the short rains) and March through May (long rains). From June to October – the cool, dry season – animals congregate around limited water resources. During the long rains, some park areas may be impassable and many camps close, although migratory birds are present and there's abundant greenery. While Tanzania can be rewardingly visited for wildlife-watching year-round, it is well worth tailoring your choice of park or reserve to the season. Some parks, such as Tarangire and Katavi, are classic dry-season destinations, while the southeastern Serengeti, for example, teems with wildebeests during the rains.

WILDLIFE HIGHLIGHTS
» Listening to the hooves of thousands of wildebeests pound across the Serengeti plains (p108) » Being mesmerised by the pink mass of flamingos feeding in Ngorongoro Crater's lake (p104) » Boating down the Rufiji River past countless hippos in Selous Game Reserve (p118) » Gazing over huge herds of buffalo grazing on Katavi National Park's Katisunga floodplains (p139) » Seeing an elephant silhouetted next to a baobab tree at Ruaha National Park (p134) » Diving around the Zanzibar archipelago (p114) amid a plethora of colourful fish » Listening to the hooting of chimpanzees while trekking through the forests of the Mahale Mountains (p139)

GIRAFFES GRAZING 'PRUNE' A TREE

TANZANIA ITINERARIES

1. NORTHERN TANZANIA CLASSIC Starting from Arusha, take in **Serengeti National Park** (p108) and **Ngorongoro Crater** (p104), plus **Lake Manyara National Park** (p128) for

waterbirds and hippos and **Tarangire National Park** (p122) for elephants. Allow at least a week, ideally longer, to visit all four. Then, travel eastwards via plane or bus and boat to the **Zanzibar archipelago** (p114) for some diving, snorkelling and relaxing. Try to include an excursion to **Chumbe Island** or **Misali Island**. With extra time in northern Tanzania, work in some trekking on **Mt Kilimanjaro** (p132) or a visit to **Arusha National Park** (p126) with a trek up Mt Meru.

2. OFF THE BEATEN TRACK Katavi (p139) and **Mahale Mountains National Parks** (p139) make an unbeatable combination – Katavi for wilderness and wildlife,

and Mahale for its remoteness, beauty and chimpanzees. The park is called Mahale *Mountains* for a reason – chimp tracking on the steep slopes can be sweaty and strenuous. Another rewarding combination is **Selous Game Reserve** (p118) and **Ruaha National Park** (p134), with their markedly different terrains and wildlife. For something more off-beat, visit **Mikumi National Park** (p1300), followed by hiking and birding in **Udzungwa Mountains National Park** (p136) and, again, time in **Ruaha National Park** (p134). Continue southwest to **Kitulo National Park** for wildflowers.

3. BIRDWATCHER'S SPECIAL From Arusha head to **Lake Manyara National Park** (p128), with close to 500 bird species. Continue to **Ngorongoro Crater** (p104) and the surrounding

highlands, then on to **Serengeti National Park** (p108) for a contrast with Manyara's waterbirds and lake scenery. The route continues through Serengeti's western corridor to Lake Victoria and **Rubondo Island National Park** – well away from most travellers' itineraries, but a birder's delight. In southern Tanzania, **Udzungwa Mountains National Park** (p136) is notable for its many endemics, while **Selous Game Reserve** (p118) offers some 400 bird species, including a wealth of waterbirds along the Rufiji River.

TANZANIA

NGORONGORO
CONSERVATION
AREA

TANZANIA

LOCATION 165km west of Arusha on a good sealed road; 4WD is required to enter the crater; access is possible year-round. Private vehicles must take a Ngorongoro Conservation Area (NCA) guide when entering the crater; an NCA guide is required for hiking in other areas of the Crater Highlands.

FACILITIES Maps and small interpretive centres at Lodoare Gate and Olduvai Museum; most lodges have maps and books.

ACCOMMODATION Five lodges on or near the crater rim, one public camping ground. Numerous special camping areas in the NCA.

WILDLIFE RHYTHMS During the dry season (late June through October), large animals concentrate around watercourses such as Mandusi Swamp and the Hippo Pool; migratory birds arrive in November and December.

CONTACT NCA (☎ 255-27-254 4625; 255-27-250 3339; www.ngorongoro-crater -africa.org).

NGORONGORO CONSERVATION AREA

The most famous feature of this World Heritage Site and Biosphere Reserve, Ngorongoro Crater, makes up only 3% of the Ngorongoro Conservation Area (NCA). NCA also protects the Crater Highlands (a chain of extinct and collapsed volcanoes) and includes the eastern part of the Serengeti Plain. Ngorongoro Crater is the largest unbroken caldera (collapsed volcanic cone) in the world. Its rim is around 2200m above sea level and the drop to the floor of the animal-rich crater is 600m. From the viewpoint on the rim you can, with clear weather, see right across the 20km-wide crater floor and identify the main habitat features – Gorigor Swamp, Lake Magadi, Lerai Forest and the open plains. With binoculars you can make out columns of **plains zebras** and **wildebeests** and groups of **buffaloes**. Buffaloes began to use the crater floor only in the 1970s, when the Maasai moved out their livestock and ceased burning – now around 4000 use the crater.

One major road descends into the crater and one climbs out again – both one-way – and there is a third route for ascents and descents. A 4WD is recommended for all. At the bottom of the main descent road you will see **rufous-tailed weaver** nests dangling from acacias (this is one of the birds endemic to northern Tanzania). Near here are the Seneto Springs, where the local Maasai herdsmen still bring their stock into the crater for water and salt licks.

There are 120km of roads to explore in the dry season. The freshwater pools in the Mandusi Swamp are a dry-season home for **hippos**, and sometimes they can be seen out feeding during the day. The surrounding marshy grasses and reeds are worth searching for **waterbirds**, and this is one of the few places in Tanzania where you can find the **African water rail**.

WILDLIFE HIGHLIGHTS
» **Ngorongoro Crater is fabulous for wildlife, with around 25,000 large animals entering and leaving the crater at will** » **Lions, spotted hyenas, wildebeests, plains zebras, gazelles and buffaloes in abundance, with buffaloes especially numerous during the rainy season; only bull elephants occur in the crater** » **One of the best spots in Tanzania for spotting black rhinos** » **The animals are used to vehicles and carry on their business with total disregard for observers, making for outstanding wildlife-watching**

TANZANIA

TANZANIA

BLUE WILDEBEEST, NGORONGORO CRATER

FRACAS AT THE CARCASS

You are more likely to encounter predators at a kill rather than witness a hunt itself, but the frenzy of feeding carnivores is a dynamic scene well worth watching as the pecking order is played out. Lions are invariably the heavyweights, but spotted hyena clans in the crater can number up to 80 individuals and can compete successfully against lions by weight of numbers. A pack of hyenas on a carcass can seem both noisy and aggressive, but hyenas don't actually fight over food. With the lions gone, a dozen or more jackals – most commonly black-backed and golden – dart into the kill when they can, even among hyenas. The golden jackal reaches the southern limit of its African range in northern Tanzania, so keep an eye out for it here (it is the most common jackal in NCA). Hyenas and jackals try to steal food from one another, while vultures wait in the wings – white-backed and hooded being the most numerous.

The Lerai Forest, rich with fever trees (yellow-barked acacias), is the place to look for **vervet monkeys**, **olive baboons**, **elephants**, **elands**, **bushbucks** and **waterbucks**. The surrounding area is a good place to look for **black rhinos** browsing on the shrubby vegetation. Ngorongoro Crater is the only place in Tanzania where you have a realistic chance of seeing black rhinos (although present in other parts of the country, rhinos are often inaccessible to visitors). Around 20 rhinos occur in the crater and you should have little difficulty seeing one or more. Don't feed the habituated and bold vervets at Lerai picnic site – as you leave you will also see them sitting by the road. You'll also need to watch out for the hungry wildlife at the packed lunchtime picnic spot at Ngoitokitok Springs: **black kites** here are as bold as baboons and will swoop down and relieve you of your food instantly. However, Ngoitokitok is a pleasant spot at which to see **hippos**.

A HIGH DENSITY OF PREDATORS

Ngorongoro Crater is believed to have one of the highest densities of predators in Africa and provides excellent chances of seeing the big cats in action. **Lions** and **spotted hyenas** are abundant, totalling around 450 altogether; **cheetahs** are occasionally seen; and **leopards** are present, though they are cryptic and more confined to the forested rim. Also, all seven of Tanzania's **vulture** species occur in the NCA – around 25% of the world's population of **Rüppell's griffon vulture** resides here and in the surrounding ecosystem. Keep an eye out for **Egyptian vultures** (usually seen singly or in pairs): they reach the southern end of their range in Tanzania, and nest on the cliffs of the crater rim.

Spotted hyenas – there are an estimated 400-plus in the crater – lollop across the flat grassland, but look for them also on the edge of Lake Magadi or other wet areas, flopped in the muddy water to cool off. They sometimes hide food underwater and have been observed hunting the **flamingos** that seasonally crowd this lake.

On the crater plains you'll probably notice **Masai ostriches**, the solitary **kori bustard**, **secretary birds** and **grey crowned cranes** (as many as 110 cranes have been recorded in a single group). One species restricted to this highland region is the **northern anteater chat**, common near areas of disturbed ground and termite mounds. On the grass plains live **Jackson's widowbirds**, which are similarly restricted to highland areas of northern Tanzania and southern Kenya. From January to April this sociable bird transforms from small and drab into a dark, long-tailed bird that dances about frantically to attract a mate. Frederick Jackson, after whom the species was named, described the antics of the 'Dancing Whydah' as 'a truly ridiculous sight': males set up a small area in long grass in which they repeatedly jump up and down, with jumps getting well over 50cm in height. They dance like this all day, most enthusiastically in the early morning and late afternoon.

Crowned and **blacksmith plovers** are everywhere, while **Kitt-litz's plover** is limited to the water's edge. The marshy areas are home to **cormorants**, **grebes**, **herons**, **egrets** and **pelicans**. The pelicans visiting the crater are a little unusual in that they mostly live on a diet of frogs – there are no fish in the crater. Another frog-eater is the **hammerkop**, a bird that never strays far from water. In the Lerai Forest, one of the special species to watch out for is the endemic **Fischer's lovebird**. The grounds of the lodges on the crater rim are excellent places to look for forest birds – stunning **golden-winged** and **eastern double-collared sunbirds** are common.

HOTSPOTS Between the crater and the Serengeti is Olduvai Gorge. Although Olduvai is mainly about fossils, the thornbush around the museum is good for birds – two species you won't see in Ngorongoro Crater are the **red-cheeked cordon-bleu** and the vividly coloured **purple grenadier**; the colourful **red-and-yellow barbet** is also resident. Olduvai is just 20km from the boundary of Serengeti National Park, and the Serengeti Plains that fall within the NCA are seasonal home to one to two million **wildebeests**, **plains zebras** and **Grant's** and **Thomson's gazelles** as they complete their annual 800km migration (see the boxed text, p111).

On the southern route to Ngorongoro Crater, a stop-off or stay at Gibbs Farm, near Karatu, is highly recommended. The flower-rich garden attracts lots of birds, including **sunbirds**, **weavers**, **robin-chats**, **mousebirds** and **tropical boubous**. A bird list is supplied and the feeding platform in the garden is an ideal place to take tea. From here, there is a two-hour walk up to an enormous elephant salt lick (the gouged walls help explain why elephants' tusks become worn down). **Cinnamon-chested bee-eaters** have their nest holes in the red banks of the lick.

Other areas within the NCA are relatively inaccessible in comparison, but with some organisation and an adventurous bent, it's quite possible to hike in the Crater Highlands. Just outside the NCA is Ol Doinyo Lengai, Tanzania's only active volcano, and you can even go up to its rim (it last erupted in 1983). Several of the highland mountains are over 3000m and support diverse habitats – moorland at high altitude; dense montane forest lower on the wetter eastern sides; and acacia woodlands and plains on the drier, rain-shadowed western sides. This variety gives rise to a diversity of birds and in various areas you will see mammals, including **monkeys** and **buffaloes**. Two of the peaks (Empakaai and Olmoti) are craters and their floors provide good grazing for antelopes such as **bushbucks.**

TANZANIA

👀 WATCHING TIPS

Ngorongoro Crater is extremely busy, and visits are currently limited to six hours per vehicle per day to reduce congestion and environmental impact. Early morning and late afternoon are generally quieter times to visit the crater. It's also worth trying to avoid peak travel seasons (July, August and the Christmas–New Year period) if possible. If you're staying at Simba Campsite, keep an eye out for habituated zebras grazing close by; after nightfall, bushpigs often snuffle through the camp. Screeching vervet monkeys in Lerai Forest may indicate the presence of a leopard or another predator: look at where they're facing, then search for movement.

SERENGETI NATIONAL PARK

TANZANIA

SERENGETI NATIONAL PARK

Serengeti is the second-largest national park in Tanzania and one of the most famous parks in Africa: a vast expanse of plains covered with wildebeests, zebras, gazelles and giraffe-trimmed, flat-topped acacias that for many visitors epitomise the continent. But the Serengeti is the size of Northern Ireland and contains far more than the seemingly endless plains in its southeast. To the north, where the park adjoins Kenya's Masai Mara National Reserve, the terrain becomes hilly and rocky; and to the west there is a mosaic of hills, valleys, rivers, ribbons of riverine forest and plains.

Most people enter the Serengeti through the Naabi Hill Gate in the southeast. This is 20km inside the park, with the real boundary a ranch-style gate in the middle of nowhere. There is no fence and the animals graze both on the Serengeti side and in the adjoining Ngorongoro Conservation Area. In the dry season, animals are scarce here because of the lack of water, but the non-water-dependent gazelles – **Thomson's** and **Grant's** – are found here most of the year. From the end of the short rains until the easing of the long rains (roughly from January to April) there are abundant **wildebeests**, **plains zebras** and **gazelles** in the area, but as there is plenty of food and water the animals become increasingly dispersed during this time. As the area dries up (usually around May) the vast migratory herds (one to two million strong) began to form and head from the Serengeti Plains towards the Western Corridor – they won't return in numbers this far south until the following January, after the short rains finish.

The short grass plains give way to longer grass plains and the landscape becomes more varied once you pass Naabi on the way to Seronera, in central Serengeti. In addition to the gazelles, **kongonis** (Coke's hartebeests) and **topis** can be

LOCATION 300km northwest of Arusha; accessible year-round, although some areas can become problematic during the long rains in April and May.

FACILITIES The main visitors' hub is at Seronera, where there are maps, books and a shop selling basic supplies. Guides can be hired at Seronera or at the main park gates. One-hour balloon safaris (www.balloonsafaris .com) can be arranged through the website or with the Seronera lodges.

ACCOMMODATION Numerous lodges, camps and public camping grounds.

WILDLIFE RHYTHMS The migration time of wildebeests, zebras and other ungulates varies from year to year, but the animals are usually in the north of the park August to October (with most crossing into the Masai Mara in October), heading south in November and December, in the southeast of the park until May, then it's north again via the western corridor through June and July. The river crossing by the herds (and the attendant Nile crocodiles) takes place around June. From December to February, various beasts give birth and provide a magnet for predators. Bird numbers and diversity peak October to April, when migratory species return.

CONTACT Tourist warden, Seronera (☎ 028-262 1515; www.tanzaniaparks.com).

WILDLIFE HIGHLIGHTS
» Some of the best wildlife-viewing in Africa, including the famous wildebeest migration » Thanks to its open plains and the sparseness of sheltering trees, the Serengeti offers outstanding views of predators; in addition to leopards and three species of jackal, the Serengeti ecosystem is estimated to support around 2800 lions and 9000 spotted hyenas » The best place in Tanzania to see cheetahs, with about 250 in the park; however, hunting dogs and rhinos are extremely rare » Large populations of ungulates, including giraffes, topis and elands » Over 500 species of bird, including many Tanzanian endemics

seen grazing, termite mounds and **common ostriches** (this subspecies is sometimes called the Masai ostrich) appear and the depression at the granite outcrops of Simba Kopje may contain **elephants** and **Masai giraffes**. Around Seronera you will find many animals during the dry season: the rivers here provide a year-round water source and the trees and shrubs provide food for browsing animals that cannot live on the plains grass. Along the watercourse of the Seronera River you may spot **elephants**, **defassa waterbucks**, **bohor reedbucks** and **lions**.

GETTING STARTED Check out the visitors centre at Seronera. You'll undoubtedly get distracted at the picnic tables by opportunists such as **banded mongooses**, **vervet monkeys**, **rock hyraxes** and a bevy of birds, including **superb starlings** and **d'Arnaud's barbets**. The barbets (here they are a distinctive race regarded by some ornithologists as a separate species, the Usambiro barbet) often sit on branches singing duets, facing each other while wagging their erect tails to reveal a flash of red. Nearby, an interpretive walkway winds up through a koppie. The displayed information unfolds the life, death and seasonal cycles of the Serengeti and its animals. Here, as with any koppie, is an ideal place to look-out for **agama lizards** – the males have a coral-pink head and bluish tail. For those with a interest in checking out bird plumage closely, the research station several kilometres away from the visitors centre has a small museum with stuffed birds and a library.

Near the visitors centre is the Seronera Wildlife Lodge, constructed around a koppie. **Rock hyraxes** regularly run about upstairs near the dining area (book here for a unique way of seeing the Serengeti's animals – by hot-air balloon; see the boxed text, p112).

Around June/July, though the timing can vary considerably, the wildebeest migration passes through the Western Corridor, west of Seronera, on its way north. The road follows the Grumeti River, which abounds with **hippos** and **crocs**; the crocs here are believed to be some of the largest in the world (size in crocs is related to age and food availability so the pickings on the river must be good). **Black-and-white colobus** live in the riverine forest and can be seen about 30km from Seronera Lodge at the point where the road comes close to the river at Kimarishi Hill. The west is about the only place you can find the savanna woodland–dwelling **patas monkey** – this species is largely confined to west and central Africa, and the Serengeti's patas monkeys are a unique subspecies.

THE BIG CATS Along with the neighbouring Masai Mara, Serengeti is one of the best places in Africa to observe the big cats. The Wandamu River area in Seronera is said to hold the world's greatest density of **cheetahs**. Without the obstruction of trees, it is almost guaranteed that you'll see cheetahs on the plains – often alone, but sometimes a mother with young or a small bachelor group. Unlike most cats, cheetahs are daytime hunters and don't necessarily conceal themselves from their prey. They

---

👀 WATCHING TIPS

Sharing your lion and leopard viewing with 20-odd other vehicles may not be your idea of enjoying wildlife, but you can head to the less busy Lobo or Western Corridor. Alternatively, most drivers confine their safari to the earlier and later part of the day: if you head out in the heat of the day, you'll still find the lions under the trees and perhaps even see a leopard hunting – although mostly nocturnal, they sometimes take advantage of the fact that most animals are resting (and are less alert) in the midday sun. Wear a broad-brimmed hat if going on a balloon ride – the flaming of the burner is hot stuff. Serengeti and neighbouring Ngorongoro are the places to get close-up wildlife shots, so pack far more film or memory chips than you think you are going to need.

instead rely on their speed – up to 110 km/h. Watching cheetahs will give you the best chance to see big cats hunting.

Although nocturnal, **leopards** aren't too difficult to spot, as the big-branched trees in which they rest during the day are not common. Search the branches of sausage trees and bigger species along the Seronera River. But it is **lions** that most people come to see and you'll definitely spot them. Lions spend most of their time laying about in shade with their paws in the air, so search the shady patches along watercourses and the shadows of big trees. Chances are your driver will be listening on the radio and will know where the big cats are (this of course often results in a traffic jam at the sighting).

Watercourses are also good places to look for **elephants**. They are dependent on water and, in the absence of green grass during the dry season, are restricted to feeding on the bark and foliage of trees and shrubby vegetation along the rivers. **Hippos** and **crocs** are found along the narrow Seronera River, and good spots to check are Syd Downey's Dam and Kerr's Dam, both near Seronera Lodge. Further away and to the north is the Retima Hippo Pool – here you can get out of your car and picnic if you wish. If there has been recent rain, scout about for tracks of **leopards**, **hippos**, **elephants** and other animals.

As you drive about, always check termite mounds, which are favoured vantage points for **cheetahs**, while **topis**, **bushbucks** and **mongooses** use them to watch for predators. **Dwarf mongooses** also frequent termite mounds, and any shade the mound casts may be a resting spot for a **serval** or **African wild cat**.

Two antelope species you'll often see grazing are **topi** and **kongoni** (Coke's hartebeest). They are easily confused as their body shape is similar, but their colour is clearly different: topis are brick-red, kongonis are fawn-yellow. The Serengeti protects Tanzania's greatest concentration of topis and is a stronghold for kongonis. They are especially common in the Western Corridor and northern savanna woodland. While kongonis congregate in small groups, topis can form herds of up to 2000. Their main breeding ground is the Ndoha Plain, but this area is fairly inaccessible.

The northern part of Serengeti, Lobo, is the best place to see **buffaloes** and **elephants** in numbers, although they also occur elsewhere. The trees of this woodland area provide elephants with food during the dry season. Buffaloes are highly dependent on

WILDEBEEST MIGRATION

Many people associate the Serengeti migration with rumbling hooves, tossing heads and thrashing tails being nipped by predators. They might think of the migration as an intense but short phase of the year. In fact, this 800km pilgrimage is an ongoing cycle of movement and dispersal that defines the Serengeti–Mara ecosystem. Dependent on rainfall, the timing of the cycle is never totally predictable, but it is generally during May that, prompted by vanishing water and the lure of newly watered sward, over one million wildebeests, zebras and gazelles congregate and tramp west and north from the southern plains. One column passes west to Lake Victoria, another moves north past Lobo. While on the hoof (May to June) the rut commences and wildebeests mate. They reach the north, and eventually cross into Kenya's Masai Mara, between July and October. During November the herds begin to reform for the return journey. By December they are dispersing among the southern grasslands; calving starts in February. Over a million wildebeests trampling and cropping nutrient-rich grasses promotes regrowth, producing fresh graze for calving – the cycle complete.

TANZANIA

BLUE WILDEBEEST, SERENGETI NATIONAL PARK

water and will usually be found within 20km of a water source – and they benefit from the shade offered by the trees.

Serengeti also protects one of the largest **giraffe** populations in Africa (the species here is the Masai giraffe), although its numbers declined in the 1990s. It is dependent on acacia trees, which grow well near watercourses. The Serengeti also supports Africa's largest population of **common elands** (the subspecies here is Patterson's eland, distinguished by its rufous coat). This bovine heavyweight (males reach nearly a tonne) is unmistakable because of its great size, but its occurrence is difficult to predict – elands are great wanderers and have home ranges as large as 1500 sq km. They are a rather sociable species: calves like to get together so you may see groups of up to 50; and if a local area offers good pickings, groups of up to 1000 elands can congregate briefly.

With nearly half of Tanzania's bird species recorded here, Serengeti offers some great birding. The **Masai ostrich** and **kori bustard** are readily seen and the **lesser flamingo** is a visitor to the saline Lake Ndutu (Lagarja). Three Tanzanian endemics – **Fischer's lovebird**, the **rufous-tailed weaver** and **grey-breasted spurfowl** – are locally common. The lovebird prefers mature acacia woodlands, and both the weaver and spurfowl can be spotted around open woodland. While the lovebirds and weaver can be seen in places other than Serengeti, the grey-breasted spurfowl occurs only in the Seronera–Ndutu area of Serengeti and around Lake Eyasi in the Ngorongoro Conservation Area. One other species to look out for is the **brown-chested plover**, a West African migrant that sometimes turns up on the Serengeti Plains, often with **Senegal plovers**, which look somewhat similar. Migrant species are present between October and April and include **white storks**, **rollers**, **cuckoos**, **swallows**, **Montague's** and **pallid harriers** and **Caspian plovers**.

It's sometimes said that there aren't many animals in the Serengeti during the dry season. This is untrue: there are oodles of animals in the Serengeti at this time – there just aren't the vast herds of wildebeests and gazelles scattered across the plains. The wildebeest migration has its season and path (see the boxed text, p111), but at other times there is still ample wildlife to keep you ogling. The only time to think about avoiding is the height of the wet season, when the roads in some areas become problematic, although seeing wildebeests calving more than compensates.

BALLOON SAFARIS

Serengeti is currently the only place in Tanzania where you can try to spot wildlife from a hot-air balloon. During the predawn drive from Seronera Lodge to the launch point – a fun 'night drive' in itself – you may encounter genets, civets and springhares. Once airborne, you drift over the plains at the whim of the airstream and accompanied by bursts of flame. It's all silent except for the burner, and from the air you can spot otherwise invisible hyena dens. Everywhere, tracks criss-cross the plains like some gigantic web. Groups of zebras, wildebeests, hartebeests and gazelles are visible for kilometres. You'll skim over acacias full of huddling olive baboons or vervet monkeys that have not yet risen for the day. You'll look down on vultures' nests, but in flight most birds become difficult to recognise when viewed from above. One of the biggest advantages of ballooning is that it overcomes viewing problems caused by long grass. Mammals such as bohor reedbucks, which are often obscured by reeds, and caracals, servals and African wild cats may be seen below. The balloon ride ends wherever the wind has blown you, and the champagne bush breakfast that follows may be accompanied by whatever animals happen to be nearby.

LION

TANZANIA

ZANZIBAR
ARCHIPELAGO

TANZANIA

LOCATION Unguja is about 40km northeast of mainland Tanzania. Pemba is 50km east of the mainland and 50km north of Unguja.

FACILITIES Unguja has nature trails and a mangrove boardwalk at Jozani Forest. Pemba has a visitors centre and nature trail at Ngezi Forest Reserve, and walking and underwater trails at Misali.

ACCOMMODATION On Unguja, there's plenty of choice in Zanzibar Town and along the coast, with upmarket resorts on Changuu and Mnemba Islands. Pemba has limited range in towns plus several upmarket resorts.

WILDLIFE RHYTHMS Conditions for snorkelling and diving are usually best from June to February or March.

CONTACT Chumbe Island Coral Park (www.chumbeisland.com); One Ocean/The Zanzibar Dive Centre (www.zanzibaroneocean.com).

ZANZIBAR ARCHIPELAGO

The Zanzibar archipelago is made up of two major islands – Unguja (or Zanzibar) and Pemba – plus numerous smaller islands. Accessible coral reefs attract divers and snorkellers, but the islands also have a diversity of land animals, including some interesting endemic species and subspecies (many of the bird species and races reflect past changes in the natural and man-made environment). The main islands are heavily populated and intensely cultivated – especially for the cloves and other spices that made Zanzibar famous. Most of the original forest cover has been cleared, but the small stands that have been preserved are worth exploring for wildlife.

CORAL REEFS, TURTLES & DOLPHINS Fringing coral reefs with a high diversity of corals, fish and other marine life bring droves of snorkellers and divers to Unguja. Popular dive sites include those near Ras Ngunwi village, off Stone Town and around Mnemba Island (off the northeast coast), which offers a plethora of fish and is also excellent for snorkelling.

Both **green** and **hawksbill turtles** nest on Unguja. At Ngunwi you can watch female green turtles lumber ashore to lay their eggs, and under the lighthouse at Ras Ngunwi a dozen green turtles can be seen up close in a walled but otherwise natural lagoon, with zebra-striped **scissortail sergeants** swimming among them.

Humpback whales move north through the channel between the mainland and the archipelago in spring and return, sometimes with families, in September. They can sometimes be seen off Unguja and Chumbe Island. **Long-snouted spinner** and **bottlenose dolphins** live in the seas

WILDLIFE HIGHLIGHTS
» Excellent marine life, snorkelling and diving around Unguja (Zanzibar island), Pemba and surrounding islets
» The chance to observe dolphins near Kizimkazi
» Intriguing land animals, including the endemic and easily seen Zanzibar red colobus and endemic subspecies of the blue monkey and tree hyrax » World-class reef life around tiny Chumbe Island and a forest that's a reminder of how Unguja's forests once were » Introduced Aldabran giant tortoises on Prison Island » Four endemic birds (all relatively common) on Pemba, plus an endemic race of vervet monkey and camps of an endemic flying-fox whose nearest relative is found in Madagascar

TANZANIA

around Zanzibar, and watching and swimming with dolphins has become a tourist industry off Kizimkazi. Please help the village's ecotourism venture – and the dolphins themselves – by following the guidelines that have been developed for observing dolphins.

JOZANI FOREST Jozani forest – the largest area of mature forest left on Zanzibar, and now protected as part of the Jozani-Chwaka Bay National Park – is the stronghold of the endangered **Zanzibar (or Kirk's) red colobus**; **blue monkeys** (the subspecies on Zanzibar is endemic) also live here. The colobus are usually easy to see – they can occur in troops of around 100 and sometimes feed in mixed troops with blue monkeys; at midday you may see them draped over the branches of Indian almond trees having a siesta.

Jozani is also a refuge for many of Unguja's other mammals (although the **Zanzibar leopard** is almost certainly extinct). You can follow trails through several different habitats to look for them or find a fruiting tree and sit quietly nearby, especially in the early morning or late afternoon. **Red-bellied coast squirrels** scamper about in the canopy (another species, the **Zanj sun squirrel**, also lives on Unguja) and more than 40 species of bird have been recorded in Jozani: time spent here would improve your chances of seeing gems such as the **African pygmy kingfisher**, **little greenbul**, **dark-backed weaver** and, if you're very lucky, **Fischer's turaco**. You are unlikely to encounter the critically endangered **Aders' duiker** (see the boxed text, p71) or the Zanzibar race of **suni**, but listen for the activities of **black-and-rufous elephant shrews** during the day and **tree hyraxes** at night; traces of nocturnal **bushpigs** may also be seen during the day. Don't miss the mangrove boardwalk at the southern end of Jozani: **mangrove kingfishers** are resident and your guide can introduce you to mangrove ecology.

THE TIDE OF DESTRUCTION

The archipelago's wildlife has suffered greatly at the hands of introduced species. Apart from invasions of common pests such as the black rat, which has been spread around the world by seafarers, three species of mongoose have been introduced to the islands. These efficient predators compete with the native mongooses, which today are rarely seen, and almost certainly caused the extinction of two birds unique to the islands. But one pest stands out: the Indian house crow. Introduced in 1890, the crows proliferated and began to prey on small birds, eggs and nestlings. The situation became so serious that eventually a house crow eradication program was implemented by Tony Archer and a team from the Commission for Lands and Environment in Stone Town. Around 45,000 crows were destroyed in the mid-1990s, but funding has since dried up and the house crow menace could yet resurface to wreak havoc on Zanzibar's native birds.

Unguja's bird total stands at well over 200 species and keen birders will no doubt continue to improve knowledge of the island's birdlife. During low tide at the harbour you should see a few loitering **sooty gulls** and **dimorphic egrets** (of both white and grey varieties) stalking across the mud for prey. But **crab-plovers** are the prize

WATCHING TIPS

ZALA (Zanzibar Land Animal) Park is a small wildlife centre about 3km from Jozani that offers an excellent introduction to Unguja's reptiles, including the island's only species of chameleon. And in case you miss them at Jozani, Zanzibar red colobus are often heard and seen in the trees around the enclosures at ZALA Park; another small population lives near Makunduchi.

sighting: they feed on all Zanzibar's shores, together with **sand plovers, terek sandpipers, whimbrels** and **greenshanks**. A few could be seen at any time of year, although numbers peak between November and March.

One of Unguja's best birdwatching sites is Bwawani Marsh, at the north end of Stone Town, where **pied kingfishers, purple swamphens, Allen's gallinules, African jacanas** and **white-faced whistling ducks** can be seen.

ISLAND SANCTUARIES Chumbe Island, Tanzania's first official marine park (also known as Chumbe Island Coral Park – CHICOP), is a 16-hectare environmentally friendly resort and reserve. Money made from visitors to the reserve is used to educate local children about conservation, and Chumbe has gained international acclaim for its ecolodge and local environmental education programs. No one lives here except park staff – and lots of crabs: red **shore crabs** hide in dry pockets on the reef; thousands of orange-and-black striped **rock crabs** squeeze into crevices among the coral rag; and **hermit crabs** leave their characteristic trails everywhere.

Most of Chumbe's natural coastal forest has remained untouched and more than 60 bird species have been recorded on the island. **Little swifts** swirl over the greenery, returning to their nests under the lighthouse's window overhangs. Two islets just southwest of Chumbe supported a breeding colony of around 750 pairs of **roseate tern** in 1994. They are likely to be seen offshore from May to December, when they are nesting. Some 350 species of fish have been recorded from Chumbe's almost pristine reef, and **turtles** and **dolphins** are regularly seen. Snorkelling is offered and you can walk the forest trail or an intertidal trail (at low tide). Huge **coconut crabs** emerge after sunset – the compost heap is a good place to look.

Changuu – also known as Prison Island – supports several of Unguja's unique **lizard** species, but is far better known for another reptile: **giant tortoises**. Native to Aldabra in the Seychelles, the tortoises were transported to Changuu during the 18th century and thrived free from predation by dogs and pigs. There's also excellent snorkelling around Changuu and, even though it's only 5km away, the reef fish fauna is markedly different from that of Unguja.

Misali is a small forested island just off Pemba's western coast that has been declared a marine conservation area. **Green turtles**

TANZANIA

EVOLUTIONARY SNAPSHOT

Each of the Zanzibar archipelago's islands has endemic animals, but the overlap of species between the islands and the adjacent mainland is a complex puzzle that preserves a fascinating snapshot of evolution. For example, Aders' duiker (see the boxed text, p71), a species that survives only on Unguja and in coastal Kenya, is a relic of ancient West African forests that once stretched right across the continent. Likewise, the subspecies of African pygmy kingfisher on Unguja is elsewhere found only in southern Africa and probably reflects past changes in the continent's vegetation. But the Pemba flying-fox is not found on Unguja or the adjacent mainland – its nearest relative is in Madagascar, 1500km to the southeast. Undoubtedly part of another wave of invading species, the flying-fox was probably isolated on Pemba before it could spread to Unguja. The Pemba Channel prevented the flying-fox's spread to the mainland and has served as an effective barrier to natural invasions of Pemba ever since.

and **seabirds** nest on the western side, mangroves fringe the eastern side and there are underwater viewing trails through the adjoining coral reefs.

BIRDS & BATS Pemba's largest remaining patch of forest, Ngezi – now protected as part of the Ngezi Vumawimbi Forest Reserve – has been selectively logged, but the island's four endemic bird species (imaginatively named the **Pemba green pigeon**, **Pemba scops owl**, **Pemba sunbird** and **Pemba white-eye**) are reasonably common and widespread. The white-eye and sunbird are common in gardens and plantations; the green pigeon readily feeds in fruiting palms near villages; and the scops owl (more often heard than seen) inhabits woodlands and plantations.

The **Pemba flying-fox** (see the boxed text, p116) is most common on Pemba's west coast and offshore islets, and there's also a good population in Ngezi (rangers should be able to point you to a camp – and watch for that cosmopolitan bat botherer, the **bat hawk**, hunting small insect-eating bats at dusk). The Pemba subspecies of **vervet monkey** and **tree hyrax** also live at Ngezi; and the **Pemba day gecko** should be heard scuttling among leaf litter. Other patches of forest survive at Mwitu Mkuu and Ras Kiuyu.

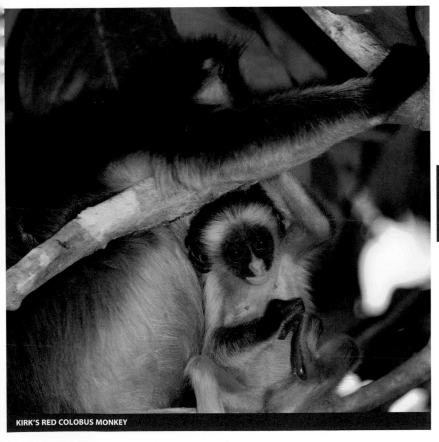

KIRK'S RED COLOBUS MONKEY

TANZANIA

SELOUS GAME RESERVE

LOCATION Park entrances 250km and 350km southwest of Dar es Salaam; often inaccessible during the long rains (March to May).

FACILITIES Boat trips, walking safaris, balloon safaris, lodges and tented camps.

ACCOMMODATION Basic camping grounds, plus various lodges and tented camps, most upmarket; budget accommodation outside the reserve gates.

WILDLIFE RHYTHMS Dry season (June to October) is best, as animals congregate around waterways.

CONTACT Chief warden (scp@africaonline.co.tz).

SELOUS GAME RESERVE

Selous is one of Africa's most important wildlife conservation areas and one of its largest, although – with one major exception – only the northern sector is open to visitors. By virtue of its size, it protects vast numbers of animals: it contains the largest **buffalo** concentration in Africa (a population put at more than 110,000 according to some estimates) and over half of Tanzania's **elephants** (approximately 57,000). The Selous ecosystem is estimated to contain Africa's largest populations of **Lichtenstein's hartebeest** (a distinct subspecies that is sometimes regarded as a full species), **common waterbuck** and **Roosevelt's sable**. However, it is not just the reserve's size that protects the animals. The presence of tsetse flies has made it unsuitable for humans and livestock, and this has undoubtedly helped to safeguard Selous' **hunting dogs** – a species that elsewhere suffers severe persecution from livestock owners. Selous is home to 25% to 30% of Africa's hunting dogs, with the reserve's population estimated at around 1300. Furthermore, most of Tanzania's **black rhinos** inhabit Selous and the park contains large numbers of **lions**, **hyenas** and **ungulates**. The Rufiji River is packed with **hippos** – which you'll hear grunting during the night – and **crocs**, and more than 440 species of bird have been recorded in the area.

It's obvious why this area was declared a World Heritage site and, with all the aforementioned, you'd think Selous would be thronging with tourists. But although visitor numbers have been steadily increasing, they are still modest in comparison with the heavily visited northern safari circuit. In practical terms the Selous is a place best visited on an organised trip. In addition to the usual game drives, escorted walking and boating safaris are allowed – both rarities in Tanzanian parks.

WILDLIFE HIGHLIGHTS

» **Fewer tourists in comparison with the northern-circuit parks and a distinct wilderness feel** » Some of Africa's largest populations of elephants, buffaloes, hartebeests, sables and hunting dogs, plus lions, giraffes and various antelopes; black rhinos are present but unlikely to be seen » Boating safaris on the Rufiji River, which is thick with hippos and crocs and offers a wealth of waterbirds » Over 440 recorded bird species, including gems such as Pel's fishing owls, African skimmers and white-headed plovers » Escorted walking safaris – the Selous is one of the few places in Tanzania where tourists can walk in a region that contains dangerous animals

TANZANIA

👀 WATCHING TIPS

The Beho area is good for elephants, which are often found in the galley forest adjacent to the river. Downstream, Lake Tagalala's banks are covered in terminalia thickets that sometimes shelter buffaloes and lions. Pel's fishing owls roost in dense, shady trees adjacent to the Rufiji: their presence is often revealed by mobbing birds, although pellets and dung littered with fish scales beneath the tree is another sign – look up!

Much of the northern Selous is flat and dominated by grassland, miombo and terminalia woodland (the pungent, sweet smell of flowering terminalias pervades the September air). Most wildlife-watching takes place on and around Selous' maze of rivers and lakes. The water is thick with **crocodiles** and **hippos**, **elephants** are a regular sight and **waterbirds** are everywhere. During the wet season the Rufiji River swells and redefines its course: the exact locations of its channels, lagoons and oxbow lakes change from year to year, and bits of camps and roads built along the river to allow great wildlife-watching often end up in the drink during the wet season.

Near the Mtemere Gate the river is edged by tall, dense trees. On foot (Rufiji River Camp conducts walks here) or on the river, this is a great area for finding **black-and-white colobus** and guides should be able to lead you to them. This is also a top area to look for one of Africa's most sought-after birds – **Pel's fishing owl**. Upstream from here many of the waterways are lined with sandbanks, and **African skimmers** plough the water's surface and mass on the shore while **vultures** wash on the beach. Further along, borassus palms fringing the water provide homes for **African palm swifts**, which can be seen darting about at sunset. Dead palms are used by **African fish eagles** as vantage points and by **Dickinson's kestrels** as nest sites. In places along the river bank, river combretum creates a wall of red flowers in November and December. **Crocs** in big numbers sun themselves on banks and **hippos** are often out grazing during the day. **Giraffes**, **waterbucks**, **elephants**, **buffaloes** and even **lions** can all be observed from the river. Interestingly, the Rufiji divides two subspecies of wildebeest: blue wildebeest is not uncommon on its northern shore, while south of the river the Mozambique (white-banded) subspecies is more often seen.

The sheer numbers of **waterbirds** on and around the river will excite even nonbirders: the **white-headed plover**, an uncommon

AFRICAN HUNTING DOGS

No terrestrial carnivore is more cooperative or successful at hunting than the African hunting dog. Although lions hunt together, in general females in a pride do most of the hunting; lions also have a low success rate, catching their prey between 20% and 40% of the time. In contrast, hunting dogs in some studies hit a success rate of up to 85%. Their cooperative pack hunting and ability to run for kilometres – an average chase of a prey is between 1.3km and 3km – is the key. The dogs select one or more targets, the pack chasing them until they can go no further. Death is swift. The dogs are cooperative, tearing and tugging on the abdomen until the victims fall. Their prey is quickly eaten – then shared. Food is regurgitated to dogs that have lost the trail, are sick or injured or stayed behind to mind the pups, and to the pups themselves.

species in East Africa, prefers the edges of waterways; the stately **saddle-billed stork** occurs in good numbers; and other treats include the rarely seen **white-backed night heron** and the migratory **squacco heron**.

SELOUS' MINI-MIGRATION Many animals live on the plains during the wet season and return to the waterways in the dry season, drifting down from the north to the five lakes in June and July. They can first be seen around Lakes Tagalala and Manze, then slowly move northeast to congregate around Manze, Nzelekela and Siwandu. Lake Mzizamia becomes an isolated lagoon when the river level drops in the dry season and has fewer animals than the others, except between September and December. However, the higher tree density here makes this area suitable for **colobus** (which aren't found around the other lakes), **trumpeter** and **crowned hornbills** and **crowned eagles**. There is also an incredible number of **hippos** and **crocs** here.

All of the lodges have local wildlife highlights in and around their grounds. Selous Safari Camp, nestled among riverside greenery, is a top spot for **elephants** – being escorted to and from your tent is entirely necessary here. The currently closed Mbuyu

Camp has a baobab 20m in circumference that was ringed by the former dining area. This tree is a hive of activity – noisy **green wood-hoopoes**, **striped ground squirrels** and **brown-headed parrots** live in the tree's hollows and carry on regardless of the people below. This camp is also a great birdwatching spot because of its position on the river. Rufiji River Camp has lots of bold **vervet monkeys** around the restaurant and this is the place to go on a walking safari to find **black-and-white colobus**. The riverine vegetation is ideal **Pel's fishing owl** habitat – this bird is rare in East Africa but is occasionally seen along the Rufiji.

One antelope you are unlikely to encounter elsewhere is **Roosevelt's sable**. This subspecies is restricted to Tanzania and southern Kenya, and Selous protects around 10,000 Roosevelt's sables – probably the largest surviving population. Sables are normally sedentary but the Selous population is fairly mobile, which can make finding them frustrating at times. They are found inside the reserve mostly during the wet season (when many areas are inaccessible) and drift out of the reserve to the south and southeast during the dry. These selective grazers and browsers are usually found in miombo, often venturing down to drink in the heat of the day.

TANZANIA

TO HUNT OR NOT TO HUNT?

Like many protected areas in Africa, Selous caters not only for photographers but also for trophy hunters. In fact, over 90% of the reserve – everything south of the Rufiji River – is given over to hunting. Ethical concerns aside (and they are considerable), it raises the question: is hunting a legitimate part of conservation? Hunters argue that their exorbitant safari fees are ploughed back into protected areas; if it wasn't for their money, wilderness would disappear under agriculture. In the 1980s, only about 10% of hunting revenue actually made it into Selous' coffers but the figure is now around 50%. Of course, the same argument could be made of nonconsumptive tourism, one the hunters counter by claiming they actually cause less damage to Selous' ecosystem. Per person, they pay far more than wildlife-watchers, so fewer of them are required to make the same profit. Fewer people means fewer lodges, vehicles, rubbish dumps and so on. Whether that's less of an impact than shooting leopards or lions is debatable.

TANZANIA

LION AT THE KILL IN SELOUS GAME RESERVE

TARANGIRE NATIONAL PARK

Tarangire is seasonally outstanding for wildlife and is second only to Ngorongoro Crater as a dry-season home for many migratory mammals. Between June and November **wildebeests, plains zebras, fringe-eared oryxes, common elands, gazelles, hartebeests, buffaloes** and **elephants** congregate around the Tarangire River, the main water source in the dry season. Once the short rains begin in November the animals start to drift out of the park, returning in June after the long rains cease. Tarangire is also a very good park for spotting **lions** and it is a stunning place for birds. Termite mounds can be seen throughout the park (and they are often the haunt of **dwarf mongooses**). Although only 30km from the Rift Valley escarpment, Tarangire falls outside the nutrient-rich volcanic belt and the annual rainfall is low (550mm): much of the park is semiarid and dominated by baobabs and acacias.

Most visitors concentrate their activity in the northern sector and around the Tarangire River. As a first port of call the patio of the Tarangire Safari Lodge is a must: it sits high on a bluff and gives a bird's-eye view over the river. Wildlife-viewing from here is excellent because you can sit and watch for hours as individuals or groups slowly come to water, weaving their way down through the baobabs and acacias. Around 3000 **elephants** occur in the park and come down to drink. With the aid of binoculars you can even make out that a rapidly moving column of dots is a family of **mongooses**. Early morning and late afternoon are the best times to watch the river, but the heat of the day offers great **raptor** watching as the birds cruise at eye level around the bluff.

Tarangire offers great birding not just because of the diversity of species here, but because of the fine viewing conditions afforded by its sparse vegetation. Highlights

LOCATION 120km southwest of Arusha; some areas of the park become inaccessible during the rainy season.

FACILITIES Visitors centre at park entrance.

ACCOMMODATION Several safari lodges and tented camps in the park and in border areas; public and private camping grounds inside and outside the park.

WILDLIFE RHYTHMS Greatest large animal concentrations August to October. Eurasian bird migrants are present October to April.

CONTACT Senior park warden (www.tanzaniaparks .com/tarangire.html).

TANZANIA

👁️ WATCHING TIPS

This is one of the best places in Tanzania to come in the dry season (July/August to October) if you want to see large numbers of ungulates (at this time, many ungulates in the more famous Serengeti have migrated north to Kenya). The Lemiyon region beyond the park's northeastern boundary offers great photographic opportunities: it is dotted with baobabs, interspersed in the dry season with wildebeests and zebras.

WILDLIFE HIGHLIGHTS
» **Dry-season home to migratory mammals, including plains zebras, wildebeests, gazelles, buffaloes, elands and fringe-eared oryxes** » **Elephants are a prime attraction along the Tarangire River during the dry season, and lions occur in good numbers** » **One of the few places where there is a chance to see hunting dogs in Tanzania** » **Fabulous for birds (more than 450 species recorded in the park and over 500 in the broader ecosystem), especially raptors; three Tanzanian endemics easily seen**

ENRAPTURED OVER RAPTORS

There are over 60 raptor species in Tanzania and 49 of them occur in Tarangire. The open habitat in the northern sector is peppered with leafless trees during the dry season and this provides perfect birdwatching conditions. From the tracks that wind along the high banks of the Tarangire River you'll readily get within photographic distance of tawny, long-crested and martial eagles as well as black-chested snake-eagles. Pale chanting goshawks are easy to spot, and keep an eye out for the gymnogene (African harrier-hawk) in more wooded areas – these slate-grey birds can sometimes be seen probing deep in hollows with their dexterous legs in search of prey. Both augur buzzards, with their orange tails, and the striking white-winged, black-bodied, short-tailed adult bateleurs are easy for nonbirders to distinguish from below. Leggy secretary birds (yes, they are raptors too) are common and unmistakable as they walk through the bush. Vultures – lappet-faced, Rüppell's griffon, hooded and African white-backed – can all be observed massed together in trees or spiralling on thermals, often in the company of marabou storks.

include the birds of prey and good numbers of three of Tanzania's endemic species – the **ashy starling**, **rufous-tailed weaver** and **yellow-collared lovebird**. Ashy (grey-brown with a very long tail) and **superb starlings** are common around lodges and camps, and noisy, twittery flocks of yellow-collared lovebirds are usually easy to locate near baobabs (they favour holes in baobabs as nesting sites). Reports of Fischer's lovebirds in Tarangire are erroneous and probably refer to escaped individuals of this popular cage bird. Rufous-tailed weavers are common in the acacia savannas throughout the park: they are bigger than most weavers (ie they are thrush-sized) and easily recognised by their scale-like plumage, pale-blue eyes and rufous tail; their large, untidy grass nests are readily seen scattered in the acacias.

Larger, ground-dwelling birds, such as **coqui**, **crested** and **Hildebrandt's francolins**, and both **red-necked** and **yellow-necked spurfowl** are regularly encountered taking dust baths along the tracks. It's easy to see why spurfowl and guineafowl are blamed for enlarging potholes! The common guineafowl here are **crested guineafowl**, but **vulturine**

guineafowl have been seen in the east of the park around Ol Doinyo Ngahari – vulturines just make it into Tanzania and are right at the edge of their range in Tarangire.

Along the Tarangire River, **Egyptian geese** and **crowned** and **blacksmith plovers** are common. The undersides of the fronds of doum palms in the river valley are festooned with the nests of **African palm swifts**; the swifts themselves are commonly seen zooming around the palms in search of flying insects, their very long, pointed tails distinctive. To see waterbirds, a trip south (a full day's effort if staying in the north) to the Silale Swamp is recommended. Lush and green, this expansive swamp attracts **egrets**, **ibises**, **plovers**, **cormorants**, **storks**, **geese** and **ducks**. Good number of **saddle-billed storks** occur here. **Pythons** also frequent the swamps and there is an increased chance of seeing one if the swamps are drying up – they hang in trees, so search the limbs of acacias. On the way south to Silale, pause at creek crossings and look around the riverbeds for **lions** and for animals digging for water. If coming from the north, you should also pass a koppie about 1km south of the Engelhard bridge across the Tarangire

TANZANIA

River – it is good for **bush hyraxes** and **klipspringers**.

Lake Burungi lies outside the park and when conditions are right, tens of thousands of **flamingos** feed in the lake. The lake shore is also a reliable place to see **fringe-eared oryxes**, which move seasonally in and out of the southern and central parts of Tarangire. Another place to find them is the Minyonyo area, which is on the river south of Kuro guard post. South from here you will find **gerenuks**, with the Mkungonero region being the best area. The semiwilderness area south of the Silale Swamp is inaccessible in the wet season, but open to off-road driving in the dry.

Around Lake Burungi you may often find **bushbucks** or **lesser kudus** browsing in thickets. The Kitabung Hill area to the south is good for viewing **buffalo** herds, which kick up dust as they mill amid the acacias and descend to drink at dusk. **Common elands** are also seen in this region.

Tarangire is also a good place in which to see **hunting dogs**. The dogs roam the whole Masai Steppe system, so sightings are unpredictable. They den on the steppe in the rains and are most likely to be encountered on the eastern side of the park in the dry season. Herds of antelope running and stotting without making alarm calls is one sign that hunting dogs are nearby.

TARANGIRE'S MIGRATIONS The movement patterns and paths of the migratory species in the Tarangire area are well known. **Plains zebras** and **wildebeests** move first, departing in October, then the **gazelles, buffaloes, elands, oryxes, hartebeests** and **elephants** move out. The bulk of these animals head northeast and some go as far as Lake Natron. **Defassa waterbucks, impalas, giraffes, lesser kudus, Kirk's dik-diks** and **warthogs** are all resident. The migratory species return in June and July – firstly the oryxes and elands, then the elephants, followed by the zebras and wildebeests; by August all the animals have returned. The migration path for many is through the Simanjiro area, so this is a good place to consider visiting once the migration begins. Operators based outside the park can offer walking safaris, driving in open vehicles, night drives and clambering about on koppies so the wildlife can be experienced close at hand. Night drives introduce nocturnal species such as **leopards, springhares, genets, civets, white-tailed mongooses** and **ratels**.

TARANGIRE'S GROWING ISOLATION

Tarangire faces an uncertain future as its migratory wildlife is almost entirely dependent on what happens outside the park – and things aren't secure. The animals are being increasingly cut off and isolated from their wet-season homes. Agricultural encroachment, farming, ranching and settlements have almost severed the migratory routes north to Lake Manyara, which is an important destination for wildebeests and zebras. There are urgent calls to have a migration corridor declared between Manyara and Tarangire, but it is almost too late. To the east the pathways are being threatening by large-scale agricultural developments between the Simanjiro area and the park. The Masai Steppe and the Simanjiro and Lolkisale Game Control Areas are the most important wet-season habitat for Tarangire animals (about 55,000 animals inhabit the area seasonally) and control of agriculture to the east is seen as imperative. The infertile soil and dry climate is not conducive to farming, although pastoralism (grazing) is seen as having the least impact on wildlife.

TANZANIA

ELEPHANTS IN RIVERBED, TARANGIRE NATIONAL PARK

LOCATION 21km from Arusha.

FACILITIES Small museum at Ngurdoto Gate; guides can be hired at Momela Gate (where all Mt Meru treks should be arranged) or at the park's main Ngongongare Gate.

ACCOMMODATION Lodges in and near the park entrance, camping grounds, two trekkers' bunkers on Mt Meru.

WILDLIFE RHYTHMS Dry season best for mammals, wet season best for migrating birds.

CONTACT Senior park warden (www.tanzaniaparks .com/arusha.html).

TANZANIA

👁👁 WATCHING TIPS

Momela Lodge is a great birding site: the hippo pools teem with waterbirds, including sacred ibises, red-billed teal, African darters, grey herons, yellow-billed storks and Egyptian geese. The garden is open to nonresidents and attracts lots of birds, including sunbirds. Giraffes, elephants and other wildlife are frequent visitors on the lawns surrounding the upmarket and atmospheric Hatari Lodge. The forest areas near Momela Gate are popular with colobus and blue monkeys.

ARUSHA NATIONAL PARK

Varying from 1500m to over 4500m in altitude, Arusha protects diverse habitats and three distinct topographical features – the inactive volcano of 4566m Mt Meru, Tanzania's second-highest peak; 3km-wide Ngurdoto Crater; and the Momela Lakes, which are great for birding. Arusha is easy to visit and although rhinos, elands, reedbucks and lions are no longer present, there are plenty of other mammals to see.

Just before you get to Ngurdoto Gate you'll see an acacia-fringed glade – Serengeti Ndogo (Little Serengeti) – that is always covered in **buffaloes**, **giraffes**, **warthogs** and **olive baboons**; it is also the only place where **plains zebras** occur in the park. From here the altitude rises and the vegetation alters dramatically to dense montane forest where **black-and-white colobus** (sometimes seen at the Ngurdoto Gate itself) and **blue monkeys** are certainties.

The road winding up to the rim of Ngurdoto Crater is flanked by tall, dense forest that is good primate habitat – look for **colobus**, **blue monkeys** and **olive baboons**. Large birds include **trumpeter** and **silvery-cheeked hornbills**. From several observation points you can see the pools, marshes and reed beds that make the crater floor a favourite of **buffaloes** and **waterbirds**. Most birds are too far away to make out, but **saddle-billed storks** should stand out.

The central road from Ngurdoto Gate leads to the Momela Lakes – shallow, ground-fed lakes that seasonally attract large numbers of **lesser flamingos**, although it is impossible to predict when and where they will be present. You should also be able to see **greater flamingos** (the two often feed in separate lakes).

Arusha's small lakes are more seasonal, but **hippos**, **elephants**, **buffaloes** and **baboons** might be seen there. **Hippos** often use El Kekhotoito, and Kusare is a good place to

WILDLIFE HIGHLIGHTS
» Picturesque landscapes with the chance of seeing savanna animals such as buffaloes, elephants and plains zebras and hippos in permanent wetlands » Almost-guaranteed sightings of black-and-white colobus and blue monkeys » Kirk's dik-diks are abundant and giraffes common near the Momela Gate » Over 400 bird species; the Momela Lakes are seasonally important for waterbirds and flamingos » Treks to Mt Meru's summit offer stunning scenery and fewer people than Kilimanjaro, and klipspringers live on the crater cliffs

spot **defassa waterbucks; Kirk's dik-diks** are common in this area. Scan the island in Small Momela Lake for **hippos** from the observation point at the edge. If you have no luck, another spot to check is about 2km along, where the lake becomes swampy: this is a hippo entry and exit point. The marshes are also good for waterbirds, especially **little grebes**.

Some 48 waterbird species have been recorded on the Momela Lakes, but diversity varies seasonally, with Eurasian migrants present between October and April (one year it was estimated that almost the entire Tanzanian population of **Maccoa ducks** overwintered here). Unlike most Rift Valley lakes, which fill by flooding and can dry up, the Momela Lakes are fed by underground streams and always contain water.

Near the Momela Gate is an area known as Buffalo Ground, an acacia-fringed, swampy area at the base of Tululusia Hill that is fabulous in the dry season. **Buffaloes**, **warthogs**, **waterbucks** and countless **giraffes** reside here, and **grey crowned cranes** sometimes feed on the plain. Hire a

KIRK'S DIK-DIK

FEEDING PATTERNS

Arusha's lakes provide ample opportunities to witness the diverse feeding techniques of waterbirds. Little grebes cruise along the surface and dive periodically, emerging almost a minute later shaking their prey. Greater and lesser flamingos swing their beaks underwater as they filter feed with their heads down. At Momela Lodge's hippo pools, sacred ibises probe the mud for molluscs with their sensitive beaks, and sometimes sway their beaks side-to-side in the shallows. The long legs of yellow-billed storks enable them to stand in deeper water and snatch small fish or snails. And hamerkops can scoop up fish in midflight or shuffle in the shallows to stir up frogs then snap them up.

guide and do the short walk to the nearby waterfall: it is very beautiful and the animals are used to vehicles. Up high, you are likely to start seeing raptors, including **bateleurs** and **tawny** and **martial eagles**.

On Mt Meru (an armed guide must escort you to the top) you may see more wildlife, and there are far fewer people than on Kilimanjaro. The lower route to Miriakamba via Fig Tree Arch has more forest and is better for animals, including **alpine birds**, **olive baboons**, **black-and-white colobus** and **blue monkeys**. The open area at Itikoni is perhaps the best place for **elephants**, but they can occur anywhere, as can **buffaloes**. Above 3000m the forest peters out and the landscape is dominated by heathers and giant alpine herbs (senecio and lobelia) that reach well over head height. There is less wildlife, but **buffaloes** and **elephants** may also be found up here; these and **waterbucks** drink at the crater pool. **Klipspringers** can be seen on the cliffs inside the crater and **lammergeiers** are sometimes seen soaring over the crater.

TANZANIA

LOCATION 120km west of Arusha; main park road is all-weather and suitable for 2WD.

FACILITIES Informative self-guiding visitors centre at the park entrance.

ACCOMMODATION A wide range of hotels and tented lodges on the escarpment and in and around near Mto wa Mbu village, where there are also budget guesthouses; camping grounds near park entrance. Camping within the park is also possible.

WILDLIFE RHYTHMS Most mammals resident year-round.

CONTACT Senior park warden (manyara@tanapa .org).

TANZANIA

WATCHING TIPS

The trees around Mto Wa Mbu village are cluttered with marabou stork nests. The flamingo population varies; ask tour operators if large numbers are present at the lake. Close-up wildlife encounters are not as frequent at Manyara as at some of Tanzania's other parks, and binoculars can be especially useful.

LAKE MANYARA NATIONAL PARK

Manyara is a shallow, alkaline Rift Valley lake 40km long and 13km wide; part of the lake and its narrow shoreline make up the national park. Even if you don't visit the national park itself, you will certainly see the lake on a trip to northern Tanzania: the only road to Ngorongoro and Serengeti climbs over the 900m-high Eastern Rift Valley escarpment and from the top you look down on Lake Manyara.

Rainfall draining through aquifers at the base of the Rift Valley wall feeds Lake Manyara and groundwater forest. For such a small park, Manyara has a diverse array of habitats and supports an enormous number of bird species. Baobabs dot the Rift Valley wall, and dense forest containing large fig trees, sausage trees and mahoganies surrounds the park entrance. As this forest survives on groundwater more than rainfall, you'll notice less moss and fewer epiphytes growing on the trees. *Acacia-Commiphora* woodland gives way to a grassy floodplain before the shoreline and lake is reached. A single road traverses the park and numerous loops take in the lake's edge.

The lake's water level is highly changeable and can dramatically affect waterbird populations. Mudflats and sandy areas are the places to look for **chestnut-banded plovers**, a species with a very restricted distribution (it has a greyish back, but look for the chestnut slash across its white breast). In very dry years the lake shrinks to a small pool too saline for freshwater-loving birds. But if conditions are right, thousands of **pink-backed pelicans** and **yellow-billed storks**, and lesser numbers of **marabou storks** and **grey herons**, congregate to breed here. **Flamingos** are an ephemeral star attraction, appearing in their hundreds of thousands one day, then leaving without warning – only to turn up at another Rift Valley lake. In very wet years the numerous streams feeding the lake can radically change the water level: dramatic flooding in 1997–98 resulted in a lake too fresh for the algal

WILDLIFE HIGHLIGHTS
» An outstanding park for birding with 487 recorded species » Depending on seasonal conditions, vast numbers of flamingos, pelicans and storks may be present » Blue monkeys in the adjacent forest, and buffaloes, plains zebras, wildebeests, gazelles, elephants and Masai giraffes in the woodland and grassland » Hippos in the lake » Lions and leopards in small numbers

FLAMINGOS OF THE RIFT VALLEY

Why are there so many flamingos in the Rift Valley lakes? For starters, much of the water that spills into these lakes leaches through volcanic ash and lava, dissolving salts. As the equatorial sun evaporates water from the lakes, the salts become increasingly concentrated. Depending on the depth and salinity, this creates ideal conditions in which huge quantities of algae and saltwater crustaceans thrive – few other organisms can compete with them or even survive in this highly concentrated brine. However, lesser flamingos also thrive because of their unique feeding technique: with tongue moving like a piston, they pump water through fine filters (called lamellae) inside their mandibles, catching algae and allowing most of the water to escape. With the abundance of food at certain times, it's no wonder that so many flamingos congregate.

growth needed to attract flamingos. The popular Hippo Pools are currently no more: they have been consumed by the lake and lie about 1km beyond the drowned tree line.

Terrestrial animals are less affected by the waterline. **Olive baboons** and **blue monkeys** can typically be seen in the lush forest near the entrance. This is also an excellent place for locating **silvery-cheeked hornbills** – just listen for their loud, raucous grunts. **Buffaloes, wildebeests, plains zebras** and **impalas** inhabit the grassy shoreline and **Masai giraffes** can be found in the acacia woodland. The Marera River area can be particularly good for giraffes, known locally for their very dark colouring. Where acacia woodland meets open areas, look out for **rollers, bee-eaters** and **shrikes** hawking insects or perched in branches. The trill of **red-billed oxpeckers** may herald the arrival of a giraffe or antelope.

Once the park was famous for its **elephants** and tree-climbing **lions**, but their numbers have declined. While poaching in the 1980s drastically reduced the elephant population, the park still remains important for elephant conservation and you should encounter some – the Msasa River area is a particular favourite for mud wallowing. But you'll have to be lucky to see lions as they are scarce on the ground as well as in the trees; many of the big trees for climbing have fallen down, probably assisted by elephants. The

Ndala River area is a good place to scout about for both lions and elephants. If this river is low, you can go on to two hot springs (Maji Moto Ndogo and Maji Moto). These may be the places to look for **flamingos** as the hot water can promote localised algal growth. They often choose to bathe at freshwater springs, ruffling their feathers and preening themselves.

PELICANS AT LAKE MANYARA

TANZANIA

LOCATION 283km west of Dar es Salaam on the Tanzam Hwy; 4WD recommended during wet seasons, when some areas may become inaccessible.

FACILITIES Small interpretive centre at park headquarters.

ACCOMMODATION Several camps/lodges, park camping grounds and bandas.

WILDLIFE RHYTHMS The best wildlife-viewing is from June to October; Eurasian migrant birds are present October to April.

CONTACT Mikumi National Park (www.tanzaniaparks .com/mikumi.html).

TANZANIA

WATCHING TIPS

Areas where Mikumi's floodplains abut savanna woodland usually offer the best birding; lions are often found resting in this fringe habitat (Mikumi's lions reputedly climb trees, possibly to escape tsetse flies). Mikumi is busy on weekends – visit on a weekday. Visitors interested in yellow baboon research may want to contact Mikumi's Animal Behaviour Research Unit (ABRU).

MIKUMI NATIONAL PARK

Mikumi is one of the largest and most easily visited of Tanzania's national parks. The southern border is contiguous with Selous, making the Mikumi–Selous complex one of the largest conservation areas in Africa. The area is home to most species of East African large mammal, and common inhabitants include **elephants, giraffes, buffaloes, plains zebras, elands, wildebeests** and **lions**. Of Mikumi's primates, **yellow baboons** are common and **vervet** and **blue monkeys** are also observed. Rarely seen, but present are **hunting dogs, greater kudus** and **sables**. This is a significant park for birds, and Eurasian migrants are present from October to April.

Most visitors see only the northern half of the park; the hilly southern half remains virtually unexplored, but protects miombo woodlands (this is where **sables** occur). Seasonal watercourses flow onto the plain from the hills and mountains that border it on three sides. The Mkata River is a central watercourse that flows through the floodplain to the north before feeding the Tendigo Swamp on the northern park boundary.

The highway and most of the tourist roads run between the floodplain and the hills, and driving into Mikumi from Dar on the causeway provides an introduction to the wildlife. **Elephants, plains zebras, giraffes** and **elands** regularly feed undisturbed near the highway and, in the wet season, **lions** have even been known to sun themselves on this road.

The park headquarters is the best place to start. Travelling northwest into the Mkata floodplain takes you to the central hippo pools on the Mkata River, home to a large group of **hippos** and numerous **waterfowl**. Watch for **African fish eagles, long-tailed cormorants, water dikkops, African jacanas** and **storks** – saddle-billed, Abdim's and **African open-billed**. In the dry season many large animals visit to drink or wallow: **elephants, buffaloes, zebras, warthogs** and **wildebeests** visit regularly, especially in the late afternoon. There are several large **crocodiles** and many small ones in the upper and lower pools.

WILDLIFE HIGHLIGHTS
» A fine park for elephants, although breeding herds are scarce » Easy viewing of hippos, plains zebras, impalas, wildebeests, buffaloes, lions, elands and giraffes » With luck, sightings of hunting dogs and sables » Over 400 recorded bird species, including palm-nut vultures and violet-crested turacos

Continuing west you leave the floodplain and turn north along Chamgore Rd, which runs along the edge of woodlands and crosses numerous small seasonal watercourses before reaching the Msole and Chamgore waterholes. In addition to seeing animals drinking or wallowing this is where you have a good chance of finding **blue monkeys** and **yellow baboons**. Further north the road divides into a circuit that visits the Chaga Wale area, with its giant grove of buttressed trees. Surrounding Chaga Wale are lots of borassus palms and at the top of this northern route is a gigantic baobab – an ecosystem in itself, with other mature trees growing from its base or within it. There is lots of wildlife around this baobab (even **leopards** are known to use its hollow interior), but be careful of the many beehives and hornets' nests. Leaving the baobab and returning south past the waterholes, a turn across the northern part of the Mkata floodplain will bring you to open short-grass areas with great views of the hills and mountains that surround Mikumi. You can do a brief side trip to Mwanambogo waterhole before returning to the park gate.

A high diversity of vegetation makes Mikumi a great place for birds, and species frequenting many different habitats occur in high numbers in a relatively small area. The circuit drive around the floodplain visits a range of habitats where birders can look for coastal species such as **Zanzibar red bishops** and **pink-backed pelicans**; woodland specialists such as **broad-billed rollers**, **white-headed black chats** and **helmet-shrikes**; and grassland birds such as **red-necked spurfowl** and **Hartlaub's bustard**. Birds of forests and mountains are represented by **purple-crested turacos** and **trumpeter hornbills**. Across the plains, savanna raptors (eg **Dickinson's kestrels** and **bateleurs**) and scavenging birds are common. Mikumi is one of the best places to see **palm-nut vultures**, and **southern ground hornbills** are abundant.

STAGGERING TRUNKS

Mikumi's luxuriant floodplains and waterways splay through this rocky region, providing welcome relief to many animal visitors. Nestled next to these waterways are clusters of palms and fruit-bearing trees, including the marula (*Sclerocarya birrea caffra*). Looking similar to the sausage tree, this thicket deciduous tree has flaky bark, broad leaves and thick foliage. Its green oval fruits are relished by monkeys, antelopes, birds and – with some notoriety – elephants. When the fruits are ripe, elephants vigorously shake the trees then 'paw' the ground with their trunks, searching for fruit. Impalas often join in, enjoying the spoils of the elephants' labour. There is considerable conjecture among scientists about whether elephants sometimes become drunk from a stomach full of fermenting fruit, but there is ample ear-flapping anecdotal evidence of erratic behaviour to suggest that they can!

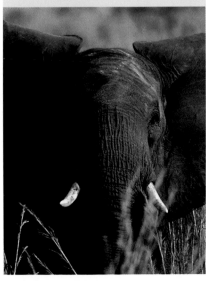

TANZANIA

LOCATION Headquarters 45km from Moshi (60km from Arusha).

ACCOMMODATION Huts and camping grounds on the mountain.

FACILITIES Maps and basic food supplies sold in the shop at park HQ.

WILDLIFE RHYTHMS Many operators don't offer Kilimanjaro treks during the long rains (March/April to June) because conditions are too wet, difficult and sometimes riskier. The June to October dry season generally brings more favourable conditions.

CONTACT Kilimanjaro National Park headquarters (www.tanzaniaparks.com/kili .html; kinapa@iwayafrica .com).

KILIMANJARO NATIONAL PARK

At 5896m above sea level, Mt Kilimanjaro is Africa's highest mountain and lures thousands of trekkers every year. Mountains create unusual and unique conditions, and are effectively ecological islands; as a result, many of the plants on Kilimanjaro are endemic. The mountain's lower reaches are savanna, with montane forest above 1800m; the higher reaches change from forest to heath and moorland, then to highland desert before finally becoming glaciers, ice and snow. The national park protects the area above 2700m, starting almost at the point where the forest ends.

For every 200m increase in altitude, the temperature drops by 1°C and near the top the temperature can be subzero at night; however, the effects of the sun are harsh and the temperature can reach 40°C or more during the day. Rainfall is at its maximum in the forest and trekkers cover their packs with large garbage bags to prevent them becoming sodden in the dense, damp forest. Above 3000m the rainfall decreases and there is little water. At the summit, oxygen is half that of sea level. This hostile environment limits plant and animal life, so the part of Kilimanjaro that is actually national park is increasingly devoid of life. The richest area for wildlife is in the forest just below.

THE ASCENT There are several routes up and around Kilimanjaro and the same types of plants, birds and animals will be seen at the same altitudes on each. The vast majority of visitors tear up and down the mountain, with the greatest numbers on the popular Marangu and Machame routes. If you take the Forest Trail near Marangu Gate you'll have a better chance of encountering forest animals because it's a quieter path. In this wet forest you may see **silvery-cheeked hornbills** or hear the shrill *kaw-kaw-kaw* of **Hartlaub's turacos** (look out for the crimson flight feathers of these mainly

👀 WATCHING TIPS

If you only want wildlife, go to Mt Meru in Arusha National Park instead – there is more wildlife and fewer people.

WILDLIFE HIGHLIGHTS

» Black-and-white colobus, blue monkeys, turacos and hornbills in the forest on the mountain's lower slopes; other wildlife is present below 2700m but difficult to see
» Good raptor and sunbird viewing on high moorlands
» A habitat diversity (forest, mountain moorlands and desert) that makes Kili a botanist's delight

green and purple birds). Less easily seen are **mountain greenbuls**, **warblers** and the **mountain buzzard** – all montane forest birds. Three of the mountain's larger primates – **olive baboons** and the arboreal **black-and-white colobus** and **blue monkeys** – should be spotted. While the forest is home to many **antelopes**, these are unlikely to be seen in the dense vegetation. Looking around will show where some common garden plants originated: impatiens, begonia and African violets are common. One of the last large mammal species to be discovered in Africa (in 1920) – the **giant forest hog** – lives in these montane forests and is sometimes encountered.

Above 3000m the forest is replaced by heathers and proteas. There is a transition into heath and moorland, which contain giant lobelias and senecios. Here the alpine birds become apparent, including the **white-necked raven**, the **streaky seedeater** and the **alpine chat**, which commonly perches on the giant lobelias. The lobelia flowers are also a favourite with one of the typical alpine sunbirds, the **scarlet-tufted malachite sunbird**. Large mammals are few up here but small rodents prosper (you'll meet the **four-striped mouse** at Horombo Hut, where it is doing especially well). **Elands** are, however, sometimes seen on the moorland, especially at Shira Plateau. The moorland is a favoured haunt of the **augur buzzard** because of the presence of the rodents; for the same reason, the **Cape eagle-owl** occurs in grassland. The most sought-after bird up here is the **lammergeier** (or bearded vulture), but as a single mountain may support only one pair of lammergeiers they are rarely seen.

Above 4000m the intense solar radiation, cold and lack of water make conditions tough for plants and animals alike, with visible life largely reduced to lichens, mosses and everlastings.

TANZANIA

KILIMANJARO NATIONAL PARK

LOCATION 124km west of Iringa; year-round access, although some park roads are impassable in wet seasons.

FACILITIES Booklet usually available at the gate. Guides must be hired for walks.

ACCOMMODATION Lodges and tented camps, basic bandas and camping grounds.

WILDLIFE RHYTHMS July to October offers greatest wildlife concentrations; migrant birds arrive October and November, and the best birding is between January and April.

CONTACT Chief park warden (www.tanzaniaparks.com /ruaha.html).

TANZANIA

⦿⦿ WATCHING TIPS

Short walking safaris are possible and these offer optimal opportunities for birding. At dusk the wild figs, tamarinds and baobabs lining the Ruaha River are buzzed by fruit-bats, some of which pollinate baobabs. During the day, watch for great white egrets cracking open freshwater oysters on the river banks. For sables, take an early afternoon game drive upstream along the Ruaha River: usually confined to woodland at the foot of the escarpment, they come to drink at the river during the dry season.

RUAHA NATIONAL PARK

Ruaha, Tanzania's largest national park, is good **lion**, **elephant** and **buffalo** country and probably the best place to spot **hunting dogs** in the country: this endangered but mobile species can often be seen here, and hunting dogs have even been seen chasing **impalas** through Mwagusi Camp. Finding hunting dogs can be a matter of luck, but they are usually seen for a few days every fortnight.

Ruaha encompasses a mixture of vegetation types and habitats and these dictate where you will most likely encounter certain species. Ruaha is located on a dry, central plateau with its central highest point forming a watershed for the park's two main rivers: the Mzombe, which forms the northern boundary, and the Ruaha, which forms most of the southern. Few visitors venture north and most confine their activities to around the Ruaha River and other sand riverbeds. This area is a centre of animal activity during the dry season (June to December) when the drying rivers may leave only isolated pools. The first of these you will encounter are the hippo pools, which lie just over the bridge as you enter the park from the south. From here you can head to the park headquarters (a popular area for **elephants**) or north to Kimiramatonge Hill. This rocky area is a good place to view pairs of **klipspringers** and also **bush hyraxes**, which form large groups and can be seen sprawled on the rocks. **Tree hyraxes** also occur in the park, but they are nocturnal and most likely to be encountered around dusk. Another species to look for around rocky hills at dawn and dusk is the **striped hyena**, although it is less commonly seen than the larger and more social **spotted hyena**.

SAND RIVERS & BAOBABS The popular Ruaha River Drive takes in the Ruaha River, from where you can carry on along the Mwagusi River. In the dry season the Mwagusi is a sand river; water lies just beneath the surface where granite rocks prevent it from sinking

WILDLIFE HIGHLIGHTS

» Around 60 recorded species of large mammals, including giraffes, elephants, buffaloes and lions » Among the best chances of seeing hunting dogs in Tanzania » A wealth of antelopes, including elands, sables and roans; Ruaha is also one of the few places where greater and lesser kudu occur together » About 425 bird species and plenty of open habitat make Ruaha a great birding destination

ECOLOGICAL MEETING POINT

Ruaha is an ecological meeting point of south, west and east Africa. Here the *Acacia-Combretum* vegetation of northern Tanzania merges with the miombo *(Brachystegia)* woodland of southwestern Africa and some animals are at the edge of their range. It is the most southerly area that you can encounter Grant's gazelles and lesser kudus, but one of the most northerly inland areas you can see sable antelopes. Roan also reach their eastern limit around here and Lichtenstein's hartebeests are unlikely to be encountered east of here except in the Selous. Even the threatened pancake tortoise, which is endemic to East Africa, reaches its southern limit in Ruaha. The striped hyena, a species that once ranged from Britain to China and down through Africa, reaches its natural limit here in central Tanzania. Even the local zebras represent the meeting point of different areas – they are a cross between the subspecies of Mozambique and East Africa.

further. In parts the sandy riverbed is sparsely fringed by tall borassus palms, and some areas support large trees such as figs, tamarinds and acacias – good places to look for **vervet monkeys** and **yellow baboons** and for **lions** resting in the shade. **Elephants** dig for water in the riverbed and excavated holes may attract **antelopes** and other species. Travelling throughout this area you should encounter **giraffes**, **buffaloes** and **impalas**, and **lions** can usually be seen daily during the dry season.

Much of the area away from the river is studded with baobabs (leafless during the dry season). Baobabs are always worth close scrutiny because they provide hollows for many species, such as **hornbills**, **lovebirds**, **squirrels** and **parrots**. Ruaha supports eight of Tanzania's 10 hornbill species, including **von der Decken's hornbill** and the **pale-billed hornbill**, which is found mostly in neighbouring Malawi and Zambia. Tanzania's endemic **yellow-collared lovebird** has a stronghold in this area. The baobab branches are also a favourite site for **red-billed** and **white-headed buffalo-weavers'** nests. At dusk, baobabs provide an ideal perch for retiring **marabou storks**, which can be seen silhouetted against the sky. They are occasionally joined by **pink-backed pelicans**, which seem entirely out of place in this semiarid environment. Among the more uncommon birds at Ruaha, **Eleonora's falcon** is a migrant that turns up during October and November before the rains begin. The **yellow-necked spurfowl** reaches the southern edge of its range around Ruaha and is frequently seen in the park.

BURCHELL'S ZEBRAS, RUAHA NATIONAL PARK

TANZANIA

LOCATION 75km from Mikumi. Local transport or rented vehicle between Mikumi and the main park gate at Mang'ula. Entry is also possible from Iringa via entry posts at Msosa and Udekwa.

FACILITIES Numerous walking trails; all require guides hired from park headquarters.

ACCOMMODATION Several basic park-run camping grounds; bush camping along the longer trails; park resthouse; local guesthouse.

WILDLIFE RHYTHMS Migrant birds are present late September to mid-December; highland forest birds may come lower to escape the cold from late May to early August.

CONTACT Senior park warden (www.udzungwa .org).

UDZUNGWA MOUNTAINS NATIONAL PARK

Udzungwa is an offbeat hotspot for hikers and birders. At its heart is the largest of the 11 Eastern Arc mountain ranges, which rises up dramatically from the surrounding flats through a range of different habitats – lowland and submontane forest giving way to montane forest and finally peaking at around 2500m in short mountain grassland covered with ericas.

While Udzungwa has many large animals, they generally inhabit areas away from walking paths. Of the smaller antelopes you may see **duikers** or **sunis** through the forest understorey, but the creatures to get excited about here are the primates and birds: the isolation of the Eastern Arc Mountains has given rise to a large number of endemic species. Much of the park is still inaccessible, although there is an increasing number of trails, but you will see plenty of birds and smaller mammals by exploring the trails around the base near the park headquarters and main park entrance at Mang'ula, or by walking up to the nearby 170m-high Sanje Falls on the Sanje River.

By wandering around the lower paths you'll invariably see **vervet monkeys**, **banded mongooses** and perhaps be scolded from a branch by a **red-legged sun squirrel**. On the way up to Sanje Falls look out for **blue monkeys** in the canopy – troops frequently occur together with troops of **black-and-white colobus**. The special species on this route – one of Udzungwa's endemics – is the endangered **Iringa red colobus**; you should be able to find it without too much trouble. Another even more endangered primate endemic to Udzungwa – recent surveys suggest it has a population of less than 1500 – is the **Sanje crested mangabey**, aptly named for

WILDLIFE HIGHLIGHTS
» A wealth of Tanzanian and locally endemic animals, including three locally endemic primates (Iringa red colobus, Sanje crested mangabey and Matundu galago), birds, reptiles, amphibians, and many plants and invertebrates » Frequent sightings of vervet monkeys, black-and-white colobus and red-legged sun squirrels » Over 400 recorded bird species, including many restricted to the mountains of Tanzania or near-endemics found elsewhere only in areas such as Zimbabwe's Eastern Highlands » No roads, but numerous hiking trails, ranging from several hours in length to several days

ARK OF UNIQUE MOUNTAIN LIFE

Udzungwa's high number of unique species is due partially to the region's constant climate over millions of years. In its continuous carpet of forests, ranging from 250m to over 2500m in altitude, over 25% of its plant species are endemic. There are numerous similarities between these forests and those of Madagascar, West Africa, Zimbabwe's Eastern Highlands and the Usambara Mountains, suggesting that these regions may have been geographically linked 165 million years ago. It is surmised that they became isolated 'islands', with species once common to the linked region subsequently evolving separately. Usambara and Udzungwa, it is estimated, have been separated for five million years. Unfortunately, there is a downside to this high level of endemicity: disturbance on even a relatively small scale can have disastrous impacts on an entire species – for example, during the 1970s, habitat destruction through forest clearing and construction of the Tazara railway led to a decline in the numbers of Iringa red colobus.

its sagittal crest. However, these are typically found higher than the falls so you are unlikely to encounter them unless you hike higher up. Several species of bushbaby live at Udzungwa, including the endemic **Matundu galago**, as does the **grey-faced sengi**, a newly discovered species of elephant shrew.

If you camp overnight look out for the strictly nocturnal **giant pouched rat**. It is nearly 1m long (including tail), but will do nothing more treacherous than scout about for vegetable matter, which it stores in its cheek pouches to take back to its burrow. The background noises of the night may include some unfamiliar pinging – caused by the resident **epauletted fruit-bats** – and the loud screams of **eastern tree hyraxes**.

A WEALTH OF ENDEMICS Udzungwa attracts birdwatchers from far and wide who come to search for the many species that occur only in the Eastern Arc Mountains; the park is also one of the best places to see a variety of near-endemic and rare birds. Most are hard to see in the thick vegetation, but easy ones to locate on the falls walk are the large and noisy **Livingstone's turaco**, **trumpeter hornbill** and, above the falls, the **silvery-cheeked hornbill**. Those wishing to see more of Udzungwa's unique birds should take a specialised trip because you need to get off the beaten track (the **Udzungwa partridge**, only described in 1992, is restricted to one locality in an inaccessible part of the park). You might be lucky and spot the **rufous-winged sunbird** (another relatively recent discovery restricted to the Udzungwa Mountains) around or below Sanje Falls when it descends lower on the mountain in winter. The **Iringa akalat** typically lives above 1500m and the **dappled mountain robin** (one of Africa's rarest birds) lives above 1200m. Although **Swynnerton's robin** and **white-chested alethe** are not restricted to Udzungwa, this area is also one of the best in which to observe them. Armed with playback, **Kretschmer's longbill** can be called out from the viney tangles right at the park headquarters.

On top of all this, Udzungwa boasts a number of local **centipedes**, **butterflies** and even a unique snake, the **Udzungwa wolf snake**, a nonvenomous, 30cm black snake with a red nose. Researchers here and in other parts of the Eastern Arc Mountains continue to turn up new animals (including birds) and plant species.

TANZANIA

LOCATION 225km from Dar es Salaam via Chalinze; access can be difficult March to May.

FACILITIES Tree hide; village tours.

ACCOMMODATION Camping and basic park accommodation; two lodges and one community-linked camp.

WILDLIFE RHYTHMS Dry season from June to January is best; very hot November to February.

CONTACTS Saadani National Park headquarters (www .saadanipark.org).

SAADANI NATIONAL PARK

At 30km long and just 7km wide, Saadani is Tanzania's smallest park and one of its least known outside the country. It is also Tanzania's only park where you can stroll along the beach between wildlife-viewing activities.

In the dense coastal thickets and palms that fringe the beach, the day begins with the morning chorus – **tropical boubous**, **common bulbuls** and **white-browed coucals** all join in. An early walk along the beach will probably reveal antelope tracks, and you'll usually see **storks**, **sandpipers**, **fiddler crabs** and a few local fishermen. On foot (escorted walks are permitted) or from a vehicle you should readily find antelopes such as **reedbucks**, **common duikers** and **common waterbucks**, as well as **yellow baboons** and **warthogs**. The airstrip and the tracks south of the village are good open areas for **Masai giraffes**, **kongonis** (Coke's hartebeests), **plains zebras** and **wildebeests**. With luck you could also see **common elands** – often found on the flats near the saltworks. To the north a circuit of tracks passes waterholes and these are the areas to look for **buffaloes**. However, most **buffaloes** and **elephants** are concentrated along the Mligazi River and in the Madete Forest area. **Lions**, **elephants**, **Roosevelt's sables** and **greater kudus** all occur in the park but are only sporadically seen.

On drives or walks you'll see common grassland and woodland birds, but don't miss birding by boat on the Wami River. The river entrance is surrounded by mangroves and, further upstream, palms and riverine forest line the banks. In the river are a smattering of **hippos** and **crocodiles** and, in the trees, **blue monkeys** and **black-and-white colobus**. Perched along the water's edge are **kingfishers** – **pied**, **giant** and the diminutive but vivid **malachite kingfisher**. **Egrets**, **grey herons**, **hamerkops** and **whimbrels** feed along the banks and sand bars, and by scrutinising the riverside vegetation you may see a **green-backed heron**. An hour upstream is a sandbank that is nearly always feather-to-feather with a mass of **African open-billed** and **yellow-billed storks**.

WILDLIFE HIGHLIGHTS
» **Masai giraffes, yellow baboons, warthogs, wildebeests, kongonis and (with luck) elephants** » **Blue monkeys and black-and-white colobus in riverine areas** » **The chance to combine wildlife-watching with beach walks, excursions to green-turtle nesting sites and boat rides to see waterbirds, hippos and crocs**

OTHER SITES

GOMBE STREAM NATIONAL PARK

Gombe is famous for chimpanzees – the chimp study started here by Jane Goodall in 1960 is the world's longest ongoing study of a population of wild animals. There are about 100 chimps in the park and you can visit the chimp feeding station and walk along the trails in order to find them. Gombe also has about 3000 olive baboons, plus red colobus, red-tailed and blue monkeys and many birds. The easiest time to track the chimps is the dry season (June to September), although the park is open year-round.
20km north of Kigoma, gonapachimps@ yahoo.com

KATAVI NATIONAL PARK

The Katisunga floodplain is the heart of this wild, sparsely visited park (Tanzania's third largest). It's at its best during the height of the dry season (July through October), when masses of hippos, buffaloes and other animals make their way to the few remaining water sources. Access is either overland via Mbeya or Tabora or with twice-weekly scheduled flights from Arusha or Ruaha National Park. These continue on to Mahale Mountains National Park, making the two an optimal combination.
40km south of Mpanda, www.katavipark.org

LAKE NATRON

This Rift Valley lake is difficult to get to, but is the world's most important breeding area for lesser flamingos. The tricky thing is that they breed in the middle of the lake, which you can't see because of the mirages that the water creates. The slopes of nearby Ol Doinyo Lengai, an active volcano, offer a chance to see fringe-eared oryxes.
25km north of Ol Doinyo Lengai

MAFIA ISLAND MARINE PARK

Most of the southern and eastern part of the Mafia Archipelago is encompassed in this marine park, currently the Indian Ocean's largest protected marine area. In addition to fine corals and nearly 400 fish species, the park is notable for its unhuried diving, and its green and hawksbill turtle breeding grounds.
120km southeast of Dar es Salaam

MAHALE MOUNTAINS NATIONAL PARK

Mahale has been a centre of chimpanzee research since the 1960s. In addition to the chimps (around 700 or so), the park is home to elephants, buffaloes, roans, plains zebras and giraffes – rarely seen on the park's western slopes where chimpanzee tracking is focused – plus two mammal species which are classic West African: the giant forest squirrel and the brush-tailed porcupine. It is also home to six endemic subspecies of birds and is the only place in Tanzania that you'll find Stuhlmann's starling and the bamboo warbler.
130km south of Kigoma, www.mahalepark.org

MKOMAZI GAME RESERVE

This reserve – soon to be gazetted as a national park – is contiguous with Kenya's Tsavo National Park and shares its semiarid features and species (including gerenuks and the large numbers of dik-diks that characterise Tsavo). Mammal numbers are not high, but the birding is fantastic. Black rhinos and hunting dogs have been reintroduced to the reserve, although both are in enclosed areas not open to the general public. Walking is possible with an armed guide.
25km east of Same

TANZANIA

UGANDA

CAPITAL KAMPALA **AREA** 236,040 SQ KM **NATIONAL PARKS** 11 **MAMMAL SPECIES** 330

Uganda is Africa condensed. Here, the best of everything the continent has to offer is packed into one small but breathtaking destination. You'll find the highest concentration of primates in the world, including the magnificent mountain gorilla, one of the rarest animals on earth.

THE LAND With its borders marked by the highest mountain range and the largest lake on the continent, landlocked Uganda straddles the vast savanna of Kenya and Tanzania, and also the biologically rich rainforests of the Congo River basin. Diverse, abundant and easily accessible wildlife offers the best of everything from East and West Africa for the intrepid nature-lover: herds of large animals in Queen Elizabeth, Murchison Falls and remote, semiarid Kidepo Valley National Parks; gorilla and primate tracking in the western rainforests; and 1017 bird species, including gems such as shoebills and African green broadbills.

Pristine rainforests in the southwest support Uganda's greatest biodiversity, and the majority of visitors head straight for the famous mountain gorilla tracking at either Bwindi Impenetrable or Mgahinga Gorilla National Parks. Locking eyes with a massive, majestic gorilla after hours of trekking through dense foliage is one of life's most amazing experiences, but you'll need to invest in a gorilla trekking permit – these cost several hundred US dollars. Chimpanzee tracking at various locations is

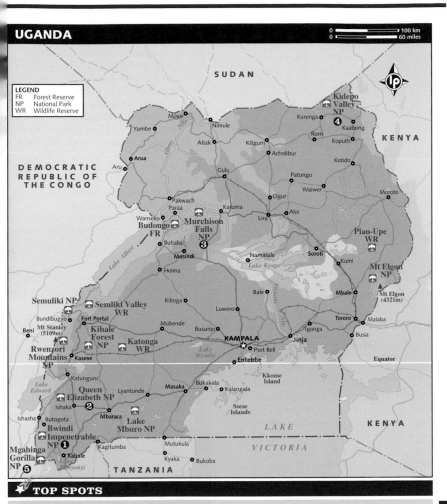

UGANDA

LEGEND
FR   Forest Reserve
NP   National Park
WR   Wildlife Reserve

★ TOP SPOTS

1. BWINDI IMPENETRABLE NATIONAL PARK (p146) Penetrate the impenetrable forest, one of the richest ecosystems in Africa and a natural sanctuary for half the world's remaining mountain gorillas.

2. QUEEN ELIZABETH NATIONAL PARK (p158) Hugging the Kazinga Channel, Queen Elizabeth is a magical mix of steamy rainforest,

open savanna and papyrus swampland, noted for its wallowing hippos and tree-climbing lions.

3. MURCHISON FALLS NATIONAL PARK (p154) Spot hippos, crocs and rare shoebill storks in what is probably the world's best water park.

4. KIDEPO VALLEY NATIONAL PARK (p165) Saffron-coloured

landscapes and open savanna host 80 mammal species, including lions and a healthy jackal population.

5. MGAHINGA GORILLA NATIONAL PARK (p166) On the black-sand slopes of the Virunga mountains, Uganda's smallest national park is a haven for golden monkeys, as well as gorillas.

UGANDA

a growing attraction, and nature aficionados often seek out the solitude and other delights of the Semuliki Valley, where the vast rainforests of the Zaïre River basin poke a toe over Uganda's western border. Cruises on the extensive wetlands surrounding many of Uganda's great lakes, on which you'll see hippos, sitatungas, crocodiles and many waterbirds, are a wildlife highlight.

The towering, often mist-shrouded Mountains of the Moon – the glacier-capped Rwenzoris – are a vast watershed on the high slopes of which grow East Africa's largest and most extensive stands of the so-called big-game plants (fleshy herbs that attain enormous size). Similar species are found in the caldera of Mt Elgon, a massive extinct volcano on the Kenyan border. From the slopes of the Rwenzoris you can see the source of the Nile, the world's longest river, which also offers some of the best white-water rafting in the world. All this and the national parks still see far fewer visitors than those in neighbouring Kenya and Tanzania.

Uganda is a great wildlife destination that is made even better by a strong reserve network, enlightened conservation policies and friendly, hospitable people. Wildlife is recovering well after decades of poaching and war, and community-based and ecotourism projects are seeing real results.

WHEN TO GO Uganda lies entirely within the tropics and experiences high rainfall in two wet seasons (April to May and October to November), except in the north, where it is dry for much of the year but wettest between April and October. Wildlife is easier to see during dry seasons when the animals congregate around water, but don't let the wet season put you off: it attracts fewer visitors and triggers breeding activity in some species, especially birds.

WILDLIFE HIGHLIGHTS
» **Catching your very first glimpse of Uganda's mountain gorillas after hours of trekking through dense foliage in Bwindi Impenetrable National Park** (p146)
» **The flash of colour as golden monkeys effortlessly swing through the forest at Mgahinga Gorilla National Park** (p166)
» **Cruising the Victoria Nile to Murchison Falls** (p154) **among super-sized splashing hippos** » **The magic of Kidepo Valley** (p165)**, a remote wilderness and refuge for jackals** » **The treetops of Ishasha** (p160)**, frequented not just by monkeys and birds but also by tree-climbing lions**

YOUNG WESTERN LOWLAND GORILLA WITH MOTHER

UGANDA

UGANDA ITINERARIES

1. MOUNTAIN GORILLAS Spotting some of the world's few remaining mountain gorillas in their natural habitat is likely to be one of the highlights of your life, not just your trip. Straight to **Bwindi Impenetrable National Park** (p146) it is then, for a once-

in-a-lifetime encounter with the beautiful, shaggy creatures. With luck you'll be able to track mountain gorillas the day after you arrive, but plan to spend at least two days and three nights here to avoid disappointment. The actual gorilla viewing must last no more than an hour for the sake of the gorillas. Head south to **Mgahinga Gorilla National Park** (p166), where you can do more gorilla trekking – this time on the black volcanic soil that marks the Rwandan border.

2. CREATURES GREAT & SMALL Starting in Kabale, travel to **Mgahinga Gorilla National Park** (p166), home to several gorilla families as well as a beautiful colony of

golden monkeys. You'll witness a colourful array of birdlife and might even get lucky with a big-cat sighting. Spend a night or two in one of the nearby lodges before hitting the road to watch gorillas in **Bwindi Impenetrable National Park** (p146), then continue north to **Queen Elizabeth National Park** (p158) and its tree-climbing lions. Wind up at **Rwenzori Mountains National Park** (p168), a mountain-flanked haven for everything from gentle forest creatures to spectacular birdlife.

3. WHITE-WATER THRILLS From Kampala, drive to **Murchison Falls National Park** (p154) via Masindi. Cut by the mighty Victoria Nile, Murchison is one of Uganda's

most diverse wildlife hotspots. Sadly, elephant numbers have dwindled but you'll come across primates, fabulous waterbirds and hippos frolicking in warm river water. From here, it's easy to arrange a white-water rafting trip at Jinga. Alternatively, if you have time to play with (at least a week), head north to the remote, savanna-coated **Kidepo Valley National Park** (p165) on the Sudanese border.

UGANDA

KAMPALA

The roof of every large building in downtown Kampala seems to have a **marabou stork** perched on it like a lone watchman perusing the street below. The storks do most of their foraging in dumps and drains further afield, returning to their nests in large trees along Nile Ave outside the Sheraton Hotel. The gardens of this hotel are actually a great spot for wandering – you'll see a few birds, including **sunbirds, eastern grey plantain-eaters** chuckling like chimps, and thoroughly urbanised **pied crows** that have been known to make nests from strands of wire. The chortlings of the ubiquitous **common bulbul** are among the first calls in the morning and often continue well after the flocks of **cattle egrets** have crossed the evening sky to roost. Groves of trees near the tourist board office are dripping with **epauletted fruit-bats**.

Apart from bats, mammals are scarce in Kampala, but troops of **black-and-white colobus** and **vervet monkeys** are resident in the excellent Entebbe Botanic Garden, half an hour south of the city on the shores of Lake Victoria. **Ross'** and **great blue turacos** and noisy **black-and-white-casqued hornbills** feed in fruiting trees in the garden's remnant patch of rainforest, and a variety of **sunbirds** and **weavers** fuss about in vegetation beside the lake, where there's a profusion of waterbirds: **hamerkops**, various **herons** and **storks**, and **cormorants** (the latter sitting with wings outstretched). **Pied kingfishers** are common and a good spot to see **giant kingfishers** is on the dock where the police launches berth. **Eastern grey plantain-eaters** are common in Entebbe Botanic Garden and **vultures** mope about on trees lining the streets.

Vervet and **de Brazza's monkeys** roam at the nearby Uganda Wildlife Education Centre (UWEC), where **hippos** can be seen from the lake's shores. UWEC grew out of the old Entebbe Zoo and now offers a chance to get close to **lions** and **leopards** as well as some of Uganda's more elusive animals, including **shoebills**, **patas monkeys**, **bushpigs** and **common duikers**.

Ngamba Island Chimpanzee Sanctuary is a rainforested island 23km south of Entebbe, purchased by an international conservation trust for the release and rehabilitation of **chimpanzees** orphaned or confiscated from the illegal wildlife trade. The project works with local communities, which will eventually supply food for both chimpanzees and visitors. A boat trip around the island is highly recommended –

chimps sometimes play at the water's edge.

Around 54km east of Kampala is Mabira Forest, the largest tropical forest in the Lake Victoria region. **Black-and-white colobus**, **grey-cheeked mangabeys** and **red-tailed monkeys** are all easily seen along an extensive trail network leading deep into the forest. **Monkeys** also loiter near the camping ground, watchful of **African crowned eagles** soaring over the canopy where **Boehm's bush** and **giant forest squirrels** rustle about, but are hard to track along limbs and branches (the raised viewing platform at the

visitors centre will help get you on their level). Another tree dweller, the **western tree hyrax**, is nocturnal and unmistakable with its screeching calls. Spotlighting could also locate an **African wood owl** or **African civet** near the camping ground, and **leopards** are seen occasionally. **Blue duikers** might be startled along trails, although they normally freeze to avoid detection. The 3km Grassland Trail offers good birdwatching through tall forest and glades where **African pied hornbills**, **great blue turacos** and a variety of **barbets** linger.

KAMPALA CITYSCAPE

UGANDA

UGANDA

BWINDI
IMPENETRABLE
NATIONAL
PARK

LOCATION 108km northwest of Kabale, 514km southwest of Kampala. Both roads meet at Butogota, 17km from the Buhoma entrance gate. 4WD is recommended during the rains.

FACILITIES Information board and permit information at Buhoma, though acquiring permits in Kampala is far simpler.

ACCOMMODATION Two upmarket tented camps, a lodge, backpacker accommodation and camping are available near the Buhoma entrance gate.

WILDLIFE RHYTHMS Gorillas are tracked year-round. Birdwatching is best September to March. June to July is good for butterflies emerging after heavy rains. Orchids flower September to October.

CONTACT Uganda Wildlife Authority (☎ 256-414-355000; www.uwa.or.ug /bwindi.html).

👁👁 WATCHING TIPS

Gorilla tracking groups leave early in the morning, after park rangers have identified gorilla movements from the previous day. Depending on the location of the gorillas, you can expect to trek for 30 minutes to a few hours. Once you've reached the site, relax and revel in the moment, keeping as quiet as possible so as not to disturb the animals.

BWINDI IMPENETRABLE NATIONAL PARK

Relative isolation, frequent rainfall and remarkable terrain have ensured the preservation of large tracts of pristine rainforest most famous for its **mountain gorillas**. The park has 90 mammal species, of which 11 are primates, including the zebra-coloured **black-and-white colobus**. Lowland and montane rainforest with a dense understorey of herbs, vines and shrubs (Bwindi means 'dark') support 150 to 250 **chimpanzees** and six other diurnal primates; 251 species of **butterfly** and 360 species of **bird** (23 of which are endemic to the Albertine Rift Valley and eight are not recorded anywhere else in East Africa).

Gorilla-tracking is the main attraction and it is estimated that half the world's population of **mountain gorillas** – just over 300 individuals – live in Bwindi. The population is currently stable but fragile, and has been come under threat from poaching and conflict in the past. Overall, Bwindi contains nine globally threatened species: **mountain gorilla, common chimpanzee, I'Hoest's monkey, African elephant, African green broadbill, Grauer's rush warbler, Chaplin's flycatcher, African giant swallowtail** and the **cream-banded swallowtail**.

There are four habituated gorilla groups that don't usually mind visitors – the Mubares (11 gorillas, one silverback), Habinyanjas (18 gorillas, one silverback), Rusheguras (10 gorillas, one silverback) and Nkuringos (19 gorillas). Two more groups are currently part of a 'mock tourism' scheme, which will eventually see them becoming habituated. Other wildlife, especially birds, is encountered on forest trails and the rainforest is magnificent: 200 species of tree, including some giant buttressed mahoganies, and 105 species of fern have been recorded; ferns and at least 80 species of orchid sprout from deep cushions of moss on branches and rocks; red balsam flowers and begonias splash

WILDLIFE HIGHLIGHTS
» **Half the world's remaining population of mountain gorillas** » **Around 360 species of bird, eight of which are not recorded anywhere else in East Africa** » **Nine endangered species, including African elephants and threatened bird species** » **Rare flora, including over 80 variations of orchid** » **More than 250 types of brightly coloured butterflies**

colour into the undergrowth; and myriads of fungi sprout from trunks and rotting logs. Streams and pools echo with the *tik-tik-tik* of **tree frogs** and the canopy constantly rustles with movement of **monkeys**, **squirrels** and **birds**. Patches of sunlight on the ground swirl as sunning butterflies take off, Highlights include the iridescent **blue mother-of-pearl butterfly**; various large, fast-flying **charaxes** (there are 35 species in Bwindi); and huge swallowtails, such as the endemic **cream-banded** and **East African giant swallowtails**.

WORTH THE CHARGE Mountain gorilla groups move daily, and may be as close as 15 minutes from the park entrance, or they may be several hours' trek away. Altitude is not a problem – the park headquarters (Buhoma) is at 1450m and the gorillas are usually seen between there and 2000m – but there can be a lot of steep hills and narrow valleys. Guides watch the gorillas daily and note where they nest for the night; leaving early next morning, a beeline is made for the nest sites and the tracking begins. Bwindi's gorillas sometimes feed close to the plantain and maize crops growing on the hillsides below the park and are not averse to raiding fields now and then (realising the importance these animals now play in the local economy, retribution is rare and farmers are usually compensated for their losses).

If you're lucky, tracking may involve negotiating only a few plantations. More often, however, it's a scramble up hillsides and along slippery paths. The latter, while tougher, is infinitely more rewarding, because nothing beats the feeling of catching a glimpse of black fur after hours of nothing but leaves. Once the previous night's nests are located the going can get difficult;

IDENTIFYING GORILLAS

Members of a gorilla group tend to resemble one another, especially along matrilineal lines. But just as the fingerprints of every human being are unique, no two gorillas have the same nose print – each has a distinctive pattern formed by the indentations above the nostrils and the shape of the nose itself. Once a group is contacted, researchers sketch the nose prints of more forthcoming individuals with the aid of binoculars. These simple line drawings are an invaluable aid to identifying group members, especially when they are similar in size, and are refined as habituation progresses until close-up photos are possible. Nose-print sketches are supplemented by written notes on variations in behaviour and vocalisations – traits that also help to identify individuals.

UGANDA

gorillas move easily through the dense undergrowth but people with bags and cameras generally don't. Trackers cut a path following the trail, 'talking' frequently to the gorillas as you get closer with soothing belches to let them know people are about and mean them no harm.

Despite his massive size, an adult male – the silverback – is usually placid and gentle unless he feels threatened. His reaction to danger – and sometimes strangers – is to scream loudly and charge at the intruder. A charge is very exciting, but it is important not to lose your nerve – stay still and look away from the silverback. He may come close but the chances of him actually harming you are very small.

SILVERBACKS ON SLIPPERY SLOPES
The Mubare group is composed of a silverback, five females and six juveniles or infants, with the silverback known as Ruhondeza – 'one who sleeps a lot'. His group can be very approachable. Ruhondeza is enormous and signs of his resting spots – flattened vegetation – are usually obvious. When glimpsed through a curtain of leaves his bulk is difficult to assess; the black fur of what appears to be his torso from a distance turns out to be his massive head and sagittal crest. In gorilla body language, staring can be taken as a threat, but Ruhondeza is a gentle giant and an approach to within 5m is usually possible. Despite their bulk, gorillas can easily move through the dense vegetation and pass with hardly a rustle. Your allotted hour of viewing time may involve more slipping and scrambling on the slopes to get into a good position to photograph various family members or to keep up with playful juveniles.

FEEDING PARTY ANIMALS
Excellent birdwatching is second to the great apes among Bwindi's attractions. First-timers can expect to see dozens of new species in a day and the secondary growth surrounding camps at Buhoma is a great place to start: **cinnamon-chested bee-eaters** hawk from exposed perches and **black-and-white-casqued** and **white-thighed hornbills** flap noisily across the canopy; **black-faced rufous warblers** call stridently from the forest edge; **blue-headed coucals** bounce down the path near tall grass; and **sunbirds, African paradise flycatchers** and **finches** all dart among the undergrowth.

To get the most out of the forest, spend a day on the Waterfall Circuit or one of the park's other trails (one follows the Munyaga River below Buhoma) with one of the knowledgeable local guides. The variety of birds is almost overwhelming – feeding parties, known as bird waves, comprising many species and perhaps dozens of individuals, move through the foliage at all levels from ground and trunk to canopy. It's a visual scramble to find and identify the procession of **flycatchers, barbets, sunbirds, cuckoos, weavers, starlings** and **warblers. Fruit-eating pigeons,** such as **African green** and **eastern bronze-naped,** call from high perches but are well camouflaged and among the hardest birds to spot. **Squirrels** or **monkeys** attracted to fruiting trees also rustle about and add to the confusion. **Forest weavers** (several species) in bold black and yellow colouring feed next to **montane orioles,** and star attractions are **black-billed turacos** and the splendid **black bee-eater** – look for the latter high up where fallen trees have created clearings.

AFRICA'S MOST WANTED
Red-tailed monkeys crash through the foliage and **l'Hoest's monkeys** – common near the forest edge – often travel along the ground and might streak across your

path in a line. Up to six species of squirrel, including **Boehm's bush** and **Carruthers' mountain tree squirrels**, scamper through the canopy; Bwindi's largest, the **giant forest squirrel**, is partly nocturnal. **Bushpigs** are sometimes seen around Buhoma; less frequently seen forest mammals include **giant forest hogs** and antelopes such as **bushbucks** and **black-fronted** and **yellow-backed duikers**. **African civets** and **servaline** or **large-spotted genets** might be seen by spotlighting around Buhoma. Rarely seen predators include **African golden cats** – melanistic (black) individuals have been reported – and **side-striped jackals**. Other possibilities are nocturnal primates – **dwarf** and **Matschie's** (or needle-clawed) **galagos** have both been recorded.

To really winkle out Bwindi's bird gems, try to get to Ruhizha. This forest sector lies at a considerably cooler and wetter 2300m, where **l'Hoest's** and **blue monkeys** and **black-and-white colobus** occur, and spotlighting could reveal a **potto** and **dwarf** or **Matschie's galagos**. The 6km walk to the bamboo zone southeast along the road to Kabale is highly recommended for birdwatching: dense secondary vegetation is frequented by finches such as **Shelley's crimsonwing**, and the ground-loving **handsome francolin** is sometimes seen on the track catching early sun. **Peters'** and **yellow-backed duikers** might also be seen on tracks in the early morning. Bwindi's 20 to 30 **elephants** frequent an extensive stand of bamboo at Mubwindi Swamp near Ruhizha and for the avid birder a walk to the swamp is a must. This wetland is the number-one location for the **African green broadbill**, possibly the most elusive – and endangered – bird on the continent. The extensive reed beds are home to other localised species, such as **Carruthers' cisticola** and **Grauer's rush warbler**.

RED AND YELLOW BARBET ON A TERMITE MOUND

LOCATION Fort Portal lies 320km west of Kampala along a mostly sealed direct road, or an hour's drive from Kasese. Kanyanchu Visitors Centre, 35km from Fort Portal, is along a dirt road and can be reached by matatu.

FACILITIES Visitors centres (with binocular hire) and forest lookout towers at Kanyanchu and Bigodi. Self-guided walk (1km) at Kanyanchu Ecotourism Centre.

ACCOMMODATION Primate Lodge (former Kanyanchu Rest Camp), with a luxury tented camp and upmarket lodge; nearby camping and bandas at Kanyanchu; lodges in crater fields west of Kibale; budget lodges at Bigodi, the crater lakes and Fort Portal.

WILDLIFE RHYTHMS Chimps can be tracked year-round. Elephants move into the Kanyanchu area during the wet seasons (March to May and September to November), which are also the best times for birding.

CONTACT Uganda Wildlife Authority (☎ 256-414-355000; www.uwa.or.ug /kibale.html).

KIBALE FOREST NATIONAL PARK

Kibale is a rich slice of rainforest where several vegetation zones overlap. The main attraction is the high density of primates that inhabit the forest (in particular, a large community of **chimpanzees**), but birdlife is prolific and a nature trail has been developed at Bigodi Wetland (a nearby swamp). Around 250 tree species have been recorded in the park, all festooned with dense mats of moss on crooks and boughs. Massive fruiting figs attract birds, **chimps**, **monkeys** and other primates, bracket fungi cling to broad tree trunks, and orchids grow high up in the canopy. Permanent streams cut through the forest, and swamps fill low-lying areas; the northern and southern boundaries support stands of grassland and west of the park is a scenic field of volcanic craters.

The elusive **forest elephant**, smaller and hairier than its savanna relatives, moves seasonally into the developed part of the park, but is seldom seen – although sometimes heard. Antelopes such as **bushbucks** and three species of **duiker** are more commonly encountered, and two species of squirrel – **montane sun squirrel** and **giant forest squirrel** – scurry through the canopy. Several hundred **chimpanzees** live at Kibale and are the subject of long-term studies. The community at Kanyanchu has been habituated and primate walks (essentially chimpanzee tracking) are conducted daily; organised night walks from Kanyanchu search out nocturnal primates such as **galagos**.

BUTTRESS BONGOS Entering the forest you might come across **red-tailed monkeys** or **grey-cheeked mangabeys** at the edge, or **olive baboons** loitering on the ground – sometimes all three species may be seen together. **Bushpigs** also favour the forest edge and you'll probably see their rootings in the undergrowth; small, pellet-shaped dung indicates where **duikers** have been. Birds are hard to see in the gloom, but **eastern nicators**

WILDLIFE HIGHLIGHTS
» Thirteen primate species, including the endemic red colobus and endangered l'Hoest's monkey » Good chance of spotting habituated groups of chimps » The 335 recorded bird species include the endemic Prirogrine's ground thrush and owl species » Ground creatures include giant forest hogs, hippos and leopards » A plethora of hoofed mammals such as buffaloes and bushbucks

and **little greenbuls** complain stridently from the foliage.

Although at times they can be silent and difficult to locate, **chimps** are by far the noisiest of African primates. From the time they leave their nests in the early morning – which they often announce by drumming on a tree buttress – until settling again at night, the forest echoes with their hoots and screams. Tracking these drama queens is largely a matter of following their sounds, but chimps can move at a fair pace on all fours and by swinging from vine to trunk, shimmying up trees and jumping across clearings. Telltale signs of their progress include knuckle prints in the mud along the trails, abandoned nests, broken branches and discarded fruits and seeds. First glimpses are nearly always tantalising – the back of a head as a chimp lopes off through the undergrowth or seeing those huge, muscular arms propelling their owner along; sometimes the noise is deafening but the chimps remain hard to see. Despite their great size, immense strength and agility, chimps are wary of people; if your tracking is rewarded with prolonged views, it is a rare privilege.

RELAXING ON THE EVOLUTIONARY TREE Chimpanzees are engaging animals whose antics are deservedly famous. If you are lucky enough to locate a party that can sit still awhile, your hour will be memorable and highly entertaining. A big male – the Kibale chimps are large, healthy animals – hunkered down on a fallen trunk may be joined by a couple of subordinates who sift through his coat for salt particles and parasites. High above, the canopy rings with bird calls: the liquid whistling of the **black-headed oriole**, the metallic *tonk-tonk-tonk* of **yellow-rumped tinkerbirds**, the *it-will-rain* call of the **red-chested cuckoo** and the chortling of **Ross' turacos**.

The chimps settle down to feed, groom and relax. The sun picks out flecks of colour

OLIVE BABOON WITH BABY

in their fur and markings that make every chimp unique: individuals can be told apart by face colour – some are black and some pink, some have freckles or scars, and others are missing digits or even a hand. Researchers are trying to monitor and name each individual in the Kanyanchu community. Grooming over, the big male might swing his legs like a child at a

UGANDA

👁 WATCHING TIPS

A forest observation tower near Kanyanchu overlooks a clearing in which elephants are sometimes seen. The northern side of Bigodi Wetland is best for seeing Central African red colobus. Multicoloured butterflies and monkeys become more active as the forest warms up, reaching a crescendo in the late morning.

playground, stretch back with hands folded behind his head and doze off, or climb a tree and make a day nest for a siesta.

A RICH SWAMP COMMUNITY A nature trail has been developed at Bigodi Wetland a few kilometres southeast of Kanyanchu Ecotourism Centre. This is the best place in Kibale to look for **Central African red colobus**, although seven other primate species (including occasional **chimps**) visit the swamp, and Bigodi also offers very good birdwatching (140 species have been clocked up). This papyrus-choked wetland is ringed by a walking trail through farmland and dense stands of figs and palms. Arrange a guide at the Bigodi Visitors Centre and start as early in the morning as possible. **Great blue turacos** and **silvery-cheeked hornbills** fly between fruiting figs in the swamp and tall trees among the surrounding crops, stands of rank grass attract **mannikins** and other **finches**, and parties of **weavers** fly over to their feeding grounds. A lookout on the edge of Bigodi is a good place to search for some of the specialised papyrus birds, such as **papyrus gonoleks** – often heard but rarely seen – and **papyrus canaries**. **Bushbucks** and **sitatungas** live in the dense vegetation, and **Congo clawless otters** patrol the waterways; **marsh mongooses** might be seen at night. **Black-and-white colobus** are common at Bigodi and **olive baboons** raid surrounding crops.

NIGHT STALKERS What is seen while spotlighting along the main access road near Kanyanchu and on jungle trails during night walks is always a matter of chance, but four nocturnal **primates**, a variety of **owls** plus the possibility of predators such as **African palm civets**, **small-spotted genets** or even a **leopard** should be temptation enough to try. A **frog** chorus from streams and ditches

after sundown adds to the already strident insect calls. A **potto**, that slow-moving relative of the monkey, might be seen stalking insects hand-over-hand along branches. In contrast, **galagos** (**needle-clawed, dwarf** and **Thomas' galagos** live in Kibale Forest) leap about in the foliage with great agility. **Lord Derby's anomalures** glide between trees by extending the loose folds of skin between their front and rear legs. Owls include **Verreaux's eagles, African wood owls** and **red-chested owlets**; and **fiery-necked** and **pennant-winged nightjars** hawk insects around clearings in the forest at dusk.

COLOURFUL & DIVERSE FOREST BIRDS Birdwatching is superb at Kibale. **Black-necked** and **Vieillot's black weavers** construct nests around Kanyanchu, where **African pied wagtails** strut about on rooftops and open patches of ground and **grey parrots** fly over, their scarlet tails and silvery-grey plumages reflecting the sun. **Sunbirds** are attracted to flowering trees, and figs attract a profusion of **pigeons, hornbills, barbets** and **starlings**. Along the road to Fort Portal (the main entrance road) **crested guineafowl** scuttle across the road in the early morning, their heads adorned with a mop of black feathers; seed eaters such as **francolins, waxbills** and **mannikins** feed in the rank grasslands and clearings along the road; **pigeons** sun themselves in treetops and the dazzling **black bee-eater** watches for its favourite prey from exposed branches. Birds of prey might include an **African goshawk** gliding across a clearing or an **African crowned eagle** looking to snatch a monkey from the canopy for breakfast. Encounters with any or all of Kibale's primates, including **chimps**, are possible along the Fort Portal road. The trails around Kanyanchu are also worth exploring for forest birds, such as **thrushes, robins** and both **African and**

green-breasted pittas. Butterflies are abundant, especially on the forest edge, gliding through sunny clearings or settling on animal dung and urine. Among the 250 species recorded are many **charaxes** and **swallowtails**, the latter including the very elusive **giant swallowtail**, mimicked by the **mocker swallowtail**.

COMMUNITY-BASED ECOTOURISM

Local communities have traditionally harvested an array of native plant and animal foods, medicines and plant products from Kibale Forest. The forest is under even more pressure now from the 900 communities that surround it, but hunting and indiscriminate harvesting are no longer allowed in the forest. Instead, the national park assists communities by employing local people as rangers, guides and receptionists. In 1992 a community-based environmental organisation was formed – Kibale Association for Rural Environmental Development (KAFRED) – to promote social and economic development of local communities through the wise use of natural resources. KAFRED's main activity is ecotourism at Bigodi Wetland Sanctuary: locals are trained as wildlife guides and accompany visitors on walks; handicrafts are made from local plants and sold as souvenirs; and funds raised have paid for community facilities. Both the Bigodi Wetland Sanctuary and the Kanyanchu Ecotourism Centre now generate revenue and employ many local people.

OLIVE BABOONS

UGANDA

LOCATION 97km north of Masindi, 354km north of Kampala.

FACILITIES Information centre, basic and more upmarket eating options.

ACCOMMODATION Two upmarket lodges and a luxury tented camp, plus chalets run by Red Chilli. Camping is permitted in some regions.

WILDLIFE RHYTHMS Grass is shorter and wildlife easier to spot in dry seasons (January to February and June to July), when mammals concentrate near permanent water. Grazers establish territories on higher ground with the onset of the wet (March to May).

CONTACT Uganda Wildlife Authority (☎ 256-414-355000; www.uwa.or.ug /murchison.html).

UGANDA

👀 WATCHING TIPS

Take the first boat cruise in the morning to get the best light and sit on the left-hand side; if you miss shoebills on the cruise, scour the dense papyrus beds of the Victoria Nile delta area from the north bank. Leopards are sometimes seen in trees along the Pakuba Track and the road to Pakwach. Patas monkeys are most often seen in grassland south of the Victoria Track.

MURCHISON FALLS NATIONAL PARK

The mighty Victoria Nile spears this park (Uganda's biggest park), squeezing through a 7m-wide rocky cleft and dropping 43m over the western edge of the Albertine Rift Valley at Murchison Falls before continuing to Lake Albert at the park's western boundary. Large-animal viewing opportunities and birdwatching are excellent in rolling grassland, savanna and vast swamps along the Victoria Nile and in dense stands of papyrus where it empties into Lake Albert.

Murchison's once-famous wildlife herds are still recovering from the devastation of war: from an estimated 14,500 **elephants** 30 years ago there are now around 1000 left in the park. However, signs of recovery are apparent and numbers of large animals are slowly building up again: there are about 1000 **buffaloes**, 300 to 500 **Rothschild's giraffes**, and **antelopes** (including **Uganda kobs**, **Jackson's hartebeests**, **defassa waterbucks** and **oribis**) are more abundant and collectively number in the thousands.

LIFE FLOATING DOWN THE NILE A boat cruise to the foot of Murchison Falls is a must. Most of the park's 1000 or so **hippos** live downstream of the falls and line the shallows by the dozen, roaring, dozing, feeding and wallowing; females are usually seen with young in February and March. Hugging the bank for part of the way, the vessel passes **Nile crocodiles** basking on sandy shelves; newly hatched crocs are sometimes seen in March. **Elephants** and **buffaloes** venture down to the water's edge to soak or drink, and small parties of **warthogs** – wary because of the large crocs in this reach – join **defassa waterbucks** and **bushbucks** for a drink. About halfway along the cruise to the falls, a sheer sandbank holds colonies of **red-throated bee-eaters**

WILDLIFE HIGHLIGHTS
» **Spectacular Murchison Falls, where the world's longest river explodes violently through a narrow cleft in the Rift Valley escarpment to plunge into a frothing river inhabited by many species of fish** » **One of the densest hippo and croc populations in Africa, as well as a healthy number of Rothschild's giraffes and lions** » **Rabongo Forest is home to chimps and other forest dwellers** » **Primates are represented by chimpanzees, vervet, red-tailed and patas monkeys, olive baboons and black-and-white colobus**

(which nest between January and March) and **pied kingfishers**; the smaller, blue-and-orange **malachite kingfisher** perches on low vegetation, especially reeds.

As the cruise continues, look out for the usually dry Nyamsika River, which wildlife uses as a highway – **elephants**, **lions** and **spotted hyenas** are sometimes seen at its sandy mouth. Birdwatching can also be good here and the rare **Egyptian plover** has been recorded. Papyrus and water hyacinth–fringed islands upstream support (literally) **weavers** and waterbirds such as **jacanas**, **gallinules**, **herons**, **ducks** and **plovers**; **shoebills** are regularly seen on a large papyrus island about halfway to the falls. **Darters** nest on fallen trees and perch along the banks of the Victoria Nile, their wings held outstretched; **black crakes** scuttle among the vegetation, even clambering up into riverside branches; and **African fish eagles** – in rich mahogany and black, with white bellies – sit atop euphorbias and acacias, calling stridently. **Olive baboons** and **vervet monkeys** forage along the banks and in large trees near the falls.

Gulu, to the north of the national park, has long been in conflict with Joseph Kony's Ugandan rebel group, Lord's Resistance Army (LRA). At the time of publication the area was recovering but violence may still flair up occasionally. Check the local news before travelling north of the park.

TRACKING PRIMATES & BIRDS ON FOOT Animals encountered south of the Victoria Nile may include **defassa waterbucks** and **warthogs**, and birding is good: **Heuglin's francolins** feed along the tracks, and flocks of **northern carmine bee-eaters** are present seasonally. Walking trails from the top of Murchison Falls follow the southern bank of the river. **Red-tailed monkeys** live in the forest near the cliffs and **black-and-white colobus** sometimes sit

STALKING THE SHOEBILL

For anyone with a keen interest in birds, there is no more important bird to see in Uganda than the unique shoebill stork. Also known as the whale-head stork, this peculiar-looking bird has a gigantic, broad bill that aids it in catching prey in the water. Its favoured diet is the lungfish, but it also eats amphibians and small reptiles, including baby crocodiles (assuming mum and dad aren't around) and snakes. Shoebills are not all that common in Uganda. However, if you visit an area where they're found, there is a good chance of a sighting, as they hunt by waiting motionless around papyrus swamps and marshes. The best places to see the shoebill stork in Uganda include: the Nabajjuzzi swamp just out of Masaka on the way to Mbarara; the banks of the Victoria Nile River in Murchison Falls National Park; the shores of Lake Albert in Semliki Valley; and around Lake Kikorongo in Queen Elizabeth National Park. Should all else fail, try the Ugandan Wildlife Education Centre in Entebbe for a guaranteed sighting.

UGANDA

over the water high on branches. **Rock pratincoles** sitting on flat rocks – particularly at the top of the falls – periodically hawk for insects; thousands of **swallows** and **swifts** of several species also feed over the water and cliffs.

Thousands of **bats** roost just below the falls on the southern bank at the so-called Bat Cliffs, emerging at dusk to feed; birds of prey such as **bat hawks** and **falcons** wait for the feast, while **black kites** can usually be seen wheeling about at any time of day. Overhanging branches are also used by **giant kingfishers**, which patrol this reach of the river, and at night by **Pel's fishing owls**. These large, rare owls are sometimes seen roosting in large trees along a dry stream bed that enters the southern bank near the bottom of the falls. **Pennant-winged nightjars** pass through the park from November to February and may be seen around the Top of the Falls camping ground. A network of trails through Rabongo Forest, a stand of ironwood in Murchison's southeast, can also be explored on foot: **black-and-white colobus, red-tailed monkeys, olive baboons** and sometimes **chimpanzees** may be seen here, and **buffaloes** are common. Birds along the waterways include **shining-blue kingfishers**.

THE BEST OF MURCHISON The best wildlife viewing is by vehicle north of the Victoria Nile, where most of Murchison's **elephants, buffaloes** and **Uganda kobs** are found and sightings of **patas monkeys** are most frequent. Take at least an afternoon to explore the Queen's, Pakuba, Victoria Nile and Albert Nile Tracks through tall grassland and savanna woodland, and papyrus swamps at the river delta. The Nyamsika Cliffs – up to 30m high in places – are a good spot to scour grassland for large mammals (elephants can often be seen from here) and birds such as **bee-eaters**.

To the west, **oribis** are abundant among the grass and regenerating acacias, grazing among **Grant's gazelles** and **Jackson's hartebeests**; the remaining tall acacias are browsed by **Rothschild's giraffes**. **Buffaloes** feed in marshy hollows and there is a large resident herd here; if you can't spot them, the telltale calls of the **piapiac** (its call sounds like its name is spelled) should give them away – flocks of this long-tailed member of the crow family often associate with buffaloes and elephants. Swathes of grassland are dotted with sausage trees, their bloated fruits swaying in the breeze coming off Lake Albert, and hundreds of distinctive borassus palms make lookouts for **martial**

'ALWAYS LOOK ON THE BRIGHT SIDE...'

Although it seems like sacrilege to say it, the mass slaughter of wildlife that took place in Murchison Falls National Park in the 1970s and '80s may have been a good thing from an ecological viewpoint. Before Idi Amin's regime the park was carrying many more animals (particularly elephants, with herds of more than 500 commonly seen) than it could sustain. The elephants alone, which numbered more than 14,000, chomped their way through 1.4 million tonnes of vegetation each year! Add to this the 26,000 buffaloes, plus herds of hartebeest, kobs and hippos, and the scale of the ecological problem can be appreciated. The wiping out of most of the large animals has given the environment here a breather and, while it was obviously a major disaster from a wildlife point of view, it means that the park's ecology is now in excellent condition and the animals are on the increase. Despite this new beginning, however, the concentrations of game are relatively low, so don't come to Murchison expecting a scene from the Serengeti.

eagles and **red-necked falcons. Abyssinian ground hornbills** – the female has a blue face – waddle along looking for small animals and **secretary birds** hunt snakes. **Lions** hunt **antelopes** and **warthogs** in the rolling grassland, and **Uganda kobs** graze on flatter ground nearer the rivers: bucks spar on the short turf among bushes and termite mounds. **Butterflies** sip moisture in huge swirling flocks, and birdlife is abundant and varied: several sorts of **bee-eaters**, including **swallow-tailed** and **little bee-eaters**, perch on low shrubs and wait for insects. Look out also for **Denham's bustards**, large, powerful birds with a reddish hind neck – Murchison is one of the best places to see these beautiful birds.

JUMBO LANDSCAPE GARDENERS

Appealing though they are, **elephants** can be incredibly destructive animals and Murchison's once-huge herds helped shape the park's modern landscape. An average elephant eats around 100 tonnes of grass, herbage and other vegetation annually, and in the 1960s Murchison's 14,500 elephants consumed an awful lot of greenery. Grasses are favoured during wet seasons, but during dry seasons elephants strip leaves, branches and insulating bark from trees and bushes. By pushing down trees and trampling saplings and small bushes their activity opens up woodland and thickets, allowing grasses to invade and making them vulnerable to fire. Hemmed in by the protection of the national park, the damage was compounded and eventually Murchison's dense woodland became grassland.

HERD OF BUFFALO WITH CATTLE EGRETS AND NILE RIVER BEHIND

UGANDA

UGANDA

QUEEN ELIZABETH NATIONAL PARK

LOCATION 64km south of Kasese, 482km west of Kampala; 4WD recommended in the park.

FACILITIES Museum, education interpretation centre and bird observatory at Mweya.

ACCOMMODATION At Mweya there is an upmarket lodge plus camping and budget accommodation. There is also a camp at Ishasha, while another upmarket lodge hugs the crater lake in Maramagambo Forest.

WILDLIFE RHYTHMS Hippos are usually seen with young from March to May. Uganda kobs seek higher ground during wet seasons. African skimmers are present on their southward migration from December to May. Numbers of northward-migrating birds peak February to March.

CONTACT Uganda Wildlife Authority (☎ 256-414-355000; www.uwa.or.ug /queen.html).

👁👁 WATCHING TIPS

Sit on the left-hand side of the boat on the Kazinga Channel cruise for best viewing and photo opportunities as it heads towards Lake Edward. Warthogs can be approached on foot around Mweya, where banded mongooses charge through camp daily. Shoebills are sometimes seen in seasonal swamps along the Northern Circuit in the Ishasha sector.

QUEEN ELIZABETH NATIONAL PARK

Much of QE, as it's known, sits between Lakes Edward and George, which are connected by the broad, 34km-long Kazinga Channel. The tracks traversing the north side of the Kazinga Channel provide good wildlife-viewing in savanna, with thickets dominated by candelabra euphorbias: **defassa waterbucks** and **buffaloes** are common, **hippos** wallow in shady mud baths and **warthogs** can only be described as abundant. Dense thickets in this area are also probably the best place to look for **leopards**. **Spotted hyenas** and **large-spotted genets** scavenge around Mweya some nights. **Giant forest hogs** are easy to see along the Royal Circuit, especially late in the day when they venture out of thickets; **banded mongooses** (some the subject of long-term studies) charge about looking for prey; and the solitary **ichneumon** (or Egyptian) **mongoose** also frequents this area.

Further north, herds of **elephants** and **buffaloes** graze on the grassy slopes of volcanic craters that rise towards the distant Rwenzori Mountains. Crisscrossing tracks of **buffaloes** and **antelopes** show where they descend to the shores of saline lakes in the craters; several lakes, such as Nyamunuka, are frequented by **flamingos**, **storks** and other **waterbirds**. The so-called Baboon Cliff, the lip of another crater, is a good spot to watch **birds of prey**. Across the main Kampala–Kasese road, **defassa waterbucks** and **lions** are common along the Kasenyi Track, and most of QE's 31,000 **Uganda kobs** are concentrated in this area. Extensive leks (combat arenas where kob bucks stake out territories and challenge all comers for the right to mate with females) near the track are recognisable by dozens of bucks resting and sparring where the grass is worn short like a playing field. Chattering groups of **grey-backed fiscals** glide in single file from branches; flocks of **Abdim's** and **woolly-necked storks**

WILDLIFE HIGHLIGHTS
» Ninety-five mammal species with a West African spin include good numbers of buffaloes, hippos and Uganda kobs » An amazing 612 species of bird, including prominent pied kingfishers » Warthogs and banded mongooses are abundant and this is the best place in Uganda for giant forest hogs » Hippos in the Kazinga Channel » The tree-climbing lions of Ishasha

LIONS ON THE KOB BREEDING GROUND, ISHASHA SECTOR IN QUEEN ELIZABETH NATIONAL PARK

feed in marshes; and **Temminck's coursers** run low and fast when approached. **Flappet larks** high in the sky are difficult to see but the drumming of their wings is easily heard.

HIPPO CHANNEL Water is a feature of QE: **hippos** are abundant, **waterbirds** are a highlight and **sitatungas** live in papyrus swamps fringing the lakes. A boat trip along the Kazinga Channel is a must. In the late afternoon **elephants**, **buffaloes** and **Uganda kobs** drink from the shores; some of the buffaloes might also be lolling about in the water. **Hippos** are always present (most of QE's hippos are concentrated in this stretch) and late in the day there's a chance some will be grazing up on the bank. **Nile crocodiles**, including some large specimens, bask on the banks, although they usually slide into the water when approached (crocodiles have only recently colonised this part of the park).

The Kazinga cruise offers great birdwatching: mixed flocks of waterbirds –

ibises, **spoonbills** and **storks** – feed in the reed beds and shallows; **ducks** and **geese** loaf on exposed mud; the nests of **Jackson's golden-backed weavers** dangle from tall papyrus stems; and dozens of **pied kingfishers** perch on overhanging branches. Birders should watch carefully in the reed beds for skulking **warblers** and the **papyrus gonolek** (though you'd probably need a tape recorder to entice it from hiding).

Near the entrance to Lake Edward a sand bar on the south bank is a favourite hang-out of **buffaloes**, **hippos** and hundreds more waterbirds: **African skimmers** – black and white ternlike birds with a scarlet and yellow bill; **great cormorants** vibrating their throats to keep cool; and **pelicans** of both species loafing about among **terns** and **grey-headed gulls**. Hundreds of **swallows** and **martins** hawk for insects a few feet above the water.

TREE-CLIMBING LIONS The largest herds of **buffaloes** and **elephants**, some of which have probably moved across from the Democratic Republic

UGANDA

of the Congo to escape poaching, and nearly all the **topis** are concentrated in the southern, Ishasha sector of the park. This area of savanna woodland has QE's highest diversity of mammals and excellent birdwatching. **Defassa waterbucks**, **bushbucks** and **warthogs** are abundant, and **giant forest hogs** might be seen in wooded areas. **Hippos** and **crocs** live in the Ishasha River, where gallery forest supports **black-and-white colobus**. A community of **chimpanzees** lives along the forested Ishasha River Gorge, but they are not habituated and the area is only accessible on foot. Large numbers of **Uganda kobs** attract Ishasha's most famous inhabitants: tree-climbing **lions**, best seen by driving along the northern circuit. **Kingfishers** patrol the Ishasha River and birdwatchers should also work the forest and adjacent savanna; **bee-eaters** and **snake-eagles** use exposed snags as lookouts for their respective prey.

VALLEY OF THE APES Dropping dramatically from the surrounding plain, Kyambura Gorge marks the boundary of the Kyambura Game Reserve, which adjoins the eastern side of QE. About 1km across at its widest point, the 100m-deep gorge is drained by the Kyambura River (with resident **hippos**) and the permanent water supports a dense forest that is home to **chimpanzees**, **red-tailed monkeys**, **black-and-white colobus** and **giant forest hogs**. Looking over the canopy from the gorge rim, it is sometimes possible to see chimps in the trees – and even occasionally venturing out to fruiting figs on the adjoining savanna (the sight of chimps standing semi-erect to see above the grass is one you'll never forget). Chimp tracking is conducted daily along the gorge, which

is also excellent for birdwatching: prize sightings could include **black bee-eaters** or **blue-breasted kingfishers**. Crater lakes east of the gorge support large numbers of **flamingos** of both species plus other waterbirds. The Maramagambo Forest is a large area of dense forest stretching up the escarpment of the Albertine Rift Valley into QE's southern reaches. Walking trails from the ranger station at Nyamasingiri lead through the forest, where **l'Hoest's**, **blue** and **red-tailed monkeys** may be seen as well as **chimps**, and forest birding is excellent. Five species of forest **duiker** and numerous **squirrels** live in Maramagambo, and **fruit-bats** emerge at dusk from a cave near the camping ground. Be sensible and exercise caution when visiting areas frequented by fruit-bats; there has been at least one recent case of a tourist contracting Ebola from contact with guano.

QUEEN ELIZABETH BIRD OBSERVATORY With a bird list topping 600 species it is not surprising that a permanent ornithological research facility should be set up, and in 1997 the Queen Elizabeth National Park Bird Observatory (QENPBO) was established to study resident and migratory birds in the park. Bird observatories are centres for the collation of data and the coordination of field observations. At QENPBO staff are particularly interested in a long-term study of annual bird migration along the Albertine Rift Valley, but they're also involved in raising local awareness, training guides and developing facilities such as hides, walkways and trails in the park. QENPBO is located next to the Institute of Ecology Hostel at Mweya and visitors are welcome to drop in.

UGANDA

WARTHOG, QUEEN ELIZABETH NATIONAL PARK

UGANDA

LAKE MBURO NATIONAL PARK

LOCATION 121km southwest of Masaka, 230km southwest of Kampala; 4WD recommended in park.

FACILITIES Visitors centre and boat hire at Rwonyo Rest Camp. Rest camp at Lake Mburo can prepare meals with notice.

ACCOMMODATION Four camps, three public camping grounds. Two luxury options at Mbara.

WILDLIFE RHYTHMS Mammals stay close to lakes and permanent swamps during dry seasons. Impalas, zebras and waterbucks disperse during the wet and elands move into southern and eastern parts of the park.

CONTACT Uganda Wildlife Authority (☎ 256-414-355000; www.uwa.or.ug /mburo.html).

LAKE MBURO NATIONAL PARK

Herds of **common elands, buffaloes** and **plains zebras** graze among **impalas** (Lake Mburo is the only Ugandan park where impalas survive), **topis, bohor reedbucks** and **defassa waterbucks** in rolling grassland; acacia woodland pierced by candelabra euphorbias harbours **warthogs** and small antelopes such as **common duikers, oribis** and **bushbucks**. The savanna is broken by koppies, but permanent and seasonal wetlands are the park's main focus for wildlife-watching: a vast swamp fed by the Ruizi River links Lake Mburo and five other lakes, and seasonal rains fill adjoining temporary swamps. During the rainy seasons temporary swamps in low-lying areas attract birds such as **rufous-bellied herons** (not recorded in any other Ugandan park) and the rare **saddle-billed stork**.

Bushpigs scavenge around Rwonyo Rest Camp at night and spotlighting along the tracks nearby could reveal opportunists like **side-striped jackals, African civets** or **large-spotted genets**, as well as **lesser galagos** in trees. Other lucky sightings could include **spotted hyenas** or **leopards**. Birders should listen for **fiery-necked nightjars** and owls such as **African scops owls** and **Verreaux's eagles** in this area. **Olive baboons** are found in savanna near Rubanga Forest (west of Lake Mburo) and a ranger can guide you on foot through the forest itself for birdwatching.

The Zebra and Ruroko Tracks pass through some of the best areas to search for wildlife. Clouds of yellow, white and blue **butterflies** of a half-dozen species drink at puddles in wheel ruts; an assortment of **doves** – chiefly **red-eyed, laughing** and **ring-necked** – explode into flight from just under the wheels; and **crested francolins** make suicidal dashes across the track. **Oribis** emerge from cool grassy hollows in the late afternoon to graze in pairs among bigger animals –

WILDLIFE HIGHLIGHTS
» **Five varied lakes attract Nile crocs and hungry hippos**
» **Zebras, impalas, buffaloes, common elands, defassa waterbucks, topis and warthogs roam the plains**
» **Waterbirds feature among 315 recorded bird species; among the prize sightings are shoebills (rare) and African finfoots** » **Predators include leopards and spotted hyenas**
» **Primates are represented by olive baboons and vervet monkeys**

UGANDA

👀 WATCHING TIPS

Hire a canoe to comb the papyrus swamps for sitatungas. Arrange with the warden to do a night drive along one of the tracks. Lake Mburo itself is one of the best places to see the rare shoebill stork; scan the water from breaks in the dense lakeside vegetation in the early morning.

HAMERKOP

approach too closely and they usually whistle an alarm before bounding off with a peculiar rocking-horse gait (better seen than described).

Waist-high termite mounds (like red-earth milestones next to the track) are used by **red-necked spurfowl** as lookouts and by male **topis** watching for predators, although Mburo's lions were killed off long ago by local farmers. **Plains zebras** mingle with **impalas** and **topis** – and with Ankole cattle grazing illegally in the park. **Common elands**, although abundant, prefer the shelter of wooded hillsides, and **klipspringers** stake out their territories on high koppies. The twisted, pale trunks of boscia trees make nest shelters for **barbets** and **hornbills**, including the **red-faced barbet** – the Kigambira Loop is the best place in Uganda to see this localised species.

Healthy populations of **hippos** and **crocodiles** inhabit the wetlands – both can usually be seen from camping grounds on Lake Mburo's shores (watch for **buffaloes** in adjacent woodland) – and three species of otter (**African**, **Congo clawless** and **African spot-necked**) patrol the lakes and swamps, but waterbirds are the most abundant inhabitants. The evocative call of the **African fish eagle** carries through morning mist – pairs nest in tall trees where **darters** and **long-tailed cormorants** loaf

with wings outstretched. **Hamerkops** and **water thick-knees** feed along the shore; **pied** and **malachite kingfishers** dive for tilapia and tadpoles; **pelicans** – usually **pink-backed** but occasionally **great white** as well – dip for fish further out, and a variety of **herons** ranges from the skulking **green-backed** to the **goliath** – the biggest of all – spearing fish in deeper water. A dense papyrus swamp choking the northern end of Lake Mburo is ideal habitat for **sitatungas** and home to **papyrus yellow** and **white-winged warblers**, **papyrus canaries** and the **papyrus gonolek**. Prized bird sightings have included **shoebills** and **African finfoots**.

IN THE THICKET OF THINGS

The flat river valleys of Lake Mburo feature dense thickets of vegetation that can offer productive wildlife-viewing. They usually grow where euphorbia becomes established on an abandoned termite mound, where it escapes the worst of wet-season flooding or dry-season grass fires. Other plants, such as climbing vines, succulent aloes and sanseverias, soon sprout beside the euphorbia; and seeds from fruits carried by birds from other thickets take root and thrive in the shade of any emergent trees – such as olives – that also become established.

The mounds become thickets – dense islands of vegetation – which become sizeable enough to shelter large animals such as **buffaloes** and **bushbucks**. They also make a home for a host of smaller creatures (such as rodents, **mongooses**, reptiles and insects) and provide nest sites for birds such as **white-browed robin-chats**, **tropical boubous**, **white-browed coucals** and **black-headed gonoleks**. Thickets live and die over many years; eventually the old euphorbias and trees die off, letting in more light and grass, and fire sweeps through once again.

UGANDA

LOCATION Kaniyo Pabidi is 29km north, and Busingiro 40km west, of Masindi.

FACILITIES Information centres and walking trails. The Budongo Conservation Field Station, funded largely by Edinburgh Zoo in Scotland, was set up to help protect the chimpanzee population but does not allow visitors.

ACCOMMODATION Camping grounds and other rural accommodation at Busingiro and Kaniyo Pabidi; hotels in Masindi.

WILDLIFE RHYTHMS Bird breeding and activity is highest during rains (February to April).

CONTACT Uganda Wildlife Authority (☎ 256-414-355000; www.uwa.or.ug).

BUDONGO FOREST RESERVE

Tracking **chimpanzees** in East Africa's largest remaining stand of ironwood forest is the main attraction at Budongo. Parts of the forest have been logged, but biodiversity remains high. Savanna woodland abuts Budongo to the north, and **elephants, defassa waterbucks, Uganda kobs** and **buffaloes** might be seen from the road into Murchison Falls National Park. Staff at the Budongo Conservation Field Station (www .budongo.org) say much of the land around Budongo Forest is under cultivation with houses, villages, schools and markets. Snares are set to catch duikers, which can cause serious injuries to the chimpanzees.

Walks along the Royal Mile offer what is probably Uganda's best forest birding. **Chocolate-backed, blue-breasted** and **African pygmy kingfishers** are particularly common; **greenbuls, sunbirds** and **apalises** keep birders looking into canopy flocks; fruiting trees attract a variety of **hornbills, barbets** and **starlings**; and **crested guineafowl** and **Nahan's francolins** are sometimes seen crossing the road.

Trails around Busingiro are also productive: both **African** and **green-breasted pittas** occur (green-breasted pittas breed in Budongo from April to May – listen for their bell-like whistling); various **illadopses** are common in undergrowth; and swifts such as **Sabine's** and **Cassin's spinetails** soar over forest clearings. Mammal encounters could include **chequered elephant shrews**, and spotlighting could yield **pottos, tree pangolins, hammer bats** or any of five **owl** species.

The network of forest trails at Kaniyo Pabidi Ecotourism Site is good for sighting **chimps** and **black-and-white colobus**, and birding includes **blue-throated rollers, tambourine doves, black-billed turacos** and **black-and-white-casqued hornbills**, and **forest francolins** and **crested guineafowl** in undergrowth. **Olive baboons** and **Abyssinian ground hornbills** feed along the road to Murchison Falls in the early morning.

WILDLIFE HIGHLIGHTS
» **Largest group of chimps in Uganda; frequent encounters with three habituated groups** » **Black-and-white colobus and red-tailed and blue monkeys are common; spotting a chequered elephant shrew is also a possibility** » **First-class forest birding, with 350 species recorded; feathered highlights include francolins, pittas, spinetails, nine species of kingfisher, 11 of barbet, plus forest starlings and hornbills**

👀 WATCHING TIPS

Kaniyo Pabidi is the only known site in Uganda where Puvel's illadopsis can be seen.

KIDEPO VALLEY NATIONAL PARK

Herds of **elephants** are common in the Narus Valley, as well as **buffaloes**, and smaller numbers of **common elands, plains zebras, cheetahs** and **Rothschild's giraffes** are easily seen in the shallow valley and around Apoka Rest Camp. Antelopes include **Jackson's hartebeest, defassa waterbucks** and **bohor reedbucks; oribis** and both **Kirk's** and **Günther's dik-diks** shelter in dense thickets on stony ridges; and **olive baboons** and **patas** and **vervet monkeys** forage over the savanna. **Bright's gazelles** have recently been seen near Moru Apol and rumours of **black rhinos** persist around Mt Zulia. The predator list includes **Nile crocodiles** in the Narus River; **lions, leopards, spotted hyenas** and **bat-eared foxes; caracals** stalk **striped ground squirrels** and ground birds; and **hunting dogs** have been reported near Mt Lomej. A ruined lodge on a ridge at Katurum makes a good vantage point from which to scan for animals during dry seasons, when the Narus is the source of the park's only permanent water. Spotlighting near Apoka could reveal **Senegal galagos, side-striped jackals** or a **white-tailed mongoose**, and **elephants, buffaloes** and sometimes **lions** are nocturnal visitors to a nearby waterhole.

Birdwatching is sensational: **piapiacs** and **oxpeckers** hang around grazing herds; **secretary birds** and good numbers of **Somali ostriches** strut among **Abyssinian ground hornbills, helmeted guineafowl** and five species of bustard, including **Denham's bustard. Abyssinian rollers, yellow-billed shrikes, Clapperton's francolins** and **black coucals** live in grassland around Apoka; and **fox kestrels, white-shouldered cliff chats** and various **swifts** frequent the cliffs at Katurum. Kigelia woodland along the Narus attracts **northern carmine bee-eaters, rollers** and **rose-ringed parakeets**, and the Kidepo Valley offers exceptional dry-country birding, with **pygmy falcons, white-bellied go-away birds** and **little green bee-eaters** (the latter at the southern limit of their distribution).

Note that at the time of publication, Kidepo Valley National Park was open but the situation in neighbouring Sudan can be volatile, so check news broadcasts or call the Uganda Wildlife Authority before travelling.

LOCATION 840km north of Kampala (4WD essential); access by chartered aircraft is recommended due to the potential dangers of passing through rebel-run villages when travelling overland.

FACILITIES Information board.

ACCOMMODATION Park-owned (book through Uganda Wildlife Authority). Frugal options include camping and hostels; fancier beds are at Apoka Rest Camp.

WILDLIFE RHYTHMS Mammals and waterbirds concentrate near pools in the Narus River during dry seasons.

CONTACT Uganda Wildlife Authority (☎ 256-414-355000; www.uwa.or.ug /kidepo.html).

WILDLIFE HIGHLIGHTS

» **Arid hotspot with zebras, oribis and elephants**
» **Uganda's only park with wild cheetahs** » **Exceptionally good for birdwatchers (475 species)** » **Somali ostriches and little green bee-eaters**

🐾 WATCHING TIPS

Stone partridges inhabit a rocky outcrop at the Imilliny ranger station. Karamoja apalis (an endemic warbler) occurs on the Kanatorok Plains north of Kidepo River. Avoid the Link Road between Hluhluwe and Umfolozi in the early mornings and late afternoons: it's the main thoroughfare for staff vehicles heading to work at the lodges and the traffic tends to frighten off animals.

UGANDA

LOCATION 14km south of Kisoro (4WD necessary), 510km southwest of Kampala.

FACILITIES Information board and scenic viewing platform. Rangers give free birdwatching tours along the edge of the park (5pm to 6pm most days; book ahead).

ACCOMMODATION Bandas and camping grounds at the park gate; good number of hotels in Kisoro.

WILDLIFE RHYTHMS Mountain gorillas usually present March to May and September to December. Alpine birds may move to lower slopes during wet seasons.

CONTACT Uganda Wildlife Authority (☎ 256-414-355000; www.uwa.or.ug /kgahinga.html).

UGANDA

MGAHINGA GORILLA NATIONAL PARK

Tracking **mountain gorillas** that live on the volcanic slopes is the main attraction, but other primates that can be seen are **golden monkeys** (a localised form of the blue monkey) and **black-and-white colobus. Elephants, buffaloes** and **giant forest hogs** also inhabit the densely forested slopes, and **black-fronted duikers** and **bushbucks** live in Mt Gahinga's swampy crater. Traces of nocturnal hunters like **African civets, servaline genets** and **spotted hyenas** may be seen on the lower trails. Other predators – rare in the park – include **leopards, side-striped jackals, servals** and **African golden cats.**

GORILLA POSITIONING SYSTEMS About 50 **mountain gorillas** in five groups inhabit the park; a group of nine called the Nyakagezi – the group includes two silverbacks, three adult females, two juveniles and two infants – is tracked daily and its position recorded with a GPS (global positioning system). Gorilla-tracking is generally less physically demanding than at Bwindi Impenetrable National Park, but Mgahinga's gorillas are international travellers that wander seasonally into neighbouring Rwanda and the Democratic Republic of the Congo. Mt Sabinyo supports stands of bamboo and wild celery, much favoured by gorillas, and an encounter with a solitary male is possible; **golden monkeys** are often seen here.

The once-cultivated slopes leading to the foot of Mts Muhavura, Gahinga and Sabinyo support abundant birdlife: **common stonechats** flit among the boulders, **augur buzzards** perch on branches, and **regal, bronze** and **malachite sunbirds** dip into the flowering spikes of red-hot pokers. Crossing fast-flowing streams you enter thick bamboo and moss-festooned forest about 1km above the park entrance, where **golden monkeys** and forest squirrels – **Boehm's bush, Carruthers' mountain tree** and **montane sun squirrels** – may be seen; **buffaloes** are also common. The localised **Rwenzori turaco** inhabits dense forest and **scarlet-tufted malachite sunbirds** sometimes feed alongside other **sunbirds** on lower slopes.

WILDLIFE HIGHLIGHTS
» **Mountain gorillas head the bill** » **Forests support golden monkeys and black-and-white colobus** » **Forest elephants, buffaloes and giant hogs** » **Good spot for viewing localised birds (115 species recorded)**

UGANDA

MT ELGON NATIONAL PARK

Most of the mountain's **elephants** have disappeared. **Bushbucks** and **buffaloes** live deep in forest and are generally seen far from the intensively cultivated lower slopes. Apart from rodents and shrews, primates are the most common mammals. **Olive baboons** can be found in the forest above the park's boundary, where **blue monkeys** and **black-and-white colobus** are also encountered. The mountain's swamps are frequented by **defassa waterbucks**, **sitatungas** and **de Brazza's monkeys** and you could startle a **bushpig** or a **common duiker** along one of the trails. Predators include **spotted hyenas** and **leopards** but they're rarely encountered. The three marked trails radiating from the Forest Exploration Centre offer good birdwatching, while **tree hyraxes** and **red-legged sun squirrels** also live in the canopy. A checklist of over 300 birds includes many species not seen anywhere else in the country. **Swallows** wing over valleys where **tacazze** and **golden-winged sunbirds** stand out among several other bird species competing for nectar. Figs attract various **pigeons** and **starlings**, **Hartlaub's** and **Ross' turacos** and **crowned**, **African grey** and **black-and-white-casqued hornbills**; **cinnamon-chested bee-eaters** hawk from perches; and tail-bobbing **mountain wagtails** flit along streams.

Elgon is a 4321m-high extinct volcano which, in prehistoric times, was taller than Kilimanjaro today. Stunted heath and moorland grow above 3000m and are accessible only by hiking overnight. Up here grow the so-called 'big game' plants – such as lobelias and groundsels – that can reach to 6m in height and are most profuse in Mt Elgon's vast caldera. There are few mammals, but **Chanler's mountain reedbucks** are sometimes seen. Most outstanding of the birds of prey is the **lammergeier**, but other raptors include **Verreaux's eagles** and **mountain buzzards**. **Scarce** and **alpine swifts** range widely after insects, and **moorland francolins** feed among grass tussocks. Other attractions include ancient cave paintings close to the trailhead at Budadiri, and labyrinthine caves and hot springs close to the crater.

LOCATION 78km from Mbale to the Forestry Exploration Centre (FEC); three to four hours from Kampala along a good sealed road. The trailhead at Budadiri, 20km from Mbale, is accessible by matatu.

FACILITIES Guides and marked trails from FEC.

ACCOMMODATION Upmarket lodge at Sipi Falls; midrange hotels in Mbale; budget lodging at Sipi Falls, Mbale and Budadiri; within the park, camping on mountain trails.

WILDLIFE RHYTHMS High-altitude birds may move lower down slopes during wet seasons; the drier months (June to August, December to March) are best for hiking.

CONTACT Uganda Wildlife Authority (☎ 256-414-355000; www.uwa.or.ug /elgon.html).

UGANDA

WILDLIFE HIGHLIGHTS
» **Mammals include olive baboons, black-and-white colobus and blue monkeys – all common in tall forest areas of the park** » **Rock hyraxes at higher altitudes** » **Defassa waterbucks and bushbucks are the most common antelopes**

👀 WATCHING TIPS

The Sasa and Piswa Trails above 3000m give the best chance of seeing lammergeiers.

LOCATION On the Democratic Republic of the Congo border, 25km from Kasese; Nyakalengija trailhead is located off the Fort Portal road, 22km from Kasese. Transport can be arranged in Kasese.

FACILITIES Walking trails. The seven-days loop is a tough but rewarding hike taking in all vegetation zones bar the glacial peaks. Shorter hikes can be arranged. Serious peak climbing for seasoned climbers.

ACCOMMODATION Hostel and camp site at the trailhead, basic hiking huts along the loop trail; nearby Kasese has a midrange hotel, several budget lodgings and a camp site; hotels in Fort Portal.

WILDLIFE RHYTHMS Alpine birds move lower down slopes during wet seasons (March to May and August to November). Dry seasons (December to February and June to August) are best for hiking and climbing.

CONTACT Uganda Wildlife Authority (☎ 256-414-355000; www.uwa.or.ug /rwenzori.html).

RWENZORI MOUNTAINS NATIONAL PARK

The 120km-long Rwenzori mountain range has long been dubbed the Mountains of the Moon. Peaking at 5109m, it is also Africa's highest range, exceeded in altitude only by the single entities of Mts Kenya and Kilimanjaro.

Blue monkeys and a race of **black-and-white colobus** are common along the trail through the Mubuku Valley; **l'Hoest's monkeys** are less so and **chimpanzees** are usually only heard. **Black-fronted duikers, bushpigs, giant forest hogs** and **bushbucks** may be startled if you walk along the trail.

Excellent forest birdwatching features the conspicuous **regal** and **purple-breasted sunbirds**, skulking **handsome francolins, olive pigeons** and 'click-cawing' **Rwenzori turacos**. Spotlight for **southern tree hyraxes**, easily located by their nocturnal screeching, and for **Rwenzori otter shrews** feeding in mountain streams.

FORESTS OF BONSAI GONE MAD The endemic **Stuhlmann's double-collared sunbird** is common above 2500m. Between heavy showers, **black-fronted duikers** pick their way over soggy ground. Calls of **white-naped ravens** pierce the misty silence and, at dusk, endemic **Rwenzori nightjars** flit about the clearings.

Giant groundsels and lobelias become more common between 3000m and 3800m. **Scarlet-tufted malachite sunbirds** pick insects from the 7m-high, powder-blue flower spikes of Wollaston's lobelias. **Rwenzori red duikers** (which replace black-fronted duikers at these heights) live among the vegetation. The tarns themselves are frequented by **African black ducks**, and **swifts, mountain buzzards, Verreaux's eagles** and **lammergeiers** cruise at the greatest heights.

At the time of publication Rwenzori Mountains National Park was open but the situation in the Democratic Republic of Congo remains volatile, so check with the Uganda Wildlife Authority before venturing into the area.

WILDLIFE HIGHLIGHTS
» Luxuriant forest with abundant flowering plants and the biggest and most extensive stands of alpine big-game plants in East Africa » Mammals include tree hyraxes, blue monkeys, black-and-white colobus and black-fronted duikers and the endemic Rwenzori red duikers » Forest and alpine birds star among 195 species » Rwenzori turacos, handsome francolins and 20 species of sunbird

WATCHING TIPS

Nyabitaba Ridge is a good place to look for Rwenzori turacos.

UGANDA

SEMULIKI NATIONAL PARK

A slender finger of the vast Ituri Forest, stretching from the Zaïre River over the Ugandan border into Semuliki National Park, offers sensational lowland rainforest birdwatching with a West African flavour. Among the mammals there's a chance of encountering any of eight species of **primate**, or larger species such as **elephants, buffaloes, pygmy hippos** and **leopards**. Animal lists total 400 birds (including 12 **kingfishers**) and 53 mammals – a high percentage of both are found nowhere else in Uganda. Mammal enthusiasts could spotlight for West African nocturnal specialities such as **water chevrotains, Zenker's flying mice** and **Beecroft's flying squirrels**.

BIRDS RUNNING HOT & COLD Primates and birds are attracted to fruiting trees along the main road: you'll almost certainly see **black-and-white colobus** here. **Central African red colobus** are rare, but other possibilities include **grey-cheeked mangabeys** and **red-tailed, blue** and **de Brazza's monkeys. Olive baboons** and **vervet monkeys** prefer grassland adjoining the forest. Birding is excellent along the main road: fig trees attract **turacos** (including the spectacular **great blue** and **Ross' turacos**), **pigeons, starlings** and up to eight of the park's nine species of **hornbill**. The forest also shelters **bushpigs, white-bellied duikers** and **pygmy antelopes**, but you are more likely to see the tree-climbing **fire-footed rope** and **red-legged sun squirrels**.

A trail to the Kirumia River is excellent for birdwatching: outstanding attractions in forest and secondary growth include **rufous-sided broadbills** and **African piculets** (East Africa's smallest species of woodpecker).

Note that at the time of publication, Semuliki National Park was open but the situation in neighbouring Democratic Republic of the Congo remains volatile, so check with the Uganda Wildlife Authority before venturing into the area.

LOCATION 52km northwest of Fort Portal, 371km west of Kampala.

FACILITIES Observation tower and boardwalk to hot springs.

ACCOMMODATION Camping grounds at Sempaya and Ntandi; guesthouse in Bundibugyo; hotels and lodges in Fort Portal. There is an upmarket camp site being developed inside the park at Bumaga.

WILDLIFE RHYTHMS Bird courting and breeding is at its peak just after drier months (January to February). Migrant waders visit the hot springs from November to April.

CONTACT Uganda Wildlife Authority (☎ 256-414-355000; www.uwa.or.ug /semlikinat.html).

UGANDA

WILDLIFE HIGHLIGHTS

» Of eight primate species, black-and-white colobus are most commonly seen » Hippos inhabit rivers and sitatungas frequent swamps » Rainforest hides elephants, buffaloes and bushpigs » Peerless lowland rainforest birding – over 400 species – features nine hornbills (three found in no other Ugandan park) and Nkulengu rails

WATCHING TIPS

African open-billed storks roost in large trees en route to the 'female' hot springs.

LOCATION 30km from Fort Portal to park boundary, 60km to accommodation.

FACILITIES Guided walks and boat trips on Lake Albert can be arranged at the accommodation site.

ACCOMMODATION Good upmarket lodge inside the park (Semliki Safari Lodge) but no other accommodation.

WILDLIFE RHYTHMS Mammals gravitate to river valleys at height of the dry season (December to February). Huge flocks of Abdim's storks arrive October to November.

CONTACT Uganda Wildlife Authority (☎ 256-414-355000; www.uwa.or.ug).

SEMLIKI VALLEY WILDLIFE RESERVE

The floodplains of the Semliki and Wasa Rivers in the north and west are grazed by **Uganda kobs**, **defassa waterbucks** and **bohor reedbucks**, and thorn thickets shelter **oribis** and **bushbucks**. **Jackson's hartebeests** live among stands of borassus palms along the entrance road; **warthogs**, **olive baboons**, **banded mongooses** and **Abyssinian ground hornbills** also forage here, and **red-necked falcons** use the palms as a lookout from which to hunt abundant grassland birds. **Elephants** concentrate in woodland in the park's south, where they can be approached on foot with a guide.

HOOTING GALLERIES A community of about 40 **chimpanzees** has been habituated and can be tracked on trails through gallery forest along the Mugiri River. Large groups of up to 30 individuals gather at fruiting cynometra trees in January and February. Encounters in this forest might include **elephants** or **buffaloes** (the smaller forest races of both occur), **Harvey's duikers** or **bushpigs**, while **black-and-white colobus** and **blue** and **red-tailed monkeys** are observed. Birdwatching is highly productive; look for **blue-breasted kingfishers**, **crested guineafowl** or the vocal **leaflove**. An unhabituated community of **chimps** lives along the Wasa River.

A few **lions** survive in the reserve and other predators that might be seen include **leopards**, **servals**, **spotted hyenas** and **African golden cats**. Forest along the Wasa River shelters **buffaloes**, which also frequent adjoining marshes, and **giant forest hogs**. **Hippos** wallow in the margins of Lake Albert and the odd **Nile croc** basks on the bank. Boat cruises (organised by Semliki Safari Lodge) search for **shoebills** and other bird specialities including **red-throated bee-eaters** (breeding January to March) and **pied kingfishers** nesting in sandbanks, as well as **lesser** and **African jacanas** and **African pygmy-geese**. **Goliath herons**, **hamerkops** and **yellow-billed storks** are all normally seen.

WILDLIFE HIGHLIGHTS
» Habituated chimps are the big hitter and there are other primate species » Forest and savanna elephants and buffaloes » Hippos and Nile crocodiles in Lake Albert » Savanna mammals such as Uganda kobs, bohor reedbucks and Jackson's hartebeests, plus lions, spotted hyenas and leopards » Brilliant birding – 350 species recorded; shoebills and other waterbirds are a speciality

👀 WATCHING TIPS

Night safaris are most productive during dry seasons, when mammals emerge from their daytime shelters in riverside vegetation to forage.

UGANDA

OTHER SITES

BUGUNGU WILDLIFE RESERVE

Savanna woodland supporting black-and-white colobus and olive baboons abuts the southern boundary of Murchison Falls National Park and surrounds the Weiga Swamp (approximately halfway between Butiaba and Bulisa). Look for buffaloes, defassa waterbucks and bohor reedbucks.
40km north of Butiaba

KALINZU FOREST RESERVE

Relatively intact rainforest on the Albertine Rift Valley escarpment. Chimpanzee groups can be found, 11km of forest trails has been developed and trained guides lead walks to look for nocturnal primates and birds.
10 km west of Ishaka on the main Mbarara–Kasese highway

KATONGA WILDLIFE RESERVE

Uganda's newest reserve hugs the Katonga River. You'll find pretty good canoe safaris here, with sightings of many of the 40 mammal and 150 bird species. Katonga is one of the best places in East Africa to track the elusive sitatunga, a semi-aquatic swamp-dwelling antelope with webbed hooves.
200km west of Kampala

KIGEZI WILDLIFE RESERVE

This reserve is a buffer between Queen Elizabeth National Park's Ishasha sector, Maramagambo Forest and heavily populated areas to the south. Dense forest contiguous with Maramagambo supports unhabituated chimpanzees, black-and-white colobus and some Central African red colobus. Kigezi is a refuge for elephants that move east from the Rwindi Plain in the Democratic Republic of the Congo and south from Queen Elizabeth National Park at the start of the wet season.
130km west of Mbarara

LAKE BUNYONYI

Large freshwater lake supporting otters, sitatungas and waterbirds. Pied kingfishers, swallows and various weavers are abundant around open water near Kisoro, and the papyrus-choked outflow 41km south of Kisoro is particularly good for papyrus birds, grey crowned cranes and waterbirds.
10km west of Kabale

MPANGA FOREST

Tiny but intact tall rainforest and swamp community with 205 tree species, eight large mammal species, including red-tailed monkeys and bushpigs, and 78 butterfly species. Walking trails make an ideal introduction to Ugandan forest birding.
40km west of Kampala

PIAN-UPE WILDLIFE RESERVE

The most important game reserve in the Karamoja region. The greatest animal diversity is in the southeast, between Mt Kadam and Greek River, where herds of buffaloes and Jackson's hartebeests roam among elands, giraffes, plains zebras and roan antelopes. Other large animals include Grant's gazelles, bushbucks, Uganda kobs, topis, defassa waterbucks and warthogs.
350km northeast of Kampala

SSESE ISLANDS

Group of 84 mostly uninhabited islands in northern Lake Victoria. Well-forested Buggala supports black-and-white colobus and vervet monkeys. Bukasa also has resident monkeys; and various papyrus-fringed islands are good for otters, hippos, crocodiles, sitatungas and many waterbirds. Different-forms of the African paradise flycatcher are abundant on Buggala and Bukasa Islands.
45km south of Entebbe

UGANDA

RWANDA

CAPITAL KIGALI **AREA** 26,338 SQ KM **NATIONAL PARKS** 3 **MAMMAL SPECIES** 170

Look beyond Rwanda's tortured past and discover East Africa's up-and-coming wildlife destinations. Home to the descendants of the *Gorillas in the Mist*, the country is a veritable primate paradise that is once again back on the tourist map.

THE LAND Rwanda's 26,338 sq km of land is one of the most densely populated places on earth and almost every available piece of land – with the exception of the national parks – is under intense cultivation. Known as the Land of a Thousand Hills, most of the country is mountainous, which necessitates a good deal of terracing. The banded hillsides are similar to those in Nepal and Tibet or the High Atlas of Morocco, and are planted with everything from bananas and potatoes to coffee beans and tea crops.

As a result of its small land area, as well as the high demand for cultivatable land, Rwanda only has three national parks, though the country's varied topography and habitat support a biological richness well out of proportion to its size. Dormant, 4500m volcanoes in the northwest and montane forests on the shores of Lake Kivu slope to rolling savanna and swampy lowlands in the east, creating diverse regional climatic conditions and a highly variable annual rainfall. In total, there are 170 different species of mammals, more than 400 different types of butterflies and a mind-blowing 670 species of birds.

On the northern border, the slopes of the Virunga volcanoes support the planet's largest remaining population of eastern mountain gorillas – tracking these gentle animals is one of the greatest wildlife

RWANDA

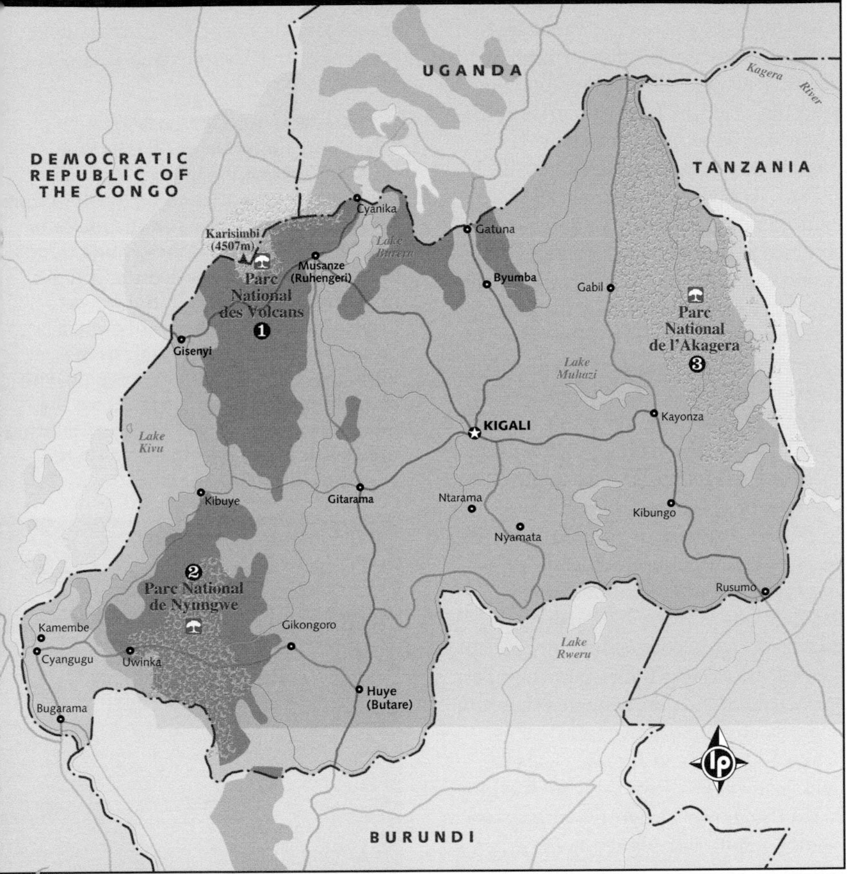

0 ⊏⊐ 50 km
0 ⊏⊐ 30 miles

UGANDA

Kagera River

DEMOCRATIC
REPUBLIC OF
THE CONGO

TANZANIA

Cyanika

Karisimbi
(4507m)

Gatuna

Lake
Burera

Musanze
(Ruhengeri)

Byumba

Gabil

Parc
National des Volcans ❶

Parc
National
de l'Akagera ❸

Gisenyi

Lake
Kivu

KIGALI

Lake
Muhazi

Kayonza

Kibuye

Gitarama

Ntarama

Nyamata

Kibungo

Parc National
de Nyungwe ❷

Rusumo

Kamembe

Cyangugu

Uwinka

Gikongoro

Lake
Rweru

Bugarama

Huye
(Butare)

BURUNDI

★ TOP SPOTS

1. PARC NATIONAL DES VOLCANS (p179) The high slopes of these towering volcanoes are the protected habitat of the critically endangered eastern mountain gorilla, the largest primate on the planet.

2. PARC NATIONAL DE NYUNGWE (p178) One of the oldest rainforests on the African continent, Nyungwe protects 13 species of primates, including habituated troops of colobus and roaming bands of chimpanzees.

3. PARC NATIONAL DE L'AKAGERA (p176) Rwanda's sprawling eastern plains foster large populations of grazers and offer a small but definitive slice of the classic East African safari experience.

experiences imaginable. Rwanda's eastern border is marked by the Akagera River and the country's largest reserve, Parc National de l'Akagera, where substantial herds of plains zebras, topis, impalas and buffaloes graze the savanna. The vast swamps of the Akagera basin support important populations of sitatungas and shoebills.

Parc National de Nyungwe rates the highest priority for conservation in continental Africa, combining high biodiversity and endemicity and significant threatened species. This montane forest is home to many species of primate, including large troops of black-and-white colobus, plus chimpanzees, Central African red colobus, owl-faced and l'Hoest's monkeys. Outstanding birdwatching includes the chance to look for rarities such as the Congo bay-owl, long thought to be extinct.

Thanks to more than a decade of relative peace and stability, environmental conservation is a high priority for the Rwandan government. Although past decades of civil strife and rampant poaching have taken a toll on wildlife, game numbers are increasing and stabilising, and there are hopes that traditional migration routes between Akagera and Tanzania will take hold again. Indeed, Rwanda is an emerging ecotourism hotspot where plastic bags are banned, responsible development is promoted and mountain gorillas are protected, cared for and revered by both young and old.

WHEN TO GO

Rwanda can be visited at any time of year – if you don't like getting wet, however, avoid the long rains of mid-March to mid-May. The dry season from mid-May to September is easier for tracking mountain gorillas, but the endless hills can look quite dry and barren, a contrast to the verdant greens of the wet season. Peak season for gorilla tracking is July and August, though travelling outside this time means it is easier

to arrange a permit. The average daytime temperature year-round is about 24°C with possible maximum of 30°C. In the higher mountains, the daytime range is as low as 10°C to 15°C.

WILDLIFE HIGHLIGHTS
» **Tracking mountain gorillas at high altitudes among the mighty Virunga volcanoes** (p179) » **Scanning herds of topis congregating at sunset on the plains of l'Akagera** (p176) » **Watching huge troops of habituated black-and-white colobus leap through the trees in Nyungwe** (p178) » **Catching a rare glimpses of golden monkeys, which are endemic to the Virungas** (p179) » **Trying to keep up with chimpanzees as they scurry across the forest floor of Nyungwe** (p178) » **Counting thousands of lumbering hippos in the swamplands of l'Akagera** (p176)

CHIMPANZEE

RWANDA ITINERARIES

1. PRIMATE TRACKING If you fancy the thought of traipsing up hillsides and ducking beneath limbs in search of mankind's closest ancestors, then spend some time in the capital

of Kigali arranging all of the necessary tracking permits. With these crucial documents in hand, head to **Parc National des Volcans** (p179), bunker down for a good night's rest and spend the morning hours searching for gorillas in the mist – or golden monkeys in the treetops. For a decidedly different experience, head to **Parc National de Nyungwe** (p178) and see if you're fit enough to keep up with agile chimps in their forestal domain.

2. ENDEMIC BIRDING If you want to tick off Rwanda's resident bird species, you're going to need time, determination and a good spotting scope. The gorillas in **Parc National de**

Volcans (p179) may steal the spotlight, but there are also endemic Rwenzori turacos as well as countless other fine-feathered friends in the hagenia forest. Rwanda's top birding destination is **Parc National de Nyungwe** (p178), which is home to around 275 different species of birds including the increasingly rare Congo bay-owl. **Parc National de l'Akagera** (p176) is home to vast marshlands that attract seasonal migrants from all across Africa.

3. SAFARI NJEMA For Rwanda's take on the East African safari experience, spend a few days exploring the varied landscapes of **Parc National de l'Akagera** (p176). While it grabs less of

the spotlight than more classic destinations, Akagera is much less trafficked, which means you'll share the road with more animals and fewer vehicles. The grassland is contiguous with eastern Tanzania and harbours much of the same wildlife, whereas the lakes and rivers support colonies of waterbirds and hippos and crocs galore.

PARC
NATIONAL
DE L'AKAGERA

RWANDA

LOCATION 75km east of Kigali.

FACILITIES An extensive network of 4WD tracks and trails.

ACCOMMODATION Camping grounds and the upmarket Akagera Game Lodge in the park.

WILDLIFE RHYTHMS Grazers seek high ground during wet seasons (October to November and March to early May), moving to valleys in driest times (January to February and late May to September). Crocs nest June to July.

CONTACT Rwandais du Tourisme et des Parcs Nationaux (Rwandan Tourism Board or ORTPN; ☎ 576514; www.rwandatourism.com).

PARC NATIONAL DE L'AKAGERA

The Kirara and Kamakaba plains support the largest concentrations of grazers and their predators: Kamakaba is a favoured haunt of **defassa waterbucks** and **bohor reedbucks**; **buffaloes** seek permanent water on the plains during the dry season; and **impalas**, **topis**, **plains zebras** and **oribis** graze further from water. **Lions** and **side-striped jackals** are seen stalking at the edges of these plains (**spotted hyenas** are primarily nocturnal); jackals and hyenas also loiter near the Akagera Game Lodge at night. Smaller animals include **warthogs**, **white-tailed** and **marsh mongooses**, **vultures**, **bateleurs** and other raptors, and **lilac-breasted rollers**.

PRIZES OF THE SWAMPS Hippos can be found along the track that skirts the network of lakes, swamps and channels on the park's eastern edge. Several **lion** prides hunt Akagera's population of **sitatungas** through the marshes between Lakes Kivumba, Hago and Mihindi. Sitatungas themselves are most active around sunrise.

Crocodiles can also be seen at Plage aux Hippos and basking at Lake Mihindi and Lake Kivumba. **Elephants** are rarely seen, but frequent the Rurama peninsula on Lake Ihema, and the Nyampiki peninsula between Lakes Hago and Kivumba. **African clawless otters** are sometimes seen during the day in sheltered bays, but the **African spot-necked otter** is mostly nocturnal. The **shoebill**, the prize bird of the swamps, is best sought along the channels connecting Lakes Mihindi, Hago and Gishanju, or Hago and Ngerenke.

ABUNDANT & DIVERSE WATERBIRDS The waterside habitats support **African fish eagles** and **malachite** and **pied kingfishers**; an assortment of **herons**, **ibises**, **storks** and **egrets**; **crakes** and **rails** skulking in the reeds; and, in open water, **cormorants**, **darters** and **pelicans**. Seasonal visitors include large flocks of **white-faced**

👀 WATCHING TIPS

African finfoots frequent the waters of Lake Ihema, especially where overhanging branches of ambatch trees trail in the water.

WILDLIFE HIGHLIGHTS
» Herds of topis, plains zebras, impalas, common elands, oribis and bohor reedbucks » Water-loving defassa waterbucks and sitatungas » Vegetated lakes with hippos, Nile crocodiles and waterbirds » Carnivores include lions, leopards, spotted hyenas and side-striped jackals » Specialities include roan antelopes, black rhinos and elephants

whistling ducks between December and February; **carmine bee-eaters** from April to September; and **white-winged terns** passing through on migration (November to December and March to April). Lakes Ihema and Mihindi are the places to look for papyrus endemics, such as the striking **papyrus gonolek**, vocal **white-winged warbler** and **Carruthers'** and **winding cisticolas**. **Water thick-knees** and **Gabon nightjars** nest on ground trampled by **hippos**, while **spur-winged geese** and **spur-winged plovers** live on the grassy edges. Colonies of **darters** and **cormorants** breeding on islands in Lakes Ihema and Mihindi are joined by nesting **herons**, **egrets** and occasionally **yellow-billed** or **African open-billed storks**.

LIFE ON THE HIGH GRASSLANDS The high, grassy plateaus of the Mubari are grazed by **oribis** and small numbers of **bohor reedbucks** during the wet seasons. At the end of the rainy seasons, **buffaloes** may be seen among the sausage trees on Mutumba, and herds of **topis** and **plains zebras** gather on the plateaus. **Defassa waterbucks**, **lions** and **side-**striped jackals also ascend the slopes of Mutumba, and small herds of **common elands** graze the plateaus of Mutumba, Mucucu and Kitabiri. This is the best part to look for the **roan antelope**. **Klipspringers** abound on Rurama and also on the slope leading to Lake Ihema from Akagera Game Lodge. The mountain savanna is rich in grassland birds: **striped pipits** on large rocky outcrops, **ring-necked** and **Shelley's francolins** (Rurama) and **Souza's shrike** (Rurama and Kitabiri).

Vervet monkeys and **olive baboons** are the only large mammals commonly seen in the woodland near Lake Kivumba, although parties of **banded** and **dwarf mongooses** might be seen on the track as you approach. **Leopards** also are quite common, but like the smaller predators – **servals**, **genets** and **African civets** – are most likely to be seen at night. This woodland is particularly good for birds: **red-faced**, **crested**, **black-collared** and **double-toothed barbets**; flocks of **white-crested helmet-shrikes**; and dry-season visitors including **African and Eurasian golden orioles**, **Madagascar lesser cuckoos** and **grey-headed kingfishers**.

AKAGERA – QUELLE TRAGEDIE!

Although Akagera once protected nearly 10% of the country, and was among the best reserves in Africa, in 1997 the park was reduced to a mere 1085 sq km due to increased population pressures brought on by returning refugees. In an effort to resettle landless Rwandans, the government slashed the park's borders by two-thirds, which virtually devastated this once pristine ecosystem. In response to substantial habitat loss, as well as depleting water supplies resulting from increased farming and ranching, Akagera's wildlife fled to Tanzania. Poachers, who carried out their illegal activities with virtual impunity, quickly decimated animal herds that chose to stay put.

For almost a decade, Akagera was something of a vegetarian safari, given that most animals on four legs were taking an extended holiday in neighbouring Tanzania. However, the Rwandan government has since implemented strict conservation laws aimed at protecting Akagera, which are certainly complementary to the government's increased push for tourism in Rwanda. Furthermore, the once decrepit Akagera Game Lodge has been rehabilitated by South African investors and now stands as testament to the future potential of this once-great safari park.

RWANDA

PARC NATIONAL DE NYUNGWE

LOCATION 210km southwest of Kigale, 90km west of Huye (Butare).

FACILITIES 50km of hiking trails.

ACCOMMODATION Camping grounds and basic ORTPN resthouse in the park.

WILDLIFE RHYTHMS Most birds and mammals breed in wet season (September to May).

CONTACT Rwandais du Tourisme et des Parcs Nationaux (Rwandan Tourism Board or (ORTPN; ☎ 576514; www.rwandatourism.com).

This is the region's single most important area of biodiversity and rated the highest priority for forest conservation in Africa. **Giant forest hogs, bushpigs** and **duikers** can be found along the many trails, and squirrels include **giant forest, montane sun** and **Boehm's bush squirrels. Tree hyraxes** can be heard after dark throughout the forest, and spotlighting along the sealed road between Butare and Cyangugu offers a chance of seeing mammals such as **side-striped jackals, civets, African palm civets** and **large-spotted** or **servaline genets. Marsh mongooses** and **Congo clawless otters** can also be seen on a guided walk to Kamiranzovu Marsh.

MONKEY FOREST Angolan colobus, Dent's monkeys (a local race of blue monkey) and **grey-cheeked mangabeys** are virtually guaranteed on walks from Uwinka Tourism Centre. Other monkey possibilities include **l'Hoest's** and **diademed monkeys. Olive baboons** and **vervet monkeys** loiter near Nyungwe's eastern edge, and **chimpanzee** habituation is under way. **Golden** and **owl-faced monkeys** live in the bamboo stands in the southeastern part of the reserve, and **eastern needle-clawed** and **greater galagos** are nocturnal prosimian attractions.

The dirt road leading to Rangiro (particularly on the far side of the pine plantation), and the Red, Blue and Kamiranzovu Trails are all highly recommended for birding. The sealed road through the park permits viewing at all levels of the forest: expect **mountain buzzards** and **cinnamon-chested bee-eaters** perched along here, plus numerous **sunbirds, wagtails** and flocks of **waxbills. Handsome francolins** are common along the trails, and **turacos** include **great blue** (Green Trail) and localised **Rwenzori turacos** (Grey Trail). Other large forest specialities are **African crowned eagles**, known to nest near Uwinka, and **crowned** and **black-and-white-casqued hornbills**. Spotlighting is also recommended – the **Congo bay-owl** was rediscovered at Nyungwe.

WATCHING TIPS

Grauer's and short-tailed warblers are sometimes seen in undergrowth along the Red Trail, between the Green Trail turn-off and the first waterfall.

WILDLIFE HIGHLIGHTS

» **Thirteen different types of primates, including roaming bands of chimpanzees** » **Habituated troops of Angolan colobus, Dent's monkeys and grey-cheeked mangabeys** » **Three duiker species on the rebound from poaching** » **More than 50 mammal species, including giant forest hogs and bushpigs** » **Twenty-four Albertine Rift Valley endemic birds, 13 sunbirds and four turacos**

PARC NATIONAL DES VOLCANS

PARC NATIONAL DES VOLCANS

RWANDA

Seven habituated groups of **mountain gorillas** inhabit Parc National des Volcans in groups numbering three to 35 individuals. The first half-hour of tracking normally involves a steep climb and fording mountain streams, during which **bushbucks** and **black-fronted duikers** are sometimes startled in the undergrowth. **Bushpigs**, **giant forest hogs** and **yellow-backed duikers** are encountered only rarely and large predators almost never – leopards have not been seen since 1979, although **African golden cats** and **spotted hyenas** probably still hang on in small numbers.

Mt Gahinga is almost entirely covered with thickets of bamboo – habitat favoured by **gorillas** and **golden monkeys**. **Duikers** climb as high as Mt Visoke's crater to feast on bamboo shoots. Look for **antelopes** taking a drink at Lake Ndezi or in Mt Muside's crater lake. Large stands of hagenia form a parkland with a rich undergrowth on the Mt Visoke saddle area – prime **gorilla** habitat. Hollows in the massive trunks shelter **tree hyraxes**, **genets**, **African common dormice**, **giant forest squirrels** and **forest pouched rats** – camp overnight and spotlight to have a chance of seeing some.

The park's bird attractions include the localised, canopy-dwelling **Rwenzori turaco**; **handsome francolins** foraging for seeds along trails; and **Chubb's cisticolas** duetting in undergrowth. The richest bird zone is the hagenia forest, in which may be seen **greater double-collared** and **regal sunbirds**, and three brilliant **waxbills: dusky, Shelley's crimsonwings** and **black-headed waxbills**. Birds of prey include typical forest bird-hunters such as **rufous-breasted sparrowhawks** and, in more open country, **mountain buzzards**. Birdlife drops off at higher altitudes, although stands of giant alpine herbs (especially on Mts Karisimbi and Visoke) are notable for **scarlet-tufted malachite sunbirds**. **Maccoa** and **African black ducks** feed in crater lakes, and **buff-spotted flufftails** skulk in the surrounding marshes.

WILDLIFE HIGHLIGHTS

» Habituated eastern mountain gorillas are the number-one attraction » Rare golden monkeys share the montane forest with their more famous primate brethren » Black-fronted duikers and bushbucks are slowly recovering from poaching » Hard to spot but present in small numbers are bushpigs, giant forest hogs and tree hyraxes » Avian specialities include the localised Rwenzori turaco, handsome francolins and scarlet-tufted malachite sunbirds

LOCATION 15km northwest of Musanze (Ruhengeri).

FACILITIES Walking trails ascend the peaks.

ACCOMMODATION Hotels and lodges covering all price ranges in Musanze (Ruhengeri).

WILDLIFE RHYTHMS Birds and large mammals move off the high peaks during the wet season (mid-March to mid-May), when freezing temperatures and hail are prevalent.

CONTACT Rwandais du Tourisme et des Parcs Nationaux (Rwandan Tourism Board or ORTPN; ☎ 576514; www.rwandatourism.com).

👀 WATCHING TIPS

Gorillas frequent the giant lobelia zone on Mt Visoke's high slopes during drier months, when the high mountain vegetation retains moisture from night mists. When you encounter the gorillas for the first time, it's important to establish your presence – don't make loud and spontaneous movements, remain calm and in control and keep an appropriate distance.

RWANDA

WILDLIFE GUIDE
FINDING, RECOGNISING & UNDERSTANDING WILDLIFE

EAST AFRICAN MAMMALS

EAST AFRICA'S MAMMALS come in an incredible assortment of sizes, shapes, colours and patterns. Those that range widely through the world's oceans, such as whales and dolphins, and the night-flying, insect-eating bats are well represented, but East Africa is most famous for its land mammals, including the world's heaviest (African elephant), tallest (giraffe) and swiftest (cheetah). Apart from boasting the greatest concentration of large land mammals on earth (the Serengeti migration), East Africa has one of the highest mammal diversities in Africa – around 400 of the continent's 1150 or so mammal species have been recorded here.

All animals classified as mammals, including humans, are united by several common features. From elephants to elephant shrews, all mammals are warm-blooded, ie they regulate body temperature through internal mechanisms, rather than relying on the sun's rays as reptiles do. Birds are the only other warm-blooded vertebrates, but only mammals have hair or fur; and whereas all birds lay eggs, all African mammals give birth to live young that have developed (gestated) for some weeks or months in the female's placenta or womb. Female mammals produce rich milk, dispensed through teats (modified sweat glands called mammae – hence the name

'mammals'), for the prolonged care of offspring until they become independent. Parental care is a trait most developed in mammals (and reaches its greatest extent in humans) but is such a labour-intensive process that only small numbers of offspring can be cared for at a time.

For a few species at the top of the food chain (such as lions and leopards) and some vegetarian giants (such as elephants and giraffes), adult life can be comparatively relaxed. But every mammal at some stage in its life is vulnerable to predation, and consequently most have at least two acute senses to warn of threatening danger: hearing – its corollary being the

PLAINS ZEBRA, SERENGETI NATIONAL PARK

MAMMALS

development of complex vocalisations; and smell, which is usually developed so far beyond our own abilities that we can only guess at the wealth of information it communicates. Many mammals, particularly predators, also have acute eyesight – and others make up for any visual deficiency with strategies such as having a tanklike physique (such as rhinos) or escaping underground (like naked mole-rats). Weapons of attack include some fine sets of teeth and claws, deadly speed and stealth; but despite the sometimes amazing weaponry carried by antelopes, their horns are generally used in the perpetual struggles among males for dominance.

All mammals exhibit basic behaviours such as eating, drinking (in most cases) and resting, which take up much time but, once fulfilled, give way to a new agenda of courtship and mating. More subtle behaviours include play, territorial marking and displacement, and life-or-death encounters involving defence, bluff and attack. Such interactions are highlights of mammal-watching, and there is no better place to begin than East Africa. A high percentage of mammals are easy to see because they are at least partially active during the day. The following pages introduce the key players of the East African wildlife experience, how they interact and why – with as little jargon as possible.

PRIMATES

ANCIENT RELATIVES East Africa is a hotspot for primate diversity, an evolutionary cauldron from which forest monkeys spread out onto the plains, and from which the great apes and we humans developed. From an ancestral, squirrel-like animal, evolutionary pressures modified a basic tree-climbing body pattern – long back, short neck and five-fingered hands and feet for clinging to trunks, branches and food – into today's diverse primate forms. Represented in East Africa are the 'primitive' bushbabies (or galagos), gorilla and chimpanzee, two species of baboon and 17 species of monkey (primate taxonomy is complex and opinions vary on these figures).

The basic monkey form (common examples among many are red-tailed and blue monkeys) speaks volumes on agility in a three-dimensional habitat: slender limbs make virtually any branch or foodstuff accessible and a long tail provides balance when jumping across gaps in the canopy. But there are many variations of this body plan, including the arboreal colobus monkeys, which have only a rudimentary thumb; others with even longer limbs that spend much time on the ground, such as patas and vervet monkeys; and the baboons, with their long, rather doglike snouts. All primates can sit and stand, and many can walk; all have furless digits, palms and soles; and, apart from bushbabies and the nocturnal owl-faced monkey, all primates are diurnal and mainly vegetarian, although insects and other small animals are eaten to varying degrees.

For primates, sight is the best-developed sense, and smell the least. All species have bifocal vision and expressive faces; many, such as de Brazza's monkey, have bold facial markings that visually reinforce communication. Touch is also highly

OLIVE BABOON

MAMMALS

developed, an opposable thumb in most species enabling them to grip a wide variety of food morsels and groom each other (something primates do a lot of). Grooming is an important part of social interaction and individuals vie for the privilege of grooming their superiors. A colobus that desires grooming stretches out in front of another, even slapping its face if the expected attention is not forthcoming; and should one desire to groom a recalcitrant, it grabs it by the forelock and smacks its head until it cooperates.

Just as squirrels offer clues to the physical origins of primates, primate behaviour (and misbehaviour) shows unequivocally the origins of our own behaviour. All diurnal primates are highly sociable, forming troops (monkeys) or communities (chimps) where both sexes vie for dominance in hierarchies of usually shifting alliances. Social structure varies among species, but usually involves a stable core of females, the female offspring of which stay in the group for life; males leave to join other groups as they mature. Nearly all species forage, sleep and range together, and fundamental to primate societies is the intense care lavished on infants. Playing as a youngster with other infants and juveniles (young chimps play tag and run round in circles till they're dizzy) builds lifelong friendships and social bonds and reinforces hierarchies. Jealousies and rivalries inevitably develop, but then there are sometimes elaborate rituals of appeasement: chimps offer a palm as supplication and bow to superiors; and dominants put a hand on the head of a lower-ranked member as reassurance.

POLITICAL ANIMALS

Status is big among chimps; males constantly vie to dominate a clan for the benefits it confers. For example, being the alpha male means you get to monopolise the sex scene, scoring most of the matings (a challenge since females are promiscuous). But other male chimps may gang up and try to oust the alpha male, so he relies on a network of buddies for help and rewards them with, for example, a share of the meat taken on hunts. Squabbling among lesser ranks goes on all the time, and all males must maintain allegiances and friendships throughout their lives. When two adults fight, a third party may bring the rivals together for a reconciliation, which inevitably involves mutual grooming. But (a very human twist, this) they also use deception to lure a rival to reconciliation, then punish him for past transgressions.

MAMMALS

⭐ HOTSPOTS

- Kibale Forest NP (p150) An extraordinary concentration of primates (13 species – including chimpanzee) in pristine rainforest.
- PN de Nyungwe (p178) Another centre of high diversity, including huge troops of colobus and chimpanzees.
- Kakamega Forest NR (p76) Kenya's monkey hotspot – a relict of West African rainforests.
- PN des Volcans (p179) Made famous by Dian Fossey, Rwanda's tract of equatorial forest harbours rare Eastern mountain gorillas.

GREATER GALAGO

RECOGNITION Vaguely catlike, with large, leathery ears and a bushy tail. Upperparts variable: silvery grey to brown; melanistic (black) forms occur. Belly fur paler.

HABITAT Dense vegetation in woodland, forest, savanna and cultivation, from sea level to 1800m.

BEHAVIOUR Exclusively nocturnal. Can rotate head through 180-degrees when searching for prey. Visits feeding stations at safari lodges. Rarely drinks. Very vocal during breeding season.

BREEDING A single young born in a leafy nest or hollow (births peak in September) is weaned at three months.

FEEDING Eats mainly fruit (especially figs), nectar, seeds, flowers and acacia sap; also insects and larvae, snails and occasionally eggs, nestlings and small reptiles.

VOICE Very vocal. Most common contact call is a babylike crying, repeated up to 100 times per hour.

SWAHILI Komba mkubwa.

PRIMITIVE PRIMATES Galagos (or bushbabies) are 'primitive' tree-dwelling primates (called prosimians), which closely resemble 60-million-year-old fossils, but barely resemble today's more familiar monkeys and apes (prosimians are only primitive in the sense that they evolved before modern primates). The 14 or so species found in East Africa range in size from squirrel galagos that could sit comfortably in a cupped hand, to the largest – cat-sized greater galagos (sometimes referred to as large-eared or thick-tailed greater galagos – both are apt descriptions).

All galagos are exclusively nocturnal, waking up at dusk and emerging from their nest after dark. They can see and accurately judge distances in what to humans is almost-total blackness: smaller species have enormous eyes, and can leap up to 7m propelled by long, powerful back legs. Greater galagos have comparatively small eyes and typically walk along branches like a monkey, only jumping to avoid danger or to cross from tree to tree. On the ground, where they are more vulnerable to leopards, greater galagos hop on their hind legs or walk on all fours, tail held erect like a cat's.

Galagos are widespread, and can live in high densities in suitable habitat. The territories of dominant males contain the home ranges of several females and their offspring. A combination of their loud, distinctive calls (some of the larger galagos' calls resemble a baby crying – hence the name 'bushbaby') and complicated scent-marking of treetop pathways helps individuals to avoid confrontation and direct competition for food. Galagos are readily seen by spotlighting (two or more species may coexist in some areas); most calling occurs in the first hour of night – a good time to look for them.

Galagos' slender digits cannot be moved independently – a feature that compromises grooming ability, so several lower teeth and the second toe of each hind foot are adapted for combing their woolly hair.

MAMMALS

★ HOTSPOTS

- Masai Mara NR (p62)
- Ngorongoro CA (p104)
- Kibale Forest NP (p150)

VERVET MONKEY

AGILE CLIMBERS If any species epitomises East African monkeys, it is the widespread, active and agile vervet. Equally at home in trees and on the ground, troops are commonly encountered foraging, playing and resting where grassland meets the trees, and can become pests at camping grounds and lodges. The savanna edge provides both rich pickings and shelter, but is shared with competing blue monkeys and baboons. Foraging some distance into the grassland, vervet troops move slowly, investigating holes and turning over dung and small rocks for insects, standing up straight or jumping above tall grass to get their bearings, and ducking back to the trees should danger threaten. Crossings between trees are made in single file with little straying – this is when they are most vulnerable.

A troop is mainly comprised of females and young, which work together to defend an ancestral home range, assisted by males that compete among themselves for mating rights and dominance. Female rank is inherited and rigorously enforced. Those of lower status showing obsequiousness to even juveniles of the dominant ranks (and risk chastisement if they don't). Ruling families get precedence at food, while subordinates vie to groom their social superiors and handle their infants, and to enlist their support in squabbles.

Males develop a startling blue or turquoise scrotum and scarlet penis as they mature – appendages that dominant individuals display prominently to neighbouring troops (behaviour that isn't tolerated from subordinates). Eventually young males are forced to transfer to other troops, usually during the mating season – a dangerous process that leaves them vulnerable to predation, rejection or even fatal aggression from the new troop. But the urge to migrate is compelling and to ameliorate the danger, brothers often transfer to other troops as a group, or join a troop to which an older brother already belongs.

RECOGNITION Small, slender monkey with long tail, grizzled greenish fur, black face and hands and bluish belly skin that shows through whitish belly fur.

HABITAT A variety of woodland and adjoining savanna, including miombo and yellow acacias along rivers.

BEHAVIOUR Variable daily routines. Troop size averages 11 to 25. Babies are born black and suckle both mother's teats simultaneously. All ages expressive – 60 visual gestures have been identified.

BREEDING Timing varies. A single infant is born after 165 days and clings to mother for four months.

FEEDING Mainly vegetarian, especially seeds, gum, leaves and flowers of acacias and figs and other fruits; grass and insects are eaten mainly during rains.

VOICE Complex – 36 distinct sounds have been identified, including alarm calls that identify different predators.

SWAHILI Tumbili.

MAMMALS

★ **HOTSPOTS**

- Samburu NR (p84)
- Amboseli NP (p74)
- Tarangire NP (p122)
- Queen Elizabeth NP (p158)

MAMMALS

OLIVE BABOON

SAVANNA PIONEERS Intelligent and opportunistic, baboons appear to be expanding their range in the face of human settlement. Large troops of up to 150 olive baboons fan out to forage across the savanna, some walking on all fours, others sitting upright when they find a morsel. Infants peep out from their mothers' breast fur, juveniles play and adults feed and watch for danger – large males standing out by their 'cape' of dense fur. A full-grown male olive baboon is a formidable animal that bares 5cm-long canine teeth in threat displays and defence; groups of males can kill a leopard, and their presence in troops enables baboons to forage in lion country. The approach of a predator usually sends baboons scurrying into the trees, from where they may shower it (or an unlucky person) with liquid excrement.

Baboon social lives are subtle and complex, but fun to watch: they stare into space or avert their gaze when being submissive; shrug their shoulders when startled; and females signal their readiness to mate by presenting hindquarters, showing their eyelids and smacking their lips. Females and young form the core of a group, and stay in it for life unless the troop subdivides. Female rank is family based, inherited and strict, and juveniles from high-ranking families can threaten adults from lower ranks. Long-term alliances develop between females as they grow, and each adult female has close ties with two or three males, with whom she forages and sleeps, normally mating with the most dominant. Males that associate with females become godfathers to their infants and will protect juveniles and mothers from bullying by other troop members. Sexually mature subadult males transfer to other troops or form loose associations (cabals) – despite her consorts, females in oestrus tends also to be receptive to dominant male 'strangers'. All members of a troop find the black infants irresistible: females vie to handle them and males hold them out to appease attacks from bullies.

RECOGNITION Large, greenish monkey with shortish, broken-looking tail and bare, doglike muzzle. Mature males have a thick, erectile mane and grey cheeks.

HABITAT Widespread in woodland, savanna, forest and cultivated land; has become an agricultural pest in some areas.

BEHAVIOUR The most terrestrial monkey. Diurnal with erratic daily patterns; sleeps in trees, rising late and retiring early, and foraging, resting or grooming at any time. Adult males band together to defend the troop.

BREEDING Year-round after six-month gestation. Soft black fur of newborn changes to adult colour at six months.

FEEDING Omnivorous; mainly grass and fruit but also seeds and animals as large as fawns. Digs for roots, shellfish and crocodile eggs.

VOICE A wide range of grunts and barks, becoming louder and more strident when threatened.

SWAHILI Nyani.

★ HOTSPOTS

- Nairobi NP (p82)
- Kibale Forest NP (p150)
- Masai Mara NR (p62)

BLACK-AND-WHITE COLOBUS

TREETOP ACROBATS Although they are common in montane forests, the first time you see a black-and-white colobus (also called a guereza or mantled colobus) will probably be when it leaps head first from one tree to another – tail and long hair flowing behind and front legs extended to break the fall – before catapulting off another branch and disappearing into the foliage. Bold, pied markings stand out among the greenery from a distance and, in the early morning, troops of colobus sun themselves high up in a favourite tree where they can be seen by neighbouring groups. Flaunting tails and cape-like frills, and occasionally shaking branches, demonstrates each troop's size and prowess; the dominant male in each periodically lets loose a chorus of raucous roars that echoes around the valleys as far as 2km away. It seems an excessive performance for a vegetarian primate, but the male has good reason to show his strength: bachelor troops are watching and waiting for an opportunity to displace him and take over his harem.

Black-and-white colobus can be seen in virtually any habitat with trees, typically sitting hunched up, stripping leaves off twigs. Close-to, their rather sad faces are topped by a 'matador's hat,' and when their long tail hangs down, the tufts look remarkably like beard moss that sways in the swirling mists of montane forests. The secret to the success of this very wide-ranging monkey is a complex digestive process that can break down old, hard and fibrous leaves; colobus may consume up to a third of their body weight daily, but must rest for long periods for digestion (during which bacterial fermentation, similar to that in ruminants, breaks down cellulose and detoxifies leaves and seeds). These consummate vegetarians don't visit the ground very often, taking water from hollows on branches, but when they do, they climb down trunks head first. The various species of red colobus are also leaf eaters, and where black-and-white and red colobus coexist, each eats different parts of the same plants.

RECOGNITION Entirely black with long, white frills on flanks, and white or white-tipped tail. White brow and 'beard' surrounds naked black face.

HABITAT Common and widespread in forests, from lowland rainforest and dry riverine forest to montane forest.

BEHAVIOUR Sociable in small territories. Family groups of six to 10. Only dominant male displays and mates, although the oldest female mostly leads the troop. Infants are born white, turning dark at three to four months.

BREEDING A single infant born during rains after a six-month gestation becomes independent at 10 months.

FEEDING Strictly vegetarian, eating a very wide variety of leaves, including old and fibrous ones, but also unripe fruit and seeds.

VOICE Males roar loudly as a territorial proclamation, especially at dawn and dusk.

SWAHILI Mbega mweupe or Kuluzu.

MAMMALS

★ HOTSPOTS

- PN de Nyungwe (p178)
- Kibale Forest NP (p150)

GORILLA

RECOGNITION A huge ape completely covered in thick black hair except for face, chest, soles and palms; mature males have a 'silver' back. Silverbacks weigh 160kg or more.

HABITAT Regenerating secondary forest, valley floors, rainforest clearings and edges and adjoining cultivation up to 3400m.

BEHAVIOUR Lives in nonterritorial harems averaging 10 members. Builds nests on ground or trees at night and for siestas. Older offspring are driven out, females frequently change groups or gravitate to solitary silverbacks to form new harems.

BREEDING Single infant born after 8½-month gestation is nursed until 1½ to two years old.

FEEDING Vegetarian; mostly leaves, shoots and stems of *Galium* vine, wild celery and thistle; also flowers, fruits, bark, bamboo shoots and occasionally insects.

VOICE Loud, 90% by silverback. Most commonly deep hoots followed by chest beating; also screams and barks.

SWAHILI Ngagi

GENTLE GIANTS Largest of the great apes, the gorilla sits comfortably on an evolutionary limb onto which it climbed just before its ancestors evolved into chimpanzees and humans. Thus, although our kinship with these gentle animals is unquestioned (gorillas are prone to colds, arthritis and heart disease, among other human ailments), they actually show more differences than similarities. These are the lifestyle apes, to whom comfort is all-important: gorillas spend more time on the ground than other apes; they are the only apes that have never been seen using tools; and they are almost exclusively vegetarian. Each family group is dominated by a large silverback: he decides when it's time to move and eats the choicest morsels, regardless of who found them (only youngsters are agile enough to climb and feed out of his reach). But when threatened, this normally gentle giant will defend his impish offspring with his life. Intruders are met with roars, chest beating, thrashing vegetation and terrifying charges that are usually enough to send any other animal packing. Of course they aren't to know that it's mainly bluff and the correct response is to do nothing – to flee will almost certainly incite his violence.

Much gorilla time is spent eating and resting – males develop a massive paunch from the sheer bulk of vegetation consumed – and you'll probably encounter a group lounging about together in the undergrowth, dozing or basking during sunny spells. A silverback is very indulgent with his offspring, allowing them to crawl all over his huge bulk, and can become quietly tolerant of humans – which is why you are able to get into the gorillas' formerly inaccessible habitat and enjoy one of the world's great wildlife experiences. Guides soothe the troop by imitating gorilla noises, but much harder to replicate are the loud farts that gorillas frequently vent, sometimes in answering volleys like puerile teenagers.

HOTSPOTS

- Bwindi Impenetrable NP (p146)
- PN des Volcans (p179)

MAMMALS

CHIMPANZEE

OUR CLOSEST COUSINS Young chimps laugh, turn somersaults, tickle each other, play tag and cry real tears. Juveniles play with infants and with small monkeys – ironically, because adults mount organised hunts for red colobus and other species. The terrified victims are ripped apart and eaten; subordinate males beg with hands out and females grant sexual favours for a share of the prized meat. Monkey hunts are everywhere among chimp communities, but food traditions and the use of tools vary greatly from area to area: famous examples include using rocks to break open nutshells and stems to extract termites from holes. Other behaviour that varies between chimp 'cultures' includes grooming leaves to get attention; using moss to soak up drinking water; using a leaf as a napkin; making cushions to sit on; and eating medicinal plants when feeling poorly. Chimps drum on tree buttresses to advertise a food source, sit and gaze at waterfalls, and break into frenzied drumming and hooting during rainstorms. But it's not all play: a baboon seen threatening a chimp with its impressive canine teeth at a food source got a quick smash in the guts for its pains, followed by an uppercut to the jaw as it doubled over. Not surprising, then, that geneticists have discovered we share 98% to 99% of our genes with chimps. Not convinced? Rain dances aside, a captive group was witnessed shuffling around in a circle stamping out a rhythm. Still not convinced? The discovery that chimps systematically murder individuals and even whole communities in neighbouring territories sent shock waves through the scientific world. Parties on these lethal raids jump and kill lone males, and drag females back to their community.

Most of the aforementioned has been revealed after decades of research at Tanzania's Gombe Stream and Mahale Mountains and Uganda's Kibale NP. Chimp tourism is still in its infancy, but watching these fascinating apes in the wild is likely to be one of the highlights of any trip to East Africa.

RECOGNITION An agile, muscular ape, blue-black to dark brown, with bare, expressive face and low brow and naked palms, soles and butt region. Adults can have silvered backs.

HABITAT Primary or secondary forest, and gallery forest adjoining miombo and savanna in which they forage.

BEHAVIOUR Communities of nine to 120 forage in territories protected by males that spend their entire lives on ancestral turf in shifting hierarchies. Females disperse to other communities. Adults weave arboreal nests for sleeping and siestas. Average group size is three to eight. Watch for reciprocal grooming sessions after meals.

BREEDING Infant born after an eight-month gestation is weaned at five and dependent until six to eight years.

FEEDING Opportunistic omnivores, eating fruit in season (especially figs) plus leaves, bark, insects, eggs and live animals as large as bushpigs and guineafowl.

VOICE Can be incredibly noisy. Has 34 recognisable sounds, the loudest being pant-hoots and excited screams. Best heard in the hour after dawn.

SWAHILI Sokwe mtu

MAMMALS

⭐ **HOTSPOTS**

- Kibale Forest NP (p150)
- Queen Elizabeth NP (p158)

DOGS

SIDE-STRIPED JACKAL

MAMMALS

SOCIABLE PREDATORS The ancestors of domestic dogs are alive and well on the plains of Africa, complete with the unmistakable repertoire of sounds and body language that humans understand instinctively (the golden jackal even barks and yelps like a domestic dog). Built for an active life, their entire body shape suggests hunting on the move (such as long legs that are suited to coursing through open country). Their pointed muzzles are full of sharp, tearing teeth (including splendid

canines) and their blunt, nonretractile claws make them fine diggers.

Many dogs are social killers, eg jackals usually hunt as resourceful pairs that also scavenge from other predators' kills. All dogs have finely developed senses: acute smell that detects food and other dogs (and its corollary; scent glands to mark out territories); keen vision to sight pack members, prey and predators; and exceptional hearing – canids have the most complex calls of all carnivores.

Most distinctive of the three jackal species, pairs of black-backed (also known as silver-backed) mate for life and stoutly defend a territory marked with scats, urine and howling choruses. Sociability is central to the success of all East African species: all young are born (whelped) underground in dens and receive intense parental care until weaned – jackal offspring may cohabit with their parents long enough to help rear another brood. As they develop, pups become lively and playful (traits that extend into adulthood); playfulness and appeasement – like showing their white belly as a sign of submission – mitigate the dangers inherent in social contact among killing animals.

But all dogs face competition and hardships: leopards in particular are well known to like dog meat. Defence consists of speed, those fine teeth and loose, erectile fur on the back and tail that seem to enlarge their profile (body extremities such as ears, tail and back are highlighted with black in many species, which exaggerates a cornered dog's movements and size).

★ HOTSPOTS

- Ngorongoro CA (p104) All three jackals coexist where their preferred habitats overlap (golden jackal dominates during the day, black-backed at night).
- Queen Elizabeth NP (p158) Side-striped jackal is common on the Ishasha Plain.
- Serengeti NP (p108) Bat-eared foxes rest, play and groom from about 4.30pm onwards.

HUNTING DOG

TEAM PLAYERS Despite their relatively small size compared with their prey (one antelope can be twice the weight of an individual dog), the superb pack-hunting skills of hunting dogs make them one of the most efficient predators on the plains. Unlike lions and leopards, which use their weight to help bring an animal down, hunting dogs rely exclusively on their numbers and ability to wear their victim out. Breasting a rise at full pelt, they bowl into surprised antelopes on the other side, scattering the herd while the leader selects the weakest and runs it down, the others following in close order to rip it apart. Almost exclusively diurnal, hunting dogs chase prey by sight, making up for a lack of speed with endurance – coursing game in open country for several kilometres, harassing it with nips until it is exhausted, then knocking it down and swiftly devouring it. As long as it is kept in sight, prey seldom escapes: in some studies up to 85% of prey chased was eventually brought down. In thicker habitat, packs may split and pursue several animals.

Sight plays a pivotal role in hunting dog society – each of these sociable dogs is uniquely marked in blotches of tan, black and white, too loud for camouflage, but thought to reinforce their inclusion in a tight, ordered hunting unit. Upon emerging from the den, every dog's day begins with an elaborate 'meet' ritual, in which the pack assembles with excited, high-pitched twittering; pups try to coerce adults into regurgitating food, and adults outdo each other in elaborate shows of submission and mobbing (mobbing appears to be an important process of socialisation, reinforcing pack membership).

Karen Blixen, author of *Out of Africa*, reported seeing a pack of hunting dogs numbering 2000 early in the 20th century. Such sights are gone: modern packs can still number between 40 and 60 animals, but 10 is the average in East Africa. The hunting dog's former abundance and diurnal habits led to its prosecution by pastoralists, and canine diseases spread from domestic dogs to decimate wild packs. The end has already come for most packs, and unfortunately the hunting dog is now the rarest large carnivore in East Africa.

RECOGNITION Long-legged dog. Fur is ochre, tan, black and white. White tail tuft. Prominent, rounded ears over black muzzle and face.

HABITAT Woodland, savanna and grassland with sufficient prey.

BEHAVIOUR Most sociable and diurnal canid, with large, overlapping home ranges. Packs consist of same-sex hierarchies subordinate to a breeding pair; all help rear young by regurgitating meat. Females emigrate at 18 months to three years of age.

BREEDING Up to 18 pups born during rains; they follow the pack after nine weeks.

FEEDING Strictly carnivorous, running down small or medium-sized antelopes; larger and smaller animals are taken opportunistically.

VOICE A repetitive, bell-like *hoo* carries over long distance as a contact call.

SWAHILI Mbwa mwitu.

MAMMALS

HOTSPOTS

- Selous GR (p118)
- Mikumi NP (p130)

MAMMALS

CATS

YAWNING LEOPARD, KENYA

EXPERT STALKERS Cats are so well known as to almost obviate any description. There are seven species in East Africa, three of which rate among the most glamorous wild animals on the planet. The standard cat package consists of short fur, long body, rounded head, long canine teeth for gripping prey, and sharp carnassial teeth (at the back of the mouth) for shearing flesh. Variations among the smaller cats include a short tail and long legs, with further refinements such as the extra-long back legs of caracals for powerful leaps (up to 3m vertically!).

Although cats have a rather poor sense of smell, their other senses are highly developed: excellent bifocal vision, even in dim light; acute hearing, amplified in servals and caracals by very large ears; and sensitive whiskers. All (except for the cheetah) have sharp claws that can be retracted into sheaths and pads on the soles of their feet for silent stalking, and all climb well – although the heavyweight lions don't go in for it much. Cats are at the top of the food chain and are almost exclusively carnivorous. Except for short periods of consorting and when females have young, the majority hunt and live alone to ensure an adequate share of food resources.

Cats are expert stalkers that kill by clamping their jaws around the throat of prey until it suffocates, or biting to sever its spinal cord. Most lie up for much of the day, but start hunting by late afternoon. The smaller cats aren't so easy to spot from a distance – muted colours help them blend in – but peak sighting times are early morning and evening. Watch for ears poking up over the grass (dark markings behind the ears act as signals for kittens following behind their mother); likewise, that little black bird sitting on a grass head in the distance could be the tail tuft of a lion on the prowl. A serval's prodigious leaps after prey are a giveaway; and swatting birds in flight is a caracal speciality. The African wild cat is widespread and chance sightings could occur anywhere you can spotlight. If you don't see one while on safari you won't have to go far to study one in detail, for this is the direct ancestor of nearly every household cat on earth – you can tell them apart by the unmarked, ginger-coloured backs to the wild cat's ears.

★ HOTSPOTS

- ○ Serengeti NP (p108) Classic lion country where you can easily watch the drama of the hunt unfold.
- ○ Samburu NR (p84) A dry and flat country accentuated by acacia trees where leopards are prone to lie.
- ○ Ngorongoro CA (p104) Good for all savanna cats from large to small.
- ○ Aberdare NP (p86) Servals, including black forms, are regularly sighted in alpine grassland.

CHEETAH

SURREPTITIOUS SPEED Charismatic and least catlike of the big cats, cheetahs usually hunt shortly after dawn, resting up in long grass during the heat of the day and resuming the hunt in the late afternoon. Much time is spent moving surreptitiously into position before bursting from cover and running down prey – shadowing its jinks, then tripping it up or knocking it off balance. Cheetahs do not have retractable claws (a feature which adds traction during sprints) and once prey is caught, it is suffocated with a bite to the throat. The cheetah's incredible bursts of speed can reach 112km/h (during which it takes 7m-long bounds), but can be maintained for only 200m to 300m; cheetahs try to get within 30m to 50m before attacking.

The least aggressive and weakest of the big cats, cheetahs drag prey to cover before feeding and wolf it down to avoid losses to lions, hyenas and even vultures. Groups of lions, dogs and hyenas may kill an adult cheetah, and more than 50% of cubs are taken by predators within their first three months. But there's a still more insidious threat: around 30,000 to 40,000 years ago the grassland of Africa virtually disappeared under forest and it is estimated that the cheetah population fell to only a few individuals, including perhaps only one female, so today's population has a greatly diminished gene pool and inbreeding is a concern for the cheetah's long-term well-being. Ironically, cheetahs are often dogged by onlookers – it is not unusual to see one surrounded by safari vehicles – which sometimes forces them to hunt during the heat of day.

Cheetahs are generally solitary, although males sometimes live in small groups that can last for years. Females raise their young alone, caring for them for up to two years, and even going without food to ensure they eat. Unlike other cats, which have innate hunting skills, cubs must learn how to stalk and catch prey – females bring them dazed or half-dead young animals and teach them how to hunt.

RECOGNITION Rangy cat with long tail ringed at the tip. Fawn or cream with evenly spaced spots. Black stripes between eyes and mouth.

HABITAT Widespread in savanna, grassland and semiarid plains with patchy cover.

BEHAVIOUR Males and females socialise only during oestrus, but two to three independent males may band together to defend territory. Uses termite mounds, vehicles and leaning trees as observation posts.

BREEDING Cubs (three to four) born after three-month gestation, feed at kills after five to six weeks and catch prey at nine to 12 months.

FEEDING Hunts gazelles, impalas, oribis, hares, warthogs, duikers and calves of larger antelopes. Groups may take zebras, wildebeest or young buffaloes.

VOICE Generally silent. Cubs called to feed on a kill with soft, birdlike chirps.

SWAHILI Duma.

MAMMALS

★ HOTSPOTS

- Masai Mara NR (p62)
- Samburu NR (p84)
- Buffalo Springs NR (p84)
- Serengeti NP (p108)

LION

RECOGNITION Fawn or tawny coat. Black to golden mane. Cubs' spots fade with age.

HABITAT Grassland, savanna and woodland; uses cover to ambush prey and hide cubs.

BEHAVIOUR Prides of related females defend territories. Prey ambushed normally within 30m. Females mate two to three times per hour for two to six days to conceive, and suckle each other's young.

BREEDING Cubs (two to six) born in a hidden den after 3½-month gestation, joining the pride after four to eight weeks.

FEEDING Ambushes medium-large ungulates and suffocates victims by biting throat. Follows vultures to kills and steals from hyenas.

VOICE Deep roar can carry up to 8km.

SWAHILI Simba.

KING OF THE JUNGLE This is the big cat of Africa, larger and more powerful than any other predator: lions' jaws bite easily through muscle and bone, often leaving little more than the head and spine of their prey intact. Some prides specialise in toppling buffaloes, others prey on giraffes, but most usually hunt impalas, wildebeest, zebras and other common herbivores (although a curious or hungry lion will eat rodents, lizards and even ostrich eggs). A few notorious rogues have killed dozens of people (although attacks are rare and usually made by old or injured lions). While lions are active mainly at night, many hunts occur just after dawn, so get out there early to see them at their best. Most of the day is spent lazing around in the shade before the hunt begins again in the late afternoon; females often play with cubs and suckle late in the day before setting out.

Two things make lions stand out from other cats: the differences between males and females (most apparent in the male's shaggy mane and size), and their sociability. Prides of about 12 lions defend territories, with one or more dominant males sharing mating rights and food with several females and their offspring. Females do most of the killing, cooperatively stalking and ambushing prey, but around the kill every cat becomes a snarling, hissing competitor for the choicest meat – the adult males inevitably getting their proverbial share.

The trade-off? Resident males cooperatively ward off attacks by nomadic males looking to dominate a pride. Nomads are usually related subadult males that have been kicked out of their home pride; if they can drive off another pride's resident males, they can appropriate their females, and will kill as many cubs as they can catch. Females come into oestrus shortly afterwards and the victors enjoy their spoils – fatherhood and a hunting pride. New litters are usually born at the same time and the pride continues as a cooperative group once again – displaced males don't usually get a second chance.

MAMMALS

⭐ **HOTSPOTS**

- Masai Mara NR (p62)
- Serengeti NP (p108)
- Ngorongoro CA (p104)
- Queen Elizabeth NP (p158)

LEOPARD

SILENT STEALTH The leopard's reclusive habits make finding it difficult, and even if you do, chances are it will melt into the undergrowth or flatten itself against a branch to become less conspicuous. But it's worth the effort – they are more common than most people think and are, in fact, still the world's most widespread big cat. Adults are solitary most of the year, with males and females associating only long enough to mate. During the day they typically lie up in a lair – such as a rock overhang, cave or dense thicket – but rarely in the same place two days running: check cliffs, kopjes and large riverine trees, and look for a twitching tail hanging from a branch or animal remains wedged in a forked bough. Listen for a rasping groan (like wood being sawed) after sundown and before dawn – often given on the move, it warns other leopards to avoid contact.

By dusk, leopards are active, and at night they are in their element, hunting by stealth and ambush, pouncing from a few metres away or leaping from a tree onto prey that can include guard dogs or domestic goats. This powerful cat can bring down a topi and drag an impala up a tree – so lions or hyenas won't steal it – and occasionally one develops a taste for human flesh. They pluck fur and feathers from small prey, and drink water when available, but otherwise can survive by drinking blood and bodily fluids. Baboons are a favourite, and as primates see poorly in the dark they are vulnerable after sundown. But by day, baboon troops mob leopards and several males may gang up to kill one. Lions will kill a leopard if it blunders into a pride. Female and male leopards have overlapping ranges, but defend exclusive territories. A male's territory may overlap that of one or more females, and he marks his turf by spraying urine on bushes, rocks and fallen branches; with secretions from anal glands; and by clawing the bark of trees.

RECOGNITION Pale yellow to tawny; dark rosettes on flanks, back and tail; solid spots on the face; whitish below. Black forms occur.

HABITAT Semiarid scrub, savanna, mountains and lowland rainforest. Favours riverine forest, woodland and rocky outcrops.

BEHAVIOUR Solitary. Mainly nocturnal, hunting during the day when undisturbed or when females have cubs. Suns on termite mounds or large rocks. Can swim.

BREEDING Year-round; two to six cubs born after 90 to 112 days, becoming independent at 18 to 22 months.

FEEDING Carnivorous. Hunts small antelopes, warthogs, hyraxes and monkeys; also arthropods, birds and reptiles. Individual tastes vary.

VOICE Cubs contacted with a loud sniff ('prusten') or meow.

SWAHILI Chui.

MAMMALS

★ HOTSPOTS

- Queen Elizabeth NP (p158)
- Samburu NR (p84)
- Lake Nakuru NP (p91)
- Serengeti NP (p108)

MONGOOSES

SLENDER MONGOOSE

FAST STRIKERS A lack of colourful markings readily distinguishes most of East Africa's 13 mongoose species from other small predators, such as civets and genets. Three or four common species (particularly Egyptian, slender and the two social mongooses – banded and dwarf) that forage during the day are often seen slinking through long grass or pausing to stand on hind legs and sniff the breeze. Mongooses vary greatly, with basic body plans ranging from elongated, slender species with short legs that prey largely on vertebrates; to the stockier, long-legged cusimanses and 'dog-mongooses'.

Most mongooses are normally solitary, nearly all are primarily ground-dwelling (only slender and Egyptian mongooses can climb well) and many are nocturnal. However, all have in common a more or less pointed muzzle, inconspicuous ears and a grizzled, shaggy coat. The small size indicates that mongooses subsist on small prey and explains why they are East Africa's most abundant and diverse carnivores; nonetheless, that so many terrestrial mongoose species can survive side by side (and compete with genets, civets and small cats) is testament to the abundance of small prey.

Mongooses feed on small animals ranging from insects and spiders to rodents and lizards, caught opportunistically or by digging, which are then chewed up on the spot. The slender mongoose is an extremely agile predator of vertebrates, including birds and hyraxes, and can leap 1m vertically to snatch prey. Mongooses are perhaps best known as fearless killers of snakes, a reputation not entirely undeserved: slender and Egyptian mongooses can overpower even dangerous cobras with lightning strikes, although the tables are readily turned if a mongoose is caught unawares.

Good mongoose country features burrows and shelters, particularly abandoned termite mounds, but don't look too early in the morning – mongooses like to lie about in the sun or play before heading out on the hunt. Nocturnal species, such as white-tailed mongooses, are readily spotlit. Watch for birds mobbing slender mongooses (they ignore most other mongooses), and for parties of hornbills feeding with dwarf mongooses.

★ **HOTSPOTS**

- Masai Mara NR (p62) A variety of habitats exploited by the sociable and nocturnal species.
- Serengeti NP (p108) Home to both slender and Egyptian mongooses.
- Lake Mburo NP (p162) Thickets, marsh and savanna support the six common species.

MAMMALS

BANDED MONGOOSE

LOYAL COMRADES Solitary mongooses make a tempting treat for eagles, cats, dogs and large monitor lizards. So it makes sense to band together for protection, which is exactly what banded mongooses do (although the name refers to the stripes on their rumps). When danger threatens, the would-be predator is confronted with a writhing mass of mongooses snapping and spitting – one male was observed to climb a tree to force an eagle to drop one of its comrades. Yet only two species of mongoose in East Africa have adopted this behaviour (the other is the dwarf mongoose), the downside of a social life being that food resources must be spread among group members.

The banded mongoose is the most commonly seen mongoose species: family groups, sometimes numbering as many as 40 members, shuffle through the savanna with a bouncing gait, occasionally standing on hind legs to scan over the grass or climbing a termite mound for a better vantage point. A typical pack includes three or four breeding females and males, plus offspring, whose day starts well after sunrise: the usual routine is to wander around their home range foraging, scent-marking rocks, branches, termite mounds and each other. Hot spells are spent resting under bushes.

Nosing in burrows, crevices and under bark, banded mongooses snap up virtually any animal too slow to get out of the way – difficult or dangerous prey is shaken or thrown against the ground to immobilise it before swallowing. But when food is encountered, it's every mongoose for itself (food is shared only with juveniles).

What other advantages are there in being a social mongoose? Breeding is synchronised within the pack so the season's young can be fed and protected together: any lactating female will suckle newborn young, regardless of parenthood; all pack members groom and play; and adult males babysit the den while the pack is out foraging. Larger packs also dominate bigger territories, and thus greater food resources, hounding off smaller groups during boundary disputes.

RECOGNITION Robust mongoose with long legs, pointed snout and long claws. Grey-brown upperparts with dark bands on rump; paler below. Length 45cm to 75cm.

HABITAT Savanna, woodland and grassland, especially with termite mounds; also cultivated land.

BEHAVIOUR Diurnal. Packs typically number 15 to 20 and sleep in abandoned termite mounds. Forage over 3km to 10km a day, usually led by a senior female. Packs may produce four litters a year; many young don't survive and subadult males disperse to other packs.

BREEDING Usually four young born in a den (mostly in rains) after a two-month gestation; they join the foraging after five weeks.

FEEDING Omnivorous, eating small animals of all types: insects, millipedes, spiders, scorpions, rodents, birds and eggs, plus fruit and berries.

VOICE Constant contact calls: chirps, twitters and churrs.

SWAHILI Nguchiro miraba or Kicheche.

MAMMALS

★ HOTSPOTS

- Masai Mara NR (p62)
- Serengeti NP (p108)
- Ngorongoro CA (p104)
- Queen Elizabeth NP (p158)

SPOTTED HYENA

RECOGNITION The only hyena with spots. Sloping hindquarters with short black tail. Rusty or tan with dark spots. Round face and ears. Broad black muzzle.

HABITAT Open savanna, thorn scrub and montane grassland with abundant prey. Dens in rocky country.

BEHAVIOUR Female-dominated but competitive clans, sometimes numbering 100 animals. Socialise before setting out to hunt. Males aged two years disperse to other clans. Cubs weaned in communal dens, with higher-ranking offspring weaned faster.

BREEDING Usually two cubs born in a den after a four-month gestation. Suckled at eight months, weaned at 12 to 16 months.

FEEDING Carnivorous; carrion (even desiccated corpses), human refuse. Hunts large and small mammals, especially wildebeest, Thomson's gazelles and young of other antelopes. Steals kills.

VOICE Complex; most commonly a far-carrying, rising wooo-up; also eerie 'laughter'.

SWAHILI Fisi madoa.

⭐ HOTSPOTS

EFFICIENT KILLERS Long maligned as misshapen, giggling cowards, spotted hyenas are now recognised as deadly and efficient hunters of the plains. They are certainly opportunistic scavengers, but research is showing that many kills previously attributed to lions are actually spotted hyenas' kills stolen by lions. Hunts usually start with one or two hyenas that keep up that deceptively loping stride for hours at a steady 10km/h, wearing down their victim by nipping at its heels. Eventually the prey is stopped by the hyenas biting its legs and belly, and clamping their massive jaws around the victim's genitals and tail. The chase attracts other clan members, and even more when a kill occurs – the consequent squabbling also attracts lions and rival hyena clans, and pitched battles between both can end in deaths.

Spotted hyenas can intimidate cheetahs, leopards, and lions (although rarely full-grown male lions). Powerful jaws are their main weapon and tool, and those teeth can shear through bone and thick hides. Active mainly at night, they cool off by lying in puddles, but if they spot vultures homing on a kill, they will quickly follow.

Male hyenas are only significant during the height of female oestrus – females have higher testosterone levels than the males themselves: they dominate males at kills, determine clan structure, protect communal dens and initiate hunts and territorial disputes. But the females' most unusual feature, which gave rise to a hermaphrodite myth, is an enlarged clitoris that can elongate like a penis (up to 19cm long) with a foreskin and fibrous tissue that mimics a scrotum. Not only does the male mate through this 'female phallus', but the cubs are born through it. And the killer instinct is there at birth: pups are born with fully formed front teeth and, if female, the first-born tries to kill the second if it is of the same sex – in the darkness of a den it makes sense for every hyena to act like a male.

STRIPED HYENA

The two East African hyena species are distinct in appearance, behaviour and food preferences. The pugnacious spotted hyena dominates the plains and is most easily seen, while the smaller striped hyena is essentially nocturnal – best sought by spotlighting, but with luck, flushed accidentally by day. An opportunistic, solitary hunter, the striped hyena's behaviour is affected by the presence of its spotted cousin: where the latter is present, striped hyenas tend to keep to open woodland – if they do meet, the striped hyena is submissive, surrendering food and making a quick exit. Although striped hyenas will drink if they can, they can live in waterless areas. Foraging alone, they most often pursue large insects (including grasshoppers, beetles and moths) but will also eat small animals such as gazelle fawns and hares if they can catch them. Striped hyenas are social creatures; several animals live together and defend the same home range or territory. It is thought that several related females (with the aid of grown offspring) cooperate to rear cubs in shared dens in kopjes, ravines and rocky hills. One to six cubs are born per litter and are fed by all family members as the adults return to the den with food. Although striped hyenas show little fear of leopards and cheetahs, they keep well away from lions.

AARDWOLF

Lacking the massive jaws and teeth of spotted and striped hyenas, the aardwolf's small, peglike teeth are adapted to a highly specialised diet consisting almost exclusively of termites, including species that other termite specialists rarely touch because they squirt noxious chemicals as a defence. No other termite eaters consume so many either: an aardwolf in a typical night spends up to six hours lapping up around 250,000 termites. Watch for this usually solitary animal on heavily grazed and trampled grassland with lots of termite mounds, walking in a zigzag with head low to the ground as it listens for termites moving about on the surface. Good signs of its presence include latrines, in which their partly buried scats (smelling strongly of ammonia) show soil and remains of termites. Aardwolves are thought to live as monogamous pairs sharing a territory with their most recent offspring. Family members enthusiastically scent-mark their territorial boundaries by smearing their anal glands on grass stems, bushes and other objects. Young are generally born during the wet season, staying at the den for three months before venturing out to hunt termites.

RECOGNITION Grey to golden with black stripes, long hair and large, pointed ears.

HABITAT Scrub and woodland.

BEHAVIOUR Strictly nocturnal.

BREEDING One to six cubs.

FEEDING Eats small invertebrates, carrion and fruit.

VOICE Giggles, whines, growls.

SWAHILI Fisi miraba.

⭐ HOTSPOTS

- Masai Mara NR (p62)
- Serengeti NP (p108)
- Ngorongoro CA (p104)
- Ruaha NP (p134)

RECOGNITION Buff to reddish brown. Snout bare.

HABITAT Open savanna and heavily grazed grassland.

BEHAVIOUR Nocturnal. Male babysits while female hunts.

BREEDING Two to three cubs.

FEEDING Harvests termites; some other small animals.

VOICE Growls, barks or roars.

SWAHILI Fisi ya nkole.

⭐ HOTSPOTS

- Masai Mara NR (p62)
- Serengeti NP (p108)

MAMMALS

RECOGNITION Black with white crown, back and tail.

HABITAT Forest and grassland.

BEHAVIOUR Nocturnal. Hunts alone or in pairs. Climbs well.

BREEDING One to four cubs.

FEEDING Eats virtually any small animal (even deadly snakes); also eggs and carrion.

VOICE Rattling roars.

SWAHILI Nyegere.

HOTSPOTS

- Masai Mara NR (p62)
- Serengeti NP (p108)
- Queen Elizabeth NP (p158)

RECOGNITION Chocolate-brown to tan; white cheeks, chin and chest. Around 1.5m in length.

HABITAT Hunts in freshwater.

BEHAVIOUR Excavates dens in overhanging banks.

BREEDING Up to three cubs.

FEEDING Mainly crabs.

VOICE A startling *aah*.

SWAHILI Fisi madji.

HOTSPOTS

- Saiwa Swamp NP (p97)
- Lake Mburo NP (p162)

RATEL

Much the same size and shape as badgers everywhere, the ratel (also called the honey badger) has a reputation for ferocity far outstripping its size. Some Africans say they would rather face a lion than a ratel and, incredible as it sounds, ratels have been known to rob lions of their kill. And if a man should get too close, well, they're just the right size to jump up and hang onto his testicles with their vicelike jaws. Normally, though, they prefer to dig out scorpions, rodents and other burrowing animals and are adept at extracting difficult items, such as honeycomb from beehives and tortoises from their shells. For a mammal that eats mainly small animals, the ratel is well equipped: its forelimbs end in massive claws for digging; thick, bristly fur protects it from dangerous prey; and its skin is loose so that any overconfident hyena or leopard that grabs hold can be turned on and bitten back. When eating stinging insects, such as ants or bees, ratels knock them out by releasing unpleasant secretions from their anal glands (ratels are related to skunks). Ratels are reputed to break open beehives located by honeyguides (small birds that feed on beeswax) for their mutual benefit. But, although greater honeyguides certainly seek out people, and lead them to hives, to date there has been no authentic record of a ratel being guided.

AFRICAN CLAWLESS OTTER

The odd dour researcher may resist the idea of animals having fun, but it is otherwise hard to explain an otter somersaulting down a mud bank when walking would be simpler and running faster. Likewise, the African clawless otter has been known to drop a pebble into the water and catch it before it hits the bottom, and even to swim about with one balanced on its head.

But otherwise, otters are serious aquatic carnivores propelled by webbed hind feet and a long, rudderlike tail. Superb divers with waterproof fur and prominent whiskers, they locate prey by groping about underwater with unwebbed 'fingers', gripping fishes or frogs and sometimes eating while treading water. Signs of their presence include scats with broken crab shells or fish bones; smooth paths down mud banks where they habitually slide into the water; and middens where shellfish have been smashed against a rock. If you wait quietly in likely habitat, you'll probably see one break the surface to take a breath, or be able to follow its progress as it swims just below the surface.

AFRICAN CIVET

For centuries, people have known of the secretion made by African civets from their perineal glands (a pair of glands situated near the anus in some mammals). Known as civetone, it is still harvested, particularly in Ethiopia, from captive specimens and used as a floral scent. Civets are solitary, pugnacious animals and smell seems to play an important role in keeping them out of each other's way: civetone is used to mark a home range and is smeared on rocks, branches and trees. Civets also make conspicuous, strongly scented dung middens, called civettries. Common and mainly nocturnal, civets are usually found when spotlighting along trails and roads, although they may also be abroad during the early morning. Essentially ground animals, they climb and dig poorly, and rely on holes dug by other animals for nurseries and dens in which to lie during the day. Civets wander nightly through their home range, trotting or walking with head down. Any small animals encountered are killed by lunging and biting, shaking and tossing. Perfect opportunists, they can digest poisonous plants and distasteful invertebrates, and kill dangerous snakes. When cornered, they bluff by erecting a spinal crest, which increases their apparent size by around 30%, but they also swim well and readily take to water to escape.

RECOGNITION Doglike. Black with creamy blotches.

HABITAT Forested mosaics, cultivated and marshy areas.

BEHAVIOUR Young freeze until detected.

BREEDING One to four kittens in den.

FEEDING Eats roots, shoots, fruits and small animals.

VOICE Contact call: *ha ha ha.*

SWAHILI Fungo.

⭐ HOTSPOTS

- Saiwa Swamp NP **(p97)**
- Lake Mburo NP **(p162)**

COMMON GENET

Attractively marked, common genets are widespread, mainly nocturnal carnivores that show great variation in coloration and pattern among several regional populations. About the size of a large domestic cat, they hunt alone in trees or on the ground, patrolling up and down branches and through undergrowth to stalk or pounce on large insects and small vertebrates. Look for these common savanna predators along roads shortly after nightfall (particularly on moonlit nights) – the shine of their eyes is easy to pick up, and when they slink into the bushes the long tail (about half the total body length) is usually distinct.

Common genets have learned to scavenge from humans and they may become semi-tame around camping grounds and lodges at night. It is not known whether they hold territories – several may be seen foraging nearby, and females almost certainly have smaller home ranges than males. Young are born in a tree hollow, burrow or nest of leaves. They begin hunting between 11 and 18 weeks, catching their own prey at six months of age. Common genets mark their territories with urine and scent secreted from their perineal (anal) glands, and by leaving scats on branches.

RECOGNITION Catlike. Yellow, dark-brown spots, banded tail.

HABITAT Savanna and woodland; rocky or hilly areas.

BEHAVIOUR Mainly nocturnal.

BREEDING Two to three young.

FEEDING Eats invertebrates, small vertebrates and fruit.

VOICE One or more coughs.

SWAHILI Kanu.

⭐ HOTSPOTS

- Tsavo NP **(p66)**
- Samburu NR **(p84)**
- Serengeti NP **(p108)**

MAMMALS

RECOGNITION Scaly exterior, long muscular tail.

HABITAT Woodland, savanna.

BEHAVIOUR Uses natural shelters. Can climb trees.

BREEDING A single offspring eats ants after three months.

FEEDING Licks up ants and termites with sticky tongue.

VOICE Hissing or puffing.

SWAHILI Kakakuona.

⭐ HOTSPOTS

- Serengeti NP (p108)
- Masai Mara NR (p62)

GROUND PANGOLIN

Also known as scaly anteaters, pangolins are small (reaching just over 1m in length) and seldom seen on safari, although they are not uncommon. If you do bump into one, it's worth a closer look: pangolins' upperparts are entirely covered in broad, overlapping scales, which make them look like a huge pine cone. The weight of their ambling gait is entirely supported by the back legs, and when threatened a pangolin rolls itself up into a ball, presenting any would-be attacker with a slippery sphere of horny scales on which it can't easily get a grip. However, the pangolin's face and underparts lack scales, and lions and hyenas make a quick meal of one if they can breach its defences. The wall of scales is a pangolin's primary defence: their powerful foreclaws can also be used against an attacker, but they are essentially for ripping open soil and hollow logs to get at their main prey – ants. Their narrow heads are small, the snouts long, narrow and toothless and their sticky tongues – as long as their heads and bodies combined – shoot into underground passages to recoil covered in insects. Young pangolins cling to their mother's back, sidling under her tail or belly at the first sign of danger.

DUGONG

Strands of seagrass floating to the surface of shallow coastal waters are a subtle sign that dugongs are grazing below. Also known as sea cows, these marine herbivores graze exclusively on meadows of seagrass that grow along the East African coast. They look like no other animal, but are probably most closely related to elephants and are thought to have inspired legends about mermaids and sirens. With a face dominated by a wide, bristly, piglike snout, dugongs have sweet voices that fill the water with chirping and twittering. They pose no threat to anyone or anything, yet will probably be the next large animal to become extinct in East Africa. Their habitat is increasingly being encroached on by fishermen – dugongs drown when they get caught in fishing nets. They swim slowly and herds may be visible beneath the surface, rising in unison to breathe every 80 seconds or so; sadly, many dugongs also die from injuries inflicted by propellers on boats. Their sole feeding grounds, the seagrass beds, are easily damaged by people walking across at low tide. Nobody knows how many dugongs are left, nor what long-term effects their demise will have on coastal ecology, but their disappearance will be a tragic loss to the wildlife kingdom and the natural world.

RECOGNITION Bulbous, grey-brown with blunt face. Around 3m in length.

HABITAT Sheltered waters with seagrass meadows.

BEHAVIOUR Forages and rests alone or in small herds.

BREEDING Single calf

FEEDING Grazes on seagrass.

VOICE Chirps and twitters.

SWAHILI Nguva.

⭐ HOTSPOTS

- Malindi Marine NP (p93)
- Watamu Marine NP (p93)

MAMMALS

AFRICAN ELEPHANT

INTELLIGENT TERRESTRIALS Besides being the largest land animal, African elephants show some amazing signs of intelligence and what looks like compassion. For example, they can use their tusks to short circuit an electric fence to get to forbidden fruits beyond; and a sick or wounded elephant is sometimes propped up by two comrades – should it fall over they'll break tusks in their efforts to raise it up again. Elephants recognise their dead, feeling the bones while standing quietly – they cover dead kin in dirt and branches, and have been known to do the same for a human they have killed. With elephants, the key points to watch are the trunk – often nonchalantly draped over a tusk, it does the grasping, drinking, spraying and trumpeting; those huge, leathery ears – which stand out when they're annoyed; and their long tusks – which act as both tools and weapons. Also look out for breasts on females, located between their front legs.

Matriarchal herds, made up of several related adult females and their offspring, are dominated by the oldest cow (the matriarch) that leads the herd well after she stops calving at age 45 or more. Young bulls are ousted from matriarchal herds at 10 to 14 years of age and drift between family units or into bachelor herds. Herds are very sociable and vocal, greeting each other (and other herds) with trumpeting, pirouetting and the placing of trunks in each others' mouths. Low-frequency sounds below human perception allow elephants to maintain contact for up to 10km, and advertise to males when a female is on heat (which brings them running).

Males come into musth one month per year and it's a sight: liquid oozes from the temporal gland, leaving dark stains on the side of the face; the massive penis turns green, drags along the ground dribbling and exudes a strong smell. Several bulls compete for dominance and when one eventually mounts (for a knee-trembling 60 seconds), other females gather round with much trumpeting and ear flapping.

RECOGNITION Huge – bulls can stand 3.4m high and weigh 6300kg (forest elephants are much smaller). Variably grey coloration is affected by dust baths.

HABITAT All major habitats with shade and water, from semidesert to rainforest and montane grassland.

BEHAVIOUR Herds have huge home ranges and make seasonal movements led by the matriarch. Active 16 to 20 hours a day, they drink and bathe daily. Large herds congregate during rains. Bulls get 'green penis syndrome' and bad-tempered in musth.

BREEDING Single calf born after 22-month gestation (mostly in rains); it may remain with mother for 10 years.

FEEDING Eclectic browsers and grazers, consuming up to 150kg in 24 hours. They recycle huge quantities of vegetation and reshape entire landscapes.

VOICE Herds are highly vocal, with deep contact rumblings, squeals, roars and snorts. Trumpeting signals annoyance and pleasure.

SWAHILI Tembo or Ndovu.

MAMMALS

HOTSPOTS

- Amboseli NP (p74)
- Tsavo NP (p66)
- Ruaha NP (p134)
- Semliki Valley WR (p170)

PLAINS ZEBRA

RECOGNITION Stocky with variable broad black-and-white stripes extending onto belly (browner in mares) and an erect, striped mane.

HABITAT Widespread in grassland, savanna and woodland near permanent water. Avoids wet ground.

BEHAVIOUR Nomadic, it's the first to graze tall grassland (followed by wildebeest and other migrating animals). Rests in the open at night and files to water at midday.

BREEDING Peaks in rains; one foal born after 12-month gestation; suckles for six months.

FEEDING Can eat tall, coarse grasses not normally consumed by other herbivores.

VOICE Noisy at night, when stallions rally mares with a loud barking bray.

SWAHILI Punda milia.

MAMMALS

STRIPED STALLIONS Among the most easily recognisable of all animals, the plains zebra is also variously known as Chapman's, Burchell's and common zebra (another species, Grevy's zebra, also lives in East Africa – where their ranges overlap the two mingle freely but never interbreed). Zebras are savanna horses whose ancestors evolved in North America and spread via land bridges to Africa during the last three million years. Zebra stripes are as individual as a human fingerprint, but their function is a matter of controversy: they effectively break up a zebra's outline (even from a short distance away), and probably act as a general antipredator pattern. But they may also be a bonding feature (an attractive visual stimulus imprinted at birth that helps keep herds together) – in keeping with this theory unstriped horses, such as wild asses, are not nearly so gregarious. Another theory is that stripes are a defence against biting tsetse flies, whose great compound eyes see many different images at once and can't easily make out a zebra's outline; running in a straight line then zigzagging is said to further confuse the flies. Living outside the tsetse zone, wild asses are unstriped.

All zebras are highly sociable with each other and other herbivores, such as antelopes (especially oryxes and elands), giraffes and buffaloes. Intelligent, fast and adaptable, zebras have been seen sliding under wire fences to reach grazing land and can be unpopular with pastoralists. A plains zebra stallion looks after up to six mares and their foals, fighting off male rivals (as many as 18 can gather when a filly first comes into oestrus) and following behind the herd when it moves – to discourage predators. Males form bachelor herds and try to abduct females from harems when they reach maturity. Watch for the mutual nibbling of legs, shoulders and neck among family members; facing in opposite directions to help spot predators; and lining up to roll in dust or rub against trees or termite mounds, which probably dislodges parasites and conditions their coats.

★ HOTSPOTS

- Masai Mara NR (p62)
- Serengeti NP (p108)
- Ngorongoro CA (p104)
- Lake Mburo NP (p162)

GREVY'S ZEBRA

FINER STRIPED STALLIONS East Africa's other zebra, Grevy's, is a large, striped ass of semiarid country that commonly associates with giraffes, oryxes, elands, impalas and buffaloes. Both plains and Grevy's zebras frequently occur together in mixed herds, especially in the dry season, but seen side by side the two cannot be mistaken (Grevy's have finer stripes that do not extend onto the belly, and large, rounded ears). Evidently they have no trouble telling the difference because they never interbreed. In fact, the two have entirely different social systems: Grevy's mares associate in loose herds that share a home range while stallions stake out territories on good pasture near water. Any mares on heat are waylaid as they pass through a male's territory to drink, the stallion fending off the advances of bachelors loitering near his boundaries. But although intolerant when mares are in heat, stallions actively consort with bachelor herds on their turf at other times (unlike plains zebras).

The precocious foals are born with their mane extending along both back and belly; this is shed as they grow to resemble more conventional manes. Foals can stand within 11 minutes, and run in about 45 minutes, and their legs are so long they must splay them to touch their noses to the ground. A foal follows its mother faithfully, even suckling from behind, but stays behind in a crèche guarded by an adult while she goes to water to drink.

Zebras have never been popular with pastoralists because they compete with livestock for pasture and water, and the range of Grevy's zebras is fast contracting. From a population of 13,700 animals in 1977, this species has experienced a 70% decline, and since the start of the new millennium its numbers have hovered around 5000. Sadly, Grevy's zebra remains an endangered species and its future on the continent remains uncertain.

RECOGNITION Finely striped zebra with white belly, large ears and tan muzzle; stripes are wider on the neck and chest, and form a bullseye on the rump.

HABITAT Mosaics of semiarid *Acacia-Commiphora* thornbush and grassland, preferably with permanent water and pasture.

BEHAVIOUR Diurnal and nocturnal. Herds disperse during dry seasons, stallions remaining on territories where possible, digging and defending waterholes in stream beds; otherwise they migrate to areas of higher rainfall. Mares foal at a traditional place year after year.

BREEDING A single brown-and-white foal born during rains after 13 months gestation is weaned by nine months.

FEEDING Can subsist on grass too tough for cattle, browsing when grass disappears.

VOICE Most common sound is a donkeylike braying.

SWAHILI Kangaja.

MAMMALS

HOTSPOTS

- Samburu NR (p84)
- Buffalo Springs NR (p84)

MAMMALS

WHITE RHINOCEROS

RECOGNITION Massive. Long, low-slung head with wide mouth. Prominent shoulder hump when head raised. Dark grey to tan overall, sometimes dust-coloured.

HABITAT Short, open grassland near water with some trees and mud wallows.

BEHAVIOUR Active day and night, alternating between grazing and resting. Temporary groups may gather in shady areas or ridges during hot weather. Drinks daily when water available. Females follows calves when fleeing. Males create dung middens.

BREEDING One calf born after 16-month gestation; grazes at two months, driven away at two to three years.

FEEDING Grazes well-drained, well-trampled short grass almost exclusively, including regrowth after dry-season fires.

VOICE Usually silent, although males squeal, grunt and snort when challenging and courting.

SWAHILI Kifaru ya majani.

SQUARE-LIPPED GIANTS White rhinos are no more white than black rhinos are black: the name is a corruption of *weit*, a Dutch word meaning 'wide', referring to the shape of its mouth (white rhinos have broad, squared-off lips for grazing whereas those of black rhinos are pointed for plucking leaves). The white rhino's relatively docile nature means that in reserves where they can still be seen, you should be able to get close enough to see this distinctive feature. You can also admire its great size, second only to African elephants (male white rhinos can weigh up to 3600kg, more than twice as much as the biggest black rhino). It takes practice to tell white and black rhinos apart at a distance, but they are shaped differently: the highest point on a white's back being a prominent shoulder hump; on a black it's the haunches. Also, black rhinos tend to stay closer to cover, while white rhinos often feed in the open in the company of others of their kind, even veering close to gregariousness at times.

A female white rhino shares her home range with her most recent calf (and sometimes with unrelated juveniles). Her home range overlaps with those of other females, and several may graze side by side. Males defend territories and can be belligerent and very vocal, especially when seeking out a female on heat. Since two charging males could do great damage, encounters on territorial boundaries often involve two males staring at each other awhile before backing off.

White rhinos were once widespread in grassland over sub-Saharan and Southern Africa. The Southern African race was all but wiped out early in the 20th century, but at the 11th hour was protected and bred back from less than 100 individuals to around 6000 animals at the millennium. The northern subspecies was not so lucky: discovered only in 1903, it was poached to probable extinction in East Africa, except where small numbers have been transported to strictly protected reserves.

★ HOTSPOTS

- Tsavo NP (p66)
- Lake Nakuru NP (p91)

BLACK RHINOCEROS

ON THE BRINK Long before the invention of firearms, black rhinos were highly successful plains mammals: long-lived, highly mobile and able to reach a broad variety of vegetation with their relatively long necks (for rhinos). Weak eyesight was no handicap for such a massive animal and compensated for by keen hearing and sense of smell. Their horns are made of solid keratin – the same substance that makes up toenails and horses' hooves. Normally there are two, the larger at the front, but occasionally a rhino will have rudimentary third or even fourth horns, harking back to extinct ancestors that had several.

Although dark from afar, black rhinos appear black only after rain or bathing, and can be as pale and grey as a white rhino if they have been rolling in sand or ash during the dry season. Where several animals coexist, scuff marks and rubbings on trees or termite mounds are good signs of their presence; otherwise you'll be lucky to find them, although if the accounts of famous hunters are anything to go by, black rhinos were not rare 100 years ago. In fact, there were still 40,000 black rhinos in Kenya during the 1970s, but despite the warnings of conservationists, Kenya's black rhino population plummeted to an estimated 400 animals by the start of the new millennium. The reason: its horns were at one point worth more than gold, with people across the Arabian peninsula using them as carved handles for their *jambiyya* daggers. While political and spiritual leaders have discouraged this practice, it will take decades before black rhinos can re-emerge from the brink.

A controversial method of discouraging poachers has been the removal of the horns from living rhinos. But horns regrow and rhinos must be dehorned every couple of years – tranquillised rhinos have a high casualty rate. Whether dehorned rhinos can survive for long in the wild is another question: far from being merely decorative, horns can be used as effective and lethal weapons (known to kill lions) in defending calves and are used by males in courtship battles. And, in the dense cover favoured by black rhinos, a poacher may not be able to tell whether it has been dehorned or not.

RECOGNITION Huge (males weigh up to 1400kg), with thick hide, short legs and massive horned head. Upper lip is pointed and muscular – almost beaklike.

HABITAT Mainly savanna with thickets and abundant shrubs; also semiarid thorn scrub to montane forest.

BEHAVIOUR Mainly diurnal. Breaks branches and loosens soil with horns. Females with young sometimes associate with others in home range. Males mark territories with dung middens and urine sprays. Calves reputed to run behind mother.

BREEDING One calf born, usually during rains, after a 15 to 16 month gestation; tended by mother for two to three years, until she next gives birth.

FEEDING Browses on leaves, twigs and branches taken low down or broken off with horns. Seeks daily access to water.

VOICE Usually silent; grunts, snorts and screams when alarmed or fighting.

SWAHILI Kifaru.

MAMMALS

⭐ HOTSPOTS

- Serengeti NP (p108)
- Ngorongoro CA (p104)

MAMMALS

ROCK HYRAX

ELEPHANT'S TINY COUSIN Groups of what look like football-sized guinea pigs sitting around on koppies and cliffs are in fact hyraxes, a uniquely African group of herbivores. The rock hyrax is one of the most commonly encountered species and can readily be seen on rocky outcrops, which it often shares with bush hyraxes. Three species of hyraxes live almost exclusively in trees. Hyraxes share an ancient ancestry with aardvarks and elephants, but to make sense of this assertion it's probably best to imagine them as herbivores that were pushed off prehistoric savannas by the highly successful antelope family into other niches. Unlikely as it sounds, hyraxes have some elephant-like features, such as teats between their forelegs and a long gestation period. More obvious features to look for include blunt feet with rounded, nailed 'toes'; and upper incisors modified into tusks (sometimes seen when they yawn), which can deliver lethal damage during aggressive territorial encounters.

Rock hyraxes live in colonies on kopjes and cliffs; bush hyraxes are browsers that shelter in colonies side by side with rock hyraxes (their associations are in fact among the closest in the mammalian world). Both are savoured by leopards, genets and rock pythons; and Verreaux's eagles eat virtually nothing else. But hyraxes are a successful and widespread group: sweat on their rubbery foot pads creates a sticky surface that allows them to scale near-vertical rocks and trunks, and thus rely on permanent shelter with accessible food.

Rock hyraxes are social and gregarious, sleeping together for safety and warmth – look for them sunning in huddles on ledges in the early morning (white stains on boulders, caused by urine, indicate active colonies). Colonies are dominated by an aggressive, breeding male (submissive hyraxes flatten their body and present their rump) – hyraxes typically enter holes, groups and conflicts backside first to avoid those tusks. For such small animals they make some mighty noises, including high-pitched warning shrieks. Territorial male rock hyraxes may call on moonlit nights, and tree hyraxes utter penetrating screams shortly after dark.

RECOGNITION Rabbit-sized with short, rounded ears and no tail. Brownish coat of short, coarse fur with yellowish oval patch in the middle of the back.

HABITAT Widespread in savanna and semiarid country wherever koppies, cliffs and rocky outcrops provide shelter.

BEHAVIOUR Mainly diurnal. Colonies number 10 to 30 animals, comprised of different families of related females, each with a territorial male. Grooms regularly with clawlike inner toe on hind foot. Males usually call in the early morning and evening.

BREEDING Young (one to four) are born furred with open eyes after 7½-month gestation. Most births are in rainy season.

FEEDING Grazes quickly with large mouthfuls; can climb trees to browse. Young graze almost at birth, although are not weaned for one to five months.

VOICE Males utter far-carrying territorial yaps. Alarm call is a high-pitched scream.

SWAHILI Pimbi.

⭐ HOTSPOTS

AARDVARK

A LIVING FOSSIL Seeing an aardvark twice presages a long life, according to one traditional African belief. But although they are relatively common, they are entirely nocturnal and notoriously difficult to see, so you'd probably have to live a long time to see two anyway. In any case, any aardvarks seen are usually eaten (chances at longevity notwithstanding). And aardvarks aren't too popular among farmers because they dig holes large enough to endanger vehicles, stock and earthen dams. These pig-sized animals (the name in fact comes from the Afrikaans word for earth pig) are referred to in some books as ant-bears (although entirely unrelated to bears, which don't occur in Africa). In fact, the aardvark's lineage can be traced back 50 million years to *Phenacodus*, an ancestor it probably shared with elephants and hyraxes.

During the day, aardvarks shelter in burrows, emerging a couple of hours after dark to hunt termites and other insects. When their huge ears pick up movements above and below the soil, they dig furiously with stout forelimbs and powerful claws to uncover termite or ant nests, then quickly lap the insects up with a long, sticky tongue (which can protrude 30cm), swallowing with little chewing. As diggers, aardvarks are second to none in Africa: to escape predators, such as pythons, an aardvark bolts into a hole – of which there may be several in its territory – and in a pinch it can completely bury itself in 10 minutes. In the morning, fresh diggings are often in evidence and show how common these animals can be. Extensive, deep warrens with almost a dozen entrances may be shared by several breeding females. More commonly, though, they dig a fresh 'camping' hole most nights, only a few metres long, and plug it with earth. Aardvark burrows are important refuges for other animals, such as bats, mongooses and warthogs, and their disappearance from an area can have a flow-on effect on many other creatures.

RECOGNITION Compact and vaguely piglike with long tail. Long tubular snout and huge ears. Thick limbs with powerful front claws. Grey, seminaked appearance. Length 1.5m.

HABITAT Widespread in grassland and savanna. Adapts to many habitats, but absent from rainforests.

BEHAVIOUR Mainly solitary and strictly nocturnal. Active from one or two hours after dusk. Digs and shelters in extensive burrows (may be used by several animals) or overnight 'camps'.

BREEDING Naked young (one or two) born after a seven-month gestation; follow mother after two weeks; independent at six months.

FEEDING Termites, ants, beetle larvae and pupae are excavated and swept up with their long, sticky tongue.

VOICE Usually silent; grunts very occasionally.

SWAHILI Muhanga or Kukukifuku.

MAMMALS

HOTSPOTS

- Masai Mara NR (p62)
- Serengeti NP (p108)

WARTHOG

RECOGNITION An almost naked, grey pig with long, lank mane, massive facial growths, upward-curving tusks and thin, tufted tail held high when running.

HABITAT Common and widespread in savanna, open woodland and grassland, especially where aardvark burrows provide shelter.

BEHAVIOUR Diurnal. Sounders usually consist of sow and current brood. Bask in sun and huddle for warmth. 'Walk' on callused knees when rooting. Wallow daily in hot, dry weather. Males disperse after four years. Mature boars solitary.

BREEDING Female gives birth to two to five piglets in a burrow after a 160- to 170-day gestation; weaned in six months.

FEEDING Grazes a variety of grasses during rains, rootling for bulbs and tubers in dry seasons; occasionally eats fruit and carrion, and soil for minerals.

VOICE Piglike grunts in alarm and squeals in distress.

SWAHILI Ngiri.

PORTLY PORKERS The sight of a line of young warthogs trotting behind mother with heads high, manes flowing and skinny tails held erect probably inspired their popular name 'Kenya Express'. But, then again, it may have been the sight of a salivating boar chasing a sow in oestrus while muttering a guttural *chug-chug-chug*. Imagine it – the sow beds down for the night in an abandoned aardvark burrow, which she has comfortably lined with grass, while outside boars are still sniffing about after dark to see if she's in heat. If she fits the bill, at least one suitor will waylay her when she emerges in the morning. With such enthusiasm, it's not surprising that warthogs are prolific breeders, which is perhaps just as well because lions are smart enough to wait outside an occupied burrow too – and if they're really hungry, they'll even dig the warthog out.

Burrows are the key to warthog survival – they are most abundant where many burrows offer protection from inclement weather and predators and provide secure birthing dens. Sounders (groups of females and their current broods) use up to 10 burrows in their home range, and knowing where the nearest one lies can be a matter of life and death – all except large boars are popular prey for lions, cheetahs and hyenas, and infant mortality is particularly high. When pursued, they bolt to the nearest hole, where an adult will turn at the last second to face the predator, backing down the hole and lashing out with those big tusks. Tusks (actually greatly enlarged lower canine teeth) also explain the gross facial 'warts': in trials of strength for mating rights, boars push face to face, then break off suddenly to swipe sideways with their tusks; the huge fatty growths protect the face from serious damage. Tusks are also useful digging tools when, on bended knees, warthogs rootle in soil with their hard, flexible snout disc.

HOTSPOTS

- Amboseli NP (p74)
- Tsavo NP (p66)

MAMMALS

GIANT FOREST HOG

Despite its large size and startling appearance, the giant forest hog was one of the last large animals to be discovered in Africa. Its singular appearance gives clues to its ecology: the shaggy coat shows a tolerance for cold (giant forest hogs live as high as the upper slopes of Mts Kenya and Kilimanjaro); the wide mouth is designed for grazing (unlike other pigs, giant hogs rarely root for tubers, and then only in soft ground); and the massive facial growths indicate a propensity for fighting – this usually involves charging and ramming, and if two meet head-on, air compressed between the concave areas of their facial pads goes off like a gunshot.

Whereas warthogs are the dominant savanna pig and bushpigs inhabit dense forest, giant hogs occupy a niche between the two. Thus, although they rely on dense vegetation for shelter, they graze in adjoining glades and sward – often in the company of buffaloes (a precursor of the modern barnyard). Sounders are usually composed of a boar and sow with offspring from previous litters that live in overlapping home ranges. Very young piglets are straw-coloured and lie flat when mother sounds the alarm; nonetheless, predators take up to 50% of piglets each year.

BUSHPIG

Bushpigs are a favoured prey of leopards and spotted hyenas, chimpanzees will eagerly tear one up for food if they can catch it, and piglets are vulnerable to eagles and pythons. But in favourable conditions, a bushpig population can increase quickly: sows mature at 18 months and give birth after only a four-month gestation. Piglets are farrowed in a den among vegetation or piles of boulders and branches. Dark brown with rows of light spots at birth, piglets remain hidden for up to two months – freezing to avoid detection when danger approaches – and stay with the sounder for about a year.

Even adult bushpigs are generally retiring, staying in cover during the day and usually venturing from cover only after dark. But it's easy to see where they've been by the trail of soil tossed with their tusks and upturned with their strong nasal disc (guineafowl sometimes forage among rootling pigs). These opportunists will also scavenge carrion and eat small animals. Bushpigs make a mess of crops and, ironically, the persecution of predators has allowed them to become a serious agricultural pest in certain areas. But bushpigs are also widely hunted by people for food, and domestication has been proposed as a way of alleviating hunting pressure.

RECOGNITION Large. Covered with coarse black hair.

HABITAT Dense forest and savanna mosaic.

BEHAVIOUR Uses shallow scrapes under logs as beds. Huddles in cold, basks after rain and fog. Wallows.

BREEDING Two to 11 piglets.

FEEDING Grass and herbage.

VOICE Grunts and barks.

SWAHILI Nguruwe nyeusi.

★ HOTSPOTS

○ Queen Elizabeth NP (p158)
○ Aberdare NP (p86)

RECOGNITION Grey, brown or reddish. Paler head, spinal crest, ear tufts and 'beard'.

HABITAT Woodland, forest.

BEHAVIOUR Holds tail down when running.

BREEDING Three to seven piglets.

FEEDING Sniffs for roots, bulbs, fruit, fungi.

VOICE Soft grunts.

SWAHILI Nguruwe.

★ HOTSPOTS

○ Lake Mburo NP (p162)
○ Ngorongoro CA (p104)

MAMMALS

HIPPOPOTAMUS

RECOGNITION Huge and bloated with short legs, massive head and broad snout. Shiny grey with pink 'highlights'. Males weigh up to 3200kg.

HABITAT Widespread in lakes and slow rivers with pools, shallow banks and adjoining grassland.

BEHAVIOUR Gregarious in groups of 10 to 15 females with young, led by dominant male. Males enlarge puddles to make temporary waterholes in rains. Large numbers congregate in dry seasons.

BREEDING Single calf born underwater, mostly during rains, after eight-month gestation; suckles for eight months.

FEEDING Grazes up to 45kg of grass a night with wide, muscular mouth. Doesn't feed on aquatic vegetation.

VOICE Noisy in water, giving loud, distinctive wheeze-honks. Bellows and roars when fighting.

SWAHILI Kiboko.

RIVER PIGS A hippo out of water resembles a huge, naked bladder. Its skin is very thin and devoid of sweat glands – which means a hippo can rapidly dehydrate and overheat – so most of its day is spent underwater with only eyes, ears and nostrils showing. Listen along a likely stretch of water for sighs as they surface and exhale; hippos can stay submerged for up to five minutes and remain virtually hidden among water weeds, suddenly emerging in a flurry of jaws and tusks. Evening and early morning are good times to see them on the move (especially if it's overcast), when they follow well-worn trails to and from nocturnal grazing areas. Lazing about in water burns very little energy and keeps hippos safe from predators (although crocs may take calves); however, it can lead to overcrowding and violent territorial disputes.

'Yawning' is a challenge to all comers – those jaws can open to 150 degrees and chop a croc in half. Territorial males back up and shower each other with urine and faeces as a sign of respect, but also fight often, and their sharp, 50cm tusks leave deep scars and sometimes fatal wounds. Sounds also play an important role in hippos' social lives: males, spaced apart in territories, advertise their dominance with loud and repeated honking. Previously believed to be exclusively vegetarian, researchers recently observed hippos devouring a dead impala in a waterhole and even behaving aggressively towards crocodiles and hunting dogs at a carcass. You don't want to get too close to their back end either: hippos mark territories and grazing trails by spraying dung and waving their paddle-shaped tail at the same time, spreading it all over the place (including safari tents). But that's no deterrent to an enterprising parasite: clinging to the skin of these amphibious animals would be a precarious existence, so large freshwater leeches feed and breed while attached to the inside of hippos' rectums!

MAMMALS

GIRAFFE

LONG-NECKED BROWSERS That neck is the longest in the animal kingdom, but still has only seven bones – the same as you and every other mammal. The biggest plus of such a towering reach is that it puts giraffes above all competition for food (except elephants). The downside is getting a drink, which, to achieve, a giraffe must splay its front legs and bend down – a position that makes it vulnerable, but must be risked at least once a week. (To prevent fainting, the arteries have special valves that stop blood rushing down to the head – and back when it stands up again.) Massive shoulders are needed to hold the neck up, and young bulls also use these to jostle, intertwining necks and delivering blows with their heads to assert dominance. 'Necking' thus establishes social hierarchies from an early age, and adult males rarely contest seriously at mating time. It looks like slow-mo, but a swing from a bull's head can break his opponent's neck or jaw.

Despite their great size, giraffes blend in well with the surroundings and aren't always easy to see, with just head and neck showing behind a tree. In dry seasons, they are more likely to be seen feeding along drainage lines on evergreen foliage, dispersing across the plains during the rains. Their coat markings follow several basic arrangements, but the pattern of each animal is unique, remains constant throughout life and tends to get darker with age. The three distinct races in East Africa, distinguished by their coats, are reticulated, Masai and Rothschild's giraffes (restricted to a few parks).

Giraffes never seem to be in a hurry, browsing placidly on even the thorniest acacias with agile lips and an amazing 45cm-long tongue. Even when walking they look relaxed, with both left legs then both right legs moving alternately – it's deceptive, for in full flight they can outrun any predator.

RECOGNITION Immensely tall (up to 5.2m) with long neck, legs and tail. Variable orange to dark-brown blotches on white to corn-gold background. Tapered head with short horns.

HABITAT Widespread and common in savanna, open woodland and plains with thickets.

BEHAVIOUR Diurnal and partly nocturnal. Nonterritorial and loosely gregarious, spending most of the day chewing cud. Herds can be mixed or single-sex, but large bulls monopolise matings. Cows calve in the same area year after year.

BREEDING Year-round. Calf born 1.8m-high; after two weeks joins others in crèche for three to four months. Weaned at 12 months.

FEEDING Exclusively browsers, mainly on acacia leaves, buds, shoots and fruits, gathered high in trees and thickets.

VOICE Normally silent, but utters snorts and grunts. Musical notes occasionally reported.

SWAHILI Twiga.

MAMMALS

★ HOTSPOTS

- Masai Mara NR (p62)
- Samburu NR (p84)
- Serengeti NP (p108)
- Lake Nakuru NP (p91)

AFRICAN BUFFALO

RECOGNITION Stocky and cattle-like. Black or dark brown with thick, up-curved horns on central boss. Reddish 'forest buffalo' are smaller with backswept horns.

HABITAT Mosaics of grassland, woodland and savanna within 15km of water; also swamps, floodplains and forest edge.

BEHAVIOUR Highly gregarious. Presence of herd often given away by cattle egrets. Drinks daily and licks termite mounds for salt. Bulls wallow to cool off and remove parasites.

BREEDING One calf born (mostly in early rains) after an 11½-month gestation; weaned at approximately 10 months.

FEEDING Grazes a wide variety of grasses, including coarse grass left by other species; browses herbs and foliage when grass is scarce.

VOICE Usually silent but for explosive snorts in alarm. Calves bleat and cows grunt to call calves.

SWAHILI Nyati or Mbogo.

BULLISH BOVIDS Perhaps no other large animal has the African buffalo's reputation: a big bull stands 1.7m at the shoulder and could easily toss a Land Rover if it wanted. Lone bulls can be extremely dangerous animals, and even blind or injured buffaloes can survive for years because of their size and bellicosity. If you do have the misfortune to be chased – you'll know it when the bushes explode and 850kg of beef comes hurtling out at 55km/h – by the time your brain catches up with your legs, it should direct you to climb a tree (on the side away from the buffalo or you'll be propelled into it). But otherwise, African buffaloes are basically cattle and, like their domestic counterparts, generally live in docile, grazing herds.

Ironically, unless you see bulls fighting or fending off lions, African buffaloes are pretty inactive. Most of a buffalo's day is spent grazing or chewing the cud. Highly social, buffaloes form large nonterritorial herds, which can number as many as 1500 members, although herds of several hundred are more common. The activity and movement of the herd is tightly coordinated by a variety of signals including lowing calls (similar to those of domestic cattle) and smells (presumably for recognising individuals and predators).

If you approach a herd, several individuals strut forward with their heads up to test the wind – a challenging pose that seems to presage a charge. Meanwhile, the remaining adults form a line with young sheltered in between before they turn and run with heads tossing. However, they will charge a predator en masse and rally to protect a stricken animal.

Herds reach their greatest size during the rains; dry seasons see them break into smaller 'clans' of 12 or so cows and their offspring, accompanied by adult bulls. Cows in oestrus attract bulls who posture for dominance, circling, pawing, thrashing bushes and sometimes charging head-on in violent clashes. Bulls past their fighting prime join bachelor herds – this is when they're dangerous, but also most vulnerable to lions.

★ HOTSPOTS

- Masai Mara NR (p62)
- Serengeti NP (p108)
- Ngorongoro CA (p104)
- Semliki Valley WR (p170)

MAMMALS

ANTELOPES

GRACEFUL GRAZERS Where there's greenery, there's usually an antelope to eat it. Some may lack charisma, but each is a piece of the ecological jigsaw, and East Africa's 40-odd species range from duikers barely 35cm high to oxen-sized eland. Think of them as deadly predators of plant life – not all of which is defenceless (many antelopes browse selectively because plants can send a toxic surge into leaves being attacked). Antelopes promote the cycle of growth by adding manure to the soil, and themselves provide a perpetual larder for all those glamorous meat eaters.

Antelopes chew the cud; nearly all young hide for a few weeks after birth before joining the herd; and females remain with a herd from birth, dominated by males whose competitiveness forces bucks to disperse as they mature. Antelopes' horns are permanent, although frequently damaged in fights, and never branched like the antlers of deer. All bucks have them (and females of some species) – ridged (annulated), twisted, straight or backswept – but they are mainly for competition, rather than defence (by the time a predator gets that close it's usually too late): it's mainly the males who strive for rank (and always for mating rights).

Male antelopes are usually called bucks and females does. Bucks of course are mainly interested in does when they're in oestrus, in which case they're ready to rut – the end result of which is usually the birth of a single fawn. All antelopes have interdigital glands between their hooves, which are used

BONGO ANTELOPE

for scent-marking territories with details of the owner's sex, age and social and reproductive status (other territorial behaviour includes piling dung in middens). Some species leave black, tar-like secretions ('black pearls') by inserting twigs into the pit-like preorbital glands in front of their eyes. After a period of lying out in the grass, many fawns join a crèche with others. Playful young antelopes leap into the air, known as stotting (or pronking), which, when performed by adults, is thought to discourage would-be predators by demonstrating the antelopes' fitness.

MAMMALS

★ HOTSPOTS

- Serengeti NP (p108) Up to 17 different species, and often several are seen feeding together.
- Masai Mara NR (p62) Numbers reach a crescendo during the wildebeest migration.
- Samburu NR (p84) Dry country species such as oryxes, gerenuks, kudus and dik-diks thrive in semiarid scrub.
- Queen Elizabeth NP (p158) Extensive wetlands are suitable for Uganda kobs, waterbucks and sitatungas.

SPIRAL-HORNED ANTELOPES

MAGNIFICENT SEVEN Forest or dense bush offered some tempting benefits for evolving antelopes, such as cover to hide in and a year-round food supply, but it came with some inherent problems – cover can be used just as effectively by predators, for example. A group of seven antelopes, collectively known as tragelaphines (spiral-horned antelopes is easier to say), has evolved various strategies that both overcome and exploit such habitats. Among them are the largest of all, the elands; some of the most distinctive, such as greater kudus; and the unique, semiaquatic sitatunga. All are browsers of young, nutritious vegetation and immediately stand out from the crowd with flanks strongly marked in blotches and vertical stripes, and more blazes on head, chest and legs.

Females of most species are hornless and show a generic resemblance, but males carry distinctive, smooth, keeled horns that spiral or twist to some degree (most dramatically in greater kudus). Stripes and blotches can make excellent camouflage, for example on the flanks of bongos and bushbucks they almost perfectly mimic sunlight dappled through the canopy, making these antelopes very difficult to detect until they break cover. But an unfortunate corollary of superb camouflage is losing sight of your family, so these highly visual animals communicate with subtle signals from an early age: females approaching their hidden young bob their heads, throat flashes showing vividly in the gloomy light; and when raised in panic, their bushy tails show a white flag.

Spiral-horned antelopes are closely related to buffaloes and, like them, are built for

SITATUNGA

MAMMALS

neither speed nor endurance. All have a nonterritorial herd structure, although only elands, which live in more open country, have a highly developed herd instinct. The rule with tragelaphines is low aggression in open, flexible societies where males dominate without confrontation, instead of staking out a territory. Large males do most of the mating, their dominance enforced by side-on displays that enhance their markings. Further refinements include a spinal crest, which can be erected in threat or courtship, and horning vegetation and soil as a mark of status.

Horns of the well-armed males are occasionally used in defensive wrestling, but bucks of most species are generally solitary and experience surges of testosterone that lead to aggressive phases, known in Swahili as *ukali*. *Ukali* may be a cyclical phenomenon that encourages other males to disperse for their own safety (lethal clashes sometimes occur when two bucks are *ukali*). Life in the open compels elands to seek security in large, mobile herds where females also establish a hierarchy and calves are vulnerable to male aggression. As a consequence, both male and female elands have horns. Doing their best to remain hidden doesn't help an antelope buff to find them of course, but at least all tragelaphines signal with barking calls. There seems to be a neat inverse correlation between the vibrancy of markings and their vocal aptitude; for example, sitatungas are weakly marked, but call often from the safety of their swamps. Living in dense bush, distinctively marked kudu bulls are more vulnerable to ambush and posture more or less silently.

THE SWAMP ANTELOPE

One of the most remarkable of all antelopes is the sitatunga, a long-legged tragelaphine adapted to exploit the abundant food resources in swamps: its shaggy coat is oily and water repellent; it is a good, if slow, swimmer; and extraordinarily elongated and splayed hooves allow it to walk on submerged vegetation. So specialised are its feet that a sitatunga can outrun predators through swamps, but on dry ground it walks rather clumsily with a spread-eagled stance. Sitatungas move slowly and deliberately to avoid detection, typically entering the water, gently sinking, then feeding with most of the body submerged. To more effectively conceal themselves from predators they can submerge until just their snouts and part of their heads show above the surface. Watching and waiting are the tricks to seeing sitatungas: they are most active between 6pm and 10am – watch along the paths and tunnels they form through reeds and rushes.

MAMMALS

★ HOTSPOTS

- ○ Lake Mburo NP (p162) For bushbucks (found wherever there are thickets), elands and sitatungas.
- ○ Saiwa Swamp NP (p97) Was proclaimed largely to protect sitatungas.
- ○ Tsavo NP (p66) Semiarid scrub is a favourite haunt of lesser kudus.
- ○ Ruaha NP (p134) Greater kudus are elusive, but this park offers the best chance of seeing one.

TOPI & HARTEBEESTS

TOPI, SERENGETI NATIONAL PARK

BUILT FOR SPEED The group of large antelopes known scientifically as alcelaphines includes topis, hartebeests and wildebeest. All are grazers whose most outstanding features are elongated jaws (their eyes always seem to be set higher up than you expect), sloping hindquarters and powerful shoulders (wildebeest look like no other antelope). All live on the open plains in large herds and rely on speed and stamina to escape predators. Life in the open demands long, strong legs for sustained, fast flight and a herding instinct for safety, and the evolution of a long face enabled these antelope to graze without the encumbrance of a long neck. Dense herds tend to create intense competition among males, and the short, muscular neck also cushions the blows when males drop to their knees for headbutting jousts.

Both topis and hartebeests are often seen standing watch on top of abandoned termite mounds. If conditions are stable, enough small herds live in a permanent home range, but when grassland dries out, mixed herds aggregate and move on. At these times, males display on the run with stylised gaits and postures, and dispense scent with vigorous kicks, capering and stamping – hence the eccentric cavorting of wildebeest.

The hartebeest shows much variation in colour and horn shape over its wide distribution – the variations are so marked that several populations go under different names, eg Coke's (also known as the kongoni) and Jackson's hartebeest. The fossil record shows that hartebeests have evolved only over the last million years or so; as their distribution becomes fragmented by agriculture, the different races will most probably evolve into new species within the next million years – should they last that long. The hirola, formerly known as Hunter's hartebeest, now has the dubious distinction of being the world's rarest antelope. Numbers plummeted from 10,000 or so in the 1970s to under 1000 and as few as 600 by the year 2000. Hirolas appear to have suffered with the massive increase in cattle, with which they compete directly for food.

★ HOTSPOTS

- Masai Mara NR (p62) Large numbers of topis and kongonis.
- Tsavo NP (p66) Last chance to see hirolas – many have been transferred here and appear to be holding their own.
- Murchison Falls NP (p154) Jackson's hartebeest is common north of the Victoria Nile.

MAMMALS

WILDEBEEST

THE FAMOUS MIGRANTS Probably no other antelopes spark as much excitement as wildebeest on their famous year-long cycle of grazing, rutting and calving known as 'the migration'. Up to 500,000 of them (along with 250,000 plains zebras) cross the Serengeti grassland to the fertile volcanic plains of the Masai Mara in a vast, constantly moving herd. The catalyst is the short grasses on which wildebeest depend – their wide mouth is perfectly suited to select nutritious leaf growing close to the ground, but they can't survive for long on anything else, and must keep circulating as pasture becomes exhausted.

Gregariousness is a great asset for an animal permanently exposed on the sward, and thousands of hooves probably confuse predators. But, unique among antelopes, wildebeest make even the arrival of the next generation a crowd spectacle. Females in the Serengeti synchronise the dropping of some 750,000 calves to within a few weeks of each other to coincide with the flush of grass in the rains. As conditions dry out, herds congregate in a massive, continuously moving stream that stimulates hormonal changes in both sexes. Females come into oestrus and males respond by staking tiny territories that usually last only a few days and are defined by little more than a bull's behaviour – the head shaking, cavorting and leaps that earned wildebeest their common name.

Bulls mate with as many cows as they can before the herd moves on, mothers travelling with calves towards the centre, 'single' females further out, dominant bulls on the edge and males trying to establish harems on the outside or trailing behind (it's all much clearer from the air). The migration is a time of plenty for lions and crocodiles waiting in ambush, and hundreds of wildebeest drown where noisy, thrashing bottlenecks form at river crossings. A few weeks pass and the cycle begins again – the plains can be bereft of wildebeest for up to eight months at a time before predators and safari operators alike hear that unmistakable bleating on the breeze and start licking their lips.

RECOGNITION Large with thick neck, shaggy horse-like mane and tail. Elongated head has white 'beard', black muzzle and cowlike horns. Grey to tan overall with darker brindling.

HABITAT Short grass plains within about 20km of water.

BEHAVIOUR Diurnal and nocturnal. Cows congregate with young among territorial bulls during rains. Calving occurs between late January and mid-March. Females come into oestrus as they lead herds in annual migration. Old and sick animals are left behind.

BREEDING Young born synchronously during wet season after eight-month gestation; can walk and run within minutes.

FEEDING Grazes nutritious short grasses until exhausted; cannot survive long on coarse grass.

VOICE Bulls give loud, froglike belching grunts when displaying.

SWAHILI Nyumbu.

MAMMALS

★ HOTSPOTS

- Masai Mara NR (p62)
- Serengeti NP (p108)

IMPALA

RECOGNITION Grant's gazelle–sized. Fawn or tan above, paler on flanks (which lack stripes), with white belly. Black stripes on haunches. Males have backward-sweeping ridged horns.

HABITAT Open woodland near short to medium grassland on well-drained soils. Avoids steep slopes.

BEHAVIOUR Active by day, feeding mostly at dawn and dusk, resting in shade to ruminate in between. Lies down in overcast weather. Bachelor males mix with females in dry seasons. Often associates with baboons. Can go without drinking.

BREEDING One fawn is born in a sheltered spot after a 200-day gestation.

FEEDING Consumes almost 100% grass during rains, switching to browse (70%) such as shrubs (especially acacia and *Combretum*), seed pods and herbage in dry seasons.

VOICE Loud snorts in alarm.

SWAHILI Swala pala.

HIGH-KICKING 'GAZELLE' You may see an impala and think 'gazelle', but in fact the impala is thought to be most closely related to topis, hartebeests and wildebeest. It's an understandable mistake, for the impala is about the size of a Grant's gazelle and among the most agile and graceful of all antelopes. When a predator approaches (and lions, cheetahs and hunting dogs often do), a herd of impalas explodes in all directions. Well known for their leaping ability, impalas can clear 3m in height, and 11m at a bound. Part of the bucks' strategy for dispersing scent is to high kick, which releases pheromones from unique glands on their rear fetlocks (easily seen as black hair tufts). Such behaviour is reminiscent of wildebeest, but male impalas also show unique tongue-flashing behaviour when courting or competing with other males for dominance. Like gazelles, you can expect to see impalas in groups, but you won't necessarily see them out on the plains – impalas seek woody areas on the savanna edge, where they browse when the grass gets too dry.

An abundance of provender encourages gregarious behaviour and the impala does form 'clans' numbering 30 to 120 in overlapping home ranges. Males are also highly sociable and often drift to different clans (something does hardly ever do). Such large herds of females promote keen competition among bucks: these testosterone-driven pawns spend up to 25% of their time shepherding does into their territories and fighting off bachelor wannabes. In East Africa, the impala rut is virtually continuous and rutting bucks are very vocal – you'll probably hear their predatorlike roars in suitable habitat and even see bucks with injuries from stronger rivals. This is a good time to get close as impala bucks are often preoccupied. The rut is so strenuous that most males are exhausted after about three months, by which time a dominant male from the ever-ready bachelor herd is able to oust him from his territory. Vanquished bucks return to the bachelor herd where they regain condition and status, upon which they usually set out to reclaim their territory.

★ HOTSPOTS

- Masai Mara NR (p62)
- Serengeti NP (p108)
- Lake Manyara NP (p128)
- Lake Mburo NP (p162)

MAMMALS

HORSE-ANTELOPES

WARRIOR HORSES Three species of large, gregarious antelope are among the most striking of large mammals, with long, pointed or backswept horns, boldly patterned coats and black-and-white 'war paint' on their faces and muzzles. Tall stature, long tail, large hooves (and in sable and roan antelopes, an upright mane) give them a rather horse-like look, and their collective name, hippotragines, stems from Latin meaning 'horse-goat'. These antelopes are adapted to hard country with unpredictable rainfall – country with few large competitors, but marginal enough that large home ranges with sufficient fodder must be defended.

Unusually for antelopes, the females' horns are well developed (although thinner than bucks') and are an effective deterrent to other mares competing for food. Adults are rarely taken as prey, relying on speed and agility to outmanoeuvre predators, although hyenas, hunting dogs and lions take a toll of their young. But as a last resort, the horns can double as formidable weapons, especially the spearlike, 75cm-long horns of oryxes, which have been known to impale lions and kill people.

These rare exceptions aside, horns are mainly used in ritual combat, or when striving for rank in a herd, and all three species have evolved various means of lessening fatal clashes. Roan bucks fight on their knees to lessen the chance of serious injuries, but fights between sable males sometimes lead to fatal gorings. This is where the sable's bold, easily seen markings come into play: young male sables resemble females and only the dominant male is black –

ROAN ANTELOPE

another black animal on his turf would present an immediate challenge. Adapted to follow infrequent rains in search of green growth, a territorial life is not usually possible for oryxes; instead, a breeding bull dominates a nomadic herd and tolerates the presence of other males. Should he show aggression to calves, females are well equipped to discourage him.

Young of all three species spend much time playing – staging mock duels and generally charging about, especially in the early morning before feeding starts in earnest. Oryxes in particular put on some showy high-stepping at dawn and during showers.

MAMMALS

⭐ HOTSPOTS

- Samburu NR (p84) This semiarid reserve makes ideal country for beisa oryxes.
- Tsavo NP (p66) The fringe-eared race of oryx can be seen south of the Tana River.
- Ruaha NP (p134) Roans and sables favour woodlands.

GAZELLES

THOMPSON'S GAZELLE

GRACE AND SPEED Gazelles conjure up images of grace and speed, and all three East African species have these attributes in spades. The two common medium-sized gazelles of the plains, Thomson's and Grant's, are grazers and browsers; the third species, the gerenuk, is common in semiarid country.

Life on open plains allows (and for safety's sake obliges) a herbivore to congregate in larger numbers than would otherwise be possible: herds of Grant's and Tommies often gather in hundreds – sometimes with each other or with other herbivores, such as zebras, topis, impalas and wildebeest. A great percentage of the 400,000 Tommies on the Serengeti Plains are migratory, mingling with zebras and wildebeest – a sight that could evoke thoughts of the former abundance of plains mammals.

All of the large predators will take gazelles when the opportunity arises: Tommies are a favourite of cheetahs and wild dogs; male olive baboons will tear a young gazelle apart for a bit of extra protein; and martial eagles take fawns. Survival in the open requires all antelopes to be constantly alert and able to flee with split-second warning. Even topping 80km/h in flight, and dodging and jumping with great agility, gazelles are not quite a match for cheetahs and run the risk of overheating when being pursued by wild dogs or hyenas.

Herd members communicate with signals to warn of predators: Tommies flicker that bold, black flank stripe by twitching their torso just as they are about to run for it; and Grant's have a flashy white rump that stands out like a beacon in flight. All gazelles have a dark stripe through the eye and pale eyebrows, and other signal patches are visible when they flag their heads, wag their tails or leap about.

Gazelles live in flexible societies with little ranking, herds of does grazing and ruminating in large, shared home ranges, walking to water, lying up together and migrating in sometimes huge aggregations. Bucks fight in defence of territories where females graze and even maintain their territories after the females have moved on. Young are hidden for a few weeks after birth, with female Tommies remaining nearby or joining 'maternity herds', which ably fend off marauding jackals.

⭐ HOTSPOTS

- Masai Mara NR (p62) Great herds of Tommies and Grant's, often mixed with other herbivores.
- Serengeti NP (p108) Tommies and Grant's
- Tsavo NP (p66) Peters' gazelle – a distinctive race of Grant's – is common in semiarid bush.

MAMMALS

GERENUK

GIRAFFE-NECK Gerenuks (from the Somali for 'giraffe-neck') are gazelles adapted to life in semiarid bush. Such habitat favours only small herds and, consequently, more than 12 gerenuks are rarely seen together. Long, slender legs and an extraordinarily elongated neck enable gerenuks to browse on the small, nutritious leaflets of acacias high up in the foliage; and a narrow snout, tiny mouth and long, pointed tongue help them pluck flowers and seed pods from between the longest spines. But gerenuks further outstrip the competition by standing on their hind legs to feed, thus attaining a height of 2m from the ground, where only very young giraffes might compete. Gerenuks can be active at any time of day, although to avoid detection they freeze, blending in with the thorny scrub.

Only male gerenuks have the distinctive forward-tipped horns – which grow up to 44cm. Young males associate with each other, and with females, but become increasingly intolerant of other males as they reach maturity. Like Thomson's gazelles, adult males mark their territories with black pearls of scent from their preorbital glands, a behaviour not seen among male Grant's gazelles. Females breed year-round and, for the first six weeks, fawns conceal themselves by hiding motionless in vegetation to avoid marauding predators such as hunting dogs, cheetahs, jackals and leopards.

RECOGNITION A gazelle with very long limbs and neck. Red-brown saddle with buff body and white underparts. Large rounded ears, wedge-shaped head and long tail with black tuft.

HABITAT Semiarid to arid bush, especially open, flat thornbush.

BEHAVIOUR Able to feed standing on its hind legs. During courtship, male scent-marks the female with his preorbital glands.

BREEDING Year-round. Single fawn born after 6½ to seven months. Fawns can stand bipedally after one month.

FEEDING Browses small-leaved, thorny trees and shrubs.

VOICE Generally silent. Snorts to signal alarm. Males 'hum' during courtship.

SWAHILI Swala twiga.

MAMMALS

⭐ **HOTSPOTS**

- Samburu NR (p84)
- Meru NP (p95)
- Tsavo NP (p66)

REDUNCINE ANTELOPES

DEFASSA WATERBUCK

WATERSIDE DWELLERS If there is any antelope you are virtually guaranteed to see on safari, it is the waterbuck, and despite a shaggy coat and sometimes pungent smell, this large, often approachable animal somehow maintains a stately bearing even when grazing up to its belly in water. Two subspecies are commonly seen: the defassa waterbuck, which has an all-white rump (used by mothers to signal their calf to follow); and the common waterbuck, in which the rump patch is so reduced it looks like the animal has just sat on a freshly painted toilet seat (it has the same signalling function, but looks more like a bullseye). Waterbucks belong to a group of antelopes called the reduncines, which lumps them with the Uganda kob and three reedbucks (southern, bohor and the less frequently seen mountain reedbuck – the East African race is called Chanler's mountain reedbuck). Reedbucks are mostly nocturnal and bohor reedbucks often give themselves away at night with whistles.

Only male waterbucks and reedbucks have horns, albeit strongly ridged (annulated) ones, which point forward at the tips, but both sexes have many skin glands that make their coat greasy – possibly as an insulation from temperature extremes – and pungent (it is sometimes stated that the waterbuck's strong scent deters predators, but plenty get eaten by lions and hyenas). As their name suggests, waterbucks are never found far from water, and all reduncines are more or less attached to it (although mountain reedbucks seek a living on valley sides); bohor reedbucks and waterbucks, in particular, rely on waterside vegetation for cover when pursued. The attraction is a year-round supply of food on waterside grassland; the price is a habitat that swings dramatically between floods and dry-season fires. As a consequence, most reduncines have broad ecological tolerances (eg bohor reedbucks stray as far as 25km during drought) and a flexible herd structure to accommodate crowding during difficult times. All males are territorial, but in waterbucks at least, females appear to have no hierarchy. But a buck will tolerate several bachelors on his turf – as long as they show correct appeasement behaviour when he expects it.

HOTSPOTS

- Hell's Gate NP (p87) Rocky slopes make a likely stakeout for Chanler's mountain reedbucks.
- Masai Mara NR (p62) Sekenani Valley Chanler's live here.
- Lake Nakuru NP (p91) Woodlands fringing wetlands are ideal for the defassa race of waterbuck; bohor reedbucks are also abundant.
- Samburu NR (p84) Common waterbucks resident.

UGANDA KOB

SWARD FIGHTERS Kob bucks have a distinctive look when they're trying to attract a doe's attention, strutting with head held high and horns pointing back horizontally. In fact, if it weren't for its mating habits, the Uganda kob would probably be a fairly unremarkable beast, looking superficially like an impala and inhabiting floodplains like other reduncine antelopes. It's recovering well after Uganda's civil war and is easy to see in some reserves, grazing on green belts near waterways during the dry season and moving to higher ground during the rains. Bucks usually hold territories some distance apart and females live in small herds with no apparent hierarchy, coming and going as they choose. But seasonal movements and the need to drink regularly force females into herds, sometimes totalling thousands of animals. Where these herds become resident, sheer weight of numbers keeps the grass short in recognisable 'kob fields'. But look closely at some of these fields and you'll see mainly males strutting about in that distinctive pose, like so many jocks in a gym.

This is where things start to get interesting: stimulated by the presence of female herds, the bucks (sometimes 40 per hectare) concentrate on leks – areas of sward, often enclosed by longer grass – where they stake out territories radiating from one or more hubs of accumulated dung and urine-soaked soil. Here, they fight all challengers for the privilege of mounting a doe, rarely retaining their court for more than a few days and often exhausting themselves within hours. Herds of bachelors wait nearby to fight, but it's not the bucks alone that attract the does – when researchers removed sections of turf and placed them outside the lek, does (and bucks) moved to the old turf in the new position. Turf soaked with oestrogen-charged urine attracts both sexes to the leks, and 90% of females enter an arena on their day of oestrus to mate with a few males that have won centrally placed courts.

RECOGNITION Like a stocky impala. Reddish or ochre with white markings on face and throat. Black on hocks. Females lack males' lyre-shaped horns.

HABITAT River flats and short grassland, especially those trampled by other grazers or created by fires.

BEHAVIOUR Diurnal and nocturnal. Gregarious, sometimes forming large herds within a short walk of water, but avoids flooded areas. Moving en masse when threatened confuses or intimidates predators. When pursued, seeks refuge in water or reed beds.

BREEDING Calves born year-round after eight-month gestation; remains hidden for six weeks then joins others in crèche.

FEEDING Grazes short grasses cropped by other species, green flushes after fires and 'kob fields'.

VOICE Whistles and grunts to advertise territory.

SWAHILI Mraye.

MAMMALS

⭐ **HOTSPOTS**

- Queen Elizabeth NP (p158)
- Murchison Falls NP (p154)

SMALL ANTELOPES

MAMMALS

ORIBI, UGANDA

ANTELOPES IN MINIATURE The ancestral antelope looked very similar to a number of rather solitary and small antelopes (some are miniature – blue duikers stand only 32.5cm at the shoulder) that exploit small niches from rainforests to cliff faces. Size apart, dik-diks, klipspringers, the savanna-dwelling steenbok and oribi, and the nine species of forest-dwelling duiker, bear the hallmarks of most larger antelopes, including white signal patches on the rump (a good way to detect duikers as they move through the forest gloom). All bucks have horns, albeit small and spiky ones, but ironically in territorial disputes they seem more inclined to use them and inflict more serious injuries than larger species.

Most species live in strongly bonded pairs and defend a home range marked extensively with their preorbital glands – modified in duikers as 'smear glands' along the muzzle – that keep others of the same species posted with details of the marker's age, sex and breeding condition. Although small antelopes feature regularly on the menu of many predators, they make size work in their favour by heavily scenting their territories and using the resulting invisible map to bolt to safety through dense undergrowth. Females and males keep each other interested with pervasive physical and airborne scents strong enough for one species, the suni, to be known as the musk antelope. All except duikers also mark territorial boundaries with dung middens.

Although rather common in places, small antelopes typically escape detection by freezing until danger passes – the bold markings of many duikers break up their outline in dappled forest light. Nimble enough to climb sloping trunks and tangles of vegetation, duikers have a subtle but intimate awareness of their environment, relying for sustenance on fruit, flowers and leaves dropped or dislodged from the forest canopy by monkeys, birds and fruit-bats. Listen for foot stamping as a warning and, if your vocal skills are up to it, an imitation of their bleat can attract duiker bucks. Snorts or whistles in alarm are other giveaways for small antelopes – oribis in particular are vocal whistlers and easily recognisable when they flee by stotting (modified in a distinctive rocking-horse movement).

⭐ HOTSPOTS

- Lake Mburo NP (p162) A mosaic of thickets and grasslands make this an ideal location for oribi
- Arabuko-Sokoke NP (p70) Supports four duiker species, including the rare Aders' duiker.
- Hell's Gate NP (p87) Steinbucks thrive among thickets and rocky ground.

KLIPSPRINGER

Even if you thought to look for antelopes high up on a cliff face, you could easily overlook klipspringers because of their small size and nondescript coloration. Living as high as 4000m on Mt Kilimanjaro, their dense fur is made up of hollow hairs that retain heat and enable klipspringers to withstand extreme cold. But they still like to take in the morning sun and this is when they are best seen, standing motionless and alert on rock ledges. When alarmed, klipspringers (from the Afrikaans 'cliff-springer') lightly bound away across boulders, landing on all fours on the tips of their modified hooves.

Typically in pairs, when they feel safe again they perform a whistling duet, the female calling straight after the male; klipspringers are very faithful to their territories and whistling probably also advertises to other pairs nearby. Inaccessible rock faces and agility are their main protection against predators, although danger can still come from above in the shape of eagles, and the male invariably acts as sentry while the doe feeds or suckles their single kid. Klipspringers typically spend their entire adult lives on one territory, but should disaster strike their patch, they can survive for a time in adjoining habitat such as valley floors.

KIRK'S DIK-DIK

Antelopes don't come much smaller than Kirk's dik-dik – despite its long, slender legs, the largest adult stands only 45cm high. Kirk's dik-diks always live in monogamous pairs, the buck whistling persistently when danger approaches, while the doe and fawn hide – reunions that follow an escape include much nuzzling and scent-marking. They are commonly seen in the early morning and evening, quivering stock-still near a bush before bolting through the undergrowth.

It is remarkable that a browser so small can be so successful, but the secret to a dik-dik's survival is a thorough knowledge of its turf, enabling it to escape through low tangles of vegetation. Territories are actively marked with black pearls of scent on twigs and stems, and middens of their tiny dung pellets mark boundaries – where a midden overlaps two territories, both families add to it on their respective sides. Any strange new droppings in their territories are detected by that flexible nose and are added to (including those of elephants!). The inside of their nose is lined with blood vessels and also acts as a heat regulator: Kirk's dik-diks can increase their breathing rate from one to eight breaths a second, sending cooled blood back to the heart.

RECOGNITION Compact, goat-like. Grizzled grey-brown.

HABITAT Cliffs, rocky slopes.

BEHAVIOUR Rests during day.

BREEDING Single kid born after six-month gestation.

FEEDING Browses on herbs and foliage.

VOICE Pairs whistle.

Swahili Mbuzi mawe.

★ HOTSPOTS

- Aberdare NP (p86)
- Arusha NP (p126)
- Lake Mburo NP (p162)

RECOGNITION Tawny upper.

HABITAT Bushy savanna edge.

BEHAVIOUR May stand on hind legs when feeding.

BREEDING Single fawn born after six-month gestation.

FEEDING Browses on shoots and foliage.

VOICE A high *zik zik*.

SWAHILI Dikidiki.

★ HOTSPOTS

- Samburu NR (p84)
- Meru NP (p95)
- Arusha NP (p126)

MAMMALS

SMALL MAMMALS

RODENTS, INSECTIVORES & HARES
A vast assemblage – both in species and individuals – of small mammals plays an important role in nearly every ecosystem, eg as food for predatory mammals, birds and reptiles; and as predators of insects and other invertebrates. Among them are the familiar (though hardly glamorous) rodents, a large group – numbering 150 species in East Africa alone – that includes rats, mice and interesting variations such as squirrels, springhares, porcupines and anomalures (flying mice). Other, unrelated small mammals that may be encountered on safari include several families of small carnivorous mammals loosely termed insectivores: the shrews, elephant shrews and hedgehogs; and the vegetarian hares, known scientifically as lagomorphs.

All rodents have a dental arrangement that features prominent incisors (gnawing teeth). Squirrels are essentially arboreal rodents (although one or two are primarily ground dwelling) and most are active during the day; they reach their greatest diversity in rainforests, where some species are attractively coloured. Anomalures are extraordinary rodents adapted to life almost exclusively in the treetops. A loose flap of skin stretching between the front and hind legs can be extended to become a gliding membrane, which enables anomalures to leap and sail between tree trunks, thus obviating the need to visit the ground. Like the more famous beaver (not found in Africa), anomalures shape their environment to suit their lifestyle. But instead of felling trees like beavers, flying mice prune the forest

MAMMALS

LESSER ELEPHANT SHREW

canopy to create flyways, and prune young trees near their food trees to eliminate competition. Apart from their outrageous behaviour, two common species also have outrageous names: the widespread Lord Derby's anomalure; and the fabulous-sounding Zenker's flying mouse, which is restricted to the Semliki Forest.

Porcupines are the largest rodents (the crested porcupine can weigh 25kg) and are armed with long, loose quills that act as a spiny deterrent to would-be predators. Life for a small rodent has many perils, so various families, such as blesmols, root-rats and mole-rats, attack plants from below and live almost permanently underground. Most extraordinary of the underground rodents is the naked mole-rat (also called sand-puppy), an almost hairless burrower that lives in underground colonies of up to 75 individuals in semiarid areas. Sand-puppies, like bees and termites, have a distinct social order that includes a large, dominant female, 'drones' and workers. Drones attend the 'queen'; she produces pheromones that suppress the sexual development of her offspring, who then become workers that dig tunnels, forage and carry food. Small mounds of earth on tracks reveal the presence of colonies and if you approach quietly, you may see workers digging near the surface in the early morning, throwing up puffs of earth like miniature volcanoes.

The insectivores are a loose grouping of insect eaters that includes hedgehogs and many species of shrew, the smallest of all mammals. Shrews look superficially similar to rodents, but feed voraciously by ploughing through leaf litter and chewing up large numbers of insects, which they detect with a sensitive snout. Variations on the shrew theme include the aquatic otter shrews and the amazing hero shrew, whose backbone can support a man's weight. African hedgehogs look much the same as their European counterparts and roll up into a protective ball when threatened.

Elephant shrews aren't actually shrews or even insectivores. They belong to their own separate (and uniquely African) group – some are almost as big as a rabbit. Hares live in open, scrubby country where they eat coarse grasses and herbage. They are common, but usually seen only when they break from cover.

GET HOPPING

Hopping is a fast, economical mode of travel utilised by two groups of burrowing rodents: the desert-dwelling jerboas and the springhare, a rodent large enough to resemble a hare – if it weren't for its even more striking resemblance to the kangaroos of Australia. Like the kangaroo, the springhare is a prodigious jumper, clearing up to 4m in a bound while their long tail acts as a counterbalance. They also have in common large ears and huge feet, on which most weight is carried by the enlarged third toe. Like most kangaroos, springhares are nocturnal and hop semierect with the forelegs held up. However, unlike springhares, kangaroos are marsupials (carrying their young in a pouch) and their similarities have evolved through similar environmental constraints – a phenomenon called convergent evolution.

MAMMALS

★ HOTSPOTS

- Samburu NR (p84) These sandy, semiarid parks are ideal for naked mole-rats.
- Kibale Forest NP (p150) Offers nightly spotlighting walks where Lord Derby's anomalure is regularly seen.
- Masai Mara NR (p62) Springhares can be seen by spotlighting just outside the reserve.

EAST AFRICAN BIRDS

BIRDS ARE AMONG the most widespread and abundant of vertebrates. One or more species is found in every habitat on earth but, above all, they are the supreme masters of an environment that few other animal groups have exploited: earth's vast atmosphere. This invisible medium fills every space, from still glades in dense forests to raging storm fronts. Birds in their many forms – and there are well over 1200 species in East Africa alone – use air as a hunting ground, a courtship arena and an observation post.

A few salient characteristics instantly distinguish birds from all other life forms. The key to their ecological success is feathers, a unique adaptation shared by all birds, but by no other creatures. Birds evolved from reptiles, and feathers from scales. Like reptilian scales, feathers overlap to serve as waterproof insulation but, unlike scales, they keep birds warm enough to maintain a high level of activity and have further diversified to provide, for example, waterproofing, insulation against extreme heat or cold, and showy courtship plumes. But as organs of flight, feathers are unsurpassed: they adjust subtly to the lightest breeze and compensate instantly for wind strength, direction and lift. Each group has differently shaped wings to exploit their preferred habitat, and the independence afforded by aerial manoeuvrability has allowed the evolution of diverse hind legs, with feet adapted, for example, to swimming, grasping or running.

Despite the bewildering differences in colour and shape, all birds are structurally similar – indeed, more so than any other class of land vertebrates. All birds are warm-blooded, and although lightweight bones riddled with air sacs help them remain airborne for long periods, even the most peripatetic must return to land to lay eggs.

FLAMINGOS, TANZANIA

Mouth parts always feature a toothless bill that varies according to food preferences, eg hooked for tearing flesh. Behaviour is also broadly similar across the world's 9000 or so species and usually includes courtship rituals between sexes; nest-building and intensive parental care while raising young; and the defence of feeding or breeding territories by physical or vocal displays. Many species regularly undertake long migrations to escape inclement seasonal changes at their breeding or foraging grounds.

OSTRICH

WORLD'S TALLEST BIRD Ostriches don't bury their heads in the sand, although they sometimes sit on their nests with necks outstretched on the ground to protect their eggs or chicks. Being the world's tallest living bird (up to 2.75m) with the largest eyes of any land animal (50mm in diameter – check out the lashes), they normally detect danger from afar. That includes you, but these huge birds can usually be spotted some way off in open country. They generally seek safety in flocks (watch for chicks trotting at the heels of adults); look among herds of antelopes or zebras, where they often mingle to lessen the chance of being surprised by a big cat. If threatened, they're off, clocking up sprints at 70km/h in 3.5m-long strides, and outpacing any predator at 50km/h for up to 30 minutes. In a tight spot, an ostrich can kill a lion by kicking with its massive feet – the inner claw is modified into a 10cm spike.

The ostrich is a ratite, part of an ancient group of flightless birds distributed across the southern hemisphere. Two distinct races inhabit East Africa: the common and Somali ostriches. Males of the latter have blue-grey necks, and legs that contrast with their pink bills. During courtship displays, males crouch while rotating outstretched wings and sway their neck from side to side; the neck and legs glow bright orange-pink (common) or deep blue (Somali). Several females – normally two to five, but up to 18 – lay eggs (the world's biggest, weighing 1.5kg) in the same nest, although only the male and major hen (she who lays first) incubate, he by night and she by day.

An incredible total of 78 eggs was recorded in one nest, but only 20 can be incubated at a time, so the major hen rolls away those that aren't hers (perhaps recognising her own by the size, structure and shape of pores in the shell); the other eggs are scavenged by hyenas and jackals. Chicks leave the nest within three days and follow the parents. When two families meet, a dispute usually ensues and the winning pair adopts the other crèche – groups of 100 to 300 young can thus aggregate.

RECOGNITION Huge bird with long, featherless neck and muscular legs. Loose plumage is black and white in male, grey-brown in female.

HABITAT Dry, open savanna, desert and semidesert; not dependent on water.

BEHAVIOUR Alone or in groups. Runs from danger; males aggressive to people and predators. Young follow parents for 12 months. Sexually mature at three to four years. May live 30 to 40 years.

BREEDING Nest a shallow scrape; about 20 eggs incubated for six weeks. Chicks run well and form crèches.

FEEDING Seeds, fruits, leaves, insects, lizards and small tortoises. Sand, stones and even coins and nails are swallowed to help digestion.

VOICE Usually silent. Snaps bill and hisses. Breeding males utter a deep, descending boom.

SWAHILI Mbuni.

BIRDS

★ HOTSPOTS

- Samburu NR (p84)
- Masai Mara NR (p62)
- Serengeti NP (p108)
- Nairobi NP (p82)

GREAT WHITE PELICAN

Pelicans are readily distinguished by their pouch: an elastic flap of skin slung under the massive bill, which, in the breeding season, glows with colour (as does the bird's bare facial skin). Great white pelicans love a crowd and are often seen loafing on banks with cormorants and the smaller pink-backed pelican (which looks silver-grey – the pink traces aren't always visible). For most of the day, they sit or stand around preening or pulsating their pouch to cool off. But cooperative feeding by both species is a fascinating sight: up to 40 pelicans form a horseshoe and simultaneously dip their bills in the water to drive fish into the shallows; in a river they form parallel rows and move towards each other with a similar effect. With the prey corralled, each pelican scoops fish and up to 13L of water into the pouch. The water is then forced out through the closed bill and the fish are swallowed. These heavy birds require a great effort to leave the water, taking a long run up along the surface with laboured flapping, and stalling in a long skid when they come to land (not surprisingly, pelicans are most abundant on large bodies of water). But, if ungainly on land, they are graceful in flight, soaring high on thermals in V-shaped flocks where each bird flaps its wings in turn.

RECOGNITION 3m wingspan. White with black flight feathers, yellow bill.

HABITAT Lakes and rivers.

BEHAVIOUR Breeds in colonies.

BREEDING Lays two eggs.

FEEDING Corrals fish.

VOICE Grunts and moos.

SWAHILI Mwari Mweupe Nakuru.

★ HOTSPOTS

- Lake Natron (p139)
- Lake Manyara NP (p128)
- Lake Nakuru NP (p91)

AFRICAN DARTER

Check branches overhanging freshwater lakes and slow rivers for an all-dark bird sitting with wings draped open. When wet, the African darter's poorly oiled feathers become waterlogged, which decreases buoyancy while it swims underwater. The feathers must be conditioned by long spells of drying in sunshine, hence the characteristic pose; closely related cormorants also hang their wings out to dry. Like cormorants, the darter hunts fish, its powerful webbed feet acting as oars underwater. But rather than pursue their prey, darters swim slowly underwater with wings partly outstretched, inviting fish to take shelter beneath them, then spearing them with a dagger-shaped bill. Small prey is swallowed underwater, but larger fish are impaled through the side and, when the darter surfaces, are shaken free and juggled in the bill until they can be swallowed head first. The darter usually feeds and swims alone, with only its head and slender neck showing, earning it the alternative name of snakebird. Darters perch for long periods, usually chasing other birds from their immediate vicinity, although they nest in colonies in association with cormorants and herons. Darters' bulky nests are built in trees and nestlings are white (cormorant nestlings are black).

RECOGNITION Sinuous neck, long, stiff tail and pointed yellow bill. Rufous throat and white eye stripe. Length 75cm.

HABITAT Wetlands.

BEHAVIOUR Usually solitary. Fishes in quiet waterways.

BREEDING Two to six eggs.

FEEDING Spears fish.

VOICE Harsh croaks at nest.

SWAHILI Mbizi.

★ HOTSPOTS

- Marsabit NP (p94)
- Murchison Falls NP (p154)

BIRDS

HERONS, EGRETS & BITTERNS

BLACK HERON

WATER MARGIN FEEDERS Most of the 19 species of heron, egret and bittern in East Africa are common and easily recognised, but different enough to make watching them worthwhile. All have long legs, toes and necks and dagger-shaped bills; differences are chiefly in coloration and size, although the all-white egrets can be difficult to tell apart: bill and leg colour are clues. At times the picture of still grace, at others angular and brittle-looking, all are deadly hunters of fish, frogs, rodents and other small animals. The long neck can be folded in a tight S-shape (and is invariably held thus in flight) and the bill harpoons prey with speed and accuracy.

Most species feed at water margins and at least one is usually present at every waterway, including mudflats and mangroves; several species can feed side by side without competing directly, and their techniques are interesting to watch. All hunt by posing stock-still for long periods before striking, some even from a perch; other techniques include running, stirring mud with their feet or flapping their wings to startle prey. The 1.5m-tall goliath heron, the world's largest hoeron, spears fish furthest from shore; the 30cm-long green-backed heron snaps up tadpoles and insects. The black heron has an amazing cloak-and-dagger technique of spreading its wings in a canopy over the water then spearing fish that shelter under it. Night-herons are nocturnal, and bitterns are solitary, well-camouflaged inhabitants of dense reed beds. Several species attend locust plagues to feed on the insects: a flock of 40,000 egrets was once recorded at a swarm in Tanzania. Cattle egrets snap up insects disturbed by buffaloes and elephants – behaviour that has been shown to be much more effective than hunting alone.

During courtship, several species of heron, egret and bittern grow long, fine plumes and patches of bare facial skin change to intense colour. Watch for preening behaviour: herons comb their plumage with a special serrated claw on the middle toe. Usually silent, herons often make harsh territorial calls at the nest; most species nest communally and heronries can be noisy places. Most species also roost communally, sometimes flying great distances in V-shaped flocks at dusk.

★ HOTSPOTS

- Lake Nakuru NP (p91) Rift Valley lakes are especially good for seeing a wide variety of species.
- Murchison Falls NP (p154) River cruises are recommended for great views of several species.

SHOEBILL

Also known as the whale-headed stork, the shoebill's most striking feature – its bulbous bill – measures around 19cm in length, and is almost as wide. Although unique, the shoebill shares with herons the habit of flying with neck retracted; it has a small crest at the back of its head like a pelican; and shows storklike behaviour such as emptying bills full of water onto the nest to cool its young. And while it may look like a large, silver-grey stork, pelicans may be its closest relatives. This solitary and stately bird is avidly sought by birdwatchers, even though most of the time it stands stock-still and stiff-legged on floating vegetation, or at the water's edge, waiting for prey. Lungfish are its favourite meal, and when a likely victim surfaces all hell breaks loose: the massive bill is jerked forward, causing the bird to overbalance, collapse and submerge its entire head. Using its wings and bill, it then levers itself upright, manipulates vegetation out of its mouth and swallows the victim – usually decapitated by the bill's sharp edges. Accuracy is everything, for its bill cannot usually be manoeuvred for a second strike. Incredibly, this all-or-nothing fishing method is also practiced in flight on occasion – the bird collapsing bodily into the water.

RECOGNITION Large (1.2m high), storklike and blue-grey with a massive bill.

HABITAT Papyrus swamps and marshy lakes.

BEHAVIOUR Solitary. Walks on floating vegetation.

BREEDING Lays one to three blue-white eggs in long rains.

FEEDING Grabs mainly fish.

VOICE Bill clapping at nest.

⭐ HOTSPOTS

- Murchison Falls NP **(p154)**
- Semliki Valley WR**(p170)**
- PN de l'Akagera **(p176)**

HAMERKOP

Related to herons and storks, and commonly seen with them, the hamerkop's distinctive profile earned it an Afrikaans name meaning 'hammerhead'. During courtship, and often at other times, hamerkops engage in unique false-coupling behaviour where one bird sits on the back of another (male or female) – mating doesn't always occur and birds may even face in opposite directions. Feeding is more conventional: prey is snatched from shallow water. For unknown reasons, hamerkops make a massive nest of twigs, sticks and even bones, usually in the fork of a tree, in which is secreted a brood chamber accessible only through a narrow tunnel. These huge constructions can weigh 40kg and be 1.5m deep; some pairs build and abandon several nests in close proximity – various owl species readily take over their vacant nests. But perhaps the hamerkop has got it right: with so many nests to choose from, a would-be predator probably stands more chance of facing a genet, spitting cobra, monitor lizard or bee swarm (all of which use abandoned nests) than the bird itself. With such tenants in hamerkop nests, it's no wonder traditional African beliefs imbued hamerkops with supernatural powers.

RECOGNITION Bronze-brown. Length 50cm to 56cm. Crest offset by heavy bill.

HABITAT Lakes and rivers.

BEHAVIOUR Usually solitary, roosting in groups. Associates with large mammals.

BREEDING Lays three to six white eggs year-round.

FEEDING Frogs and fish.

VOICE Strident yelping *yip-pur, yip-yip-pur-pur-yip*.

⭐ HOTSPOTS

- Nairobi NP **(p82)**
- Amboseli NP **(p74)**

MAMMALS

BIRDS

STORKS

YELLOW-BILLED STORK

STATELY SENTINELS Stately and often colourfully marked, storks are generally found near wetlands, although some species are far less dependent on water for food resources than other waterbirds. Superficially similar to herons, they share with them the long legs, toes and neck, although the latter is generally thicker and the overall body shape is bulkier. All storks fly strongly with necks outstretched and they can often be seen soaring high in thermals, where their distinctive bill shapes make identification fairly easy. Marabou and saddle-billed storks are among the largest of flying birds, the latter with a 2.7m wingspan.

All eight species found in East Africa are predominantly white, black or black-and-white and all have large bills adapted to a carnivorous diet consisting of small animals such as frogs, fish and rodents. The more generalised feeders, such as white and Abdim's storks, snatch insects, small rodents and reptiles with dagger-shaped bills; saddle-billed storks jab at fish in the shallows; and yellow-billed storks find aquatic prey in muddy water by the touch of their long, sensitive bills. Marabou storks, the most predatory, have a massive 35cm bill used to pick over carrion and slay other animals, including birds as large as flamingos. Marabous readily adapt to a scavenging life in cities and are often seen close to rubbish dumps in Nairobi or Kampala. Most specialised of all is the African open-billed stork: this all-black species has a distinctive tweezer-shaped bill, which it uses to remove snails from their shells.

White storks are famous in Europe for arriving en masse in spring and nesting on rooftops; large flocks return to East Africa between November and April. The arrival of another migrant, Abdim's stork, is usually associated with rains. Of the resident species, only woolly-necked and saddle-billed storks are solitary nesters; all others nest in colonies, sometimes in association with herons or cormorants. All species construct large, untidy platforms of sticks in trees, often near or over water; adults empty bills full of water over their chicks to keep them cool. Marabous have a strange habit of defecating on their legs to cool off – a habit they share with vultures.

★ HOTSPOTS

- Masai Mara NR (p62) Flocks of white and Abdim's storks arrive between October and April.
- Lake Turkana (p92) Supports African open-billed storks.
- Lake Naivasha (p90) Yellow-billed and saddle-billed storks are widespread along the Rift Valley lakes.

IBISES & SPOONBILLS

SACRED WATERBIRDS Essentially waterbirds, ibises and spoonbills are biologically akin to herons and storks by dint of their long legs, toes and necks; the differences lie mainly in the shape of their sensitive bills. The most obvious feature of spoonbills – a flattened, spoonlike bill – is swept from side to side as they feed on microscopic water creatures, filtered through fine, sieve-like lamellae (bony filters). The bills of ibises are not flattened and curve strongly downwards – designed for probing the mud for prey. Despite their different bills (and the fact that spoonbills are more tied to wetlands), the two groups are close relatives: occasionally ibises are seen sweeping their bills from side to side, and spoonbills poking in soft mud.

The African spoonbill is common in shallow, slow-moving waterways in the company of other waterbirds, although Eurasian spoonbills also occasionally stray to East Africa (especially at Lake Turkana in northern Kenya – it can be told apart by its black bill). Spoonbills and most ibises nest colonially in trees (often in association with herons, storks and cormorants), where they build untidy stick nests.

Ibises use their long, bowed bills to probe for crustaceans, snails and tadpoles. The most widespread species commonly forages on lawns and grassland and adapts readily to agriculture: on occasion it has averted devastation to crops by consuming plague locusts. In fact, this common, black-and-white bird was worshipped by ancient Egyptians, who associated its migration with the arrival of the fertile floodwaters of the Nile River every year. Mummified specimens have been found in ancient

GLOSSY IBIS

tombs, it is accurately depicted on wall friezes and, to this day, it is still known as the sacred ibis.

While sacred ibises are gregarious waterbirds, nesting in colonies and flying to communal roosts in V-shaped flocks at dusk, pairs of hadada ibises nest alone and often feed well away from water. The hadada's brash *ha-haha* call is one of the most distinctive sounds of the savanna, especially at dusk and dawn, and can be heard even in the parks and suburbs of cities. The closely related African green ibis is an inhabitant of mountain forests and is even less dependent on water, foraging in clearings, nesting in trees and even running along large branches.

BIRDS

⭐ HOTSPOTS

- Lake Nakuru NP (p91) Rift Valley lakes are regular haunts of all bar the green ibis.
- Kilimanjaro NP (p132) The high slopes of this mountain are the best places to seek green ibises.

RECOGNITION Greater flamingo is tall (1.5m), white or pale pink with long pale pink legs and S-shaped neck; lesser flamingo is shorter (90cm) and deeper pink with darker bill and red legs.

HABITAT Salt lakes, estuaries and coastal lagoons.

BEHAVIOUR Highly nomadic and gregarious. Flock-synchronised courtship. Flies with neck and legs fully extended.

BREEDING Sporadic. A single egg is normally laid on a semiconical nest of mud surrounded by water in inaccessible mudflats.

FEEDING Greater flamingo eats aquatic insects, crustaceans and molluscs. Lesser flamingo eats algae. Both filter food by sweeping the beak from side to side underwater.

VOICE Goose-like honking; constant low murmuring while feeding in flocks.

SWAHILI Heroe.

BIRDS

GREATER & LESSER FLAMINGOS

FLOCKING PINK Masses of pink birds shimmering through the heat haze – audible but inaccessible across fields of treacherous mud – make a tantalising sight, and early Christians considered the flamingo to be the Phoenix, the legendary red bird that rises from the ashes of its own funeral pyre. Flamingos are instantly recognisable by their combination of pink coloration and long, slender neck and legs. Where the two are found together, the pale-pink greater flamingos tower above the deep rose-pink lessers.

Few large birds are as gregarious as flamingos: great numbers concentrate in shallow lakes too alkaline or saline to support fish (which otherwise compete for the tiny water animals or algae sought by flamingos), and food resources occur in such quantities that competition between individual birds is limited. Flamingos may spend hours standing or floating motionless, but their feeding method is unique among birds: while walking through shallow water with head upside down and submerged, they sweep their angular bill from side to side. Food is caught in lamellae (fine bony filters) and excess water and mud are forced out by the tongue acting as a piston. Flamingos have been estimated to consume 60 tonnes of algae a day.

Courtship rituals are conducted en masse: hundreds or thousands of birds stretch their necks and twist their heads in unison, stretch wings and legs and strut through shallow water before abruptly changing direction. These displays synchronise hormone production and ensure a colony takes simultaneous advantage of optimum conditions to raise their young. However, breeding sometimes fails catastrophically and rising water levels can wipe out an entire season's efforts.

Adults flamingos have few predators, although their tongues were considered a delicacy in ancient Rome, marabou storks take a toll on eggs and chicks, and African fish eagles sweep over a flock to induce a panicked stampede then pick off injured birds.

★ HOTSPOTS

- Lake Bogoria NR (p89)
- Lake Nakuru NP (p91)
- Lake Turkana (p92)

DUCKS & GEESE

GRAZERS AND DIPPERS Thanks to their long history of domestication, few birds are as universally recognisable as ducks and geese (collectively known as waterfowl); indeed few groups are so similar, with a broad, flattened bill at one end and strongly webbed feet at the other. Several of the 14 resident or nomadic species grace nearly all lakes, swamps and rivers in East Africa, and migrants from Eurasia swell local numbers from November to March. All waterfowl are adapted to an aquatic life, with insulating down beneath waterproof feathers, and most are strong flyers, taking off explosively and quickly attaining fast, level flight (among the fastest of flying birds) with necks outstretched. Food is typically vegetation and small invertebrates; each species of waterfowl occupies a slightly distinct feeding and breeding niche and thus several can coexist without competing directly.

The most common species are easily identified by their bill colours, but look out for their different feeding behaviour. The so-called dabbling ducks (including red-billed teal and yellow-billed duck) upend in shallow water, paddling like mad to stay under and grazing weed from the bottom. In deeper water, Maccoa and white-backed ducks dive for a living, propelled by legs set well back, and swim with bodies low in the water. Egyptian geese are primarily grazers, pulling grass sometimes far from water. The African black duck inhabits forest streams and rivers and even alpine tarns, where it dips its head to take prey from beneath submerged stones. East Africa's smallest duck, the African

RED-BILLED TEAL

pygmy-goose, is at home diving among floating lilies.

Many waterfowl are nomadic, often covering vast distances to reach new waterholes as an old one dries out. Breeding is usually prolific to take advantage of favourable conditions, and numbers can build up quickly. Most are solitary breeders, laying in nests the female often lines with down. Young hatch covered in cryptically marked, waterproof down and can walk and swim almost immediately, following their parents around and catching their own food. The other great distinction of these birds is of course their vocal repertoire: the familiar barnyard quacking is de rigueur for typical ducks, but the two species of whistling-duck are aptly named for their sibilant whistling.

BIRDS

★ HOTSPOTS

- Lake Nakuru NP (p91) All common species and northern migrants can be seen on the Rift Valley lakes.
- Lake Naivasha (p90)
- Masai Mara NR (p62) Spur-winged geese frequently visit temporary wetlands.

BIRDS OF PREY

BATELEUR

BIRDS

on the same tree. They reach their greatest diversity in forests, although several species are found in every habitat. With a few notable exceptions, such as the brightly coloured bateleur, all are rather plain in coloration, although some are adorned with showy crests.

Raptor watchers should look for huddled dark shapes on top-most boughs (large species take longer to get going in the morning, and finish hunting earlier in the day, because they depend on thermals to gain altitude and soar). Note large, bulky nests in which an incubating bird may be sitting low with its mate perched nearby; listen for small birds (such as drongos) mobbing; and watch for large hawks drying their outstretched wings on exposed perches after a storm. Other giveaways include antelope legs wedged into branches (eagles' handiwork), piles of feathers where a bird has been plucked and whitewash below nests on cliffs. Rubbing styrene foam on glass to imitate a distressed rodent can have spectacular results. Watch also for hawks seizing fleeing animals from grass fires.

Varying in size from pigeon-sized sparrowhawks to mighty eagles with a 2.5m wingspan, nearly all raptors are exclusively carnivorous, with talons to grasp or snatch prey and a hooked beak for tearing flesh. Raptors have incredible eyesight, spotting a grasshopper at 100m and a hare at 1km. Forest hawks are usually on the move with the dawn, and insect-eating raptors start out once the sun makes their prey more active. Sparrowhawks and goshawks feed primarily on birds caught in mad dashes through foliage. Snake-eagles sit and wait for hours on a perch and then drop onto snakes, which they kill and swallow whole. The African harrier-hawk (or gymnogene) has long legs with which it reaches into nests, cavities and under bark for prey, even

RAVENOUS RAPTORS East Africa has around 80 species of birds of prey (or raptor) from three distinct families: the falcons; the eagles, hawks, harriers and vultures; and the secretary bird. In open savanna at least, it is not unusual to see several species in the sky at once, or perched

hanging upside down from weavers' nests to extract chicks and eggs. Harriers methodically quarter grassland, gliding on long, slender wings and dropping onto mammals and birds – their facial feathers are arranged in a disc, which heightens their hearing (like owls). And there are many other hunting strategies: bat hawks swallow bats whole in midair; Verreaux's eagles haunt cliffs and kopjes for hyraxes; African crowned eagles snatch monkeys from the forest canopy; and the martial eagle can bring down a small antelope and carry it to a perch.

Instead of elaborate plumage, raptors rely on dramatic aerial displays during courtship, such as free falling while grappling talons, and passing prey to one another while one bird flies upside down. Hawks often display late in the morning – watching for this behaviour is a good way to

MASTERS OF THE AIR

Falcons are voracious predators that kill mainly birds on the wing, although there are exceptions: kestrels hover and pounce on mice and lizards, and pygmy falcons subsist on insects. Like other raptors, falcons have a strongly hooked bill and powerful talons superbly adapted for seizing prey. But in flight they show their true mastery, their long, narrow wings scything through the air in quick beats, picking up speed as prey is approached and building to a deadly crescendo in dives known as stoops. Falcons are among the swiftest of birds (although such statistics are rarely measured accurately and doubtless have been exaggerated). The 19 species certainly have few enemies, save larger falcons, and none normally builds a nest, using instead cliff ledges and nests abandoned by other birds – the 20cm-long pygmy falcon is smaller than the buffalo-weavers, whose old nests it uses!

BLACK-SHOULDERED KITE

detect forest hawks. Each species has a different proportion of wing length to breadth, which in turn determines aerobatic manoeuvrability and speed. Thus, the broad wings of forest hawks help them manoeuvre through branches and foliage; and the great eagles have long, broad wings on which they can glide to great heights and distances. Most aerobatic is the bateleur (from the French for acrobat), a consummate glider that, in courtship displays, performs fast rocking motions on the wing.

BIRDS

HOTSPOTS

- Masai Mara NR (p62) Excellent for raptor-watching; dozens of species from sparrowhawks to eagles.
- Serengeti NP (p108)
- Hell's Gate NP (p87) Cliffs are home to augur buzzards and several species of falcon.
- Kilimanjaro NP (p132) Hunting grounds for mountain buzzards and Verreaux's eagles.

VULTURES

CARRION SCAVENGERS Think of the great plains – and the nightly carnage left by lions and hyenas – and you'll also probably get an image of squabbling flocks of gore-encrusted vultures eating the stuff few animals will touch. And fair enough because, with few exceptions, that's basically what they do. Should they need an introduction, vultures are birds of prey adapted to eat carrion, their chief difference to other raptors being a usually bald head and neck (it's easier to feed and keep clean that way), and feet better suited to walking than grasping. It may not be an appealing way of life to us, but it's an extremely profitable niche to exploit.

Look for these great, bulky birds sitting at the top of acacia trees and on large, exposed branches – larger species are usually solitary. Although ungainly on the ground, all have long, broad wings superbly adapted for long spells of soaring, and by midmorning these large birds are usually circling high on thermals. Vultures have a poor sense of smell, instead using their keen eyesight to follow other vultures and eagles, or scavenging mammals on the ground that might lead them to a kill. If vultures are circling in the air over a carcass it's usually a sign that predators are still chewing away at it: if you're on foot, beware.

Early morning is not usually a vulture's best time. After a cold night on the plains they take a while to get airborne owing to a lack of thermals, especially on an overcast day. Hunched up, most of the seven plains species are difficult to identify as anything other than vultures, but in flight their various features are more apparent. Larger species usually take precedence at a carcass, although smaller vultures may gang up and chase them away, and each species is specialised to feed differently and thus has

WHITE-BACKED VULTURE

different headgear. The largest, the lappet-faced and white-headed vultures, tear open a carcass, eating the skin as well as bones and sinews. They pave the way for vultures with a long, bare neck – Rüppell's griffon and African white-backed – to reach right into the guts to eat soft parts without getting their feathers caked in blood; they will even climb inside a rib cage. The comparatively small hooded and Egyptian vultures can't compete with larger species, instead grabbing scraps from the frenzy; crows and marabou storks also loiter for morsels.

Vultures may fast a week between kills, but it's not all gore and bloodlust. Hooded vultures pick over human refuse, and Egyptian vultures steal birds' eggs and smash them on the ground; they have learned to break open ostrich eggs with a rock. The boldly marked palm-nut vulture is superficially similar to the African fish

BONE CRUSHER

Despite its name, which means 'lamb vulture', and great size (with a 2.8m wingspan, this is one of the largest vultures) the lammergeier probably doesn't kill lambs. In fact, it rarely kills anything in the rugged gorges and alpine areas it frequents. Like all vultures it is a scavenger, but rather than tearing at flesh (something it could easily do with its hooked bill and curved talons), it eats whole bones and scoops out the marrow with its tongue. It particularly favours large leg bones, and any too large to be swallowed are dropped from a height of about 20m to 80m onto a well-used, flattish area of rock called an ossuary until they smash or splinter. Ravens in alpine areas have also been seen trying this trick, although they can't seem to manage it as well as their mentor. Also known as the bearded vulture because of its black, bristly beard of feathers around the beak, the lammergeier is Africa's rarest vulture.

PALM-NUT VULTURE

eagle (and may in fact be closely related) and, like it, feeds on fish and crabs. But, despite its hooked bill, this extraordinary vulture feeds mainly on the protein-rich nuts of palms, such as *Phoenix* and *Raphia* palms, a food source sought by many birds and mammals. All vultures are attentive parents: adults range up to 160km in a day as they follow the wildebeest migration across the Serengeti Plains before returning to the nest with food.

BIRDS

HOTSPOTS

- Masai Mara NR (p62) One of the top spots for vultures because of high concentrations of predators and prey.
- Mikumi NP (p130) Palm-nut vultures common.
- Hell's Gate NP (p87) Rüppell's griffons and Egyptian vultures nest here.
- Mt Elgon NP (p167) Good spots to look for lammergeiers.

SECRETARY BIRD

RECOGNITION Uniform grey with black thighs, flight feathers and loose crest. Bare orange facial patch and deep-pink legs and feet. Long central tail feathers and outstretched legs obvious in flight.

HABITAT Short grassland with scattered thorn trees; common in agricultural land. Avoids hilly or rocky country.

BEHAVIOUR Usually solitary or in pairs, but groups may gather at locust plagues or bushfires. Nests and roosts on flat-topped acacias. Soars high on thermals. Kicks at tufts of grass or dung for prey. Regurgitates large pellets near roosts and nests.

BREEDING Lays one to three eggs, usually in wet season; only one chick survives and fledges after two to three months.

FEEDING Mainly large insects and spiders, but also reptiles, birds up to small-hornbill size, small mammals (such as rodents, hares, mongooses and small cats) and carrion.

VOICE Generally silent; a deep guttural croaking in displays, fights, at nest and in flight.

A VORACIOUS PEDESTRIAN Stalking across grassland with jerky precision and standing 1.2m high – tall enough to be seen from hundreds of metres away – this high-stepping bird of prey is unique to Africa. Its body and head resemble those of a large eagle but, despite its hooked bill, it differs from other raptors in a number of ways. For example, its legs are three times as long as those of a conventional raptor, and jack it up to an ideal vantage point from which to look for a meal.

The secretary bird is known to stride up to 20km a day in search of prey, which it kills with a rain of swift kicks from its thick, powerful feet. When a snake is encountered – and dangerous vipers and cobras are attacked with relish – it is stamped to death in a lethal flamenco audible from some distance away. Speed and agility are the keys to handling venomous prey, and secretary birds' legs are heavily scaled for further protection. Small prey is swallowed whole – that includes snakes, but also eggs, chicks, entire wasps' nests and golf balls (by mistake); larger items are torn apart or cached under a bush for future reference.

The secretary bird's long, black crest flaps in the breeze and is said to resemble the quill pens worn behind the ears of 19th-century scribes; another theory attributes the name to *saqur-et-air*, which is French-Arabic for 'hunting bird'. Despite the obvious eagle-like features, there is behavioural evidence for other possible origins. The long legs suggest a common ancestry with storks, and other storklike traits include extending its neck in flight and head-bowing and bill-clapping displays between pairs at the nest. But courtship flights are very raptorlike and include pendulum displays where one bird drops in a graceful swoop from a great height with wings folded and then pulls out of the dive to climb slowly and repeat the show. Pairs also tumble in midair with feet outstretched towards each other.

BIRDS

★ HOTSPOTS

- Masai Mara NR (p62)
- Serengeti NP (p108)
- Murchison Falls NP (p154)

AFRICAN FISH EAGLE

THE VOICE OF AFRICA Whether perched at the top of a *Euphorbia*, head and breast glowing white, or sweeping low on a dive, few birds beg superlatives like this magnificent wetland predator. African fish eagles are common and, in some places, live in comparatively high densities. At first light their loud, ringing calls echo across lakes and river valleys – a sound so distinctive and recognisable that the fish eagle is known as the 'voice of Africa'. Pairs sometimes duet from perches, throwing their heads back until they are bent almost double. Closely related to the bald eagle of North America, fish eagles look regal wherever they perch, but these voracious raptors are so effective at fishing they can (and often do) spend as much as 90% of the day resting or preening. A hungry fish eagle stares intently at the water. When a likely fish is spotted, the bird makes a fast, sweeping dive, at the last second throwing its legs and huge talons forward to seize its slippery catch. Most prey consists of surface-feeding fish taken within 15cm of the surface, although if necessary it will plunge in bodily to a depth of 50cm. The largest catch recorded is 3kg, but anything over 2.5kg can't be lifted and must be dragged or rowed with one foot through the water to shore. Any fish it can carry are consumed at leisure at a favourite perch.

Fish eagles also rob other birds (and each other) of their catch: victims of their piracy can be as large as pelicans, herons and storks, or as small as pied kingfishers. Where there are no fish, they prey on waterbirds, killing flamingos and even wiping out entire colonies of herons, spoonbills and cormorants.

RECOGNITION Pure white head, breast, back and tail contrast with rich chestnut belly and 'trousers', and black wings. Bill black with yellow base. Length 75cm.

HABITAT Widespread near lakes, rivers and estuaries (occasionally forest); immature birds may wander far from water.

BEHAVIOUR Adults pairs sedentary and intensely territorial when breeding; may reuse the same nest for 10 years. Groups gather at fish strandings. Immatures may form loose nonbreeding populations. Will cross large arid areas to reach isolated waterways.

BREEDING Usually lays two eggs in large nest of sticks and papyrus near water. Chicks fledge at 65 to 75 days.

FEEDING A large variety of fish and waterbirds (especially young birds); also scavenges dead fish and carrion (immatures may be seen at predators' kills).

VOICE A loud and far-carrying *wee-ah, kyo-kyo-kyo-kyo* from a perch or in flight.

SWAHILI Fu kombe

BIRDS

★ HOTSPOTS

- Lake Naivasha (p90)
- Lake Baringo (p88)
- Queen Elizabeth NP (p158)
- Murchison Falls NP (p154)

FRANCOLINS

RED-NECKED SPURFOW

GAME BIRDS Francolins belong to the great order loosely known as game birds – the pheasants, quails, partridges and jungle fowl (precursors of the domestic chicken) that have been the target of hunters' activities for centuries. And it's not just humans – small cats and other predators readily stalk francolins – but these ground-dwelling birds are great survivors: they are abundant and come in many varieties. Francolins nest on the ground (although the retiring habits of some species mean that their nests are as yet unknown) and the downy, precocial chicks are well camouflaged and can run within hours.

Walking (and running) are strong francolin traits – all species have stout legs and feet and run fast to evade predators – and only when push comes to shove will they take to the wing, flying low for a short distance before dropping to the ground again.

The basic francolin design is like a large, upright quail, with heavily streaked upperparts in greys, browns and black for camouflage, although some, eg the red-necked and yellow-necked spurfowl, sport naked flesh on the face and neck that enhances their territorial displays. All have a strong, hooked bill useful for snatching small animals, picking up seeds and fruit and digging for bulbs. Like domestic hens, many rake the soil and leaf litter with their strong feet, and cocks of most species sport spurs on their legs.

Although a few species occur across Asia, Africa is the francolin stronghold and the 18 species found in East Africa range in size from 20cm to 35cm. Many are common and a day's birding in any reserve is bound to encounter at least one species. Francolins often feed along roadsides in the early morning and late afternoon, or dart across the road in single file. Two of the most abundant – red-necked and yellow-necked spurfowl – are decidedly chickenlike and are commonly seen standing atop termite mounds or roadside banks. Savanna and grassland with thornbush are francolin strongholds, although a few (such as Jackson's francolin) inhabit alpine meadows up to 4000m and others (eg Nahan's francolin) are specialised to life in dense forests.

★ HOTSPOTS

- Masai Mara NR (p62) Red-necked spurfowl cross the road here.
- Lake Nakuru NP (p91) Coqui francolin on lakeside grasslands.
- Serengeti NP (p108) A reliable location for the grey-breasted spurfowl, a Tanzanian endemic.
- Budongo FR (p164) Nahan's and other rainforest francolin species can be found here (with patient searching).

BIRDS

GUINEAFOWL

QUINTESSENTIAL GROUND BIRDS
With bare, skinny neck and head, and stout, slightly hooked bill, the three guineafowl species could be cartoon caricatures of birds. Despite their reluctance to fly – preferring instead to run at full pelt away from danger, the helmeted guineafowl doing so with wings half open – guineafowl roost in trees at night. All species are immediately recognisable by their boxlike shape and black plumage punctuated by tiny white spots, and bizarre headgear is the order of the day: the crested guineafowl sporting a dishevelled mop of black feathers, and the helmeted guineafowl a bony knob like a top hat, which probably protects it during headlong plunges into the undergrowth.

Guineafowl are opportunists that consume a wide variety of small animals such as insects and small vertebrates; plant matter such as seeds, fruit, berries and bulbs; and also raid crops. They also swallow grit to aid digestion. Helmeted guineafowl gather in flocks to drink (something all except vulturine guineafowl must do regularly) and also associate with mammals, such as rhinos, lions and mongooses, whose presence presumably discourages potential predators. Their relationship with baboons is less benevolent, for each tries to steal food from the other, but watch for the forest-dwelling crested guineafowl picking up scraps dropped by monkey troops moving through the canopy.

All species indulge in dust bathing (loosening soil by pecking then tossing it over their feathers and shuffling to get an even coat); this behaviour is thought to condition their feathers and help to get rid of

HELMETED GUINEAFOWL

parasites. Startled birds that have been dust bathing seem to explode in a cloud of dust before hightailing it. Many predators, ranging from large and small cats to chimpanzees, prey on guineafowl and, as they are as large as a farmyard chicken, the effort involved in chasing one down is usually rewarded with a good meal.

All guineafowl lay prodigious numbers of eggs (probably because of their high mortality rate) from which the chicks hatch more or less simultaneously and are led away from the nest almost immediately. As with most game birds, guineafowl chicks develop quickly and can fly within about two weeks.

BIRDS

★ HOTSPOTS

- Masai Mara NR (p62) Helmeted guineafowl are common.
- Samburu NR (p84) Support vulturine guineafowl.
- Kibale Forest NP (p150) Crested guineafowl are found here.

RECOGNITION Slaty black, pale green bill and red legs, feet and eyes. Length 20cm.

HABITAT Vegetation beside freshwater lakes and swamps.

BEHAVIOUR Often walks on floating vegetation.

BREEDING Three eggs laid in bulky nest in waterside vegetation.

FEEDING Small animals.

VOICE Harsh *krrok-krraaa*.

HOTSPOTS

- Lake Baringo (p88)
- Lake Naivasha (p90)
- Murchison Falls NP (p154)

BLACK CRAKE

Crakes and rails almost exclusively exploit the cover and feeding opportunities provided by dense stands of reeds or rushes fringing slow waterways. The downside is that they have a reputation for being difficult to see among the forest of stems (often calling near an observer but remaining invisible). However, the black crake is an exception, with this common bird readily seen on virtually any East African wetland. Black crakes have a similar shape and size to most other crakes and rails, with a rather slender body, strong legs and feet and a short bill. Using reeds as cover, crakes typically feed on mud exposed at water's edge, darting back to cover should danger threaten (the best way to see most species is to wait patiently for one to make its nervous feeding forays onto the mud). Black crakes often feed in the open for extended periods and will readily use hippos' backs as stepping stones (although they can fly and swim well). Like most of the family, they feed on a variety of small animals, ranging from worms and snails to insects, tadpoles and frogs; but black crakes also scavenge from carcasses; perch on warthogs' backs to pick off parasites; and climb waterside trees to steal birds' eggs and chicks.

RED-KNOBBED COOT

RECOGNITION Velvety black, white bill and head 'shield' with two small red knobs.

HABITAT Lakes and swamps.

BEHAVIOUR Builds floating platforms for resting.

BREEDING Five to seven eggs.

FEEDING Aquatic vegetation.

VOICE Hoots *hoo-hoo* and a metallic, nasal *kiik*.

HOTSPOTS

- Lake Baringo (p88)
- Lake Naivasha (p90)
- Marsabit NP (p94)

Coots belong to a widespread family that includes crakes, rails and moorhens. Unlike most of their relatives, coots spend most of their lives swimming – their long toes are heavily lobed for paddling and their feathers are waterproof for diving (something they do frequently to feed on aquatic vegetation). Their characteristic nasal piping is one of the most evocative of wetland sounds, and flotillas of red-knobbed coots, sometimes numbering thousands, drift among ducks and other waterbirds on freshwater lakes.

During the breeding season, the two small, fleshy knobs at the top of their white headgear (which stands out at quite a distance) become swollen and brightly coloured – hence the name. Otherwise, the red-knobbed coot is very similar to its counterparts in other parts of the world (a familiar sight on many ornamental lakes) – even the pumping motion of the head as it swims is common to coots everywhere.

Although they spend little time on land, they can run well and, when taking flight, coots patter across the water's surface for some distance. The common moorhen, which often lives closeby, is superficially similar, but at a glance can be told apart by its red head 'shield' and yellow-tipped bill.

BIRDS

GREY CROWNED CRANE

No need for superlatives – suffice to say this is one of the most elegant birds in all of Africa, and Uganda's national bird for good reason. Cultures other than Ugandan associate cranes with longevity and fidelity, and pairs of grey crowned cranes stay together until one dies. They preen each other's golden crest, perform loud duets and dance in spontaneous displays of head bobbing, bowing, stick tossing and high leaps with wings outstretched. One pair's exuberance will stimulate others in a flock to leap into the air and up to 60 birds have been seen dancing together for a few minutes before settling down again to feed.

Grey crowned cranes fly with neck and legs outstretched, often making loud, trumpeting calls as they head to roost at dusk. They are the only cranes able to perch and consequently roost and, on rare occasions, even nest in trees. Normally though, they nest in wetlands and forage in grassland, sometimes walking between the two and grazing en route or stamping the ground to scare up insects. Look for grey crowned cranes feeding in groups, and among baboon troops and herds of impalas or zebras.

RECOGNITION Slate grey with black, white and chestnut on wings. Red throat wattles. Strawlike crest. Height 1.1m.

HABITAT Marshes, grassland.

BEHAVIOUR Gregarious outside breeding season.

BREEDING Lays two to three eggs.

FEEDING Opportunist: eats grain, tubers and insects.

VOICE Trumpeting *oo-waang*.

 HOTSPOTS

- Masai Mara NR (p62)
- Serengeti NP (p108)
- Queen Elizabeth NP (p158)

KORI BUSTARD

Although all bustards can fly strongly should the need arise, they are consummate walkers – or strutters, because their habit of pointing their bill upwards as they walk away from an intruder gives them a dignified air. Two or three species are commonly seen in suitable habitat, typically decked out in greys and browns that camouflage them in the muted tones of the grassland. The kori is the biggest East African bustard (up to 1.2m tall) and Africa's heaviest flying bird, weighing up to 18kg (despite having long legs, its rather small feet render it incapable of perching in trees); look for it peering over the top of the grass. Eggs are laid on the ground and the chicks are also superbly camouflaged – the nest and eggs of Hartlaub's bustard have never been found. Koris are especially fond of toasted insects and small animals and are readily seen gathered at grassfires where pickings are good. But the best time to watch bustards is during courtship: the male kori bustard puffs out his white throat feathers in a huge bulging ruff, flips up his startling white under-tail feathers and booms loudly (this performance can last several days). The male black-bellied bustard stands atop a termite mound, launches himself into the air then falls bodily back to earth.

RECOGNITION Heavily built. Back brown, mantle black, head white. Black cap.

HABITAT Grassland and cultivation.

BEHAVIOUR Usually solitary.

BREEDING Lays two eggs.

FEEDING Fruit, seeds and small animals.

VOICE Deep *voom-voom-voom* by displaying males.

 HOTSPOTS

- Masai Mara NR (p62)
- Serengeti NP (p108)
- Amboseli NP (p74)

BIRDS

WADERS

COMMON GREENSHANK

INTERNATIONAL COMMUTERS Every autumn thousands of small to medium-sized shorebirds (commonly known as waders) arrive in East Africa to spend the equatorial 'winter' on coastal mudflats and the margins of freshwater swamps and lakes. Among them are some long-distance champions – stints, sandpipers, redshanks, Eurasian curlews, common greenshanks and ruffs – which breed as far away as the Arctic Circle and make a trip of several thousand kilometres twice annually. Here, all but one (the African snipe is resident in East African grassland) sit out the northern winter, taking advantage of the mild climate to regain condition after the rigours of

breeding and migration. In their winter outfits, most of these migratory waders are rather drab (and consequently a magnet for serious birders, who spend hours trying to work out which is which), but each has a specialised bill shape and size for probing mud, which offer clues to their identification.

The loose term wader also covers several closely related families, not all of which make these long trips; many of these are attractively marked and common. The black-winged stilt and pied avocet are black and white, the stilt's coral-pink legs matched only by those of flamingos for length in proportion to body size. The avocet's distinct upturned bill is used to scythe through shallow water for aquatic insects and crustaceans. Other closely related families include the jacanas and thick-knees (dikkops).

But East Africa has so many surprises in store for a birdwatcher that you may even rethink preconceptions about waders. For example, the large crab-plover smashes open crab shells with its chisel-like bill and is unique among waders for digging and laying eggs in burrows. The ploverlike coursers and pratincoles frequent dry land and are often seen far from water – coursers running after prey and the long-winged pratincoles hawking insects (particularly locusts). Several coursers are nocturnal, but readily seen by spotlighting, and two or three species of coursers and pratincoles can coexist in the same habitat by feeding at different times of day. Temminck's courser picks over burnt ground for insects and is so specialised to this habitat that its eggs are almost black to match the charred earth.

★ HOTSPOTS

- Arabuko-Sokoke FR (p70) Mida Creek adjoins the park and is the most important wader haunt in Kenya.
- Lake Nakuru NP (p91) Marshy ground at the lake's corners attracts migratory waders November to April.
- Murchison Falls NP (p154) Stilts along the Victoria Nile, rock pratincoles at and above the falls.

PLOVERS

GRASSLAND SENTINELS Plovers are members of the large group of shorebirds often known as waders, although many species are found far from water in grassland and cultivated fields. Several large species are often seen on savanna game drives. In fact, they are often heard well before they are seen because they protest loudly at the approach of any intruder – animal or human – and act as sentinels of the grassland. Their raucous calls may also be heard at night and are one of the most distinctive bird calls – the blacksmith plover sounds like metal banging on metal.

All plovers have a compact body, large head and short, blunt bill. The larger savanna-dwelling species tower above most others on comparatively long legs, while the smaller species – which tend to stay near the muddy edges of waterways – look decidedly dumpy but run quickly. The savanna species tend to be boldly marked with white wing-flashes visible in flight; some have coloured facial wattles (which are most developed on the African wattled plover) and the black-headed plover has a wispy crest.

The savanna specialists eat mainly large insects, but the long-toed plover forages on floating vegetation. Typical plover feeding behaviour involves standing still, running a short distance, pausing to look for food, then running to the prey and dipping their beaks to snatch it up. Smaller plovers can be well camouflaged and are first noticed when they run, sometimes virtually at your feet. With another technique (called foot trembling) plovers stir up prey by vibrating their toes through short grass or on dirt.

SPUR-WINGED LAPWING

Several smaller plovers feed on shorelines and mudflats among other waders; they include some long-distance migrants from Eurasia, such as golden and grey plovers, which winter in East Africa from October to April.

All plovers nest on the ground, although the nest is hardly more than a scrape (even in the middle of a track); savanna species aggressively protect their young, but smaller species like Kittlitz's and three-banded plovers rely more on camouflage. The eggs and young of all plovers are cryptically marked and chicks can run and hide soon after hatching. In sandy soil parents may bury their eggs when away from the nest.

BIRDS

★ HOTSPOTS

- Lake Nakuru NP (p91) Kittlitz's, chestnut-banded and migratory plovers feed on the shores of the lake.
- Masai Mara NR (p62) Savanna species (African wattled, blacksmith and crowned plovers) are resident.
- Murchison Falls NP (p154) Long-toed plovers are common on floating vegetation.

RECOGNITION Fawn upperparts spotted brown. Yellow legs, bill and eyes. Height 43cm.

HABITAT Grassland, open woodland and rocky country.

BEHAVIOUR Usually solitary.

BREEDING Lays two eggs.

FEEDING Eats small animals.

VOICE Musical *pe-pe-pe-peou-PEOU-PEOU-PEOU-pee-pi-pe-pe-pe*.

★ HOTSPOTS

- Masai Mara NR (p62)
- Serengeti NP (p108)

SPOTTED THICK-KNEE

Among the many offshoots from the large shorebirds group is a small family of mainly nocturnal waders known as thick-knees (although their knees are barely thicker than those of other birds), dikkops or stone curlews. Large for waders, long-legged and equipped with very large eyes, thick-knees hunt insects and other small animals at dusk and after dark with ploverlike walk-pause-peck behaviour. Spotted thick-knees are commonly encountered on tracks at night, but during the day they rest in dry areas under bushes; when accidentally flushed from cover their large size and sudden appearance can be startling. Normally, when danger approaches they crouch down, lying flat on the ground with neck extended; another tactic is simply to walk away and blend in with the countryside. Males and females mate for life, and both care for the young; their nest is a shallow scrape on the ground sometimes lined with vegetation, stones or animal droppings. Spotted thick-knee chicks can walk soon after hatching, their down blending superbly with rocky soil when they lie flat to avoid detection (the water thick-knee is commonly seen near water during the day and is reputed to lays its eggs near basking crocodiles as a deterrent to predators).

AFRICAN JACANA

Competition for resources is keen at the water's edge, but few birds have adapted to life on top of the water, and none as successfully as the jacanas, which live virtually their entire life afloat: hugely elongated toes spread their weight so they can run across water lilies, Nile cabbage and other floating masses as well as soft mud. When walking on submerged vegetation, they can appear to walk on water; alternatively, the back of a hippo makes a good vantage point. At a pinch they can dive and fly (clumsily) with legs dangling – often giving their harsh call in flight.

Most bodies of still water with lily pads or other floating vegetation will have a few jacanas (although they can be hard to see if a dropping water level has caused the shadows of drooping lilies to break up the view); watch for the blue headgear, wing stretches and jacanas in flight. The sexes look alike, but any aggression is likely to be from a female defending her territory – all parental care is by the male. He incubates the eggs by holding two under each wing. Chicks can walk soon after hatching, but the male carries them under his wings for protection and even moves the eggs in this manner should rising water cause the destruction of the nest.

RECOGNITION Chestnut body, white face and breast. Blue bill and 'shield'. Height 30cm.

HABITAT Swamps and lakes.

BEHAVIOUR Gregarious outside breeding season.

BREEDING Lays two to five eggs on floating vegetation.

FEEDING Insects and small water animals.

VOICE A harsh rattle.

★ HOTSPOTS

- Lake Baringo (p88)
- Lake Naivasha (p90)
- Lake Manyara NP (p128)
- Queen Elizabeth NP (p158)

BIRDS

SANDGROUSE

Unrelated to grouse, although they do look superficially like stocky, painted pigeons, sandgrouse are primarily birds of semiarid country. The five species are essentially ground birds, eating mainly seeds picked up while walking in pairs or small flocks. Subtle patterns of buff, tan and black disrupt their outline, and the well-camouflaged eggs are also laid on the ground. Strong, pointed wings enable them to fly away from danger and to survive in even the most arid country (if food is available) by transporting them long distances – they will travel up to 20km

daily to reach water. The best way to see sandgrouse is to wait by a waterhole at dawn or dusk, when flocks drift in to drink. Wave after noisy wave lines up at the water's edge, each bird dipping its bill for a few seconds before taking off again. And watch for males bathing – what they're actually doing is soaking up water in modified belly feathers, which they then take back to the nest and allow the chicks to suckle.

★ HOTSPOTS

- Samburu NR (p84)
- Tsavo NP (p66)
- Lake Turkana (p92)
- Masai Mara NR (p62)

AFRICAN SKIMMER

Of the three species of skimmer found worldwide, only one is found in Africa. Usually seen sitting on sand bars with heads pointing into the wind in the company of gulls and terns (their close relatives), on close inspection skimmers reveal an extraordinary feature: the lower half of their bill extends 1cm to 3cm beyond the tip of the upper one. While it may look deformed, it is actually a superb design for a unique fishing technique: flying in a straight line about 5cm above the surface, the skimmer's lower mandible slices through the water at a 45-degree angle while the mouth is held open, snapping shut the instant it comes in contact with a fish (an action that whips the head round under the body).

In cross section, the skimmer's bill is extremely narrow and so streamlined – to reduce drag in the water – that it can skim while gliding. The lower jaw grows faster than the upper and is worn away by abrasion with sand and objects underwater – young birds learning to skim sometimes practice on sand by mistake. Because this is a tactile and not a visual technique, skimmers can fish at dusk and even on the darkest nights (they're best seen heading out to feed around dusk). To compensate for bright reflections, a skimmer's pupils narrow to a slit like cats' eyes, unlike those of any other birds.

RECOGNITION Black upperparts, pure white below. Large scarlet bill tipped yellow. Length 40cm.

HABITAT Broad waterways.

BEHAVIOUR Breeds in colonies. Some populations migrate.

BREEDING Lays two to three spotted eggs in sand scrape.

FEEDING Skims for fish.

VOICE A repeated, sharp *kip*.

★ HOTSPOTS

- Lake Turkana (p92)
- Queen Elizabeth NP (p158)

BIRDS

PIGEONS & DOVES

NAMAQUA DOVE

species, such as the African green and olive pigeons, are also common, but usually feed on fruit in trees. Waterholes are always good places to look for pigeons and doves, since most species must drink daily.

All pigeons and doves fly well – the doves and turtle doves often breaking from just under your front wheels. Explosive take offs are one of the secrets of their survival, along with good camouflage and loose-fitting feathers, which often leave a would-be predator empty handed. They also have a rapid reproductive turnover: most species are prolific breeders (in fact it's all some of them seem to do and you'll probably see a few bowing and cooing as a preliminary to mating). Their nests are usually just a formality – a loose, untidy platform of twigs, although some nest on rock ledges – but the parents have a legendary propensity to sit tight on the nest, deserting a clutch to a predator only at the last second. And the young grow faster than just about any other birds, developing for the first few days of life on a highly nutritious solution ('pigeon's milk') of digested seeds from the crop of the parent – a trait pigeons and doves share with parrots.

Like those of waterfowl, and a few other domesticated birds, the calls of pigeons and doves are famous and many are variations on the familiar cooing. Although similar, once recognised the calls are a useful aid to identification. Forest-dwelling species can be much harder to pin down among dense foliage, but look for them at dawn winging across the canopy or sitting high on exposed snags, something they may do for long spells.

COMMON COOERS It would be hard to credit the lives of such ostensibly gentle birds with any sort of drama, but when it comes to feeding, courting and mating (all of which most pigeons and doves do a lot of) they are as competitive as any other birds. This successful family is represented by 24 species in East Africa, although many of the ubiquitous doves and turtle doves look very similar and pose some tricky identification problems for birders. Several of these mainly ground-feeding birds, including ring-necked, red-eyed and laughing doves, will commonly be seen walking along tracks at the edge of grassland. More colourful

★ HOTSPOTS

- Masai Mara NR (p62) Plenty of doves in the savanna plus African green pigeons along the Mara River.
- Kilimanjaro NP (p132) Forest and montane species; doves where forest abuts savanna edge.
- Kibale Forest NP (p150) Rainforest attracts fruit-eating pigeons.

BIRDS

PARROTS & LOVEBIRDS

The popular conception of colourful parrots screeching across the African sky is a bit misleading: they certainly screech, but only eight species live in East Africa. Virtually every aspect of parrot biology relates to life in the trees. Strong feet and claws – two toes pointing back and two forward – grasp food and clamber through foliage. Their distinctive, hooked bills crush nuts, tear bark and act as a third leg when climbing; food held in the feet is manipulated with a strong, thick tongue. Their bright colours, so obvious in flight, disrupt their outline

among greenery and blossom, and nests are usually in tree hollows where the eggs are safe from all but monkeys, snakes and tree-living mammals. Parrots often alight on exposed perches to take the early sun and are often noisy when feeding – when a threat appears the birds fall silent only to explode in all directions from the foliage in a burst of colour (behaviour that is thought to confuse predators). Lovebirds are small enough to be overlooked; some species sleep upside down, hanging on with their claws.

HOTSPOTS

- Kibale Forest NP (p150) The rare African grey parrot may still be seen here.
- Mt Kenya NP (p80) Red-fronted parrots in tall forest above 2000m.
- Serengeti NP (p108) Fischer's lovebirds common in acacia woodland.

CUCKOOS & COUCALS

Laying eggs in another bird's nest is not unique to cuckoos, but few other birds are as adept at shirking the burden of parenthood. And with around 17 species in East Africa alone, their diversity reflects the success of nest parasitism. Although most are common, some aspects of their behaviour are still a mystery. During courtship males typically call for hours on end and even at night (a colonial official once requested the removal of cuckoos for disturbing his sleep). Females lay their eggs in the nest of the 'host'

species. Upon hatching, the cuckoo chick evicts the rightful eggs or chicks and is raised by the unsuspecting parents: such are the joys of parenting that the adult hosts (often tiny warblers – watch for parties of small birds mobbing cuckoos) don't seem to realise that their pride and joy is many times their own size. Exceptions to the parasitic rule are the five species of coucal, large, mainly ground-dwelling cuckoos that build their own nests and incubate their own eggs.

HOTSPOTS

- Lake Mburo NP (p162) Widespread savanna species such as red-chested and diederik cuckoos, and white-browed coucals are commonly seen.
- Bwindi Impenetrable NP (p146) Excellent for larger rainforest cuckoos.
- Masai Mara NR (p62)
- Serengeti NP (p108)

BIRDS

TURACOS

SCHALOW'S TURACO

TREE TURKEYS The crimson wing-flashes of a large green bird gliding across the trail are often your first view of a forest turaco, for although large birds (most measure about 40cm to 43cm) and rather poor flyers, they move about branches and foliage with great agility and can be tricky to spot. Unique to Africa, turacos are often brilliantly coloured and are one of the highlights of a safari (visually, although not ecologically, they replace parrots as one of the most attractive groups). At least one species is found in most habitats and several may occur in close proximity – especially in the rainforests of Uganda and western Kenya, where turacos reach their greatest diversity and size.

The 75cm-long great blue turaco is the largest species and is common in the canopy of undisturbed rainforest. Its former epithet, tree turkey, is a gross misnomer: although it can run fast on the ground, it's hard to imagine a turkey running along branches with the great blue's agility. Despite its size it can reach fruits and berries at the end of slender branches, even hanging upside down to do so. Turacos are among the most vocal of forest birds, one call sometimes setting off a chain of responses throughout the canopy. Calls are one of the tricks to locating turacos and, once recognised, they will be found to be quite common.

Many colourful turacos also inhabit savanna and semiarid country; on safari you'll probably encounter the mainly grey plantain-eaters and go-away birds. Plantain-eaters don't actually eat plantain or bananas, but the go-away birds are noisy turacos, their calls sounding like a nasal *g'way, g'way*; the eastern grey plantain-eater makes a chimplike hooting that featured in the soundtrack to *Tarzan* movies. Savanna species are not so agile as their forest-dwelling relatives, clambering about in acacias and keeping a lookout from the treetops. The bare-faced and white-bellied go-away birds are often seen around safari lodges, bare-faced in the west and white-bellied in the east.

All turacos are almost exclusively vegetarian, eating fruits, leaves, flowers and buds – great blue turacos feed leaves to their young. Most leave the trees to drink or bathe; parties of go-away birds can be seen drinking at pools and great blue turacos eat moss near streams.

★ HOTSPOTS

- Mt Kenya NP (p80) Hartlaub's turaco is common.
- Serengeti NP (p108) Go-away birds are easily seen.

BIRDS

OWLS & NIGHTJARS

CREATURES OF THE NIGHT Most owls are essentially nocturnal and no group of birds is more successful at hunting at night. Armed with grasping talons, hooked bills and soft plumages for silent flight, a disclike arrangement of facial feathers funnels sounds to their hypersensitive ears. All are carnivorous and specialists include the white-faced scops owl, which takes a high percentage of scorpions in its diet; and Pel's fishing owl, which hunts fish along rainforest rivers – even wading to do so. Admirable though their nocturnal lifestyle is, it usually makes seeing owls considerably more difficult than hearing them. Fortunately, several of East Africa's 18 species are comparatively common. Savanna-dwelling eagle-owls, such as the pink-lidded Verreaux's eagle, can sometimes be located during the day by the mobbing behaviour of smaller birds. Not surprisingly, most are best seen by spotlighting: by driving slowly, the eye shine of one or two species can usually be picked out. Spotted eagle-owls are often on the move at dusk, their bulky silhouettes standing out against the sky; and African wood owls commonly hunt around lodges. The African scops owl is the smallest and possibly commonest species, but during the day its camouflage can render it almost invisible against bark.

On a night drive you will probably see one or several nightjars taking off from the track before you, their eyes reflecting in headlights. Also nocturnal, nightjars share owls' soft plumage and silent flight, but are essentially aerial hunters that snap up insects in flight with their wide gape. Nightjars have weak

VERREAUX'S EAGLE OWL

feet and a small body, but long, usually slender wings; most roost and all nest on the ground, a trait for which they are superbly camouflaged in intricate patterns of brown, buff and black. Nightjars cannot hunt effectively in dense forest: watch for them hawking in clearings and over fields or grassland. The problem with nightjars is getting one of the 18 species to sit still long enough to look at. Even then, the identification of most is extremely difficult and more reliably made by their distinctive calls (notable exceptions grow extraordinary wing feathers when courting, eg pennant-winged and standard-winged nightjars).

BIRDS

⚘ HOTSPOTS

- Lake Baringo (p88) Verreaux's eagle-owls and white-faced scops owls hunt here.
- Murchison Falls NP (p154) The place for Pel's fishing owls as well as pennant-winged nightjars (March to September) and standard-winged nightjars (November to February).
- Mt Kenya NP (p80) Montane nightjars are resident around the Met Station.

SPECKLED MOUSEBIRD

CURIOUS HANGERS Mousebirds are endemic to the African continent (there are four species in East Africa) and have an engaging and comical habit of hanging from branches and wires. A mechanism on their toes locks the feet in position and the articulation of their legs means the feet are held at shoulder height when hanging. Mousebirds are largely vegetarian and it is thought that by hanging, the sun warms their belly and helps them digest food. But during sleep (something speckled mousebirds do for up to 12 hours), their metabolic rate can fall by 90% and they also like to warm up in the early morning – pairs even warm each other by hanging breast to breast.

Speckled mousebirds are highly sociable, living in family groups that fly with apparent discipline in single file from one bush only to crash land in the next. Flight – whirring wing beats alternating with direct glides – looks fast but actually isn't, but strongly hooked claws help them to clamber about in trees. Large groups may visit one fruiting tree, a trait that doesn't endear them to gardeners. But garden pests or not, their resemblance to mice is owed to the texture of their soft, hairlike feathers and to their habit of running fast along branches, up tree trunks and along the ground, long tail trailing behind. When threatened, mousebirds hang in dense vegetation, dropping to the ground to hide if necessary, then climbing back up when danger passes.

Group members cluster together at times during the day and even nesting is a social affair: chicks are fed by the parents and by youngsters from previous broods that act as helpers. And adding to so many unique features is the absorbing behaviour of the chicks: when about 10 days old, they start toying with nest material; once they leave the nest they play games with other young birds (such as running, wrestling and chasing) and also engage in head shaking, sudden leaps, mutual feeding, building nests and playing with twigs and leaves.

RECOGNITION Short, stout body with very long, stiff tail. Nondescript grey-brown overall. Short, sometimes whitish crest. Thick, finchlike bill and deep-pink legs.

HABITAT Open areas with trees, such as savanna, gardens and agricultural land.

BEHAVIOUR Gregarious and sedentary. Roosts, dust bathes and basks in groups. Clusters can gather several times a day, but especially in cold weather. Males (mainly) preen each other. Mobs coucals and small predators such as shrikes and kingfishers.

BREEDING Nest is a cup in a bush or tree; has the smallest eggs of any nonparasitic bird.

FEEDING Largely vegetarian: fruit, buds, leaves, entire flowers, nectar and even dead bark. Can eat some plants poisonous to other species. Eats earth.

VOICE Whistles and chatters throughout the day. Usual contact call is a soft *siu-siu*.

BIRDS

★ HOTSPOTS

- Masai Mara NR (p62)
- Serengeti NP (p108)
- Queen Elizabeth NP (p158)

KINGFISHERS

THE HOLE STORY Common in most habitats, East Africa's 15 species of kingfisher include the world's largest and smallest species, but the basic form doesn't vary: all have a large head with long, pointed bill, compact body and very short legs. During the breeding season, pairs make vocal displays to each other and to defend their nests – woodland kingfishers are particularly aggressive, chasing away other hole-nesting birds, small hawks and even people. But at other times, and despite their bright coloration, most savanna and forest species are easily overlooked because of their habit of perching motionless for long spells – until a large insect or small lizard walks by, in which case it will be suddenly dived upon, taken back to the perch and bashed repeatedly to remove legs, wings or pincers before being swallowed whole.

Kingfishers also use the diving approach when bathing and hunting, by crash landing in water. Pied, malachite, giant and a few other kingfishers are usually easier to see because they dive from exposed perches near water, such as overhanging branches, jetties and boats. The abundant pied kingfisher can also be seen hovering over water up to 3km from land. To catch fish, amphibians and crustaceans, kingfishers have eyes that adjust instantly from daylight to underwater vision, but they must also learn to judge depth, refraction and the likely escape route of their quarry: watch for kingfishers bobbing their head to take aim before diving.

The pied kingfisher is the only species that roosts and nests communally – sometimes alongside colonies of bee-eaters – and one in three pairs has helpers that assist with

BUFF-BELLIED KINGFISHER

feeding young and defending the nest. All kingfishers nest in holes, and their short legs are ideal for scuttling along narrow tunnels. Usually they dig a tunnel in a sand bank (a record 8.5m-long tunnel was dug by a pair of giant kingfishers), but smaller species may nest in the sides of aardvark burrows; tree-nesting species always enlarge an existing hole; and rainforest-dwelling kingfishers excavate arboreal termite mounds. All the action takes place indoors, but after the chicks fledge, adults may be seen feeding them outside the nest for a few days.

BIRDS

HOTSPOTS

- Lake Nakuru NP (p91) Pied and malachite kingfishers are common.
- Serengeti NP (p108) Good spots to look for grey-headed and striped kingfishers.
- Queen Elizabeth NP (p158)

BEE-EATERS & ROLLERS

AERIAL ACROBATS Closely related to kingfishers, the equally or even more colourful bee-eaters and rollers are bird highlights of any safari. For travellers from higher northern latitudes, where bright colours among birds are comparatively rare, their glowing range of colours are a delight to the eye and a relief from the greens and browns of the savanna.

African bees have a fearsome reputation, but being such an abundant food resource, it was inevitable that at least one group of birds should tackle them. Bee-eaters appear to do so with relish, and nowhere have they reached the diversity they boast in East Africa (16 species), although some are seasonal migrants and a few have ranges that only just reach the region. All are very similar in size (mostly 20cm to 25cm in length) and shape:

streamlined with pointed, down-curved bills and long, swallowlike wings. But their habit of perching on exposed branches to watch for likely prey makes them easily seen and identified and because all are brightly coloured, their antics are a pleasure to watch.

Many species hunt from perches (along which they may huddle in rows at night or in cold weather), chasing the bees that make up a substantial percentage of their diet, but also tackling dragonflies, cicadas and potentially dangerous wasps and hornets. After a sometimes animated chase, which can include corkscrew turns, they return to their perch and bash the insect against a branch – taking care to rub off the stings of bees and wasps – before swallowing it whole. These thrashings can often be heard from several metres away. Larger species,

LITTLE BEE-EATER

uch as the Eurasian and carmine bee-eaters, spend much time hawking insects on the wing, although the latter follow tractors and bushfires and readily perch on mobile sites, such as ostriches, bustards, zebras and antelopes – subduing prey against the bird's back or antelope's horns! Bee-eaters are so specialised at catching insects on the wing that they ignore insects crawling along the ground.

Like their kingfisher cousins, all bee-eaters nest in holes: forest species in trees, others in tunnels excavated in river banks (carmine bee-eaters) or road cuttings. Larger, more aerial feeders often live colonially in cooperative (and competitive) units of related birds. Helpers, usually blood relatives such as the previous year's offspring, assist with incubation and feeding and, in turn, gain an apprenticeship in parenthood. But helpers sometimes also lay an egg or two in the nest at which they are helping. In fact, studies of colonies have revealed complicated and shifting alliances: adultery is rife among mated pairs, females lay in the nests of other females (a practice known as egg dumping), and some birds habitually attempt to rob others of food. Pairs will also nest separately, which is the usual practice among smaller species, such as the little and Somali bee-eaters.

Although hardly musical, bee-eaters have pleasant calls (at least when compared to the kingfishers), which are transcribed as a liquid, trilling *krreep-krreep*. All species sound more or less the same and, once the basic pattern is learnt, calls are easily recognised and a good way to detect bee-eaters in the canopy or flying overhead.

ROCKING ROLLERS

The seven species of roller are colourful and several, such as the lilac-breasted and Abyssinian, sport long tail feathers. The lilac-breasted roller is in places very common, easily seen and photographed and probably elicits more admiration from visitors than any other bird in East Africa. Like most of their relatives, rollers are not known for their song – typical calls are cackling or croaks – but a male displays by 'rolling' (an aeronautical term): flying slowly upwards with languorous flaps, he coasts down again, rocking from side to side to show off his prominent pale wing patches and usually cackling as he goes. Rollers also catch prey from a conspicuous perch: savanna species pouncing on ground-dwelling invertebrates and forest species hawking flying insects in the canopy. Lilac-breasted rollers also sometimes follow and catch prey disturbed by dwarf mongooses. You might also be the target of attention from one of these flashy birds – male rollers defend a territory and become pugnacious towards other birds, mammals and even people.

BIRDS

HOTSPOTS

- Lake Baringo (p88) Hosts Madagascar (May to September), blue-cheeked (October to May) and carmine bee-eaters (September to March).
- Murchison Falls NP (p154) Red-throated bee-eaters breed January to March; also carmine, little and swallow-tailed bee-eaters, and Abyssinian rollers.
- Samburu NR (p84) Dry-country species – white-throated (September to April), little and Somali bee-eaters, plus abundant lilac-breasted rollers.

HOOPOE

DISTINCTIVE CALLERS The hoopoe is so unlike any other bird that its image is unmistakable on ancient Egyptian tombs (among several other common African birds, such as the sacred ibis). Its name comes from its call – even its scientific name, *Upupa epops,* evokes the soft *hoo-poo-poo* that can be heard from several hundred metres away, and is sometimes repeated for hours on end. Hoopoes are not rare and at times (during migration) are common in East Africa – their appearance often evokes comment from people on safari. Their most unusual feature – a large, floppy crest that is usually held flat along the crown – is held erect like an untidy fan when the birds are alarmed. But they are rather unobtrusive birds that feed on the ground and are often first noticed in flight – an undulating, butterflylike flap-and-glide that shows off the boldly contrasting black-and-white pattern of their broad wings and banded rump. Courtship displays are even more striking, with pairs flying slowly round their territory one behind the other.

When feeding, hoopoes walk jerkily along the ground on rather short legs (one feature which betrays an ancestry shared with kingfishers), jabbing left and right at loose soil with their bill, or digging vigorously enough to make sods fly. Large prey items may be snatched and beaten against a hard surface (another kingfisher trait). When a predator passes overhead, the hoopoe flattens itself against the ground with wings spread, tips almost touching, tail fanned and bill pointing straight up; the effect of the disruptive pattern on its wings and back makes it almost invisible, especially against rocky ground. Groups of hoopoes sometimes roost one to a tree in copses, using the same perches for weeks on end.

Hoopoes are strong migrants: birds that breed in Europe arrive south of the Sahara in October; and birds that breed in Africa (including East Africa) migrate seasonally across the African continent. The two subspecies have subtle plumage differences (although apparently no behavioural differences) and you will sometimes see reference to African and Eurasian hoopoes because some taxonomists regard the two as separate species.

RECOGNITION Pink-rufous or cinnamon with black-and-white wing bars and black tail; folding crest with black tips. Slender, down-curving black bill. Length 28cm.

HABITAT Flat or undulating wooded savanna with sparse ground cover; also cultivation, orchards and lawns.

BEHAVIOUR Usually seen singly or in pairs, flying into a tree when approached; loose flocks form on migration. Pairs territorial and may use same nest hole in successive years. Males usually call from elevated perch.

BREEDING Lays four to six eggs in a hole in a bank, tree, wall or termite mound.

FEEDING Probes ground for large insects, their larvae and pupae; also takes worms, spiders, molluscs, small reptiles and (rarely) eggs.

VOICE Low, soft but far-carrying *hoo-poo-poo* repeated every few seconds during breeding season.

BIRDS

★ **HOTSPOTS**

- Buffalo Springs NR (p84)
- Serengeti NP (p108)

GREEN WOOD-HOOPOE

IRIDESCENT CHATTERBOXES Noisy, gregarious and conspicuous, the presence of these agile insect hunters is typically announced by loud chattering before they break cover and fly between trees in single file. Wood-hoopoes are unique to Africa and are related both to true hoopoes and hornbills (scimitarbills differ from wood-hoopoes in name only, although they tend to be less vocal and gregarious than wood-hoopoes). All wood-hoopoes and scimitarbills are characterised by long, slender bodies with a long tail and a long, down-curved bill. Adult plumage in all species is dark but iridescent: appearing black in some lights, close-to it changes from shimmering green to blue or violet that contrasts with the vegetation. Green wood-hoopoes, the most widespread species, feed on a wide variety of insects and other small animals. Small, animated parties of these engaging birds scamper along branches and up trunks, probe crevices and lever up bark as they search for prey, or hang upside down using their tail as a brace to peer into holes.

Green wood-hoopoes (they can look very blue in dull light) display noisily to each other while foraging, chuckling, bowing and rocking with tails spread and wings partly open, and sometimes pass bits of bark or lichen between each other using their bills, before moving on. And listen for them hammering like woodpeckers, bashing prey against the bark or pecking at a beetle they've wedged in a crevice. Groups sometimes roost together in tree cavities (a scarce resource for which they must compete with other animals – including bee swarms), where they are sometimes caught by nocturnal predators such as genets and safari ants. Hollows play an important role in breeding as well: unable to excavate their own nest holes, wood-hoopoes rely on naturally occurring holes or those abandoned by barbets and woodpeckers.

RECOGNITION White wing and tail spots stand out from all-dark iridescent plumage in flight. Bright-red bill and feet.

HABITAT Common in savanna, woodland, riverine forest and gardens below 2800m.

BEHAVIOUR Gregarious, groups usually following the male as he forages. Prises off flaking bark by inserting and opening bill. Flock members jointly investigate potential breeding holes. Secretes musky odour from rump glands.

BREEDING Nests in existing cavity in tree or post, usually after long rains. Up to 10 nonbreeding helpers may assist with rearing young.

FEEDING Takes a wide variety of insects, especially caterpillars, beetles and larvae; also fruit, centipedes, small lizards and bird eggs.

VOICE Noisy: a weird chuckling chorus starts slowly then accelerates.

BIRDS

★ HOTSPOTS

- Masai Mara NR (p62)
- Serengeti NP (p108)
- Mt Kenya NP (p80)

HORNBILLS

AFRICAN TOUCANS Chameleons are a favourite food of many of East Africa's 20 hornbill species, as are other lizards, insects and fruit; and larger species eat virtually any animal they can swallow, including eggs, birds and fruit-bats. Whatever their preferences, hornbills are among the most conspicuous, noisy and engaging of large birds to be seen in savanna and forest. All hornbills have long eyelashes, but those of the ground hornbills are very long and thick and can be seen easily. And all have a large, sometimes colourful bill, which in some, such as the trumpeter hornbill, is adorned with a casque – a hollow protuberance thought to resonate when the birds call. Noise plays a big role in a hornbill's life: they call for many reasons (for example, to contact each other or establish territories) – their nasal honkings are a good way of locating them; and a unique feather arrangement makes their wing beats audible from some distance away.

Several species live side by side in most areas and up to eight may coexist in forest communities, where different species may even nest in the same tree. Early morning is the time to watch for their complex interactions: calls signal communal roosts waking up; flocks fly across the canopy to fruiting trees with a loud whoosh of wings; black dwarf hornbills hawk insects and catch prey displaced by columns of safari ants; red-billed dwarf hornbills join feeding parties of squirrels and other birds; and white-crested hornbills alert monkeys to danger in their mutual territories. Interaction with other animals is not unusual: watch for chanting goshawks taking quails flushed by ground hornbills, and ground hornbills themselves

BIRDS

SOUTHERN GROUND HORNBILLS

can give away the location of lions or a leopard.

Dwarf mongooses roam in packs, searching out small animals such as insects and lizards and retreating to their dens in abandoned termite mounds at night or during the heat of the day. Their diet is exactly the same as that of three species of hornbill (Von der Decken's, eastern yellow-billed and red-billed) and a remarkable and possibly unique feeding strategy has evolved: the hornbills walk along with foraging mongooses, snapping up food disturbed or flushed by their companions. Although there is some competition, high-leaping grasshoppers are usually too fast for the mongooses and cryptic prey are missed by the hornbills, which hunt by sight. Both also take rodents if the opportunity arises, but the hornbills never eat the rat-sized baby mongooses.

This relationship is no accident; the hornbills wait until the mongooses start foraging in the morning, chivvying them along by walking among them until they get moving. And if the mongooses take more than an hour to wake up, one or two birds peer down the mound's ventilator shafts and honk repeatedly until the mammals emerge, yawning and bleary-eyed. Both mongooses and hornbills are eaten by a variety of large hawks and, if this arrangement seems one-sided, it has been shown that the birds provide early warning of the marauders – giving mongoose guards that watch from termite mounds or trees extra eyes and more time to forage for themselves. Mongooses get decidedly agitated when their hornbills don't show, trotting up and down the mound and making half-hearted forays into the grass.

SELF-SEALING PRISONERS

All hornbills nest in cavities, usually in a tree, and pairs spend much time inspecting holes. After mating, females of most species seal themselves into a suitable nest by plastering up the entrance with mud, sticky fruit and droppings, until only a slit remains – an effective barricade against predators. There she raises the chicks, cramped with long tail bent vertically over her back, while the male passes food through the entrance. The exceptions to the rule are the ground hornbills: they also nest in hollows, but the females don't get bricked in. Southern ground hornbills are one of the few species known to breed cooperatively – up to six immature and adult helpers assist at the nest.

BIRDS

WOODPECKERS

Wood is the key to woodpecker ecology – they even drink from small puddles in tree forks – but although some species hammer vigorously to dig out grubs, others pry off flaking bark, glean insects from foliage or extract ants from crevices with a long, barbed tongue. Other physical adaptations that help them exploit the forests' rich insect resources include strongly clawed feet on short legs; stiff, pointed tail feathers that prop them up as they cling vertically to tree trunks; and a strong, chisel-like bill for excavating holes in trees (muscles at the base of the bill act as

shock absorbers and nostrils covered by feathers exclude flying woodchips). The 20 woodpecker species in East Africa exploit many subtle forest niches (eg Tullberg's woodpeckers often forage among trees that have been killed by fire) and several species can often be found in close proximity. The birds themselves play a pivotal role in wooded ecosystems: woodpeckers are among the only animals that actually create cavities in living wood, and their hole construction benefits many species of bird, mammal, reptile and insect.

★ HOTSPOTS

- Serengeti NP (p108) For common savanna species.
- Masai Mara NR (p62)
- Kakamega Forest NR (p76) Good rainforest pickings, including grey-throated and yellow-billed barbets.
- Saiwa Swamp NP (p97) Nesting double-toothed barbets.

BARBETS & TINKERBIRDS

Like their relatives the woodpeckers, barbets and tinkerbirds are usually found in trees (although a few barbets spend much time on the ground). But unlike woodpeckers, these stocky, generally short-tailed birds come in many colours and patterns. Least colourful are the tinkerbirds (the yellow-rumped tinkerbird's pervasive *tonk-tonk-tonk-tonk* call is one of the most common bush sounds). Some barbets are clad in subdued shades, but others range from black-and-

white to bright blue, red and yellow. All barbets and tinkerbirds nest in holes, which they excavate in branches or tree trunks with their strong, pointed bill (which in many is surrounded with prominent bristles). Most species eat mainly fruit, although all include some insects in their diet. Tinkerbirds are the most arboreal and forage with other birds in the canopy; many barbets perch for long periods in tall, dead trees. Fruiting fig trees are ideal places to stake out and several species of barbet and tinkerbird may gather at one tree.

★ HOTSPOTS

- Serengeti NP (p108) Cardinal and bearded woodpeckers are widespread in savanna.
- Masai Mara NR (p62)
- Bwindi Impenetrable NP (p146) Rainforest-dwelling Elliot's and buff-spotted woodpeckers.

BIRDS

LARKS

Like many other grassland birds, most of East Africa's 25 species of lark are cryptically coloured, their muted shades of brown, tawny and buff often echoing the soil colour where they dwell. Many superficially resemble pipits, and larks are also essentially ground dwellers: they are often encountered along vehicle tracks in savanna and grassland; and their nests are always well hidden in tussocks. Larks have strong legs and feet (some species have long hind claws to walk over tussocks) and readily run to escape danger, although all can fly well. Their strong, hard bills are adapted to a diet containing lots

of seeds. Larks and pipits were once believed to be closely related, but larks are possibly distant relatives of the sparrows – sparrow-larks show obvious similarities. And larks advertise their territories with long display flights, which often involve complicated – and beautiful – song sequences. The famous skylark does not occur in East Africa, but one of the most evocative sounds on the rustling grassland of the Serengeti Plains is the plaintive whistling of the rufous-naped lark.

HOTSPOTS

- Serengeti NP (p108) Grassland species such as rufous-naped and flappet larks.
- Masai Mara NR (p62)
- Lake Turkana (p92) Arid-zone specialists: crested larks and chestnut-headed sparrow-larks.

GREATER HONEYGUIDE

It's not much to look at (and this is the gem among the 14 species), but the greater honeyguide is an amazing bird. Firstly, although its standard fare is insects, it also eats beeswax, which it digests with special stomach bacteria. Secondly, it lays its eggs in other birds' nests – typically those of woodpeckers and barbets. When laying, the female greater honeyguide sometimes punctures or removes the eggs of the host; if she doesn't, her chick has a hooked bill with which it kills its foster siblings so it is raised alone – it is fed on the hosts' diet until it fledges 30 days later. And thirdly, greater honeyguides lead people to beehives so they will break them open – the only honeyguide thought to do so. It is often stated that honeyguides lead ratels (and possibly mongooses, genets and baboons) to hives, but there's little hard evidence for this. Conspicuous when 'guiding', the bird moves from tree to tree with a fluttering flight and a loud, continuous chattering, flicking its white outer tail feathers and stopping to watch the progress of its follower. After the hive is opened, it feeds on the wax, larvae and eggs – any bee stings are resisted by its thick skin. Greater honeyguides also obtain beeswax at abandoned hives without a helper if the hive has already been broken.

RECOGNITION Grey-brown with white ear patch, whitish underparts and black throat. Stubby pink bill. Height 19cm.

HABITAT Open woodland.

BEHAVIOUR Solitary. Perches for hours. Harasses drongos.

BREEDING Lays one white egg.

FEEDING Insects, beeswax, bee larvae and eggs.

VOICE Continuous bur-witt.

HOTSPOTS

- Masai Mara NR (p62)
- Serengeti NP (p108)

BIRDS

SWALLOWS & MARTINS

Swallows and martins are small, active birds, familiar to most people as messengers of seasonal change and also because several species nest in or near human dwellings. Their supremely aerial lifestyle has led to a streamlined body with long, narrow wings for powerful, sustained flight; and many species sport distinctive forked tails with long streamers (that have also given their names to a family of large butterflies – the swallowtails). All feed exclusively in flight by scooping up insects with their wide mouths, and they tend to be gregarious in flight; several species are often seen together – look for them hawking above marshes and swamps at any time of day. Many flash with iridescence and have contrasting pale underparts or reddish markings on their head and throat. The familiar and cosmopolitan barn swallow is just one of 23 resident and migratory species, including various martins and rough-wings, that occur in East Africa. Swallows and martins sometimes nest in colonies, most building a cup-shaped nest of mud pellets gathered waterside or at drying puddles.

⭐ HOTSPOTS

- Murchison Falls NP (p154) Swallows and martins feed between the high banks of the Victoria Nile.
- Lake Turkana (p92) Rock martins inhabit local gorges.

RECOGNITION Grey-brown upperparts; darker head. White belly, yellow vent. Height 20cm.

HABITAT Virtually anywhere with trees or shrubs.

BEHAVIOUR Normally in pairs, congregating at fruit trees.

BREEDING Two to three eggs.

FEEDING Fruit and insects.

VOICE Melodious chortlings.

⭐ HOTSPOTS

- Common in hotel grounds, towns and gardens

BIRDS

COMMON BULBUL

If any bird can be called ubiquitous in East Africa, it is the common bulbul (also known as yellow-vented or dark-capped bulbul). It is neither showy nor colourful and its behaviour is unobtrusive, but it readily adapts to human settlement and is common in city parks. Although common bulbuls generally avoid forest, they spread along roads and railways and will fly over the canopy to reach jungle plantations and camps. They can become a nuisance, stealing scraps from safari lodges, and are easily caught when intoxicated from eating fermented fruit.

Common bulbuls are quick to spot a predator, such as a snake or owl, which they scold noisily. But it is for their calls that they are best known: their chortlings start well before dawn, and can continue for two hours after sunrise; they sometimes congregate at dusk, and are often the last birds to sing, bedding down well after sunset with much fussing and twittering. The common bulbul is part of a complex family that includes many similar species of greenbul and brownbul (whose identification birdwatchers can scratch their heads over); the common bulbul makes a useful reference point when trying to identify unfamiliar species in a new habitat.

WAGTAILS, PIPITS & LONGCLAWS

GRASSLAND TAIL-PUMPERS Whether running along safari lodge rooftops, flitting along streams or snapping up flies from under the hooves of large animals, East Africa's six wagtail species are distinctive and common. The African pied wagtail is one of the most easily recognised, and is readily seen foraging in flower beds and on lawns, snatching insects off the ground or after a chase. All wagtails pump their tail up and down when standing still (something they don't do very often) and walk, rather than hop, with an exaggerated back-and-forth head movement.

At first sight, pipits bear little resemblance to wagtails, but they are closely related: they too forage on the ground and snap up insects, and typically pump their tails when they stand still. But, while many wagtails are boldly marked, most pipits are grassland dwellers and coloured accordingly in subdued shades of brown and buff. The widespread grassland pipit is commonly seen running down tracks ahead of a vehicle, pausing often before scooting off again. Several pipits are migratory and sometimes associate with wagtails outside the breeding season at communal roosts, gathering at dusk in tall trees and reed beds. Many pipits and larks look superficially similar, but they belong to different families and are generally not regarded as close relatives. The glorious exception among the drably coloured pipits is the golden pipit, which in flight resembles a great yellow butterfly.

The six species of longclaw – so-called because their hind claw is extremely long,

YELLOW WAGTAIL

enabling them to walk over tussocks – tend to stand more upright than pipits and have longer legs; they also have colourful underparts and don't pump their tails. Longclaws are usually not difficult to spot and often indulge in melodious territorial songs in flight or from an exposed tussock. Both pipits and longclaws build a grass nest on the ground during and after the rains, when growing grass affords more concealment for nests and young. In a remarkable example of convergent evolution, the yellow-throated longclaw is almost identical in appearance, nesting and habits to the unrelated meadowlarks, the familiar songbirds of North America.

BIRDS

⭐ HOTSPOTS

- Serengeti NP (p108) Several species of pipit and longclaw in grasslands.
- Tsavo NP (p66) Golden pipit and Pangani longclaw country.
- Aberdare NP (p86) Yellow wagtails are common around buffalo herds, African pied around lodges.
- Kilimanjaro NP (p132) Mountain and grey wagtails beside highland streams.

BABBLERS

Throughout their range in Africa and Asia, the large and varied babbler group are renowned skulkers of forest undergrowth. Fortunately in East Africa, a few species are quite easy to see and can even become semitame around lodges. Most are thrush-sized birds (20cm to 23cm in length) with strong legs and feet, and typically forage for insects and other small animals on the ground. East African species are not brightly coloured, although most are highly gregarious, feeding, resting and roosting in small flocks and lining up on branches to indulge in mutual preening. And these animated parties also draw attention to themselves with frequent vocalisations, sometimes in duets or choruses. Babblers are rather sombrely marked in greys and browns, but eye colour can be an important clue to identification, and differs for all East Africa's babblers. As their name suggests, parties of chatterers are very vocal, but the six species of illadopses are forest skulkers that pose a challenge to ardent birdwatchers.

★ HOTSPOTS

- Samburu NR (p84) Rufous chatterers common in semiarid thornbush country.
- Budongo FR (p164) Uganda's illadopsis headquarters features four species.

WARBLERS

To the uninitiated, a birdwatcher's obsession with small, nondescript birds is inexplicable when there are so many colourful and large birds to look at. But among birds, beauty does not equate rarity, and to hard-core birders the identification of every bird is important – especially the 'little brown jobs' (LBJs). Enter the warblers: small (usually up to 15cm) insect eaters that typically live in dense vegetation. Many, such as camaropteras, crombecs and eremomelas, are attractive little birds, but the harder the challenge the greater the sport and there are few greater challenges than the 32 species of grassland warbler known as cisticolas. Resplendent in buff, grey, white and brown, they all look almost identical and are best told apart by their calls when they're breeding: apart from the singing, whistling and trilling cisticolas, there's the thoroughly modern, rock-loving cisticola and the less-melodious winding, rattling, wailing and croaking cisticolas. Several names commemorate ornithologists of the British Empire, such as Hunter and Carruthers; then there's the wing-snapping cisticola and, for the prurient, the foxy and red-faced cisticolas.

★ HOTSPOTS

- Serengeti NP (p108) Several species of cisticola can easily be seen in grasslands.
- Masai Mara NR (p62)
- Bwindi Impenetrable NP (p146) For black-faced rufous warbler and Grauer's rush warbler.

BIRDS

THRUSHES, CHATS & RELATIVES

MUSIC MAKERS Apart from the thrushes – famous as songbirds around the world – this large and varied family includes the boldly marked wheatears, which in East Africa include both resident and migratory species; a few specialists of cliffs and rocky country such as the colourful cliff chats and the migratory common rock thrush); and the rainforest-dwelling alethes, akalats and ant thrushes, which forage among leaf litter for insects flushed by columns of driver ants. If the diversity weren't enough, confusion can arise because widely distributed species can go by different names in different countries.

At least one species is found in nearly every habitat and several may live in close proximity. It's hard to generalise about the 73 East African members of this enormous family, but all are usually solitary, small- to medium-sized birds with comparatively long legs and a shortish bill. Other features, such as body shape, tail length and coloration vary considerably. But among the many variables, one feature stands out in a few species at least: their vocal ability. Tuneful examples include the nightingale (this legendary singer is a migrant to East Africa); the white-browed robin-chat, a common garden bird with a fine repertoire of musical whistling; and the spotted morning thrush, which often greets the dawn around safari camps.

The olive thrush will probably be the first member of the family you encounter because, like its European and American cousins, it has adapted well to human

COLLARED PALM-THRUSH

habitation and forages while hopping across lawns. Peak baggers will almost certainly encounter the alpine chat, a confiding bird at mountain picnic sites as high as 5200m. The sooty chat is a conspicuous species of open country, where it digs nest tunnels in termite mounds (on which it frequently perches) and abandoned aardvark burrows. Wheatears also inhabit open country, where they perch in an upright stance; migrant species can be abundant en route to and from their northern breeding grounds, and the resident capped wheatear may be seen feeding on emerging termites.

BIRDS

HOTSPOTS

- Lake Nakuru NP (p91) Migratory wheatears in season.
- Masai Mara NR (p62) White-browed robin-chats and spotted morning thrushes around lodges.
- Lake Baringo (p88) White-shouldered cliff chat and brown-tailed rock chat resident at cliff faces.
- Udzungwa NP (p136) Relict forest has a high diversity of thrushes.

FLYCATCHERS

PARADISE FLYCATCHER

INSECT EATERS Three families of birds (the 'true' flycatchers, monarch flycatchers and a family of African flycatchers that includes the batises and wattle-eyes) are broadly lumped as flycatchers largely as a result of similarities in their foraging behaviour: all are small, sometimes hyperactive birds that catch insects in a variety of ways. Gleaning insects from foliage is a feeding technique common to most, but aerial pursuits launched from a perch are more characteristic of some groups. These insect-catching sallies are also used by other birds, such as drongos and some kingfishers, and are known as flycatching (appropriately enough) regardless of the species. Flycatching is entertaining to watch and can involve sudden turns and corkscrew movements during which the bill is sometimes heard snapping shut.

One or more flycatchers can be seen in most habitats and they can be quite tolerant of people. Wattle-eyes are small flycatchers of rainforest undergrowth, usually replaced in drier habitat by batises – small, shrikelike birds boldly marked in grey, black and white – which hunt in pairs or small family groups. Wattle-eyes and batises both snap their wings in flight, but are readily distinguished: only wattle-eyes have a coloured fleshy wattle surrounding the eye. The so-called monarch flycatchers are large and pugnacious and some are colourful; the true flycatchers are rather nondescript grey and brown birds of forest edges, some of which are Eurasian migrants.

Monarch flycatchers are renowned for their crests and long tails but, without a doubt, the most spectacular species is the common, easily recognisable African paradise flycatcher. The male's long tail streamers can measure more than twice his body length and are shown off to perfection in flight. Many colour variations exist for this species: rufous is the most common form, but it can also be grey or white, and all three shades can occur on the one bird. The African blue flycatcher is another restless forest monarch with a showy tail, which it fans open and shut, perhaps to startle insects. Like many flycatchers, monarchs build a neat, cup-shaped nest decorated with lichen and moss and bound with spider webs.

BIRDS

⭐ HOTSPOTS

- Kakamega Forest NR (p76) Good for rainforest wattle-eyes.
- Murchison Falls NP (p154) Silverbirds are common in thorny bush and savanna.

WAXBILLS

JEWELS IN THE UNDERGROWTH

Finch is a term that covers a multitude of forms, from sparrows to brilliant seed-crackers, and these mainly seed-eating birds are the most diverse bird group in East Africa (other finches include the weavers, whydahs and canaries). There's a lot of grass out on the savanna and a host of finches has evolved ready to pounce on heads of ripe seeds or slide down stalks to pick them off the ground. Many species have a red, waxy-looking bill, and the term 'waxbill' is commonly used to cover about 50 small, mainly colourful species with names such as twinspots, firefinches, silver-bills, crimsonwings, grenadiers and cordon-bleus. Many are also popular caged birds, known by other names in captivity.

Look for waxbills on roadsides, the edge of savanna and fields and in flocks mixed with other species, especially where grass is seeding. Many are common and some are confiding (such as red-billed firefinches and cut-throat finches), often nesting near human habitation. A number of brilliant species, including seed-crackers and crimsonwings, inhabit undergrowth of the rainforest edge; and the all-dark negrofinches are forest species that eat largely insects and berries (watch for them higher up in the canopy than other species, and often in association with sunbirds). However, despite their bright colours, waxbills can easily be overlooked; for example, when flushed, quail-finches fly a short distance then drop vertically to the ground and run like quail. And waxbill calls are often just high-pitched, sibilant whispers that can be mistaken for those of insects;

RED-BILLED FIREFINCH

indeed, the locust-finch measures only 9cm in length and looks like a large grasshopper flitting between seed heads.

Most waxbills build untidy domed nests of grass; some simply add material to the gaps under hamerkop or secretary bird nests; others, such as silverbills and some mannikins, use old weaver nests; and blue-capped cordon-bleus and bronze mannikins sometimes build near hornet nests. Bright spots, usually hardened callosities, on the gape and inside the mouth of chicks, invoke an irresistible feeding response in parents in the darkness of the nest chamber – a feature mimicked by whydah chicks that parasitise waxbill nests.

BIRDS

★ HOTSPOTS

- Kakamega Forest NR (p76) Rainforest and undergrowth favoured by negrofinches and seed-crackers.
- Mt Kenya NP (p80) Forest edge, grassland and streamside tangles for waxbills and crimsonwings.

SHRIKES, BUSH-SHRIKES & HELMET-SHRIKES

LIVING LARDERS With such an abundance and selection of thorns across the savanna, it's not surprising that something has found a use for them (albeit one that may appear gruesome to humans). Thus lizards, beetles, crickets, small birds and rodents may sometimes be seen impaled on the long, pointed spines of acacias. European settlement has also been adapted to the job, with barbed wire doing nicely too. This is the work of shrikes, perching birds boldly marked in black, white, greys and browns, often with a black 'mask' across the face.

The so-called true shrikes, some of which are migratory, are birds of open country that typically hunt by waiting on a likely perch and dropping onto their victim. Slender and upright, they have short legs, strong feet and hooked claws; at the business end, their large head supports a heavy, thick bill with an obvious hook at the tip. Several species are resident and common. When migrants pass through they can be abundant one week and gone the next.

Glamorous it ain't, but their hunting is effective: small vertebrates are pinned down and killed by repeated strikes to the back of the head – at least they're dead when they get impaled. Spikes keep prey steady while it's being eaten but, catering aside, storing food also has the advantage of providing insects on a cool day when fewer are about. It is also believed that these larders attract females, which are presumably impressed by a male's hunting skills. But other birds steal such food stores, and anything spiked on a whistling

CRIMSON-BREASTED SHRIKE

thorn bush is asking to be carried away by the ants that live in them.

In complete contrast, the many species of bush-shrike – a family whose members go under names such as brubru, boubous, chagras and gonoleks – run the whole gamut of colours from subdued browns and greys to radiant gold and scarlet contrasting with black. Some, such as the papyrus and black-headed gonoleks, are among the most beautiful of East African birds. However, although they're worth the effort, bush-shrikes are not nearly so easy to see and many are skulking inhabitants of dense foliage and thickets (although many respond well to a playback of their calls). Bush-shrikes also have stout, hooked bills, and several species are boldly marked in black-and-white, but they don't impale food on spikes and, rather than sitting and waiting, they are active hunters through foliage.

Helmet-shrikes are yet another family of shrikes that takes advantage of the abundant insect prey (although some ornithologists don't regard true shrikes, bush-shrikes and helmet-shrikes to be closely related). Helmet-shrikes are highly sociable birds with typical shrike features, such as a powerful bill. In all but one species the head is adorned with a ruff of stiff, forward-pointing feathers and some also have coloured wattles surrounding their eyes. Helmet-shrikes travelling in parties of up to 20 birds search trunks, branches and leaves for insects, on which they feed almost exclusively. They may roost communally, but only one pair in the group normally breeds at a time and in some species other group members help with nest building and feeding the chicks.

A HANGMAN BY ANY OTHER NAME...

Common fiscals are certainly common, and often seen perched on wires and posts, where their neat black-and-white plumage stands out from a distance. A fiscal was a senior judicial officer who dressed in black and white during Cape Colony days; the shrike's other common name, Jackie Hangman, is perhaps less obscure. In fact, anywhere shrikes are known in folklore, they have a reputation for cruelty and attract less than complimentary local names. For example, the scientific name *Lanius,* used for true shrikes, means butcher; *pies-grieche* is a French handle meaning 'sadistic magpie'; and the German *neuntoter* (nine dead) refers to the red-backed shrike's supposed penchant for murdering nine victims before resting. Cheery stuff but, happily, other shrike names have origins in their calls, such as boubou or gonolek; and the name gorgeous (or four-coloured) bush-shrike says it all, really.

BIRDS

HOTSPOTS

- Murchison Falls NP (p154) Several species of 'true' shrike live side by side on the savanna plains, their numbers augmented by migrating shrikes in season; bush-shrikes also resident.
- Kibale Forest NP (p150) The Bigodi Wetland supports papyrus gonoleks.

ORIOLES

Usually heard before they are seen, orioles are medium-sized, rather starlinglike birds that live virtually their whole lives in the canopy of woodland and forest. All of East Africa's seven species are golden yellow, suffused with olive or with contrasting black on their wings and tail. If you can locate the source of their liquid, fluting calls – they sound a bit like their common name – you'll also see a strongly pointed, bright-red bill and bold, red eyes. Common in woodland and gardens, orioles rarely descend to the ground and fly with deep undulations, sweeping up to a perch like a woodpecker. Watch for them plunge bathing by dropping from a perch into a puddle or pool and, during showers, tipping forward on a branch with wings outspread. Generally solitary outside the breeding season, orioles sometimes join mixed feeding flocks and congregate at fruiting trees. Their main food, large insects, is vigorously flogged against a branch before swallowing – hairy caterpillars are flayed by this method.

⭐ HOTSPOTS

- Nairobi NP (p82) Good for the widespread black-headed oriole and migrants in season.
- Bwindi Impenetrable NP (p146) Pristine rainforest supports montane, forest and migratory species.
- Arabuko-Sokoke FR (p70) The northernmost location for green-headed orioles.

OXPECKERS

The two species of oxpecker are members of the starling family specialised to eat parasites such as ticks and lice clinging to the skin of large animals. Flocks of one or both species can usually be seen on or near herds of antelopes and many other herbivores, large and small – including livestock. At first glance, the relationship seems rosy – the oxpeckers hopping over their hosts and exploring their crevices in their quest to remove parasites – but elephants are particularly intolerant of these birds, and pastoralists regard them as a nuisance. Both species certainly eat a significant quantity of parasites (100 adult ticks per day, according to one estimate), plucking them out bodily or gleaning them with a scissoring motion of their bill. But they also keep wounds open to feed on blood, pus and any parasites attracted to the gore – injured animals are particularly susceptible and often lack the strength to chase the birds off. Oxpeckers also rip mouthfuls of hair from mammals to line their nests – a comical sight, but not one necessarily enjoyed by the victims.

⭐ HOTSPOTS

- Ngorongoro CA (p104) A few oxpeckers can usually be seen wherever there are concentrations of large animals.
- Masai Mara NR (p62)
- Serengeti NP (p108)

PIED CROW

Because of their large size, mainly black coloration and often daunting calls, crows and ravens are known around the world as harbingers of death. Several species commonly associate with humans, and their apparent liking for battlefields has instilled a crow mythology in many cultures. Crows eat mainly small animals, but also carrion when available (a group of crows is called a murder) and they often arrive at a carcass even before vultures and kites assemble.

The pied crow is a consummate opportunist and readily takes food scraps discarded by people; it is now the common scavenger in many settlements, where flocks of hundreds may gather at rubbish dumps. This trait is common to many crow species, and pied crows scavenge side by side with brown-necked ravens where the two overlap. But the house crow – introduced from the Indian subcontinent, and now a common pest in coastal cities – demonstrates more than any other species this family's adaptability. Opportunistic and bold, it takes the eggs and young of other birds; kills small birds and harasses large ones; rides the backs of livestock and pecks at their sores; thrives near rubbish dumps; and in places has ousted the native pied crow.

RECOGNITION Glossy black with white saddle and belly. Length 46cm.

HABITAT Grassland, cultivation, savanna and towns.

BEHAVIOUR In pairs and small flocks; roosts communally.

BREEDING Lays four to five eggs in bulky nest during rains.

FEEDING Carrion, small animals, fruit and grain.

VOICE Harsh *aaahnk*; croaks.

★ HOTSPOTS

- Virtually any town or village

COMMON DRONGO

Another contender for ubiquity is an all-black, slightly iridescent bird that can also be quite fearless of people – the common drongo (the similar velvet-mantled and square-tailed drongos also live in East Africa). Common drongos (the name predates the pejorative definition familiar to Australians) are usually conspicuous on a horizontal branch or exposed limb. They fearlessly pursue flying predators, such as hawks and crows, sometimes in pairs, and press home their attacks with pecks or buffeting. Drongos are rather voracious predators themselves. They take mainly insects, but sometimes rob other birds of their catch and are not averse to taking nestlings. Nonetheless, other small birds readily nest in the same trees as drongos, perhaps comforted by their pugnaciousness towards other predators. Drongos typically chase likely prey from a perch, snatching it in flight or pursuing it to the ground, where it is dispatched or dismembered while being held down with the feet. Common drongos also follow bands of dwarf mongooses, seizing prey disturbed by the mongooses' progress. Rather tuneless, but at times enthusiastic singers, their loud, metallic notes can sound through the hottest part of the day and into the night.

RECOGNITION Black with blue sheen and fishlike tail. Red eye.

HABITAT Open grassy areas and forest edges.

BEHAVIOUR Solitary or in pairs. Catches small animals fleeing grassfires.

BREEDING Usually three eggs in a shallow, woven nest.

FEEDING Chiefly insects.

VOICE Metallic twanging.

★ HOTSPOTS

- Queen Elizabeth NP (p158)
- Serengeti NP (p108)
- Masai Mara NR (p62)

BIRDS

STARLINGS

SUPERB STARLING, MERU NATIONAL PARK

BIRDS OF PARADISE The oily gloss of the common starling so familiar in Europe (and where it has been introduced in North America and Australia) offers only a glimmer of the magnificence to which its cousins in Africa attain. Starlings were described by one ornithologist as Africa's birds of paradise and nowhere else on earth can show off such a colourful range of this garrulous, sociable family (of which oxpeckers also form a part). Many of the 30 species in the region are brilliantly iridescent, the various glossy starlings flashing blue, violet, indigo and bronze, and others sporting bold patterns or other features.

Starlings reach their greatest diversity in savanna, but at least one species can be seen in most habitats, from high mountain grassland and rainforest canopies to semidesert; look for the red-winged starling in cities, where it clings to the vertical faces of tall buildings like artificial cliffs. Most African starlings are omnivorous opportunists, eating insects and spiders or vegetable matter such as fruit and grain; the superb starling can become quite fearless of people, even raiding picnic tables.

Starlings inhabiting forests generally have shorter legs and a larger proportion of fruit in their diet, and longer-legged savanna species spend more time on the ground where they take live food. Wattled starlings are respected for delivering farmers from locust plagues; and some species feed in association with others, eg savanna starlings with weavers and forest starlings in bird waves. The harsh alarm calls of each species are similar and can be recognised by different starling species – even monkeys and oxpeckers' hosts (such as buffaloes and antelopes) are known to respond to them.

Most starlings nest in loose colonies, or at least in clusters of nests. A nest is usually in some sort of cavity, most commonly a hole in a tree, cliff, river bank or building, but for forest dwelling species it can be a tangle of vines or epiphytes; nest holes of barbets or woodpeckers are readily appropriated and magpie starlings are unique for nesting in termite mounds. A

THE GOSS ON GLOSS

Nearly all of East Africa's starling species show some degree of glossiness in their plumage, but these fast-flying birds don't always allow lingering views in which to flush out their identification subtleties. Four species are entirely glossy-black with chestnut wing patches; and the eight glossy starlings *(Lamprotornis)* look, well, glossy blue. The trick with the black *Onychognathus* starlings is to make a quick assessment of tail length: short tail means Waller's starling and long tail means bristle-crowned, but slender-billed and red-winged starlings are so similar that habitat and elevation are the best ways to separate them in the field – the former lives in montane forests as high as 4500m, and the latter is more a lowland species common in cities and gorges. The so-called glossy starlings are very tricky to identify and at first you'll just have to accept the word of an experienced guide. Only Rüppell's long-tailed starling has a long tail, but distribution is a clue: the greater blue-eared starling is the most widespread and the black-bellied starling more coastal. The greatest zone of overlap occurs in Uganda – good luck!

few never use holes, building instead bulky nests of grass, twigs and leaves with a side entrance; red-winged starlings make cup-shaped nests strengthened with mud on rock faces and large buildings; and slender-billed starlings nest behind waterfalls for extra protection. A few glossy starlings place shed snake skin in a nest, and many species decorate with fresh green leaves and even flowers.

Usually sociable, most species show sporadic movements related to the availability of food. Regular migrations are undertaken by magpie and Hildebrandt's starlings according to rainfall. At the end of the breeding season, family groups link with other groups while foraging to number 100 or more individuals, and even more at roosts, where thousands may congregate (known as moots). Many species gather in trees during the middle of the day and sing in 'choirs' for long spells; the purpose of such behaviour is unknown.

GLOSSY STARLING

BIRDS

 HOTSPOTS

- Tsavo NP (p66) Savanna species such as golden-breasted, Fischer's and migratory Hildebrandt's starlings.
- Mt Kenya NP (p80) Kenrick's and Abbott's starlings inhabit montane forests as high as 2500m; slender-billed starling in alpine moorland up to 4500m.
- Murchison Falls NP (p154) Six species of glossy starling have been recorded.

SUNBIRDS

IRIDESCENT JEWELS If not the biggest, sunbirds are certainly among the most colourful of East Africa's birds. At least one of the 53 species can be seen wherever there is an abundance of nectar-producing flowers, from the semiarid zone to rainforests and even near the top of the highest peaks where few other birds survive. Sunbirds reach their greatest variety in rainforests, but many are restricted in range to specific habitats, such as coastal woodland (eg the Amani sunbird, a relict species restricted to Kenya's Arabuko Sokoke Forest and isolated Tanzanian mountains such as the Usambaras and Udzungwas) or alpine moorlands (eg scarlet-chested malachite sunbird). In fact, sunbirds nicely demonstrate the amazing variety of birdlife in East Africa: closely related species that occur in adjoining areas indicate that a common ancestor evolved into two or more species under changing environmental conditions. Thus, pairs of similar species occur throughout the region, eg Hunter's and scarlet-chested sunbirds, and malachite and scarlet-tufted malachite sunbirds.

The basic sunbird body plan is small (as small as 8cm, but ranging up to 15cm in some species whose tail streamers are almost as long again), with a sharp, down-curved bill showing much variation in size and curvature. Males of nearly all species have patches of iridescence that can cover most of the body or be restricted to patches on the throat, rump or head. The combinations are dazzling, from the large malachite, bronze and tacazze sunbirds in

WHITE-BELLIED SUNBIRD

shimmering green or bronze with long tail streamers, to dozens of smaller species sporting splashes of violet, gold and amethyst. Several are also augmented with red, yellow or orange 'normal', ie non-iridescent feathers that may be exposed only during displays or preening. Many species look very similar and provide the enticing identification problems so valued by birdwatchers: females and immature males of many otherwise brilliant species have drab plumage with little iridescence. And to complicate matters, several species, such as the mouse-coloured sunbird, lack iridescent patches.

Still, identification isn't everything and sunbirds are active little birds worth watching at any time. They flit about restlessly and males pugnaciously defend territories against other sunbirds. Although all sunbirds eat at least some insects, caught in flight or while perched, the main food source for most is nectar sipped with a specialised tongue while beak-deep in a flower, or after the base of the bloom has been pierced with the sharp bill. They lean into flowers while perched next to them, or feed while hanging upside down. Usually solitary or in pairs, larger groups may congregate during seasonal flowerings of favoured plants, such as aloes, lion's-paw mints (*Leonotis*), flame trees and mistletoe.

Nesting in all species conforms to a pattern: a domed nest of woven grass and fibres of vegetation, usually suspended by several tendrils or fibres from a branch or twig. Some variations include a porch over the entrance. Most species lay only one or two eggs, which are incubated by the female, although the male also helps with raising the young.

THE 'HUMMINGBIRDS' OF AFRICA

Sunbirds are sometimes compared to the hummingbirds, a group not found in Africa, but the similarity is only superficial and they are not closely related. However, sunbirds occupy a similar ecological niche and only hummingbirds surpass them in their most remarkable feature – iridescence. Unlike 'normal' feathers, in which colour is caused by pigmentation, iridescence is caused by a modified feather structure that creates a reflective surface. Iridescent feathers have a weak structure and, therefore, flight feathers are not iridescent – iridescence typically appears as a throat patch (gorget), but in males of several species, such as the beautiful sunbird, covers almost the entire body. Iridescent feathers change colour according to the angle of the viewer. For the wearer, this may have a role in bluff or territorial display: when a male that appears black or dull side on suddenly turns to face a rival, that creature is suddenly confronted by an intimidating burst of colour.

BIRDS

★ HOTSPOTS

- Mt Kenya NP (p80) Montane specialists, such as tacazze sunbirds, and scarlet-tufted malachite sunbirds feeding at giant herbs.
- Lake Baringo (p88) Several dry-country species, such as beautiful sunbird, are resident.
- Bwindi Impenetrable NP (p146) A host of rainforest species can be seen.

SPARROWS, WEAVERS, BISHOPS & WIDOWS

INDUSTRIOUS NEST SPINNERS A few finches native to East Africa are recognisable as sparrows, even chirping and habitually living near people like their kin across much of the world. But their close relatives have evolved into an extraordinary variety of weavers, brightly coloured bishops and widows with elaborate tail plumes. The diversity of these groups is staggering – 81 species – and one, the red-billed quelea, is one of the most abundant birds on the planet: at times it is so numerous that flocks number in the millions and break branches with their weight when they land.

Weavers are mainly decked out in yellow with black, rufous, orange or brown highlights – exceptions to the colour rule are the malimbes, in which yellow is replaced by red. Confusing enough when nesting, their identification is a birdwatcher's nightmare outside of the breeding season, when many of the colourful males moult into a drab, sparrowlike plumage and form mixed flocks with females and other species. Still, they are energetic builders of intricate and distinctive woven nests; the majority nest socially and weaver colonies can become virtual cities of grass apartments smothering entire trees – they can be seen in virtually any town or village, as well as in the wild, where palms and spreading acacias might be draped with hundreds of nests.

Each weaver species has its own trademark architecture and many nests can be identified by shape alone. Some nests hang from intertwined stems like a pendulum; others are onion-shaped or have a long, narrow entrance like an upside-down flask; some are neat balls holding two papyrus stems together; and buffalo-weavers

GOLDEN PALM WEAVER

build large, untidy accumulations of grass with multiple entrances in which several pairs live and roost. Weaver colonies are noisy and constantly busy, with birds coming and going with nest material, males courting females, and rivals stealing nest material. Unlike their savanna counterparts, some forest weavers are solitary or feed in pairs and don't build colonial nests; they frequently associate with 'bird waves' moving through the forest. Malimbes are agile canopy feeders and another outstanding species is the parasitic weaver, which lays its eggs in the nests of warblers such as prinias and cisticolas.

Outside the breeding season, male bishops and widowbirds are streaked and drab like many other weavers and sometimes form large, nomadic flocks. But when courting is in full swing, they are eye-catching and colourful birds, moulting into black plumage with flashes of orange, yellow or red. Male widowbirds also grow elaborate plumes – those of the long-tailed widowbird can be three times as long as its body.

Males of most species of bishop and weaver are polygamous, mating with several females if their courtship performances are suitably impressive and building a nest for each. Male bishops stand out perched high on stems across swathes of rank grassland and perform display flights with feathers fluffed out, some becoming almost spherical in the process. Male widows stake out territories where they display, the most spectacular being Jackson's widowbird, which tramples an arena in long grass where it jumps up and down with wings and long tail spread – several sometimes performing in a small area.

CUCKOOS UP THE SPOUT

For weavers (and indeed all birds), success depends on building a nest secure enough to raise a brood and withstand the attentions of predators. And so successful are many at building such nests that other birds, such as waxbills and pygmy falcons, find abandoned weavers' nests attractive enough to shelter or even nest in themselves. Pygmy falcons are mainly insect hunters and don't bother the weavers, but there's nothing much the weavers can do about a gymnogene (also called African harrier-hawk) robbing a nest. These specialised raptors hang upside down from the nest and insert a long, double-jointed leg to extract an egg or chick. Diederik cuckoos commonly parasitise lesser masked weavers, but the weavers are fighting back: certain populations build entrance spouts so tight that the cuckoos can't get into the nest and have even been found wedged in so tightly they have died in the spout.

BIRDS

⭐ HOTSPOTS

- Masai Mara NR (p62) Savanna, marsh and grassland are varied habitats for nearly 30 species.
- Serengeti NP (p108)
- Samburu NR (p84) Semiarid acacia country heaving with buffalo-weavers, social weavers and others.
- Bwindi Impenetrable NP (p146) Several rainforest-dwelling weavers can be seen among bird feeding parties.

WHYDAHS

The eight species of seed-eating whydahs (the name comes from a town in Benin) have adopted parasitism as a breeding strategy. However, on hatching, the young don't evict or kill their foster siblings (unlike cuckoos, for example). Instead, they are raised alongside them and even associate with their foster family for some time after leaving the nest. Like their foster siblings, whydah and indigobird chicks have colourful callosities inside their mouths, which stimulate their foster parents to feed them. Adults look nothing like their unwitting hosts and feed and drink alongside them. Females, juveniles and nonbreeding males all have typical, nondescript finch plumage. But when males develop courtship colours, indigobirds are entirely cloaked in deep, satiny blue and whydahs, in true East African fashion, develop long, showy tail plumes.

★ HOTSPOTS

- Tsavo NP (p66) Straw-tailed and paradise whydahs are common in low scrubby bush.
- Nairobi NP (p82) Good chance of seeing the widespread village indigobird.

CANARIES

If you've ever wondered where those caged songsters come from, East Africa has 15 species, some of which go under the name of seedeaters. One, the oriole-finch, looks like a miniature oriole, complete with black head and red bill. Canaries are yet another part of the great assembly of finches, closely related to goldfinches and quite common in most bush habitats. The streaky seedeater is common near settlements and a few other species share its reputation as something of a pest – those stubby, almost conical bills are adept at cracking open seeds. Look for canaries and seedeaters at the edge of crops and gardens, associating in small groups with other canary species and other finches. Wild canaries bear little resemblance to their rather pallid captive relatives, although a few are also prodigious songsters – male yellow-fronted canaries gather to sing in treetops and are also caught for the pet trade. Other canary species build cup-shaped nests of grass in trees and bushes, sometimes in loose colonies.

★ HOTSPOTS

- Nairobi NP (p82) Brimstone canary is common in bush and the edge of cultivation.
- Mt Kenya NP (p80) Forest edge is ideal for several species along the Naro Moru Trail.
- Kibale Forest NP (p150) Papyrus choking the Bigodi Wetlands support papyrus canary.

PIN-TAILED WHYDAH

ROADSIDE PERCHERS When travelling between parks, you'll often see birds perched along roadsides: common fiscals are among the more obvious, and male pin-tailed whydahs perched on wires, fence posts and prominent branches – their long tail feathers drifting in the breeze – quickly become a familiar sight. These gregarious birds normally travel in small flocks numbering 20 to 30 birds; males are polygamous, typically mating with more than one female, and during the breeding season flocks are typically composed of one breeding male for every five or six females and nonbreeding males. Breeding males are pugnacious and have been know to chase birds of other species from feeding stations. Even outside the breeding season, pin-tailed whydahs are conspicuous while feeding: they jump backwards along the ground, scattering soil to expose fallen seeds (when breeding males do this, their long tail flaps with each hop).

The male's coloration is attained at the start of the long rains; afterwards he moults through motley stages to finally resemble the females and nonbreeding males. In nonbreeding plumage, the various species of whydah can be very difficult to tell apart – birders should try to visit East Africa when birds start breeding. While he's in the mood, the male pin-tailed whydah is a sight worth seeing: he sings as he flies around a perched female with gentle undulations, his tail bouncing up and down; she responds by shivering her wings. Once the formalities are over, females also work hard at reproducing: whydahs are nest parasites, ie they lay their eggs in the nests of other birds (usually waxbills), which then invest all the energy necessary to raise the whydahs' young. Each female removes one egg of the host for each egg she lays, typically laying only one or two per nest, but occasionally laying in more than one nest. After laying, the parents have nothing more to do with the raising of their offspring: the unwitting hosts feed and raise the aliens alongside their own chicks.

RECOGNITION Breeding males black and white with long (20cm) tail streamers and bright-red bill. Females similar to nonbreeding males.

HABITAT Forest edge, savanna and cultivation as high as 2500m; also in suburban gardens.

HABITS Males sing while perched on a bush, post or stalk. Parasitises common, black-rumped and fawn-breasted waxbills. Nonbreeding flocks may number 100 birds. Coloured callosities in mouth of nestlings resemble those of hosts' chicks.

BREEDING Eggs white. Nestlings fledge after 17 to 21 days. Fledglings associate with foster parents before becoming independent.

FEEDING Finds seeds by jumping backwards while raking the ground with claws; sometimes hawks insects in flight.

VOICE A high-pitched *tseet tseet tsuweet*, frequently repeated.

BIRDS

⭐ HOTSPOTS

- Masai Mara NR (p62)
- Serengeti NP (p108)
- Murchison Falls NP (p154)

OTHER CREATURES

WITH SO MANY large, highly visible and world-famous mammals and birds to see, it's not surprising that East Africa's small, reclusive and cryptic creatures often get overlooked. In fact, the majority of Africa's reptiles, amphibians and invertebrates have never been systematically studied – even though these groups are undoubtedly more diverse than mammals and birds. So while viewing large mammals and colourful birds is still the priority on most safaris, keeping an eye open for the less-obvious creatures offers an alternative but equally unique experience for the keen wildlife watcher.

Reptiles are abundant and diverse in East Africa, from giant carnivores such as the Nile monitor and bank-basking Nile crocodile to the smaller but brightly coloured agama lizards and slow-moving, swivel-eyed chameleons. Snakes are less conspicuous and include some superbly camouflaged and patterned species. The largest, the 4m-long African rock python, can suffocate and swallow a small antelope; others such as puff adders, mambas, cobras and vipers are famously venomous, but your chances of coming to face to face with one are rare. Amphibians are abundant in rainforests, where their breeding choruses can be deafening, but Kenya's Arabuko Sokoke Forest is a seasonally dry environment that supports an extraordinary diversity of frogs. Rainforests are also hotspots for butterflies – of which East Africa boasts hundreds of showy species.

Most people would rather not know about some of the smallest animals of the African bush, particularly those that might bite. But

LEOPARD TORTOISES

forewarned is forearmed and, unpleasant though some are, everything from lions to safari ants plays a role in the ecosystem. A point in case is dung beetles, whose sole reason for living is to seek out animal droppings which they bury next to their eggs. You'll probably see several dung beetles rolling perfectly spherical balls of dung much larger than themselves along paths. Upon hatching, the beetle grubs eat their way through their nursery larder before turning into pupae and hatching into adult beetles. Be grateful: the average elephant consumes 100 tonnes of herbage annually and if it wasn't for these animated poop scoops you'd need more than a 4WD to get through it.

Another group of insects that has an even greater impact on wildlife and ecosystems is termites. There's an awful lot of vegetation growing out there, more than the large herbivores can consume, and behind the scenes millions of termites are also chewing away at it, turning cellulose into protein. Less benevolent are the blood-sucking tsetse flies, but in a sense you can thank them for much of the wildlife you see on the savanna today. Tsetse flies are found only in certain habitats (bushy savanna and miombo woodland are favourites) and here they hunt large animals (including humans). Because some transmit the deadly sleeping sickness, areas that harboured tsetse flies were shunned by pastoralists, and large mammals proliferated (the Masai Mara is probably the most famous of these areas). Sleeping sickness is all but eradicated, but tsetse flies are still attracted to blue clothing.

RECOGNITION Grey-brown to olive-green with bands of yellowish spots. Up to 2m.

HABITAT Savanna, waterways.

BEHAVIOUR Solitary. Males fight for territory.

BREEDING Lays 20 to 60 eggs.

FEEDING Insects, crabs, small vertebrates and carrion.

VOICE Hisses.

SWAHILI Buru kenge.

HOTSPOTS

- Masai Mara NR (p62)
- Serengeti NP (p108)
- Murchison Falls NP (p154)

NILE MONITOR

East Africa's largest lizard is a solitary reptile typically seen ambling through the savanna or lounging on a branch overhanging water. Watch early in the day for it catching some rays on an exposed rock, sandbank or tree stump. Basking warms them up for the hunt but, like most reptiles, monitors have low energy requirements and can go for long spells without eating. Normal locomotion is a slow, meandering gait (a large one sometimes dragging its belly along the ground), but Nile monitors are proficient swimmers that readily take to water if threatened – young ones don't venture in too deep in case a crocodile is waiting.

Any nook or crevice is investigated for a morsel, and prey includes a large variety of small animals, from insects and birds to mammals as large as a mongoose. Monitors readily dig up unguarded crocodile eggs and climb trees to rob birds' nests. That long forked tongue constantly flicking in and out is completely harmless; in fact, it helps detect prey by transferring scent to an organ in the roof of the mouth (called a Jacobson's organ). However, monitors can inflict a serious bite. Adult monitors have few predators, although they are sometimes taken by pythons, crocodiles and large raptors.

NILE CROCODILE

The Nile crocodile is Africa's biggest reptile by far, an aquatic killing machine reaching a length of up to 6m. Smaller crocs eat fish underwater or snatch swimming birds, but for a large one, virtually any animal is fair game, including antelopes, livestock and even big cats. Adult crocs take many migrating wildebeest and zebras crossing rivers, such as the Mara and Talek Rivers, and are responsible for hundreds of human deaths every year. A crocodile can stay submerged with only its eyes and nostrils above the surface, waiting to ambush prey – shine a torch over a swamp at night and the reflected eye shine will show just how abundant they can be.

When an animal gets too close, the croc lunges with incredible power and speed, drags its victim underwater and drowns it. Several crocs may gather at one floating carcass, clamping teeth onto the flesh and spinning. Adult crocodiles have no predators, although territorial disputes between males can cause serious injuries, and hippos will nudge them off a sandbank and even bite one in two if it threatens a calf. But for a young croc to reach maturity, it must first dodge birds, fish and larger crocodiles.

RECOGNITION Powerful jaws and tail. Olive or dull grey.

HABITAT Freshwater.

BEHAVIOUR Basks. Female guards nest and hatchlings.

BREEDING Lays 30 to 40 eggs that hatch after 90 days.

FEEDING Strictly carnivorous.

VOICE Young yelp when hatching.

SWAHILI Mamba.

HOTSPOTS

- Lake Turkana (p92)
- Masai Mara NR (p62)
- Serengeti NP (p108)

OTHER CREATURES

LIZARDS

COLD-BLOODED CAMOUFLAGERS Like other reptiles, lizards have scales and rely on the sun to warm their bodies (despite this, many geckoes are nocturnal and actively hunt insects and other small prey). Most conspicuous are the brightly coloured agamids that run over large rocks such as koppies. The bright-orange head of the male common agama stands out from a distance to attract potential mates – look carefully nearby and you'll probably see a cluster of females watching him, although they are camouflaged perfectly against the rock. Other species are not so easy to see, but by turning over loose rocks and logs (be sure to replace them, and watch for snakes and scorpions) you may uncover a gecko – rainforest geckos are best sought by picking out their eyeshine at night with a torch.

Folklore has it that chameleons dive for cover when they hear hornbills honking. However, this would be hard to prove because they are usually well camouflaged and you'd have to find one first (locating chameleons is chancy, but they're often seen crossing roads). If hornbills strike terror into chameleons, these utterly harmless lizards scare the bejesus out of traditional African populations, who believe children will be born hideously deformed if a pregnant woman sees one. And they do look like they were designed in a boardroom, although they are in fact ideally suited to an arboreal lifestyle, with eyes that swivel independently on scaly cones; sticky, muscular tongues that can shoot out the length of their bodies to grab an insect; paired toes for clinging to thin branches; and prehensile tails coiled like watch springs.

FLAP-NECKED CHAMELEON , ZANZIBAR

Chameleons' heads are large and domed and in some species are adorned with neck shields, horns and other weaponlike growths used by males in territorial disputes. Chameleons are probably most famous for their ability to change colour and it has been speculated that one would explode if placed on a tartan rug. In truth their colour-changing abilities are often exaggerated, being generally restricted to shades of green, grey and brown and take several minutes to perform. However, some males flush with bright colour when trying to attract a mate or ward off another male straying into his territory. When males lock horns, the trees don't exactly shake with chameleon warfare as it's more a determined pushing until one gives way.

OTHER CREATURES

★ HOTSPOTS

- Lake Nakuru NP (p91) The Baboon Cliffs are a good place to get close to agama lizards, although they inhabit koppies in many reserves.

SNAKES

Although many animals feed on snakes, including secretary birds, snake-eagles and mongooses, seeing a snake is usually a matter of chance and, whatever their reputation, the majority are harmless to people. Many are nocturnal so if you particularly want to see them, you could improve your chances by spotlighting at night. The biggest East African species, the African rock python, occasionally reaches 6.1m (although 4m to 4.5m is more common) and is often abroad late in the day where rock outcrops, such as kopjes, provide cover. Rock pythons asphyxiate prey as large as a small antelope by wrapping it in muscular coils. Some snakes inject venom into their prey through hollow teeth (the well-known fangs) and names like vipers, adders, mambas and cobras will be familiar to many people. From the safety of a vehicle, you can watch them hunt and appreciate their subtle, often beautiful coloration. Normally sit-and-wait predators that strike with split-second speed, puff adders are often on the move after rain. Cobras are famous for their hood that spreads as they rear up to strike; spitting cobras have modified fangs that accurately spray venom several metres.

★ HOTSPOTS

- Tsavo NP (p66)
- Lake Nakuru NP (p91)
- Kakamega Forest NR (p76)

FROGS & TOADS

Collectively known as amphibians, frogs and toads are instantly recognisable by their large eyes, webbed feet and (usually) moist skin. All are more or less dependent on freshwater to raise their young, although there are many ingenious variations on the theme. Eggs usually hatch into tadpoles with gills that eventually develop legs and breathe air. Adults are carnivorous, snatching insects and other small animals (an African bullfrog was recorded eating young puff adders!) with their broad, sticky tongue. Arabuko Sokoke Forest is the number-one place for frogs in Kenya, with at least 25 species known; activity peaks at the start of the long rains when their loud calls make a deafening chorus in suitable breeding areas. During the day, many shelter under logs and rocks, but amphibians are best detected at night with a torch – look among vegetation in shallow water and in dense foliage for tree frogs. Calls are distinct for every species and one of the best ways to locate frogs and toads.

★ HOTSPOTS

- Lake Mburo NP (p162) Low-lying grasslands that flood during the rains sometimes have huge concentrations of frogs.
- Semliki Valley WR (p170) These rainforests can be productive 'frogging' habitat.

THE SMALL FIVE

The chase for the so-called Big Five – elephant, buffalo, lion, leopard and rhino – reputed by hunters to be the most dangerous game) is a high priority on many safaris. Nothing wrong with that, of course, but once the pressure's off, spare a moment for some of the smaller, less glamorous animals that are usually overlooked on safari.

ELEPHANT SHREW Mammals don't come any smaller than shrews and, although the smallest weighs only 2g, each has every sense and organ of an elephant 2.85 million times its weight. Elephant shrews are giants among midgets, weighing in at a leaf-trembling 440g, and even have a long, prehensile snout with which they sniff out prey in leaf litter. Some are boldly patterned and can measure 23cm from chequered rump to the end of their quivering trunk. The best places to see elephant shrews are at Arabuko Sokoke Forest Reserve in Kenya (golden-rumped elephant shrew) and Budongo Forest Reserve in Uganda (chequered elephant shrew).

BUFFALO-WEAVER So-called because of its habit of perching on the back of buffaloes and other large animals, these large (20cm), mainly black, white or black-and-white members of the weaver family build huge, untidy domed nests in which several pairs nest. Buffalo-weavers are common in savannas, sometimes in large flocks: Samburu National Reserve in Kenya has abundant white-headed buffalo-weavers.

ANT-LION Small, conical pits in sandy soil indicate the presence of these voracious (though tiny) insect predators. Ants blundering along the rim of the pit lose their footing and tumble into the open jaws of the ant-lion waiting buried in the sand below – few escape. Despite their fearsome demeanour, ant-lions are actually the larvae of lacewings – harmless flying insects with transparent wings.

DUNG BEETLE

LEOPARD TORTOISE Only grass and flowers quake at the approach of this slow-moving antithesis of the sleek, predatory cat. Its dense, bony shell protects it from most predators, although some birds (such as ostriches) swallow young ones whole or drop adults from a height to crack them open. Sex looks hilarious and males grunt audibly with the effort. A leopard tortoise could be encountered in virtually any savanna country; Serengeti National Park and Masai Mara National Reserve in Tanzania and Kenya respectively are good places to start.

DUNG BEETLE On safari you're likely to see dung beetles rolling balls of dung along tracks. An army of dung beetles of many species buries a massive tonnage of dung with their eggs – the larvae recycle the waste material and themselves become food for insect-eating animals.

OTHER CREATURES

PLANNING YOUR SAFARI
EVERYTHING YOU NEED TO KNOW TO GET STARTED

SAFARI **HAS TO BE ONE OF THE MOST EVOCATIVE WORDS ever to infiltrate the English language. In the Swahili language, safari quite literally means 'journey', though to eager visitors flocking to East Africa, it means so much more. From inspiring visions of wildebeest fording raging rivers and lions stalking their heedless prey through the savanna grass, to iridescent flamingos lining a salty shore at sunset and the guilty thrill of watching vultures tear flesh and hyenas crunch through bone, a safari into the wild is untamed Africa at its finest.**

From the open plains of Kenya and Tanzania, which support the planet's greatest concentration of herd animals, to the tropical forests of Rwanda and Uganda, which are still inhabited by our closest primate cousins, East Africa presents a vast range of primeval landscapes in which to watch wildlife. Varied topography and climatic influences have created a host of natural environments in which animals and plants have developed an extraordinary diversity, making the region's national parks and reserves among the best in the world for experiencing wildlife.

With such a choice at hand, and road conditions making efficient travel a challenge, it helps to do some planning before you set out. Fortunately, planning a safari to East Africa is a pleasure in itself: the region is so versatile that it's virtually a blank canvas, catering equally for thrillseekers and sunseekers, budget backpackers and high-end high rollers, those who like it tough and those who just want to get going.

Animals move around, seasons change and weather varies. There is no guarantee that you'll see absolutely everything you're after, but with the right directions you should see something amazing in just about any part of East Africa. And, while it may be stating the obvious, the more time you have on safari, the more you will see, and the richness of East

Africa's wildlife diversity means that even after some weeks you will encounter new species and new behaviours.

It's worth pointing out that there is absolutely no substitute for your own careful research: do as much reading as possible before you go and concentrate on the areas with the key wildlife that matches your interests. Some safari-goers become quickly obsessed with the search for the Big Five, while others seek to tally massive birding checklists, though any specific wildlife-focused pursuit requires time spent in specialised habitats.

With that said, this chapter provides a useful general overview of the safari-planning process, from deciding where and when to go, to giving author-tested tips on how to book your trip. Whether you decide in the end to organise everything through a professional operator, or do everything yourself and have a memorable go at the self-drive safari experience, this chapter will help you with each stage of your planning and set essential priorities for your trip to come.

As an added bonus, we've also outlined our favourite spots for everything from romance and adventure to luxury and family travel (see the boxed text, p000). And we've assembled some handy tables outlining which national parks offer what activities, as well as where you should head if you want to spot some of Africa's most charismatic creatures. Hopefully, these features should help you jump start your brainstorming sessions and set you on a rapid trajectory for some of the most dramatic wildlife-watching this planet has to offer.

Safari njema. We wish you a rewarding journey.

WHERE & WHEN TO GO

EAST AFRICA: COUNTRY BY COUNTRY

KENYA

For many people, Kenya is East Africa in microcosm. The region's premier tourist destination really does seem to have it all: wildlife and nightlife, cities and beaches, mountains and deserts, traditional and modern cultures, all couched in a range of landscapes as staggering in their diversity as they are stunning in their appearance.

The classic image of safari savanna is perhaps the single key selling point for Kenya's tourist industry and, with all the famous fauna, no keen animal-spotter should go home disappointed. When the annual wildebeest migration fills up Masai Mara with upwards of one million hulking herbivores, a good number of which are silently stalked by hungry felines, wildlife-watching is truly unparalleled. However, clued-up visitors face an infinite choice of alternative settings and activities, from trekking the glacial ridges of Mt Kenya to kitesurfing off the white sands of the Indian Ocean coast, and much more besides.

This sheer diversity is something to be relished and is by no means limited to the natural surroundings. The people, too, represent a wide cross-section of everything that is contemporary Africa, and everyday life brings together traditional tribes and urban families, and ancient customs and modern sensibilities. Swapping the latest political gossip with the switched-on locals is just one more small pleasure that comes with the culture.

Sooner or later on any trip, you'll look up at the starry skies and feel Africa all around you, living, breathing and fuelling a thousand dreams. Whatever your mental image of this region, and wherever you move on to afterwards, Kenya will provide a crucial part of the picture and is a microcosm not to be missed.

Internet Resources:

- **Destination Kenya** (www.destination kenya.com) Handy directory of hotels and safari operators.
- **Jambo Kenya** (www.jambokenya.com) A broad-based information website with lots of tourist information.
- **Kenya Association of Tour Operators** (www.katokenya.org) Contains the full list of KATO- approved member companies.
- **Kenya Meteorological Department** (www.meteo.go.ke) Local and national weather forecasts.
- **Kenya Wildlife Service** (www.kws .org) Up-to-date conservation news and detailed information on national parks and reserves.

TANZANIA

Few areas of the continent captivate the imagination quite like Tanzania. Snowcapped Mt Kilimanjaro towers majestically over the horizon, flamingos stand sentinel in the salt pans of Ngorongoro Crater and the hoofbeats of thousands of wildebeest echo over the Serengeti Plains. In many ways, this is the Africa of legend, where hot, dusty afternoons end abruptly in glorious blazes of sunset and velvet-black, star-studded skies enfold the hills, where Indian Ocean breezes caress white sands and where moss-covered ruins of ancient Swahili city-states dot the shoreline.

Yet, despite its attractions, Tanzania has managed for the most part to remain unassuming and low-key. It has also remained enviably untouched by the tribal rivalries and political upheavals that plague many of its neighbours, and this – combined with a booming tourism industry – make it an ideal choice for both first-time visitors and Africa old hands. The most popular areas – the northern safari circuit around Arusha and the Zanzibar Archipelago – have sealed main roads and an array of hotels and restaurants and are easily incorporated into a larger East African loop.

Throughout, Tanzania offers travellers an array of options, set against the backdrop of a cultural mosaic in which over 100 ethnic groups amicably rub shoulders. While most visitors head straight for the famed northern wildlife-watching circuit, followed by time relaxing on Zanzibar's beaches, Tanzania has much more to offer anyone with the time and inclination to head off the beaten path.

Wherever you go, take advantage of opportunities to get to know Tanzanians. With their characteristic warmth and politeness, and the dignity and beauty of their cultures, it is they who will inevitably wind up being the highlight of any visit. Chances are that you'll want to come back for more, to which most Tanzanians will say *'karibu tena'* (welcome again).

Internet Resources:
- **African Studies Center Tanzania Page** (www.sas.upenn.edu/African_Studies /Country_Specific/Tanzania.html) Heaps of links.
- **Tanzania National Parks** (www .tanzaniaparks.com) Official website of the park service, with general information and beautiful photos.
- **Tanzania On-Line** (www.tzonline.org)

An intro to all things official, with links to government sites and more.
- **Tanzania Tourist Board** (www .tanzaniatouristboard.com) The official site of the country's tourist board.
- **Zanzibar.Net** (www.zanzibar.net) An introduction to the island of Zanzibar.

UGANDA

Uganda is Africa condensed, with the best of everything the continent has to offer in one small but stunning destination. While it tends to get overshadowed by its more highfalutin neighbours, Uganda is home to the tallest mountain range in Africa, the Rwenzoris or Mountains of the Moon; it is the source of the mighty Nile, the longest river on the planet; and it has the highest concentration of primates in the world, including the majestic mountain gorilla, one of the rarest animals on the continent.

On top of all this, the scenery is so striking that it looks like a watercolour, yet Uganda's extensive network of national parks sees far fewer visitors than it deserves. While infrastructure is much more basic, and the range of accommodations much more limited, Uganda remains prime safari country, especially if you're the type of person who doesn't want to share your spot with a caravan of safari vehicles.

However, Idi Amin's antics and Uganda's long string of tragedies in the 1970s and '80s are so etched into the Western consciousness that some people wrongfully still regard the country as dangerously unstable. The reality is vastly different. Stability has returned to most parts of the country and tourists are welcomed with open arms. Ugandans have weathered the trials and tribulations remarkably well. You won't meet a sullen, bitter or cowed people. Rather, they are smiling and friendly, with an openness absent in other places – truly some of the finest folk in Africa.

RECOMMENDED PARKS & RESERVES

No two wildlife-watching experiences in East Africa are alike, which is why your choice of park should reflect exactly what it is you want out of your safari. Here are our top recommendations.

BEST FOR ROMANCE

Masai Mara Game Reserve (p62) Looking to put some passion back into your lover's eyes? A hot-air balloon ride in the soft morning light should more than do the trick.

BEST FOR BIG FIVE

Ngorongoro Conservation Area (p104) You're going to have to scour the rim if you want to spot a leopard, though black rhinos are present in small numbers and lions, elephants and buffaloes are fairly common.

BEST FOR GETTING WET

Murchison Falls National Park (p154) A boat cruise to the foot of Murchison Falls along the Victoria Nile should provide plenty of spray and mist, though watch where you swim as there are plenty of crocs about!

BEST FOR ADVENTURE

Parc National des Volcans (p179) There are few activities as adrenaline-pumping as tracking mountain gorillas through bamboo forests, especially when they just happen to inhabit slopes of soaring volcanoes along the Rwandese–Congolese border.

BEST FOR FIRST-TIMERS

Lake Nakuru National Park (p91) Small enough to be tackled in a long day, yet home to rarities such as black and white rhinos as well as a healthy leopard population, Lake Nakuru is a great training ground for honing your safari skills.

BEST FOR ROUGHING IT

Tsavo National Park (p66) If you're looking to eschew luxury in favour of bedding down on Mother Earth, Tsavo National Park has a rough-and-ready network of undeveloped camp sites.

BEST FOR LUXURY

Zanzibar Archipelago (p114) The Spice Islands are an exotic and opulent escape where you can unwind on a white-sand beach, go scuba diving in crystal-clear waters and indulge in a tropical cocktail (or two).

BEST FOR BIRDS

Kakamega Forest (p76) This ancient relict of equatorial rainforest is home to approximately 330 species of birds, from barbets and starlings to weavers and bluebills.

BEST FOR KIDS

Serengeti National Park (p108) Africa's most famous safari park is an unparalleled wildlife experience that will astound even the most finicky of children. There's an extensive network of family-friendly lodges on offer.

BEST FOR WALKING SAFARIS

Kibale Forest National Park (p150) Home to several troops of habituated chimpanzees, Kibale Forest allows you to leave behind the safari vehicle and walk alongside humankind's closest primate ancestor.

Uganda is a captivating country with a great deal to offer, and sooner or later the mainstream masses will discover its delights – make sure you get here before they do. Winston Churchill called it the Pearl of Africa. He was right.

Internet Resources:

° **African Studies Center Uganda Page** (www.africa.upenn.edu/NEH/uhome .htm) Country information and lots of links.

° **Integrated Regional Information Network** (www.irinnews.org) Regional news and humanitarian issues.

° **Pambazuka** (www.pambazuka.org) Articles on regional and continent-wide social and humanitarian issues.

° **Uganda Travel Planner** (www .traveluganda.co.ug) There isn't an abundance of useful material on the internet about Uganda, but this is the best place to start.

RWANDA

Welcome to Le Pays des Milles Collines, or the Land of a Thousand Hills: Rwanda is a lush country of endless mountains and stunning scenery. Nowhere are the mountains more majestic than the peaks of the Virunga volcanoes in the far northwest of the country, forming a natural frontier with Democratic Republic of the Congo and Uganda. Hidden among the bamboo and dense jungle of the volcanoes' forbidding slopes are some of the world's last remaining mountain gorillas and it is the opportunity to encounter these contemplative creatures at close quarters that continues to draw visitors to Rwanda.

A beautiful yet brutalised country, Rwanda is all too often associated with the horrific events that unfolded here in 1994. It has been etched into the world's consciousness as one of the most savage

WATCHING WILDLIFE – WHERE TO GO WHEN

ANIMAL	BEST PLACE TO SEE	BEST TIME TO VISIT
BLACK RHINOCEROS (P209)	SERENGETI NATIONAL PARK (P108)	VARIES YEAR TO YEAR
	NGORONGORO CONSERVATION AREA (P104)	JUL-OCT
CHEETAH (P195)	SAMBURU NATIONAL RESERVE (P84)	JUN-OCT, DEC-APR
	BUFFALO SPRINGS NATIONAL RESERVE (P84)	JUN-OCT, DEC-APR
CHIMPANZEE (P191)	KIBALE FOREST NATIONAL PARK (P150)	YEAR-ROUND
	PARC NATIONAL DE NYUNGWE (P178)	JUN-AUG
ELEPHANT (P205)	AMBOSELI NATIONAL PARK (P74)	SEP-OCT, JAN-MAR
	TSAVO NATIONAL PARK (P66)	SEP-OCT, JAN-MAR
FLAMINGO (P240)	LAKE BOGORIA NATIONAL RESERVE (P89)	OCT-APR
	LAKE NAKURU NATIONAL PARK (P91)	OCT-APR
AFRICAN WILD DOG (P193)	SELOUS GAME RESERVE (P118)	JUN-OCT
	MIKUMI NATIONAL PARK (P130)	JUN-OCT
LEOPARD (P197)	LAKE NAKURU NATIONAL PARK (P91)	APR-AUG, NOV-DEC
	QUEEN ELIZABETH NATIONAL PARK (P158)	JUN-SEP, DEC-MAR
LION (P196)	SERENGETI NATIONAL PARK (P108)	VARIES YEAR TO YEAR
	MASAI MARA GAME RESERVE (P62	VARIES YEAR TO YEAR
MOUNTAIN GORILLA (P190)	PARC NATIONAL DES VOLCANS (P179)	MAY-SEP
	BWINDI IMPENETRABLE NATIONAL PARK (P146)	YEAR-ROUND
WHITE RHINOCEROS (P208)	TSAVO NATIONAL PARK (P66)	SEP-OCT, JAN-MAR
	LAKE NAKURU NATIONAL PARK (P91)	APR-AUG, NOV-DEC

genocides in history. The country has taken giant strides towards recovery in the subsequent years, however, and Rwanda is primed to become one of the continent's leading ecotourism destinations.

Rwanda has more than the magical mountain gorillas. The shores and bays of Lake Kivu conceal some of the best inland beaches in African, which is pretty handy given how far it is to the sea. Deep in the southwest, Parc National de Nyungwe is the most extensive montane rainforest in the region and provides a home for many primates. The capital Kigali is also surprisingly safe and sophisticated.

Many visitors are unsure about travelling to Rwanda given its history. However, as long as security and stability persist, Rwanda is a refreshing place to travel, with tourists remaining a relative novelty, and the rewards of the present outweigh the risks of the past.

Internet Resources:

- **International Criminal Tribunal for Rwanda** (www.ictr.org) The official website for the genocide trials taking place in Arusha.
- **New Times** (www.newtimes.co.rw) The latest news on Rwanda in English.
- **Tourism in Rwanda** (www .rwandatourism.com) The country's

TRAVEL SAFETY

Visitors to Africa are understandably daunted by the continent's unenviable reputation as a dangerous place, though it's a grossly naive to group 53 separate and unique countries into one broadly sweeping generalisation. Each African country is as diverse and different from the others as any in Europe, Asia or the Americas and offers a varied palette of urban and rural, young and old, traditional and modern and rich and poor alike.

With that said, it is true that war and violence are daily occurrences in some parts of Africa, and that the underlying social ills behind them are unlikely to disappear in the near future. Tragically, cyclical poverty combined with diminishing natural resources can fuel crime based on opportunism, and tourists are sometimes perceived as being wealthy and easy targets.

However, government travel advisories tend to err on the side of extreme caution for Africa, as well as occasionally advising against travel to entire countries based on small areas of regional unrest. While these advisories are useful for tracking stability patterns and keeping up on the latest current events, you should always balance warnings against other sources.

Truth be told, the reality on the ground is almost always different than the international headlines, which means that your fellow travellers are often the best source of information. An excellent resource is Lonely Planet's own Thorn Tree (www.lonelyplanet.com/thorntree), an engaging online forum where you can pose questions and get answers from a dynamic range of people.

Finally, it's worth taking comfort in the fact that the overwhelming majority of travellers in Africa never experience any kind of problem. In fact, the most likely annoyance for travellers is mere petty theft, which can occur anywhere in the world and is usually preventable if you take the necessary precautions.

As a general rule, you should always take advantage of the hotel safe and never leave your valuables out in the open. And – quite simply – when you're out and about, don't take anything with you that you wouldn't want to lose. Exude confidence, practice street smarts and never let fear get the best of you.

TYPES OF SAFARI

PARK OR RESERVE	NIGHT DRIVES	WALKING SAFARIS	BOAT SAFARIS	CAMEL/ HORSE SAFARIS	BALLOON SAFARIS
KENYA					
MASAI MARA NR (P62)	•	•		•	•
TSAVO EAST & WEST NPS (P66)	•	•			
ARABUKO SOKOKE FR (P70)		•			
AMBOSELI NP (P74)	•	•		•	•
KAKAMEGA FOREST (P76)		•			
MT KENYA NP (P80)		•			
NAIROBI NP (P82)					
SAMBURU, BUFFALO SPRINGS & SHABA NRS (P84)	•	•		•	
ABERDARE NP (P86)	•	•			
HELL'S GATE NP (P87)		•			
LAKE BARINGO (P88)					
LAKE BOGORIA NR (P89)					
LAKE NAIVASHA (P90)					
LAKE NAKURU NP (P91)	•	•		•	
LAKE TURKANA (P92)			•	•	
MALINDI & WATAMU MARINE NPS (P93)		•			
MARSABIT NP (P94)	•	•			
MERU NP (P95)	•	•			
MT ELGON NP (P167)		•			
SAIWA SWAMP NP (P97)		•	•		
SHIMBA HILLS NR (P98)	•	•			
TANZANIA					
NGORONGORO CA (P104)		•			
SERENGETI NP (P62)		•			•
ZANZIBAR ARCHIPELAGO (P114)			•		
SELOUS GR (P118)		•	•		
TARANGIRE NP (P122)	•				
ARUSHA NP (P126)		•			
LAKE MANYARA NP (P128)	•				
MIKUMI NP (P130)		•			
KILIMANJARO NP (P132)		•			
RUAHA NP (P134)		•			
UDZUNGWA MOUNTAINS NP (P136)		•			
SAADANI NATIONAL PARK (P138)		•	•		
UGANDA					
BWINDI IMPENETRABLE NP (P146)		•			
KIBALE FOREST NP (P150)	•	•	•		
MURCHISON FALLS NP (P154)	•	•	•		
QUEEN ELIZABETH NP(P158)	•	•	•		
LAKE MBURO NP (P162)	•	•	•		
BUDUNGO FR (P164)		•			
KIDEPO VALLEY NP (P165)	•	•			
MGAHINGA GORILLA NP (P166)		•			
MT ELGON NP (P96)	•	•			
RWENZORI MOUNTAINS NP (P168)	•	•			
SEMULIKI NP (P169)	•	•			
SEMLIKI VALLEY WR (P170)		•	•		
RWANDA					
PARC NATIONAL DE L'AKAGERA (P176)	•	•			
PARC NATIONAL DE NYUNGWE (P178)		•			
PARC NATIONAL DES VOLCANS (P179)		•			

official tourism website, with information on national parks and local culture.

CLIMATE & SEASONS

Possibly the single most important influence on the behaviour of wildlife – and therefore your chances of seeing it – is rain. Rain affects plant growth, the seasonal availability of fruits and drinking water and the number, distribution, breeding and/or migration of prey animals and their predators, not to mention the personal comfort of the observer and the condition of roads.

The main tourist season runs during the hot, dry months of December and January and the cool, dry months from June to August, though the region can really be visited at any time of year. When the long rains fall from March to May, things are much quieter, there are fewer tourists, accommodation prices come down and some places close completely. While main routes in most areas remain passable, secondary roads are often closed, especially in parts of Uganda and Tanzania. You can expect to get drenched for at least a few hours each day and it will be too muddy in many areas for hiking, but everything will be beautifully green.

Rainfall patterns in East Africa vary considerably from habitat to habitat, which is an important consideration when planning your safari. During the dry season in savanna and grassland, animals can usually be found reasonably close to permanent water – elephants in particular remain nearby – and burnt or trampled grasses make viewing easier. Rain brings with it spurts of green growth and triggers the breeding or migration of many herbivores and predators, the courting and breeding of birds and the appearance of wildflowers.

By late in the wet seasons, visibility is greatly reduced by high grass, and wildlife has dispersed as water and food is more widely available. During this time, getting around can become difficult, and in some places impossible. On the flipside, tourists are then fewer in number, which means that you won't have to share the national parks with too many other people.

Rainforests can be very wet places at any time of year, but don't let the wet put you off – carry a light umbrella so observation can continue during showers. Dry seasons will mean easier but hotter tracking of the forest-dwelling great apes, but they are active year-round as their movement is dictated mainly by the availability of food. Bird courtship – and therefore peak activity – tends to coincide with wet seasons.

In the mountains and highlands, rain, falling as snow on the high peaks, forces antelopes, elephants and birds to lower altitudes during wet seasons. Cold and wet conditions on the great mountains can pose a physical challenge to visitors at any time of year and every care should be exercised.

BEFORE YOU BOOK

The majority of travellers prefer to get all the hard work done before they arrive in East Africa by booking from abroad, either through travel agents or directly with safari companies. This fairly common practice also ensures that you'll be able to secure a spot at the more famous lodges, especially during peak seasons when places start filling up months in advance. However, while most safari operators will take internet bookings, making arrangements with anyone other than a well-established

PLANNING YOUR SAFARI

midrange or top-end operator can be a risky business. If you're going for a budget option, you should certainly wait and do your research on the ground when you arrive.

If you want to book a safari once in East Africa, a good starting point is to visit a few of the travel agents in either Nairobi, Mombasa, Dar es Salaam, Arusha, Kampala or Kigali. For tips on choosing the type of safari you want, plus a list of tour operators, see p000.

COSTS

Most safari-operator quotes include park entrance fees, the costs of accommodation or tent rental, transport costs from the starting base to the park and the costs of fuel plus a driver/guide for wildlife drives. However, this varies enough that it's essential to clarify before paying. Drinks (whether alcoholic or not) are generally excluded and budget camping-safari prices usually exclude sleeping-bag rental. Prices quoted by agencies or operators usually assume shared (double) room/tent occupancy, with supplements for single occupancy ranging from 20% to 50% of the shared-occupancy rate.

If you are dealing directly with lodges and tented camps rather than going through a safari operator, you may be quoted 'all-inclusive' prices. In addition to accommodation, full board and sometimes park fees, these usually include two activities (usually wildlife drives, or sometimes one wildlife drive and one walk) per day, each lasting about two to three hours. They generally exclude transport costs to the park. Whenever accommodation-only prices apply, you'll need to pay extra to actually go out looking for wildlife. Costs for this vary considerably.

BUDGET SAFARIS

Most safaris at the lower end of the price range are camping safaris. In order to keep costs to a minimum, groups often camp outside national park areas (thereby saving park admission and camping fees) or stay in budget guesthouses outside the park. Budget operators also save costs by working with larger groups to minimise per-person transport costs and by keeping to a no-frills set-up with basic meals and a minimum number of staff. For most budget safaris, as well as many midrange safaris, daily kilometre limits are placed on the vehicles.

MIDRANGE SAFARIS

Most midrange safaris use lodges, where you'll have a comfortable room and eat in a restaurant. Overall, safaris in this category are comfortable, reliable and reasonably good value. A disadvantage is that they may have something of a packaged-tour or production-line feel, although this can be minimised by selecting a safari company and accommodation carefully, by giving attention to who and how many people you'll be travelling with and by avoiding the large, popular lodges during peak season.

TOP-END SAFARIS

Private lodges, luxury tented camps and even private fly-in camps are used in top-end safaris, all with the aim of providing guests with as 'authentic' and personal a bush experience as possible without forgoing the creature comforts. For the phenomenal price you pay, expect a full range of amenities, as well as top-quality guiding. Even in remote settings without running water you will be able to enjoy hot, bush-style showers, comfortable beds and fine dining. Also expect a high level of personalised

ttention and an intimate atmosphere
– many places at this level have fewer
han 20 beds.

TIPPING

Assuming service has been satisfactory,
tipping is an important part of the
safari experience, especially to the
driver/guides, cooks and others whose
livelihoods depend on tips. Many
operators have tipping guidelines and
expectations increase substantially if
you're on a top-end safari, part of a large
group or if an especially good job has
been done. Also, it's never a mistake to
err on the side of generosity while tipping
those who have worked to make your
safari experience memorable. Remember
that other travellers are going to follow
you, and the last thing anyone wants
to find is a disgruntled driver/guide
who couldn't care less whether you see
wildlife.

TYPES OF SAFARI

ORGANISED VEHICLE SAFARIS

The options here range from a couple
of days up to a month, with a week or
two being ideal. At least one full day in
either direction will normally be taken up
with travel, and after seven days you may
well feel like a rest. If you pack too much
distance or too many parks into a short
period, chances are that you'll feel as if
you've spent your whole time in transit,
shuttling from place to place, rather than
enjoying the destination.

Minivans are the most common option
throughout most of Kenya and northern
Tanzania, but if you have a choice, go
for a good Land Rover–style 4WD
instead. Apart from aesthetics, minivans
accommodate too many people for a good

experience, the rooftop opening is usually
only large enough for a few passengers to
use at once and some passengers will get
stuck in middle seats with poor views.

Whatever type of vehicle you're in,
you should try to avoid crowding. Sitting
scrunched together for several hours over
bumpy roads, or squeezed into a middle
seat, detracts significantly from the safari
ambience. Most prices you will be quoted
are based on groups of three to four
passengers, which is about the maximum
for comfort for most vehicles. Some
companies put five or six passengers
in a standard 4WD, but the minimal
savings don't compensate for the extra
discomfort.

DO-IT-YOURSELF SAFARIS

A DIY safari is a viable and enticing
proposition in East Africa if you can get
a group together to share the costs of
renting a vehicle. Doing it yourself has
several advantages over organised safaris,
primarily total flexibility, independence
and being able to choose your travelling
companions. However, it's generally true
to say that organising your own safari
will cost at least as much, and usually
more, than going on a cheap organised
safari to the same areas.

Remember to bring enough extra
petrol in jerry cans (it's not available in
most parks), as well as some mechanical
knowledge and spare parts. Many park
areas are quite remote and, if you break
down, you'll be on your own. On that
note, it's certainly not a good idea to
go on a do-it-yourself safari alone. Not
counting the everyday risks of bush
driving, if you have to change a tyre in
lion country, you'll want someone to
watch your back.

Apart from the cost, vehicle
breakdowns, accidents, security and a

lack of local knowledge are also major issues. Maps are hard to find, particularly for remote areas, and if you do break down in the wild, you're well and truly on your own. Whoever is driving is also going to be too busy concentrating on the road to notice much of the wildlife. However, there is a smug but well-deserved sense of self-satisfaction that is inherent in any successful DIY adventure.

For hiking or other safaris where you don't need a vehicle to get around the park, doing things yourself via public transport is much easier, with the main considerations being time, sorting things out with park fees, guides and other logistics and finding some travelling companions. Generally speaking, allow up to a full day at the access town or trailhead to organise food, equipment and guides.

WHICH SAFARI?

While price can be a major determining factor in safari planning, there are other equally important considerations:

- Ambience Will you be staying in or near the park? (If you stay well outside the park, you'll miss the good early-morning and evening wildlife-viewing hours.) Are the surroundings atmospheric? Will you be in a large lodge or an intimate private camp?
- Equipment Mediocre vehicles and equipment can significantly detract from the overall experience. In remote areas, lack of quality equipment or vehicles and appropriate back-up arrangements can be a safety risk.
- Access and activities If you don't relish the idea of hours in a 4WD on bumpy roads, consider parks and lodges where you can fly in. Areas offering walking and boat safaris are best for getting out of the vehicle and into the bush.
- Guides A good driver/guide can make or break your safari. Staff at reputable companies are usually knowledgeable and competent. With operators that try to cut corners, chances are that staff are unfairly paid and unlikely to be knowledgeable or motivated.
- Community commitment Look for operators that do more than just give lip service to ecotourism principles and that have a genuine, long-standing commitment to the communities in which they work. In addition to being more culturally responsible, they'll also be able to give you a more authentic and enjoyable experience.
- Setting the agenda Some drivers feel they have to whisk you from one good sighting to the next. If you prefer to stay in one strategic place for a while to experience the environment and see what comes by, discuss this with your driver. Going off in wild pursuit of the Big Five means you'll miss the more subtle aspects of your surroundings.
- Extracurriculars It's not uncommon for drivers to stop at souvenir shops en route. While this does give the driver an often much-needed break from the wheel, most shops pay drivers commissions to bring clients, which means you may find yourself spending more time souvenir shopping than you'd bargained for. If you're not interested, discuss this with your driver at the outset, ideally while still at the operator's offices.
- Less is more If you'll be teaming up with others, find out how many people will be in your vehicle and try to meet your travelling companions before setting off.
- Special interests If birdwatching or other special interests are important, arrange a private safari with a specialised operator.

Do-it-yourself travellers can camp in designated sites or hire cheap bandas in many parks: Uganda, with its community-based ecotourism projects, is best serviced in this regard, Kenya less so and Tanzania in its scramble for foreign revenue is trying to push tourists upmarket. Other forms of accommodation, such as tented camps and safari lodges, are both popular and well run in nearly all reserves. These offer a high standard of service and comfort and, although the sky's the limit for prices, they are part of the safari tradition and definitely worth trying at least once.

SPECIALISED SAFARIS

In addition to the following sections, be sure to check out our coverage of specialised safaris – birdwatching, primate tracking and snorkelling – on p000.

Walking, Hiking & Cycling Safaris At many national parks you can arrange relatively short walks of two to three hours in the early morning or late afternoon. The focus is on watching animals rather than covering distance, and walks like these are often included in organised vehicle-safari packages, especially at the top end of the scale. For keen hikers who want to minimise their time in safari minibuses, there's an increasing number of more vigorous options, usually involving point-to-point treks or longer circuits. Finally, cyclists who are in peak physical shape – and can tolerate the equatorial sun – have the option of criss-crossing the region with fellow road warriors.

DO IT AT...
» **Mt Kenya National Park (p80)**
» **Kilimanjaro National Park (p132)**
» **Hell's Gate National Park (p87)**
» **Kibale Forest National Park (p150)**

BOAT SAFARIS
Boat safaris are an excellent way to experience the East African wilderness and offer a welcome break from dusty, bumpy roads. They're also the only way to fully explore riverine environments and they'll give you new perspectives on the terrestrial scene as you approach hippos or crocodiles at close range, float by a sandbank covered with birds, or observe animals on shore from a river vantage point.

DO IT AT...
» **Queen Elizabeth National Park (p158)**
» **Murchison Falls National Park (p154)**
» **Selous Game Reserve (p118)**
» **Arusha National Park (p126)**

BALLOON SAFARIS
Drifting over the Serengeti Plains or along a riverbed in a hot-air balloon is a superb way to experience East African nature – if you have the funds. While everything depends on wind and weather conditions, and wildlife can't be guaranteed, the captains try to stay between 500m and 1km above ground, which means that if animals are there, you'll be able to see them from an unforgettable bird's-eye perspective.

DO IT AT...
» **Masai Mara Game Reserve (p62)**
» **Serengeti National Park (p108)**

CAMEL SAFARIS
Camel safaris offer the chance to get off the beaten track and into areas where vehicle safaris don't or can't go. Although you may well see wildlife along the way, the main attractions are the journey itself, and the chance to immerse yourself in nomadic life and mingle with the indigenous people. Most travelling is done in the cooler parts of the day and a camp site is established around noon.

DO IT AT...
» **Lake Turkana (p92)**

PLANNING YOUR SAFARI

GETTING AROUND

A vehicle is essential in most reserves, so even if you can get there by public transport, you won't be allowed in without a lift. Hire cars are readily available, but expensive, unless you share the costs among several people; most of the time you're as well to hire a driver/guide so you are free to watch animals instead of the road. Road conditions vary from good to abysmal; dry-season travel generally presents few problems, but in wet seasons a 4WD is advisable and sometimes essential. You are allowed into reserves in your own vehicle as long as you pay the requisite entrance fees.

BUSH DRIVING

Although there is an extensive network of both tarred and gravel roads throughout East Africa, the thrill and adventure of bush driving is unequalled. Not surprisingly, the region is a favourite destination of veteran off-road enthusiasts. However, just because you've read a survival manual doesn't mean that you're ready to head out into the wilds – 4WD driving is serious business and tourists have died in the past due to careless mistakes. Remember, real (and safe) 4WD driving is nothing like you see on TV. Following are some road-tested tips that should help you in planning a safe and successful 4WD expedition.

Although a good map and a compass may be sufficient for navigating in your own country, it is strongly advisable to invest in a good Global Positioning System (GPS) unit before travelling in East Africa. Although GPS units are *not* a substitute for a map and compass, they are useful for establishing waypoints and helping you determine which direction you're heading. As a general rule, you should always be able to identify your location on a map, even if you're navigating with a GPS unit.

Stock up on emergency provisions, even if you're sticking to the main highways. Distances between towns can be extreme and you never know where you're going to break down (and when someone is going to pick you up). Petrol and diesel tend to be available in most major towns, though it's wise to never pass a station without filling up. If you're planning a long expedition in the bush, carry the requisite amount of fuel in meta jerry cans and remember that engaging 4WD burns nearly twice as much fuel as highway driving. A good rule is to carry 5L of drinking water per person per day, as well as a good supply of high-calorie, nonperishable emergency food items.

Garages throughout East Africa are surprisingly well stocked with basic 4WD spare parts, and you haven't truly experienced Africa until you've seen the ingenuity of a bush mechanic. The minimum you should carry is a tow rope, shovel, extra fan belt, vehicle fluids, spark plugs, baling wire, jump leads, fuses, hoses, a good jack and a wooden plank (to use as a base in sand and salt), several spare tyres and a pump. A good Swiss Army knife or Leatherman tool combined with a sturdy roll of duct tape can also save your vehicle's life in a pinch.

OPERATORS

Competition among safari companies is fierce these days and corners are often cut, especially at the budget level. Some companies enter wildlife parks through side entrances to avoid park fees, while others use glorified minibus drivers as guides, offer substandard food and poorly maintained vehicles, or underpay and otherwise poorly treat their staff. Conversely, there are many high-quality companies with excellent track records, providing truly memorable and high-quality safaris.

Following are some things to keep in mind when looking for an operator:

- Do some legwork (the internet is a good start) before booking anything.
- Be sceptical of price quotes that sound too good to be true and don't rush

into any deals, no matter how good they sound.

- Take the time to shop around at reliable outfits to get a feel for what's on offer; decide exactly what you want, then visit the various companies in person and talk through the kind of package you're looking for.
- Go through the itinerary in detail and

TIPS FOR BUSH DRIVING

Still keen to give bush driving a go? If so, here are a few author-tested tips:

- Driving through high grass is a dangerous proposition as the seeds it disperses can quickly foul radiators and cause overheating. If the temperature gauge begins to climb, stop and remove as much plant material as you can from the grille.
- Keep your tyre pressure slightly lower than you would when driving on sealed roads.
- Try to avoid travelling at night when dust and distance may create confusing mirages.
- Keep your speed to a maximum of 80km/h on gravel roads, and much less on dirt roads and tracks.
- Maximise your control by keeping both hands on the steering wheel.
- Follow ruts made by other vehicles.
- If the road is corrugated, gradually increase your speed until you find the correct speed – it'll be obvious when the rattling stops.
- Be especially careful on bends – slow right down before attempting the turn.
- If you have a tyre blowout, do *not* hit the brakes or you'll lose control and the car will roll. Instead, steer straight ahead as best you can and let the car slow itself before you attempt to bring it to a complete stop.
- You don't meet other cars very often, but when you do it's like dust clouds passing in the night. When a vehicle approaches from the opposite direction, reduce your speed and keep as far left as possible. On remote roads, it's customary to wave at the other driver as you pass.
- In rainy weather, gravel roads can turn to quagmires, and desert washes may fill with water. If you're uncertain about the water depth in a wash, get out and check the depth (unless it's a raging torrent, of course) and only cross when it's safe for the type of vehicle you're driving.
- Be on the lookout for animals. Antelopes, in particular, often bound onto the road unexpectedly, resulting in unpleasant meetings.
- Avoid swerving sharply or braking suddenly on a gravel road or you risk losing control of the vehicle. If the rear wheels begin to skid, steer gently into the direction of the skid until you regain control. If the front wheels skid, take a firm hand on the wheel and steer in the opposite direction of the skid.
- Dust permeates everything on gravel roads – wrap your food, clothing and camera equipment in dust-proof plastic or keep them in sealed containers. To minimise dust inside the vehicle, pressurise the interior by closing the windows and turning on the blower.
- In dusty conditions, switch on your headlights so you can be more easily seen.

confirm what is expected/planned for each stage of the trip.

One thing to look out for, whichever company you book with, is client swapping. Quite a few companies shift clients on to other companies if they don't have enough people to justify running the trip themselves. This ensures that trips actually depart on time, and saves travellers days of waiting for a safari to fill up, but it does undermine consumer trust. Reputable companies will usually inform you before they transfer you to another company. In any case, it may not be the end of the world if you end up taking your safari with a different company from the one with which you booked; just make sure the safari you booked and paid for is what you get.

The brochures for some safari companies may give the impression that they offer every conceivable safari under the sun but, in fact, many companies also advertise trips run by other companies. While it's not the most transparent way to do business, again, it needn't be the end of the world. A reliable company will normally choose reliable partners and you're only really likely to come unstuck at the budget end of the market.

Companies recommended in this chapter enjoyed a good reputation at the time of research, as do many others. However, we can't emphasise enough the need to check on the current situation with all of the listed companies and any others you may hear about.

KENYA

Basecamp Explorer (☎ 020-577490; www.basecampexplorer.com) An excellent Scandinavian-owned ecotourism operator offering a nine-day camping itinerary to Samburu, Lake Nakuru and the Masai Mara, with walking at Mt Kenya, Lake Bogoria and Lake Baringo. The firm also runs plenty of conservation-based safaris, including trips to Lamu, Tanzania, Mt Kenya and Kilimanjaro.

Best Camping Tours (☎ 020-229667; www.bestcampingkenya.com) Offers camping safaris on all the main routes, including Amboseli and Masai Mara (three to four days) and Amboseli and Tsavo West (four days).

Bike Treks (☎ 020-446371; www.biketreks.co.ke) Offers walking and cycling as well as combined walking/cycling safaris. Its shortest safari is a three-day Masai Mara trip, and there are also six-day walking or cycling trips to the Maasai land west and south of Narok.

Bushbuck Adventures (☎ 020-7121505; www.bushbuckadventures.com) A small company specialising in personalised safaris. It's relatively expensive, but some company profits go into conservation projects. The company is also strong on walking safaris.

Eastern & Southern Safaris (☎ 020-242828; www.essafari.co.ke) A classy and reliable outfit. Safaris in Tanzania and Uganda are also available, and departures are guaranteed with just two people for some itineraries.

Gametrackers (☎ 020-338927; www.gametrackersafaris.com) Long established and usually reliable, this company offers a full range of camping and lodge safaris around Kenya. There are also short excursions, walking, Mt Kenya treks and numerous long-haul trips to Tanzania, Uganda and further afield.

IntoAfrica (www.intoafrica.co.uk) This environmentally and culturally sensitive company places an emphasis on fair trade and gets more praise from readers than just about any other. Trips on offer include a variety of routes up Mt Kenya as well as cultural treks with Maasai people.

Let's Go Travel (☎ 020-340331; www
.letsgosafari.com) This excellent travel
agent runs its own safaris and excursions
and also sells on an amazing range of
trips from other companies.

Ontdek Kenya (☎ 020-3524405; www
.ontdekkenya.com) This small operator
has been recommended by several
readers and offers walking trips catered
to women, vegetarians and birdwatchers.
Destinations include the Rift Valley lakes
and Mt Kenya.

Origins Safaris (☎ 020-312137; www
.originsafaris.info) Offers tailored
birdwatching trips and a superb range
of exclusive cultural safaris around
the country, including such rare sights
as Samburu circumcision ceremonies
and tribal initiation rites in southern
Ethiopia.

Safari Seekers (☎ 020-652317; www
.safari-seekerskenya.com) Has its own
permanent camp sites in Amboseli,
Samburu and Masai Mara and runs
camping and lodge safaris in Kenya and
Tanzania, plus trips into Uganda.

Safe Ride Tours & Safaris (☎
020-253129; www.saferidesafaris.com)
Relatively new operator consistently
recommended by readers for its camping
excursions.

**Sana Highlands Trekking
Expeditions** (☎ 020-227820; www.
sanatrekking
kenya.com) Another of the big budget
players and a regular stop on the tout
circuit. However, it has had a reasonable
reputation in the past for walking safaris
as well as the usual camping and lodge
itineraries.

Somak Travel (☎ 020-535508; www
.somak-nairobi.com) Runs the usual
range of lodge safaris and other options
such as luxury camel treks.

Southern Cross Safaris (☎ 020-
884712; www.southerncrosssafaris.com)

Long-standing operator and travel agent
with an excellent reputation around the
country.

TANZANIA
Africa Travel Resource (www
.intotanzania.com) Web-based safari
broker that matches your safari ideas with
an operator and helps you plan and book
customised itineraries.

Akaro Tours (☎ 027-275 2986; www
.akarotours.com) No-frills Kilimanjaro
treks, day hikes on Kilimanjaro's lower
slopes and a range of cultural tours.

**East African Safari & Touring
Company** (☎ 0744-741354; www.
eastafricansafari.info) Customised
itineraries for individuals and small
groups, with focus on the ecosystems
around Tarangire National Park, where it
operates a camp.

Foxes African Safaris (☎ 0744-
237422; www.tanzaniasafaris.info)
Family-run company with lodges and
camps in Mikumi, Ruaha and Katavi
National Parks, on the coast near
Bagamoyo and in the Southern Highlands.
Offers combination itineraries to these
destinations using plane, road and its own
private luxury train.

George Mavroudis Safaris (☎ 027-254
8840; www.gmsafaris.com) Exclusive,
customised mobile safaris in offbeat areas
of the northern circuit, done in vintage
style. Also offers combination Tanzania/
Rwanda itineraries.

Green Footprint Adventures (☎ 027-
250 2664; www.greenfootprint.co.tz) All
safaris are individually tailored and highly
personalised. Activities generally range
from a few hours to a half day and include
canoe safaris in Arusha National Park,
mountain biking and walking around
Lake Manyara, short hikes in the Crater
Highlands and bush-guide courses.

Hippotours & Safaris (☎ 022-212
8662/3; www.hippotours.com) Southern-

circuit itineraries, especially in Selous Game Reserve and on Mafia Island.

Hoopoe Safaris (☎ 027-250 7011; www.hoopoe.com) One of the best companies in the industry, with top-quality luxury camping and lodge safaris, plus a range of treks. It also arranges trekking and safari itineraries combining Tanzania, Kenya and Rwanda.

IntoAfrica (www.intoafrica.co.uk) Small company offering fair-trade cultural safaris and treks in northern Tanzania and Kenya, and earning consistently high marks from readers. It supports local communities in the areas in which it works, and is a fine choice if your interest is more in gaining insight into local life and culture than in experiencing the luxury-lodge atmosphere. Itineraries include treks on Mts Kilimanjaro and Meru, plus a seven-day wildlife-cultural safari in Maasai and Chagga areas.

Kahembe Trekking & Cultural Safaris (☎ 027-253 1088/1377; www.kahembe culturalsafaris.com) Small outfit offering Mt Hanang treks and a range of no-frills cultural safaris around Babati; a good choice for experiencing Tanzania from a local perspective.

Moshi Expedition & Mountaineering (☎ 027-275 4234; www.memtours.com) Kilimanjaro treks and northern-circuit safaris at competitive prices.

Roy Safaris (☎ 027-250 2115/8010; www.roysafaris.com) Highly regarded, family-run company offering budget and semiluxury camping safaris on the northern circuit, plus luxury-lodge safaris and treks on Mt Kilimanjaro, Mt Meru and in the Crater Highlands. Its vehicle fleet is the cream of the crop and safaris and treks are consistently good value for money.

Safari Makers (☎ 027-254 4446; www .safarimakers.com) Reliable no-frills northern-circuit camping and lodge safaris and treks at very reasonable prices, some of which also incorporate Cultural Tourism Program tours.

Shah Tours (☎ 027-275 2370/2998; www.kilimanjaro-shah.com) Quality Kilimanjaro and Meru treks at reasonable prices.

Sunny Safaris (☎ 027-250 8184/7145; www.sunnysafaris.com) Wide selection of no-frills camping and lodge safaris at reasonable prices, as well as Kilimanjaro and Meru treks, and day walks in the area around Arusha.

Tropical Trails (☎ 027-250 0358, 027-254 8299; www.tropicaltrails.com) Kosher treks, photographic camping safaris and other special-interest tours can be arranged, and a portion of the company's profits goes towards supporting education projects in Maasai schools.

UGANDA

Afri Tours & Travel (☎ 041-233596; www.afritourstravel.com) One of the better all-round safari companies in Uganda, offering safaris at prices for every pocket. It operates the Sambiya River Lodge in Murchison and promotes some excellent-value short safaris to what is arguably Uganda's best national park, as well as offering full safari itineraries throughout the country.

African Pearl Safaris (☎ 041-233566; www.africanpearlsafaris.com) Offers a wide range of shorter safaris around Uganda with a focus on Bwindi Impenetrable National Park, where it operates the Buhoma Homestead.

Great Lakes Safaris (☎ 041-267153; www.safari-uganda.com) One of the newer safari companies in Uganda, the team has been generating rave reviews for friendly service and flexibility. It covers all the major national parks in Uganda.

Kimbla-Mantana African Safaris (☎ 041-321552; www.kimbla-mantana

.com) Known throughout East Africa for its luxury lodges and tented camps, Mantana offers a limited range of safaris around Uganda. Most of its trips combine stays at one or more of its camps at Lake Mburo, Bwindi and Kibale Forest, plus visits to Queen Elizabeth and the crater lakes.

Uganda Safari Company (☎ 041-251182; www.safariuganda.com) Formerly Semliki Safaris, this is a specialist operator offering all-inclusive safaris throughout Uganda for around US$300 per day, including Semliki Valley Wildlife Reserve, Queen Elizabeth National Park, Murchison Falls National Park and the mountain gorillas. As well as offering tailored trips for birdwatchers, anglers and other special-interest groups, it runs the luxurious Semliki Lodge in western Uganda and Apoka Lodge at beautiful Kidepo Valley.

Volcanoes Safaris (☎ 041-346464; www.volcanoessafaris.com) Extensive choice covering the highlights of Uganda, with a particular focus on the mountain gorillas here and in Rwanda. The organisation also operates upmarket camps at Mgahinga, Bwindi and Sipi Falls. It's also possible to make enquiries or bookings through its UK office.

RWANDA
Primate Safaris (☎ 503428; www .primatesafaris-rwanda.com) Offers a range of short safaris to Ngungwe Forest National Park and Parc National des Volcans; in addition, the owners have years of experience in the Kenyan safari business.

Thousand Hills Expeditions (☎ 505151; www.thousandhills.rw) New operator with a very experienced team that has worked all over the world. Gorilla visits, national park visits and an emphasis on local culture. Its motto is 'paradise needs to be shared'.

Volcanoes Safaris (☎ 576530; salesrw@volcanoessafaris.com) The Rwandan branch office for Uganda's Volcanoes Safaris.

ON SAFARI
MAKING THE MOST OF YOUR SAFARI EXPERIENCE

UP AT FIRST LIGHT, a quick gulp of coffee and into the vehicle for an early game drive – few experiences compare with sunrise over the savanna, especially when it's teeming with African wildlife. While there's no way of knowing exactly what each day will bring, you can be assured that each day will bring *something*.

One of the finest prospects in the world for watching wildlife, a safari in East Africa ensures some spectacular viewing. Within the many parks and reserves, wildlife is not only abundant and diverse, it's also particularly habituated to the presence of people and vehicles. Visitors enjoy up-close encounters and the chance of sightings normally reserved for specialists who live and work with animals.

Every scale of experience is here, whether you want to see epic seasonal migrations of huge herds, the prolonged grooming sessions of a meerkat colony, or a pair of beetles resolutely rolling a dung ball to their nest site. From giving tips on seeing as much variety as possible, to helping you get better acquainted with your old favourite animal or park, this chapter is aimed at maximising the quality of your safari experience.

THE SAFARI EXPERIENCE

GAME DRIVES

Game drives are the backbone of most safaris, with the idea being to spend as many hours as possible in the bush searching for animals. A game drive can be done at any time of day, but early morning, mid-morning and late afternoon, with a break early on for breakfast and another in the middle of the day for lunch, is the usual plan. Night drives are also an excellent way to view

nocturnal animals, though they're not permitted everywhere.

Most organised safaris begin with an early wake-up call – usually accompanied by a hot drink and the rising sun – and then a game drive before breakfast. The same wisdom applies if you are doing it yourself: the importance of an early start cannot be stressed too highly. You will see large animals at virtually any time of day, but the earlier you set out, the better your chances of seeing nocturnal species still on the prowl, or predators gathered at a kill. There is also a greater chance of observing interesting interactions in the early hours and, practically speaking, it's usually cooler.

Savanna is an excellent environment in which to spot large animals and you don't normally go far without seeing something. The basic technique is to drive along slowly, stopping for photos as you like. After an hour or two driving around, it's back to camp or lodge for breakfast, a freshen up and then a mid-morning game drive. Again, this is a good time of day: large raptors such as eagles and vultures are starting to take to the thermals as the land warms up, many grazers are still moving about and primates have shaken off the night's chill. Activity wanes noticeably as noon approaches and animals seek shade and rest; primates also head for the shade, though they may remain active all day.

By late afternoon, things are on the move again, and afternoon game drives typically last from about 3pm until the park's closing time. Unfortunately, things tend to get most interesting just as the sun sets and it's time to leave. While darkness covers much wildlife activity normally hidden from people, in a handful of locales, night drives are the highlight of any safari and offer all the thrills of a game drive with a whole new suite of players.

An essential prerequisite for a night drive is a spotlight (preferably one that plugs into the vehicle's cigarette lighter) or a powerful torch, either of which is provided by your operator or vehicle rental company. While you're out and about, drive along slowly and look for eye-shine reflected in the light; even small animals can be detected using this technique.

VEHICLES & DRIVERS

Safari vehicles come in many permutations. You'll be spending quite a bit of time in a vehicle and, as a rule of thumb, the more money you shell out – whether going along on a tour or renting your own vehicle – the more comfortable the ride. Most vehicles are Land Rovers or Landcruisers, seating anything up to nine people (but most comfortably only four), with open sides, side windows or roll-back canvas flaps; the roof can be pop-top, flip-top, roll-back etc. A 4WD vehicle is the most desirable way to travel in the wet season, and essential in most wilderness areas.

Minivans – the target of much derision by 'serious' safari operators – are not usually 4WD, but are often driven as if they were. Again, they come in varying degrees of comfort and usually have a pop-top: those with a single, long pop-top provide the best viewing for all occupants; those with two or three smaller pop-tops offer less viewing flexibility and comfort. Those with a central aisle rather than bench seats give greater room for everyone to move around or take pictures. Minivans have the advantage of normally being cheaper than 4WDs (and most budget companies use them), but their use can be limited during the wet season.

Your driver normally doubles as your guide and is there to help you see wildlife and also to get you back to camp safely. Most will do their utmost to make sure you enjoy your safari experience (after

ON SAFARI

SPOTLIGHTING – LOOK THEN MOVE ON

A host of wildlife takes advantage of darkness to move about and feed, and the best way to see it is by spotlighting. Unfortunately it's not allowed in many reserves, but where it is possible you should take the opportunity to get out after dark. The idea is to drive (or walk) along slowly, scanning the bush on either side of the vehicle for eyeshine (the telltale reflection from an animal's tapetum – a layer of reflective cells in the eye of a nocturnal animal). There's a knack to doing it effectively and you must look directly along the light beam to see the eyeshine. Identification can be more difficult at night, with even the most familiar animal appearing quite different (although different coloured eyeshine gives a clue, eg antelope eyeshine is green-blue while bushbaby eyeshine is red). It's amazing what previously hidden wildlife and activity can be seen after dark: predators on the move, animals such as aardvarks that hide in burrows during the day; birds such as owls and nightjars; and even large spiders and scorpions. Beware that extended exposure to bright lights can damage an animal's eyes and disturb its behaviour, so look then move on.

all, their livelihood depends on it). It's a good idea to establish a dialogue early on: if you want to stop, tell them, and make it clear if you want to take photos – they may have to be reminded to switch off the engine.

You are entitled to an early start if you want one and to be at the reserve gates by opening time if necessary – arrange this the night before your game drive. Also note that unless you direct otherwise, drivers tend to follow each other to a kill, a pride of lions or whatever. If you don't want to be part of the minivan circus, let your driver know; likewise, if you are happy to spend hours watching a herd of something less glamorous, eg antelopes, just say so – you're the boss.

SPECIALISED SAFARIS

BIRDWATCHING

East Africa is one of the killer birdwatching destinations of the world. If it is your first birding trip outside Europe, America or Australia, you'll probably double your life list (for the uninitiated, a life list is the tally a birder keeps of all the bird species he or she has seen around the world). A tally of 500 species is easily achievable in an average visit and some hard-core birders clock up 700 ticks in a month-long trip to Kenya or Uganda. Birds are incredibly diverse and abundant, and groups familiar in other parts of the world take on a new significance – starlings occur in dazzling variety and iridescent colour; and the sparrow family is represented by dozens of species of weaver living in noisy colonies. Uniquely African groups such as the hamerkop, turacos and mousebird are common and those in search of a challenge can wrestle with the identification of dozens of species

of cisticolas, larks and pipits.

Read as much as possible before arriving: familiarise yourself with new bird families and prioritise sites according to the species you most want to see. Most birders try to see as many of the country endemics and unique African groups as possible, such as turacos or the shoebill, and concentrate less on cosmopolitan groups like migrant shorebirds. Prime birding locations are described in trip reports available through mail-order natural history booksellers and on websites devoted to birding. Coverage will depend on time, money and competing interests, but if your trip is restricted to one country, thoroughly work as many habitats as possible. If you are going to two or more countries, remember that rarities in one might be common elsewhere and plan accordingly. Consider hiring an expert bird guide for an area that might prove challenging - some of these guides have superb eyesight and an ear for the calls.

WHAT TO TAKE & WHERE TO GO

Make sure your binoculars are waterproof and dustproof, since a typical itinerary ranges from rainforest to dry plains. For information about selecting binoculars, see p000. Spotting scopes are probably only necessary if you're doing a lot of wader watching; most birders find a scope useful for only a small percentage of sightings, and too cumbersome for rainforest work. A tape recorder and directional mike are extremely useful for calling in forest birds, especially skulkers such as flufftails and nocturnal goodies. Avoid stressing birds with the overuse of playback.

Identification is well documented for Uganda, Kenya and Tanzania. Don't leave home without the *Field Guide to Birds of Kenya and Northern Tanzania* by

Zimmerman, Turner and Pearson; it's a superb book and the last word on the area it covers (the soft-cover version is recommended for ease of use in the field). For the rest of Tanzania plus Uganda, the *Illustrated Checklist to Birds of Eastern Africa* by van Perlo is the most useful book. As yet there is no guide covering the birds of the Zaire River basin, although those species that reach western Uganda are covered in van Perlo. Flipping through guides in search of the right section among the sheer dazzling variety can be time-consuming in the field – consider colour-coding the pages for quick reference.

Endemic Bird Areas listed by **BirdLife International** (www.birdlife.org) are good places to start planning your East African birding trip; many high-profile reserves fall into these areas, although a few are off the usual tourist circuit. For a good swipe at Kenya's 1100 species, try to cover coastal lowland forests, high grassland, alpine habitat, semidesert and Rift lakes. Tanzania has the highest number of endemics (23) among its 1040 recorded species. The presence of only one endemic among 1017 species shows Uganda's high overlap with neighbouring Kenya, but it offers the advantage of being a comparatively compact area. Rwanda weighs in at a more modest tally of 670 species, though there are notable Albertine Rift endemics and birds common to the Zaire River basin.

One last thing – don't fret about missing out on other wildlife as most good birding reserves are also good for mammals, of which you'll see plenty because birders often spend lengthy amounts of time in the field.

DO IT AT...
» **Arabuko Sokoke Forest Reserve (p50)**
» **Kakamega Forest (p76)**
» **Ngorongoro Conservation Area (p104)**
» **Semuliki National Park (p169)**

GORILLA & CHIMPANZEE TRACKING

Tracking gorillas and chimpanzees through the forests of East Africa is among the world's great wildlife experiences. National parks in Uganda and Rwanda protect important populations of both species and several of the parks run well-established tracking programs. International conservation bodies work closely with communities surrounding many of the parks; in these areas tangible benefits flow on from tourism to the local people because of their involvement in tracking, infrastructure and support.

Don't be fazed by the possible hardships – but be prepared. Wear walking shoes with adequate grip for muddy slopes (don't even think about trying it in sandals – among other things, you might run into safari ants). You can expect rain at any time of year, so carry a light waterproof jacket in your day pack (make sure it's large enough to fit over your day pack as well). While gorilla tracking, you may need both hands for the scramble up steep hillsides and through brakes of dense cane – carry gardening gloves in case you have to push your way through stinging nettles or thorny vines.

It can also get quite cold at high elevations, so take a warm top. Rain or no, tracking can be hot work: carry plenty of water (preferably 2L). If you get too hot or tired, your guide will probably carry your pack for you and cut you a walking stick if there's a steep descent. Finally, don't forget camera and memory cards, but flash photography is not permitted, so you'll need to set your digital camera to a high ISO to cope with the often gloomy light conditions among undergrowth.

HOW IT'S DONE

Gorilla tracking can involve negotiating steep hills and gullies (a reasonable level of fitness will help you to enjoy the day), but the effort is amply repaid by your allotted hour spent in the company of these largest of primates. Reserve your permits as early as you can – only a specified number of tracking permits are issued daily – and check into the park office as close to opening time as possible. You will be allocated to a group with a guide. Starting from where trackers watched them bed down the night before, you will follow the gorilla's trail – usually obvious as crushed vegetation, temporary nests and broken food plants. Trackers will clear a path for you where necessary, but gorillas can cover ground quickly: some groups of tourists are lucky enough to come across them within a few minutes, but most can expect an hour or two of hard slog. You're expected to tip guides, trackers and porters after a successful tracking.

Chimp tracking attracts far less publicity (and tourists) than gorilla tracking, but offers an exciting alternative. In your allotted hour of viewing with habituated chimps, you can expect lots of noise and some boisterous action. Organised primate walks are run regularly from some reserves with a high density of primate species and usually offer a good chance of encountering chimps. However, wild chimps are generally shy of humans and, even where parties have been habituated, contact is never guaranteed. Even when you do meet up, chimps can move very quickly through forest: if a party is on the go, you'll have to leg it to keep up – and that can be very hot work.

DO IT AT...

» **Bwindi Impenetrable National Park (p146)**
» **Parc National des Volcans (p179)**
» **Kibale Forest National Park (p150)**
» **Parc National de Nyungwe (p178)**

SNORKELLING & DIVING

Coral reefs the world over are among the great natural spectacles, and the coasts of Kenya and Tanzania offer some fine examples where snorkelling can be enjoyed in safety and comfort at a relatively low cost. Some basic equipment is all that is required to enjoy a constantly moving parade of fish in every imaginable shape and colour, crabs, shrimps and shells with intricate and outlandish camouflage, and the great reefs of coral that form the basis for this fascinating ecosystem.

The minimum requirements are a mask, snorkel and fins; those who don't carry these as part of their normal travel gear can hire them at various coastal resorts, although check their condition before forking out any money. If you wear spectacles and do a lot of snorkelling, consider getting a mask made up with glass to your eyes' prescription; these are not available in East Africa, so you'll have to get it done at home. If you have contact lenses (again, bring them from home) then you should definitely wear these when under the water.

The sun's strength can be deceptive when you're wet, so wear a T-shirt to cover your back against sunburn; lightweight diving suits perform the same task. If you really want to feel the sun on your back (especially if you're escaping a northern winter) make sure you apply liberal amounts of sunblock. And if you're heading out in a boat for a few hours, remember to take adequate drinking water. Also be aware that scuba diving is a skill requiring equipment and training outside the scope of this book.

Various field guides will help you identify marine organisms, especially reef fish. *The Guide to the Seashores of*

Eastern Africa and the Western Indian Ocean Islands edited by M Richmond is an excellent book covering many types of marine life. Unfortunately, books can't be read underwater, although you could laminate colour photocopies of fish ID sheets before leaving home. A waterproof drawing crayon and sketching board are handy for jotting down details of colours and shapes to help identify what you've seen once you're back on shore or on the boat. The coral reef is a dazzling ecosystem, which can be enjoyed just for its own sake, but learning how to identify its many inhabitants helps to piece together the ecological jigsaw and enhances your appreciation of what you see.

HOW IT'S DONE

Wade out until there's enough water in which to float, then lay your arms along the side of your body, point face and mask downwards and kick gently along with the fins. A little effort goes a long way and the stiffer the fins, the better the propulsion. The snorkel fits into the mouth and is gripped with the teeth; breathe through your mouth when floating on the surface and hold your breath for forays underwater. With practice it is possible to dive a few metres underwater: take a deep breath and duck dive (vertically) from the surface; fins work just fine beneath the surface and a surprising distance can be covered with little effort. When you surface, blow sharp and hard to eject the water from the snorkel. Mastering the basics takes a few minutes, but that's it – only stamina and curiosity will limit your exploration.

Snorkelling can give hours of pleasure for very little effort, but there are a few hazards you should know about. Sunburn, fatigue and cramp from cold water can affect anyone – check local conditions and currents before venturing out. Be aware that some marine life is dangerous; coral cuts and scrapes are the most common cause of discomfort, but don't touch anything alive underwater – certain fish and cone shells can deliver a lethal sting. Finally, note that during the wet season, underwater visibility can be reduced by silted rivers emptying into the sea, and heavy weather might make boat access to reefs difficult.

DO IT AT...

» **Zanzibar Archipelago (p114)**
» **Malindi Marine National Park (p93)**
» **Watamu Marine National Park (p93)**

HOW TO WATCH WILDLIFE

Animals are free to roam and may not be where you want them to be, but the better informed you are, the more likely you are to see what you're after. If you're on a tour, your knowledge will complement that of the guide and will often be in demand from other members of the party. Here are some vital tips.

TIME OF DAY

This is arguably the most important factor in successful wildlife watching. Learn what time of day your quarry is most active, how it spends other times and how these might vary according to season and weather conditions – and plan your days to make the most of these factors. An early start may catch nocturnal predators still on the move; birds are most active in the early morning, although raptors ride thermals as the day warms up; and nocturnal animals may be active in overcast conditions. Activity dies off during the heat of the day, especially during the dry season (large mammals shelter under trees or shrubs and birds rest in shade), picking up again in the late afternoon and peaking near sundown.

ON SAFARI

WEATHER

Daily, as well as seasonal, temperature and rainfall patterns also make a difference. For example, puff adders are often on the move after rain, lizards like to bask in early sunshine, and monkeys are more active when the day warms up. A storm can bring on a flurry of activity – swifts moving through on the front, termites swarming and, in the aftermath, predators snapping up wind-blown insects and rodents. Predators also generally hunt into the wind – this helps guides predict where they'll be the next day.

FOOD SOURCES

Food availability can change with season, and knowing your quarry's food preferences can help. Note what's about, eg trees in flower attract birds, butterflies and bats; termite swarms are snapped up by many animals, from jackals to rollers; and some lions follow the wildebeest migration.

WATER

For many animals, daily access to water is essential and, during dry seasons, they will stay close to a ready source; naturally the concentration of prey will attract predators. The daily ebbing and flowing of tides affects marine life and the roosting and feeding of shorebirds on mudflats.

KNOW YOUR HABITAT

Some knowledge of where an animal lives will be of great value in finding it. Learn what to expect in each major habitat and by patiently waiting, sooner or later something will show. For example, a cliff face may harbour klipspringers, a leopard's den or an owl's nest. Once you make the link between species and habitat, your search pattern will change and new things will reveal themselves.

The area where one habitat merges into another is usually especially productive, eg woodland abutting grassland provides food and shelter to both grazers and browsers; and in the sunny woodland edge grow flowering plants that attract birds and butterflies. Check likely shelters, such as tree hollows, cliff overhangs or termite mounds, and dead trees and overhanging branches that are often used as lookouts or perches. Remember, habitats and their species composition also vary with altitude.

PUT IN THE HOURS

Don't rely on beginner's luck – the longer you spend observing, waiting and watching in the field, the more you will see. As the famous line goes, 'The more you practice, the luckier you get'.

SEARCHING & IDENTIFICATION

Prime your senses (especially sight and hearing), keep quiet and look for clues. Watch for silhouettes against the sky in the forest canopy; body parts (eg a leg dangling from a branch or twitching ears above long grass) and shadows; movement and moving vegetation; and shapes that don't fit. Look in both foreground and background, look at the ground and into the trees and both upstream and downstream when crossing a river. Use your peripheral vision (especially at night) and watch where other creatures are looking, eg Tommies staring at a cheetah.

Listen for alarm calls (which themselves indicate that predators are nearby), rustling bushes, snorting breath, splashing water and changes in the activity of other creatures, eg monkeys screaming at a crowned eagle. Cupping your hands behind your ears helps to funnel sounds and to detect faint calls (rotate your head to judge the direction of sounds). Many large animals give off a distinctive odour or attract insects. Relax (animals can detect tension) and keep quiet and heed your own instincts, such as the feeling that you're being watched or the hair standing up on the back of your neck.

If on foot, learn to use the environment to your advantage: walk slowly, using cover such as bushes and trees; stay downwind of animals (ie keep the wind in your face); and avoid wearing strong artificial scents, which will help to give you away. Don't stare at an animal as you approach – this can be seen as a threat. Avoid making sudden movements and loud noises, which startle mammals (birds are less concerned with noise than movement); and don't point at great apes – they may feel threatened and retaliate. Don't sneak up on animals – they may think you're stalking them and react accordingly. Sit still awhile against a tree or termite mound (animals look for movement, and if you don't move, they probably won't pay much attention). Stake out a burrow or den that appears to be in use – fresh droppings nearby are a promising sign. And, perhaps most important of all, learn from the professional guides – listen to their stories, learn their techniques and ask questions.

The identification of animals is usually the first step towards finding out more about them. Most people categorise what they see without realising it, eg a jackal is automatically recognised as a member of the dog family. But the finer points of identifying East Africa's species usually requires more than a cursory examination.

The first step, usually made with no conscious effort, separates things by shape, eg an elephant, a cat, some kind of antelope. Other basic indicators are pattern or colour, eg leopards and lions have a similar shape, but different coloration; and size – both servals and leopards are spotted, but servals are much smaller. Looking for the basic differences will come naturally after a short time and, with practice, the subtle differences attributable to sex, age and geographical variation will also become familiar. Bird identification is a science in itself (and for birdwatchers an abiding passion) with its own techniques and terminology.

For birds or mammals, nothing beats practice in the field, backed up by reading (field guides are a good place to start, as is the wildlife guide provided in this book), taking field notes and, if you have the talent or inclination, sketches or photos.

THE BIG FIVE

Throughout Africa you'll repeatedly hear the phrase, the 'Big Five'. It won't take long to work out that it refers to the five most sought-after species: lion, leopard, elephant, rhino and buffalo. The term originates from the days of widespread big-game hunting when the Big Five were (and still are) considered to be the five most dangerous species to hunt. Now applied more often by lodges and reserves as part of their advertising ('Deep in the heart of Big Five country!'), it's a useful indication of the best-conserved regions: if the Big Five are there, you can generally assume all the species indigenous to the area are still present. Occasionally, you'll hear of the Big Six, a more precise term indicating both species of rhino (black and white), and just to confuse things, the Big Seven, meaning the Big Five plus cheetah and African wild dog.

ON SAFARI

ON SAFARI

BEYOND LOOKING

For many people, the simple pleasure of looking at wildlife evolves into photography, writing, art or learning more about animal behaviour (plant behaviour happens much more slowly, but is no less fascinating). The realisation that a vast, milling mob of wildebeests is actually a structured, complex community of interacting animals opens up a whole new world of watching wildlife to complement the thrill of the chase. How does one bull react to another? Why are most females in the middle of the group? Follow one animal – what does it do? To which individuals is it submissive or dominant? Each observation can answer one question and pose several more.

But if you want to keep chasing new species, ticking, twitching or listing (ie keeping a list of what you have seen and pursuing those species that you haven't yet seen) can become a lifelong hobby. Listing is a reflection of the natural desire to collect and catalogue objects and a harmless fulfilment of the hunting instinct. Should it need any justification, listing takes people to places they wouldn't otherwise visit, as they pursue the rare or unusual; it hones the senses, powers of observation and skills of identification; and it leads to an appreciation of the diversity of life. Birds and, to a lesser extent, mammals are the usual targets of twitchers, but such is the stimulation of watching East African wildlife that it is easy to start ticking other diverse, conspicuous and colourful groups, such as butterflies and tropical fish.

ADVANCED TECHNIQUES

Mastered the basics? Here are some advanced techniques for moving beyond the amateurs and playing in the same league as professional guides.

HIDES, OBSERVATION TOWERS & BOARDWALKS

A hide (also called a blind) is any artificial structure that allows the watcher to remain hidden while wildlife behaves more or less as normal. Your safari vehicle is an effective hide, simply because most animals don't make the connection between vehicles and their occupants. Stationary hides are usually covered wooden shelters with horizontal openings through which wildlife can be observed or photographed; some are just fences and others are more elaborate, eg game lodges that overlook waterholes. Bird hides are sometimes erected next to waterholes and can be great places for wildlife photography. Wooden observation towers allow you to scan across vegetation from a height and look at birds or monkeys at eye level (a great luxury). Boardwalks over water can also act as observation platforms by getting the observer deep into otherwise inaccessible habitat.

USING CALLS

Calls (vocalisations) are particularly important for locating birds and amphibians, but many mammals, including elephants, hippos and lions, also make loud or dramatic calls. Homing in on vocalisations is an important part of tracking primates, and an imitation of a bleating wildebeest can rouse a lion from slumber. Birdwatchers know that even a poor imitation of some calls can bring birds in for a closer look – a favourite trick is pishing, ie making a high-pitched kissing sound with the mouth to attract small birds (kissing the back of your hand can have the same effect). Similar sounds can be made with a squeaker (available from

irdwatching supply shops) and by
ubbing polystyrene foam against glass
eg a windscreen). High-quality MP3
layers are available with microphones
or recording a call and playing it back
o attract the animal in question. Most
irds respond well to playback and it is
ften the best way to locate and identify
ome species, such as flufftails, owls or
ightjars.

However, always use discretion and
restraint with any of these techniques.
Animals attracted to your calls are having
their normal routine disrupted, which can
potentially have seriously adverse effects –
a lion checking out your wildebeest calf
call may be missing a real opportunity
to hunt. And a bird responding to what
it perceives as a territorial challenge
may be distracted from a real intruder;
it may be deprived of valuable feeding
time; or it may fail to notice the presence
of a predator. If overused, the playback
technique can also make individual
mammals and birds so inured that they
don't respond at all.

TRACKS AND SIGNS

Animal tracks (spoor) and droppings
(scats) are a great way of finding out
what's around, especially those hard-to-
see nocturnal species, even if you don't
see the beast in question. Some signs, such
as those of elephants, are immediately
recognisable (especially the droppings),
but most others are also distinct and a few
can be learned quite quickly.

Experienced trackers can read a great
deal from spoor and scats (eg where
an animal has rested, whether it was
hunting etc). Spoor and scats change
and disintegrate over time (eg owl pellets
break down quickly in wet forests), and
years of practice are needed to pick up the
subtleties of the tracker's art.

Examples of signs to look for include
fur on fences or acacia thorns; nests of

THE NAME OF THE GAME

The word 'game' actually hails from
hunting: originally the game was the
thrill of the sport, but gradually the
quarry itself came to be called game.
Derivation notwithstanding, the term
pops up regularly in East Africa when
people refer to wildlife and doesn't
necessarily mean that some poor beast
is about to receive a lethal dose of lead
poisoning. 'Game-viewing' is the most
common local term for wildlife watching
and is usually done on a 'game drive',
a guided tour by vehicle. 'Big game' is,
of course, the Big Five whereas 'general
game' collectively refers to the diverse
herbivore community, ranging from
duikers to giraffes. While the word
'game' in its various forms is used widely,
hunters also still employ the term, most
often as 'big game' as well as 'plains
game', their term for the herbivores;
advertisements for the latter are usually
for hunting.

squirrels (called dreys) or birds; burrows
(eg those used by warthogs in abandoned
termite mounds); flattened grass where
an antelope has been lying out; a
smooth tree trunk where an elephant
has been rubbing; animal trails leading
to a waterhole, food source or shelter;
whitewash left by birds – especially
raptors – on cliffs, rocks and termite
mounds; and pellets of undigested
material regurgitated by owls and hyenas.
Carcasses can also be telltale signs of
predators, eg a dead impala dragged into
a tree by a leopard. Tracking gorillas and
chimps offers an opportunity to get to
grips with tracks and signs while on foot,
where broken or flattened vegetation,
discarded fruit, droppings and disused
nests make an interesting detective story.

WATCHING RESPONSIBLY

Watching wildlife under natural conditions at such close range is a privilege, and with this privilege comes the responsibility to ensure wildlife continues to live unhindered, both for its own survival and so that other people can enjoy the same experience. Strict ethical codes exist for game-viewing and for gorilla and chimp tracking; visitors are usually briefed before setting out. Of course you'll want quick results for all the money you've forked out, but it is important for everyone to stick to the rules; should a serious breach occur, don't hesitate to report your (or someone else's) driver or guide – it's in their interests to keep their comparatively well-paid jobs. Immense benefits – personal, aesthetic, recreational, conservation and financial – stem from the wildlife-watching industry, and it is important for all concerned (especially the animals) to ensure that wildlife tourism is carried out responsibly The following are a few particularly important points to consider.

CLOSE ENCOUNTERS

Accidental encounters with large and potentially dangerous animals are a distinct possibility, but with common sense and care, you will come to no grief. Most big animals move away as you approach, and little else can harm you. Wildlife-viewing from a vehicle is very safe, but more intimate encounters can be expected on a walking safari – it's part of the excitement, but remember to exercise extreme caution even when accompanied by an armed guide. Monkeys can become a pest around camping grounds – assert your dominance early on, before they get too cocky. All snakes should be treated with extreme caution – a few are dangerous and on no account should you try to pick one up (injured snakes can be especially dangerous).

DOS AND DON'TS ON SAFARI

- Large animals can be dangerous; don't drive too close to animals and don't drive between a female and her young.
- Don't make loud noises, such as tooting the horn or banging the side of your vehicle, to attract an animal's attention.
- Stay well clear of a predator on the hunt – it or its young may starve if the hunt is unsuccessful.
- Leave things better than you find them. Pick up other people's rubbish and keep your own rubbish until you can dispose of it properly.
- Do not drive off designated tracks - it destroys vegetation and encourages erosion.
- Do not throw matches or cigarettes out of your car. Put all fires out completely.
- Do not collect souvenirs such as bones, horns, feathers, shells etc – they play a role in the natural environment.
- Move in towards an animal gradually or in stages; that way you'll eventually get closer without disturbing it.
- Respect your own life. Do not get out of the vehicle except at designated areas and don't stand or sit on a roof or hang out a window – predators and primates can move very quickly.

ON SAFARI

DRIVING

There's a strict curfew on driving at night in most reserves, and outside the reserves it's not a good idea to be on the roads after dark because of the danger of hitting animals or of running into bandits. During the day, most of your wildlife-watching will be inside reserves, where a speed limit of around 40km/h is usually enforced and animals have right of way (if no speed limit is indicated, use 40km/h as a guide). The chances of getting bowled over by an elephant are pretty slim; however, if an elephant, buffalo or rhino charges you, it's a very good idea to get out of its way – drivers don't usually need to be told and will start the engine as soon as a large animal starts to look stroppy.

FEEDING WILDLIFE

Some lodges have feeding stations that attract birds and monkeys by day and galagos and genets at night. However, for you there's one simple rule – don't feed wild animals. Artificial feeding can foster a dependence on handouts, change natural behaviour and, in the long term, even cause malnutrition (visitors' bags usually contain sugary foods rather than beetle grubs). Monkeys and baboons are intelligent, opportunistic animals that quickly learn how to get a free feed; if one is suddenly denied a coveted morsel, it can turn ugly very fast. At best this will mean a tantrum that will convince you to deliver the goods; at worst, physical aggression that you don't want to be involved with.

ANIMAL WELFARE

Most travellers are aware of the debate over buying souvenirs made from animal products such as ivory. It might be difficult to relate that innocent-looking souvenir to a real animal, but don't fool yourself – your purchases can be one more nail in the coffin of a species. And don't assume that a product openly on sale is legal – even if it is, it does not mean that it meets any standards for wildlife sustainability or the humane treatment of animals. Many countries have strict laws about quarantine and the importation of prohibited animal or plant products, so check your own country's regulations before wasting money on a potentially prohibited import – the penalties are sometimes severe.

DISTURBING WILDLIFE

In popular reserves, animals have become used to vehicles and often behave more or less naturally a few metres from camera-snapping tourists. This has had unfortunate side effects, such as the spectacle of lions or cheetahs being literally surrounded by safari vehicles; cheetahs being so harassed that they cannot hunt effectively; the destruction of vegetation; and drivers churning up the countryside by cutting new tracks in their pursuit of animals. While it's understandably difficult not to join in the safari circus at times, especially if vehicles are swarming around a kill, resist the temptation and focus on finding your own discovery.

WHAT TO BRING

CLOTHING

Suitable clothing maximises comfort to the wearer and minimises disturbance to wildlife. Subdued colours, such as greens or browns, make your presence in the landscape less obtrusive, but avoid camouflage clothing – in Africa it's for military use. Predawn departures can be chilly, especially in open vehicles with the wind whipping past, and be prepared

ON SAFARI

for sudden storms during the wet season; dress in layers and peel off or add clothes as conditions dictate.

Cotton or cotton-synthetic blends are cooler in hot weather; wear synthetics that breathe and are waterproof in cool conditions. Sleeveless photographer jackets have many pockets, which are very useful for carrying the paraphernalia necessary for wildlife-watching (like field guides and notebooks). A hat is important: light cotton protects your head against the sun, but opt for wool or synthetics in cold conditions. A wide brim cuts down glare and helps hide your eyes (looking directly at an animal can be taken as a threat).

Gorilla and chimp tracking is usually hot, and sometimes wet, work – carry a light waterproof jacket with a hood in your day pack. Trekking in high mountains requires specialised equipment and clothing, so do your homework and come prepared.

FIELD GUIDES

Field guides are (usually) pocket-sized books that depict the mammals, birds, flowers etc of a specific area with photos or colour illustrations. Important identification pointers and a distribution map are usually provided for each species; sometimes there are also brief natural histories, summarising breeding, behaviour, diet and the like. Guides to animals are usually organised in taxonomic order, a system that shows evolutionary relationships between species and is generally consistent between guides. Plant guides often follow other systems, eg wildflowers may be ranked by colour.

Ideally you should combine your own observations, notes and sketches with what you read in field guides, but on safari the excitement and overwhelming variety often make this impractical. Don't assume that because the field guide says species X is found here, it must be species X. If you find something unusual – birds in particular often wander outside their usual range – take notes and refer to other books when you get a chance. Depending on how much you value the book's appearance, consider colour coding the outside margin of the pages so you can flip to a section easily.

Field guides are handy tools that have made an incalculable contribution to the popularity of wildlife-watching. But rarely are they the last word on a subject and further reading of weightier texts can provide valuable detail not covered in your field guide.

BINOCULARS & SPOTTING SCOPES

A good pair of binoculars is probably the most important piece of equipment on safari and the best investment a wildlife-watcher can make. Any working pair is better than none at all: a rustle in the bushes can become a brilliant sunbird, and a cheetah at full pelt after an antelope can be brought close-to. Take your own (don't expect someone else to share), but if you are serious about watching wildlife, it is worth investing in quality optics; prices range from US$100 to thousands of dollars. There's any number of brands on the market, and a few things are worth knowing before you buy.

Factors to consider are size (to suit your hands), weight (they could be hanging from your neck for hours at a time) and whether you wear glasses (special eyecups are available for spectacle wearers). Decent models also have a dial (diopter), which allows you to compensate for any focusing difference between left and right eyes. Good binoculars are hinged, allowing adjustment for the distance between your eyes.

Like cameras, you get what you pay for with binoculars. Top-end brands such as Zeiss, Leica, Bausch & Lomb and Swarovski offer superb optics, last for years and are waterproof and dustproof. More affordable brands, such as Bushnell, and midrange to upper models from respected camera manufacturers (eg Pentax, Canon and Nikon) are perfectly good for most wildlife-watching. Good-quality compact models are worth considering, but don't be tempted by super-cheap compacts or by binoculars with 'zoom' optics (they usually have poor light-gathering ability).

Your final choice of binoculars will depend on budget, likely amount of use and desire for quality and comfort. But before you spend a lot of money, talk to people and test their binoculars in the field. Read manufacturers' brochures and product reviews in birdwatching magazines. Birdwatchers carry weight in the marketplace and conduct exhaustive tests in the field; if a particular brand and/or configuration passes their (usually stringent) requirements it'll be good enough for use in East Africa. Recommendations usually come in different price categories. **Better View Desired** (www.betterviewdesired .com) is a useful website that tests new releases and has a host of background information, plus lists of retailers and manufacturers.

THE NITTY GRITTY

Numbers are usually stamped on every pair of binoculars, eg 10x50, 7x32. The first number refers to the number of times the image is magnified when you look through the eyepieces: at 10x, an object 100m away will appear as if only 10m away; at 7x, it will appear as if 14m away. The most useful magnifications

for wildlife-watching are 7x, 8x or 10x. The second number, most commonly between 20 and 50, refers to the diameter in millimetres of the objective lens (ie the lens furthest from the eye); the wider the lens (ie the higher the number) the more light enters and therefore the brighter the image.

Larger objective lenses increase light-gathering ability and hence image brightness. Higher magnification reduces brightness. Not only is a brighter image clearer, it is also more colour accurate – a sometimes crucial point for identification. Light-gathering ability can be estimated (it's not a perfect guide) by dividing the objective diameter by the magnification – the higher the result, the more light enters the binoculars. Thus, 10x50s and 8x40s perform similarly, but 7x42s often give a brighter image. Special interior coatings can also increase image brightness. Having extra light-gathering ability may not be all that useful during the middle of the day (your eye can take only so much light before your irises start to close), but in dim conditions, such as at dusk or in a rainforest, you'll want all you can get. As your irises can only open so far (and this decreases with age), opting for greater light-gathering power may be a waste. To check, test out different binoculars in dim light before you buy a pair.

Larger objective lenses also mean a larger field of view, ie the width of the area (usually indicated in degrees) that fits into the image you see. Field of view is also a trade-off against magnification, ie higher magnifications reduce the field of view. The narrower the field of view, the harder it is to locate your target, especially if it is moving.

Internal lenses can also affect quality. Most binoculars have porro prism lenses, which are offset from each other to give the familiar crooked barrels. Roof prism lenses are aligned directly behind each other and allow compact, straight barrels: cost is their only drawback. Good compromises of all factors are configurations such as 7x35, 7x40 and 8x40. Birders tend to favour 8x40 or 10x50 for the sometimes critical extra magnification.

Spotting scopes are essentially refracting telescopes designed for field use. Birders use scopes most often in open habitats, eg when watching waterbirds and waders. Scopes offer higher magnifications than binoculars (usually starting at 20x or 25x), but must be mounted on a tripod or monopod to reduce shaking (not usually feasible in a vehicle). Disadvantages include weight and bulk, and a narrow field of view makes scopes difficult to use effectively in rainforests. Again, a quality scope will be expensive: Kowa, Leica, Celestron, Nikon and Bushnell are all excellent brands.

DIGITAL CAMERAS

Wildlife photography is a highly specialised field, but the quality of today's equipment – even modestly priced, nonprofessional gear – means that excellent results are possible for anyone.

If you're buying your first digital camera, the selection is mind-boggling. Canon or Nikon are the choice of most professional wildlife photographers, largely because they offer formidable lens quality, but all established brands are good. Cameras essentially all do the same thing, though with varying degrees of complexity and technological assistance. Most digital SLRs have a full range of automatic functions, but you should select a model that also allows full manual operation. Once you've mastered the basic techniques, you'll probably find it limiting if you're unable to begin experimenting with your photography.

More important than camera bodies are the lenses you attach to them – and for wildlife, think long. A 200-300mm lens is a good starting point, though bird portraits require something longer. Lenses of 400-600mm focal length are probably out of the price range of most people, though slower lenses (lenses with a relatively small maximum aperture) are reasonably priced and very useful. Dedicated (ie brand-name) lenses have superb optical quality and are more expensive than generic brands (eg Tamron), but unless you're a pro you'll probably notice only a slight difference.

Zooms are generally not as sharp as fixed focal-length lenses (ie lenses that do not zoom), but the difference is only important if you're thinking about publishing your pictures. Many brands offer zooms around the 100-300mm range which, when paired with a short zoom like a 35-70mm, covers most situations for recreational photographers. Recently released super-zooms – 55-300mm and 100-400mm – are worth investigating. None are cheap, but they yield excellent-quality results in one versatile package.

Hundreds of accessories can be used to enhance shots, but one that's vital is a tripod. Many shots are spoiled by camera shake, particularly when using longer lenses. Tripods can be cumbersome to include in your luggage, but sturdy, compact models can easily fit into a sausage bag. Collapsible monopods are light and easy to carry, but do not offer nearly as much stability as a tripod.

Most wildlife photographers in East Africa are restricted to a vehicle, where it is impractical to use a tripod. An excellent alternative for vehicle-based photography is a beanbag. A small cloth bag with a zip opening takes up almost no room, and can be filled with dried rice when you arrive at your destination. Simply roll down your window, lay the beanbag on the top of the door and rest the camera lens on it (or, if you're a passenger in a minivan, lay the beanbag on the roof if it opens).

IN THE FIELD

Before you go anywhere, know how your camera works. Visit the local zoo or park and shoot a few dozen snaps to familiarise yourself with its controls and functions. Many good wildlife moments happen unexpectedly and pass in seconds; you'll miss them if you're still fiddling with dials and settings. For the same reason, when in reserves, leave your camera turned on (and pack plenty of batteries).

Most cameras in manual mode have shutter- and aperture-priority functions. In shutter-priority mode, you set the shutter speed and the camera selects the appropriate aperture for a correct exposure; the reverse applies for aperture-priority. These two functions are probably the most valuable for wildlife photographers – but you need to know when to use them. Shutter priority is excellent for shooting action. If you want to freeze motion, select the highest shutter speed permitted with the available light, and the camera takes care of the aperture setting. On the other hand, if you're trying to emphasise depth of field in your shot, opt for aperture priority. Large apertures (low f-stops) reduce the depth of field – a useful trick for enhancing a portrait shot by throwing the background out of focus. However, if you're shooting a scene where you want everything in focus, such as thousands of wildebeests on a vast plain,

select a small aperture (high f-stop).

Composition is a major challenge with wildlife as you can't move your subject around. Try different vantage points and experiment with a variety of focal lengths. If you're too far away to take a good portrait, try to show the animal in its habitat. A 400mm lens might give you a close-up of a seabird's face, while a 28mm will show the entire colony receding into the background – all from the same position. Try to tell a story about the animal or illustrate some behaviour. Jackal pups transfixed by grazing gazelles might be too shy for a decent close-up, but could make a lovely subject if you include the antelopes and surroundings.

Unless you're packing a very powerful flash, wildlife photography relies on the vagaries of natural light and the best shots are invariably those taken in the 'golden hour' – just after dawn and just before dusk. Where possible, get into position early, whether it's a bird hide, waterhole or scenic lookout you noted the day before. Don't always assume front-on light is the best. Side lighting can give more depth to a subject; back lighting, particularly when the sun is near the horizon, can be very atmospheric.

Above all else, when photographing wildlife, be patient. You never know what will appear at the waterhole next or when a snoozing predator will suddenly spot a chance for a kill. You cannot always anticipate when an opportunity will arise, but if you're willing to wait, you'll almost certainly see something worth snapping.

ON SAFARI

GLOSSARY

adaptation – physical or behavioural trait that helps an organism survive or exploit an environmental factor.

algae – primitive water plants.

alpha male or female – dominant animal in a hierarchy, eg a *primate* troop (a sometimes tenuous position).

amphibian – animal that lives part of its life cycle in water and part on land, eg frog.

annulated horns – ridged horns of some antelope species, eg oryxes, impalas.

aquatic – living in freshwater (compare with *marine*).

arboreal – tree-dwelling.

arthropod – invertebrate characterised by a segmented body and jointed legs, eg insects, spiders.

artiodactyl – an even-toed *ungulate*, ie hippos, pigs, giraffes and antelopes.

asynchronous – not occurring simultaneously, eg the hatching of eggs.

avian – characteristic of birds, eg avian behaviour.

bachelor group – aggregation of nonbreeding adult and subadult males, eg antelopes.

big cat – the three largest cat species: lions, leopards and cheetahs.

Big Five – The five large animals (rhinos, buffaloes, elephants, lions and leopards) regarded as the most dangerous to hunt (and therefore the most prized) by colonial hunters.

binocular vision – vision with overlapping field of view to give a 3D perception of space; best developed in cats and primates.

biodiversity – faunal and floral richness characterising an area.

biomass – total weight of living organisms in an ecosystem.

bipedal – standing or walking on two legs, eg humans.

bird wave – a feeding party of birds, especially in rainforest, containing various species.

birder – a bird-watching enthusiast.

blind – see *hide*.

bluff – behaviour to convince a *predator* or rival that the bluffer is stronger.

boar – male pig.

bolus – ball of food or dung.

boss – head covering that supports horns, eg on a buffalo.

bovid – a member of the antelope family (Bovidae).

bovine – cattlelike in appearance or behaviour.

brood – group of young animals produced in one litter or clutch.

browse – to eat leaves and other parts of shrubs and trees (hence browser).

bull – male buffalo, elephant, giraffe etc.

callosity – hardened area of skin, eg on the face of a warthog (also called callus).

camouflage – coloration or patterning that helps an animal blend into its surroundings.

canid – any member of the family Canidae (eg dog, fox, jackal).

canine – doglike; also relating to or belonging to the family Canidae (dogs, foxes, jackals etc).

canine teeth – the four large, front teeth at the front of the jaws; well developed for killing in carnivores and fighting in baboons.

carnassial teeth – the shearing teeth of carnivores near the back of the jaws.

carnivore – meat-eating animal.

carrion – dead or decaying flesh.

casque – prominent bony growth surmounting the bill of some hornbills and head of guineafowl.

cellulose – component that strengthens the cell walls of plants, supporting them and forming stems.

cheek pouch – extension of cheeks for the temporary storage of food, eg in monkeys.

class – a major division of animal classification, eg *mammals*, birds, *reptiles* etc.

climax forest – mature forest.

colony – an aggregation of animals, eg birds, that live, roost or breed together (hence colonial).

commensalism – close but independent association between two unrelated animal species.

contiguous – adjoining (eg woodland spanning two adjacent reserves).

coursing – to run down *prey* along the ground mainly by sight, eg a hunting dog.

courtship – behaviour (often ritualised) associated with attracting a mate.

crèche – young birds or *mammals* gathered for safety.

crepuscular – active at twilight, ie evening or before dawn.

crustacean – arthropod with gills that can breathe underwater or survive in damp conditions on land.

cryptic – behaviour, appearance or lifestyle that helps conceal an organism from *predators*.

cud – partly digested plant material regurgitated and chewed by resting ruminants.

decurved – downward-curving.

dewlap – loose skin (eg in eland) or feathers hanging under chin.

digit – finger or toe.

dimorphism – having two forms of colour or size, eg spotted and black leopard (see *sexual dimorphism*, *polymorphism*).

dispersal – movement of animals (eg after breeding or rains) or plants (eg seeds) across a geographic area (compare with *migration*).

displacement activity – behaviour performed out of normal context, eg grooming when an animal is stressed.

display – behaviour transmitting information from the sender to another, often associated with threat, defence of territory, courtship etc.

diurnal – active during daylight hours (opposite of *nocturnal*).

diversity – variety of species or forms in an area.

dorsal – upper (top) surface, ie the back on most animals (opposite of *ventral*).

down – loose, fluffy feathers that cover young birds and insulate plumage of adults.

drey – nest of squirrels.

dung – animal excrement (faeces).

dung midden – accumulation of dung as a territory marker, often accompanied by scent marking (see latrine).

ear-tuft – wispy hairs extending beyond ear-tips (eg on a caracal) or erectile feathers near ears (eg some owls).

ecology – scientific study of relationships between organisms, their environment and each other.

ecosystem – community of living organisms and their physical environment.

edge – transition zone between two habitats, eg savanna and forest; hence edge species (also called ecotone).

endangered – in danger of imminent extinction if trends causing its demise continue.

endemic – found only in a certain area, eg turacos are endemic to Africa.

environment – physical factors that influence the development and behaviour of organisms.

epiphyte – plant growing on another for support, eg orchids on a tree (compare with parasite).

equatorial – living on or near the equator.

erectile – can be erected, eg hair or feathers erected in defence or courtship displays.

estrus – see oestrus.

evolve – to change physical and/or behavioural traits over time to exploit or survive changing environmental constraints.

faeces – excrement.

family – scientific grouping of related genera, eg Felidae (the cat family).

farrow – litter of pigs (also verb).

feline – catlike; also related to or belonging to the Felidae (cat family).

feral – running wild, eg escaped domestic stock.

fledgling – young bird able to leave the nest, ie to fledge.

flight distance – distance at which an animal will flee from a predator or observer.

flight feathers – large wing feathers.

flock – group of birds, sheep or other herbivores (also verb).

foliage – leafy vegetation, eg on trees.

folivore – a leaf-eating animal.

fossorial – adapted for digging.

frugivore – a fruit-eating animal.

gallery forest – forest growing along watercourses, which thus may extend into an adjoining habitat.

game – wild animals, especially mammals and birds, hunted by humans for food and sport.

genera – plural of genus.

genus – taxonomic grouping of related species.

geophagy – eating rock or soil, eg elephants at Mt Elgon.

gestation – period young mammals develop in the womb before birth.

glaciations – periods during ice ages when glaciers covered large areas of the earth's surface.

gland – see scent gland, inguinal gland, interdigital gland and preorbital gland.

glean – to feed by gathering, eg along branches or among foliage.

granivore – a grain-eating animal.

gravid – pregnant or bearing eggs.

graze – to eat grass (hence grazer).

great ape – any of the large, tailless primates, ie gorilla, chimpanzee and human being.

gregarious – forming or moving in groups, eg herds or flocks.

guano – phosphate-rich excrement deposited by seabirds and bats, usually accumulated over generations.

habitat – natural living area of an animal; usually characterised by a distinct plant community.

hackles – long, loose feathers or hairs on nape or throat, often erectile.

harem – group of females that mate with one male; the male defends his harem against other males.

hawk – to fly actively in search of prey, eg insects, usually caught in the open mouth.

helper – animal, usually from a previous brood, that helps parents raise subsequent brood or broods.

herbivore – a vegetarian animal.

herd – social group of mammals.

hide – artificial construction, usually of wood, for the observation of animals while keeping the observer hidden (also called blind).

hierarchy – order of dominance among social animals, usually with a dominant individual or caste and one or more tiers of power or function, eg primates.

hive – home of bees or wasps.

holt – otters' den.

home range – the area over which an individual or group ranges over time (compare with territory).

host – organism on (or in) which a parasite lives; bird which raises young of parasitic species.

immature – stage in a young bird's development between juvenile and adult.

incisor – front (ie cutting) teeth.

incubate – to hatch eggs using warmth.

inguinal gland – scent gland in groin area.

insectivore – an insect-eating animal.

interdigital gland – scent gland between hooves, eg on antelopes.

invertebrate – an animal without a spinal column or backbone, eg insects, worms.

iridescence – metallic sheen on many insects and birds, eg sunbirds.

jinking – moving jerkily or with quick turns to escape a predator.

juvenile – animal between infancy and adulthood (mammals) or with first feathers after natal down (bird).

kali – Swahili for fierce or angry.

koppie – outcrop of rock on savanna plains.

lamellae – comblike plates in the bills of some birds (eg flamingos) that filter food particles from water.

latrine – site where mammals habitually deposit dung or urine (compare with dung midden).

leap – collective term for leopards.

lek – communal arena for mating and territorial sparring (antelopes) or courtship displays and mating (birds).

loaf – to laze about, especially used in describing bird behaviour.

localised – found only in a small or distinct area.

lying-out – remaining motionless with head flat on the ground to avoid danger (eg antelopes).

mammal – warm-blooded, furred or hairy animal that gives birth to and suckles live young.

mandible – lower part of beak or jaw.

mantle – shoulder or upper back area on birds or *mammals*.

marine – living in the sea.

matriarchal – female-dominated.

matrilineal – relating to kinship or descent down the female line.

melanism – naturally occurring excess of dark-brown pigment that produces black forms of some animals, eg leopards, servals.

midden – see *dung midden*.

migration – regular movement, often en masse, from one location to another, eg wildebeests, shorebirds (hence migrant, migratory).

miombo – fire-resistant deciduous woodland, especially that dominated by brachystegia.

mob – to harass a predatory animal, eg small birds mobbing an owl; often in response to a distress call.

monogamy – having one reproductive partner for life, eg bat-eared fox.

montane – living or situated on mountains.

moult – to shed and replace all or selected feathers, skin or fur, usually prompted by seasonal or behavioural changes, eg courtship.

musth – a frenzied state of sexual readiness in certain large male *mammals*, eg elephants (also spelled must).

mutualism – behavioural co-operation between two species where both benefit (also called symbiosis).

natal – pertaining to birth.

nest parasitism – laying eggs in the nest of another bird species and taking no further part in rearing the offspring (also called brood parasitism).

nestling – young bird until it leaves the nest (see *fledgling*).

niche – specialised ecological role played by an organism.

nictitating membrane – semi-transparent membrane that draws across eyes of birds and some *reptiles*.

nocturnal – active at night.

nomadic – wandering in search of resources such as food or water.

oestrus – period when female *mammal* is ovulating and therefore sexually receptive (also spelt estrus).

omnivore – an animal that eats both plant and animal matter.

opportunist – an animal that finds *prey* virtually anywhere while expending as little energy as possible.

order – grouping of one or more animal families, eg cats and dogs into Carnivora/carnivores.

pair bond – social ties that keep mates together, reinforced with grooming, calls etc.

parasite – plant or animal that obtains nourishment during all or part of its life from another life form, usually to the detriment of the *host*.

pelagic – living at sea, ie in or above open water.

perissodactyl – an odd-toed *ungulate*, eg rhino, horse.

photosynthesis – process whereby plants convert sunlight, water and carbon dioxide into organic compounds.

pioneer – the first species of animal or plant to colonise an area.

piscivorous – fish-eating.

plantain – large, tropical, banana-like plant.

plantigrade – walking with the whole foot on the ground, eg elephants, humans.

plumage – birds' feathers, often used to describe total appearance, eg drab plumage.

polyandry – female having access to more than one reproductive male.

polygamy – having access to more than one reproductive mate.

polygyny – male having access to more than one reproductive female.

polymorphism – having more than one adult form, size or colour.

precocial – being able to walk or run (eg wildebeest), forage (eg ostrich) or swim shortly after birth (hatching).

predator – animal that kills and eats others.

prehensile – flexible and grasping, eg tail, fingers.

preorbital gland – *scent gland* in front of the eyes, especially in antelopes, used to mark territory.

present – to show genital region as appeasement (eg apes) or to indicate readiness to mate.

prey – animal food of a *predator*.

pride – collective term for lions.

primate – a monkey, *prosimian* or ape.

primitive – resembling or representing an early stage in the evolution of a particular group of animals.

pronk – see *stot*.

prosimian – 'primitive' *primate*, eg bushbaby.

prusten – loud sniff made by female leopard to call cubs.

pug – footprint or other imprint left on the ground by an animal.

quadruped – four-legged animal.

quarter – to systematically range over an area in search of *prey*, eg jackals, birds of prey.

race – see *subspecies*.

raptor – bird of prey, eg hawk, falcon, vulture.

recurved – upward-curving, eg the bill of an avocet.

regurgitate – to bring up partly digested food from crop or stomach, particularly when feeding young.

relict – remnant of formerly widespread species, community or habitat, now surrounded by different communities.

reptile – a scaly, cold-blooded vertebrate, ie turtles, crocodiles, snakes and lizards.

resident – an animal that remains in an area for its entire life cycle.

rinderpest – a disease of cattle that can affect related animals such as antelopes.

riverine – living near or in rivers or streams.

rodent – any of the many species of rat, mouse, squirrel, porcupine etc.

roost – area where *mammals* (eg bats) or birds gather to sleep, sometimes in large numbers (also verb).

ruminant – *ungulate* with four-chambered stomach (rumen) that chews the cud (hence ruminate).

rump – upper backside of *mammal* or bird, often distinctively marked, eg antelopes.

rut – (antelopes) the mating season (also verb).

saddle – mid- to lower-back area on *mammals* and birds.

sagittal – pertaining to upper seam of skull, eg sagittal crest on male mountain gorilla.

savanna – vegetation zone characterised by contrasting wet and dry seasons where grassy understorey grows with scattered trees and shrubs.

scavenger – animal that feeds on carrion or scraps left by others.

scent gland – concentration of special skin cells that secrete chemicals conveying information about the owner's status, identity, reproductive state etc.

sedentary – animal remaining in one area for all or part of its life cycle (see *resident*).

selection – process whereby traits that don't further an organism's reproductive success are weeded out by environmental or behavioural pressures.

sexual dimorphism – differences between males and females of the same species in colour, size or form; spectacular examples occur in many birds.

sibling – related offspring with the same parents (hence foster-sibling in brood parasites).

signal – movement or trait that conveys information from one animal to another, eg danger.

skein – collective term for geese.

slough – to shed skin when growing, eg *reptiles, amphibians*.

sounder – group of pigs.

sow – female pig.

spawn – eggs of fish and *amphibians,* usually laid in water (also verb).

speciation – the process whereby species are formed.

species – organisms capable of breeding with each other to produce fertile offspring; distinct and usually recognisable from other species, with which the majority don't interbreed.

spoor – the track or tracks of an animal.

spraint – otter urine, used as territorial marking.

spur – horny growth on some birds, eg on forewing (lapwings) or 'heel' (francolins).

spy-hop – to jump above vegetation, eg grass, to check bearings, threats etc.

stage – level in development of an organism.

stalk – to pursue *prey* by stealth.

stoop – powerful dive of bird of prey.

stot – stylised high leap while bounding, especially by young antelopes in play and adults when fleeing (also called pronk); thought to display fitness to would-be *predators*.

streamer – long tail feather, eg of swallows.

subadult – last stage of juvenile development, usually characterised by near-adult coloration, size or plumage.

subdesert – semiarid area with more rainfall, and hence more vegetation and biodiversity, than true desert.

subordinate – an animal that is ranked beneath another in a social hierarchy, eg chimps.

subspecies – population of a species isolated from another population (eg by landforms) that has developed distinct physical traits (also called race).

succulent – fleshy, moisture-filled plant, eg euphorbia, aloe.

sward – grass or a stretch of grass.

symbiosis – see *mutualism*.

talon – hooked claw on bird of prey.

taxonomy – scientific classification of organisms according to their physical relationships (also called systematics).

tectonic – pertaining to changes in the earth's crust caused by movement below its surface.

temporal gland – facial glands between the eyes and ears of elephants that secrete temporin.

termitary – earthen mound constructed by a termite colony (also called termitarium).

terrestrial – living on the ground.

territory – feeding or breeding area defended against others (usually unrelated) of the same species (compare with *home range*).

thermal – rising column of air; used by large birds to gain height.

troop – group of monkeys or baboons.

tropical – found within the tropics, ie between the Tropics of Cancer and Capricorn.

tsetse fly – biting, blood-sucking fly.

tusker – large elephant or boar.

tusks – greatly enlarged *canine teeth,* used as tools, or in defence and ritual combat, eg in elephants.

ungulate – a hoofed animal.

ventral – lower (under) side of an animal (opposite of *dorsal*).

vertebrate – an animal having a backbone, ie bony fish, *amphibians, reptiles,* birds and *mammals*.

vestigial – small, nonfunctional remnant of a feature formerly present, eg vestigial horns.

vocalisation – sound made orally by an animal as a signal.

volplane – steep, controlled dive on outstretched wings, eg by vultures to a kill.

waders – shorebirds and related families, eg, plovers.

warm-blooded – maintaining a constant body temperature by internal regulation, eg birds and *mammals* (also known as homoiothermic).

warren – network of holes used as shelter and nursery.

waterfowl – water-dwelling birds with webbed feet, ie swans, geese and ducks.

wattle – fleshy, sometimes brightly coloured growth often prominent in courtship, eg on birds.

yearling – a *mammal* in its second year of growth.

INDEX

INDEX

BEHIND THE SCENES

THIS BOOK

This book was commissioned and produced in Lonely Planet's Melbourne office.

Publisher Chris Rennie
Associate Publisher Ben Handicott
Commissioning Editor Janine Eberle
Project Manager Jane Atkin
Designer Mark Adams, Nic Lehman
Cover Designers James Hardy, Nic Lehman
Layout Designer Wendy Wright
Assisting Layout Designers Paul Iacono, Wibowo Rusli, Cara Smith
Coordinating Editor Kate James
Assisting Editors Daniel Corbett, Helen Koehne, Ali Lemer
Coordinating Cartographer Sam Sayer
Assisting Cartographer Ross Butler
Prepress Production Ryan Evans
Print Production Manager Graham Imeson

Thanks to Yvonne Kirk, Shahara Ahmed, Julie Sheridan, Indra Kilfoyle, Wayne Murphy, Melanie Dankel, Darren O'Connell, Sally Darmody. Special thanks to James Hardy.

TITLE PAGES BY LONELY PLANET IMAGES

Highlights Dennis Jones p10; Environment & Conservation Karl Lehmann, p32; Destinations Karl Lehmann, p56; Wildlife Ariadne Van Zandbergen, p180; Planning Ariadne Van Zandbergen, p294 ;On Safari Ariadne Van Zandbergen p314

SOURCES

Common names for many wide-ranging African mammals and birds vary across the continent; and no two references agree completely on names (scientific or common). Mammal names used in this book follow the *Checklist of the Mammals of East Africa,* published by the East Africa Natural History Society. For birds we followed *Birds of Kenya & Northern Tanzania* by Zimmerman, Turner and Person; and *Birds of Eastern Africa* by van Perlo.

THE LONELY PLANET STORY

Fresh from an epic journey across Europe, Asia and Australia in 1972, Tony and Maureen Wheeler sat at their kitchen table stapling together notes. The first Lonely Planet guidebook, *Across Asia on the Cheap,* was born.

Travellers snapped up the guides. Inspired by their success, the Wheelers began publishing books to Southeast Asia, India and beyond. Demand was prodigious, and the Wheelers expanded the business rapidly to keep up. Over the years, Lonely Planet extended its coverage to every country and into the virtual world via lonelyplanet.com and the Thorn Tree message board.

As Lonely Planet became a globally loved brand, Tony and Maureen received several offers for the company. But it wasn't until 2007 that they found a partner whom they trusted to remain true to the company's principles of travelling widely, treading lightly and giving sustainably. In October of that year, BBC Worldwide acquired a 75% share in the company, pledging to uphold Lonely Planet's commitment to independent travel, trustworthy advice and editorial independence.

Today, Lonely Planet has offices in Melbourne, London and Oakland, with over 500 staff members and 300 authors. Tony and Maureen are still actively involved with Lonely Planet. They're travelling more often than ever, and they're devoting their spare time to charitable projects. And the company is still driven by the philosophy of *Across Asia on the Cheap*: 'All you've got to do is decide to go and the hardest part is over. So go!'